BIRTH OF A REFORMATION

LECTOR HOUSE PUBLIC DOMAIN WORKS

This book is a result of an effort made by Lector House towards making a contribution to the preservation and repair of original classic literature. The original text is in the public domain in the United States of America, and possibly other countries depending upon their specific copyright laws.

In an attempt to preserve, improve and recreate the original content, certain conventional norms with regard to typographical mistakes, hyphenations, punctuations and/or other related subject matters, have been corrected upon our consideration. However, few such imperfections might not have been rectified as they were inherited and preserved from the original content to maintain the authenticity and construct, relevant to the work. The work might contain a few prior copyright references as well as page references which have been retained, wherever considered relevant to the part of the construct. We believe that this work holds historical, cultural and/or intellectual importance in the literary works community, therefore despite the oddities, we accounted the work for print as a part of our continuing effort towards preservation of literary work and our contribution towards the development of the society as a whole, driven by our beliefs.

We are grateful to our readers for putting their faith in us and accepting our imperfections with regard to preservation of the historical content. We shall strive hard to meet up to the expectations to improve further to provide an enriching reading experience.

Though, we conduct extensive research in ascertaining the status of copyright before redeveloping a version of the content, in rare cases, a classic work might be incorrectly marked as not-in-copyright. In such cases, if you are the copyright holder, then kindly contact us or write to us, and we shall get back to you with an immediate course of action.

HAPPY READING!

BIRTH OF A REFORMATION

ANDREW L. BYERS

ISBN: 978-93-5420-383-1

Published: -

LECTOR HOUSE LLP
E-MAIL: lectorpublishing@gmail.com

Dr. Warner.

BIRTH OF A REFORMATION

OR
THE LIFE AND LABORS OF DANIEL S. WARNER

BY

A. L. BYERS

"It shall come to pass, that at evening time
it shall be light."

*TO THE
GENERATIONS
FOLLOWING.*

PUBLISHER'S PREFACE

Year 1966

This volume, a reprint of the book originally published in 1921 and out of print for many years, is in response to a long felt need that this biography of D. S. Warner, along with a brief mention of a few of his associate ministers and gospel workers, should be available to the readers of the present generation and those to follow, should the Lord extend time.

The original book is herewith reproduced without alteration or change, except a very few minor omissions, and accounts of events and conditions existing after the period of Bro. Warner's life.

The reader should bear in mind that Bro. Warner's coming out of sectism was a gradual process over a period of time leading to the climactic step, and any improper or questionable action on his part while involved in sects was merely a result of his lack of clear light and understanding of God's Word. After the light broke through, he himself renounced these practices.

In 1878 D. S. Warner wrote: "The Lord ... gave me a new commission to join holiness and all truth together and build up the apostolic church of the living God."

Bro. Warner and his associates, discerning the impossibility of the true church existing within the framework of denominationalism, declared their freedom from the "sin of sectism and division" and instituted the "evening light" restoration movement in the latter part of the nineteenth century in direct fulfillment of Bible prophecy. See Zech. 14:7. These vital Bible truths, especially on the line of holiness and the nature of the church, which those reformers proclaimed, are imperative today in preserving the church after the apostolic pattern.

Many reformations have come to the religious world since the decline of the apostolic church from its pristine glory of the first century. Yet the nineteenth century reform is more complete, radical and fundamental than any previous movement. A historian has penned this significant observation: "No sooner had D. S. Warner and others begun to preach as men had not preached for time out of mind than men saw in their message the grandest truths the mind of man is capable of receiving. They saw the church built up by Christ, led and organized by the Holy Spirit, the names of whose members are in the Lamb's book of life, which takes the Scriptures as its only discipline, and fellowships every blood-bought soul. Here is real Christian unity.

"Despised and rejected in 'religious' circles, these men preached more real Bible truth in one sermon than one would expect in months of the ordinary kind. They preached profound truths; and it created a furor wherever they went. Thousands received Scriptural light. Many joyfully embraced the great truths they heard and spared neither pains nor money to spread the message everywhere."

In his book, "The Cleansing of the Sanctuary," Bro. Warner wrote thus on the subject of exclusiveness: "Christ is an exclusive Christ; there is none beside him. The faith that he gave us is an exclusive faith; no other saves the soul. The truth of God is exclusive in its nature; everything contrary to it is false. The kingdom of Christ is exclusive. It is a stone that breaks everything else to pieces. The one church that Jesus founded and named, and which is his own body, is also exclusive, for there is only 'one body in Christ.' During the reign of pagan persecution the rulers offered to stop the bloody martyrdom and allow the Christians to worship God in freedom, if they would confess that the pagan idols were also real Gods. This they could not do, but chose rather to die. And on this very point of exclusiveness is the present offense of the cross. People would not seriously object to God's ministers setting forth the church as contained in the Scriptures, if we would recognize their earth-born institutions as being also God's churches. But this we cannot do and be honest before God and faithful to his Word. "There is but one household of faith. Christ does not have a plurality of wives. He has but one bride, and she has no sisters. Thus saith her husband, 'My dove, my undefiled is but one; she is the only one of her mother.' S. of Sol. 6:9."

"Three score and ten" years ago Bro. Warner's earthly career in the service of the Master was ended, yet God in His infinite plan has preserved a holy remnant through the intervening years which has retained and maintained those precious original reformation truths. The two witnesses (Rev. 11:11)—the Word and the Spirit—have resumed their rightful positions as Governors of the church in this "evening time" of the gospel day. Jesus Christ will find His Church "without spot or wrinkle" when He comes again for His Bride.

—THE PUBLISHERS

May, 1966

AUTHOR'S PREFACE

Year 1921

A quarter century has elapsed since the passing of D. S. Warner from the scenes of his earthly activity, and full forty years have gone since the beginning of the great reform of which his labors constituted so large a part. While there are many still living whose personal knowledge of him and his ministry will suffice to them for an encouraging testimony of Christian attainment and of God's marvelous use of human instrumentality when permitted to have his way, the time has come when the absence of any published account of this remarkable man begins to be felt. The rising generation and the generations that follow should have access to a study of such an example of Christian devotion and usefulness, as well as of God's faithfulness to one who will fully trust him. When it was announced that a biography was contemplated, the proposition at once met with hearty approval and encouragement.

That due to the lapse of years there should be some difficulty in securing the necessary data with reference to his early life is of course consequential. His brothers and sisters are all deceased. A nephew and a niece and some of his earlier acquaintances were interviewed, and correspondence was had with other relatives and acquaintances. The most valuable acquisition, however, was the use of his diaries, kindly granted by his son, D. Sidney Warner, now living in Canton, Ohio. These diaries do not cover all of his early ministerial career, but the quotations from them will reveal the Christian character of the man as well as show considerable of his itinerancy and of the facts of his life.

As to the source of information respecting the latter period of his ministry, when his work took the character of a reform, recourse has been had to the files of the periodicals he edited and also to the personal recollections of some who were pioneers with him in the movement. Of these may be mentioned as giving particular information Mrs. Allie R. (Fisher) Allen, Lansing, Mich.; William N. Smith, North Star, Mich.; David Leininger, Akron, Ind; Mr. and Mrs. J. N. Howard, Nappanee, Ind.; Mrs. Anna J. Slagle, Bucyrus, Ohio; Mr. and Mrs. B. E. Warren, Springfield, Ohio; and Mrs. Frankie Warner, Anderson, Ind.

It was my privilege to have a personal acquaintance with D. S. Warner and to be more or less closely associated with him during the last five years of his life. To one who never knew him personally no printed account can afford an adequate conception of what it was to come in contact with this wonderful ambassador of God, whose presence wrought conviction in the unregenerate, and inspired confidence and courage in the hearts of believers. The divine manifestations in his preaching, his prayers, and his ministrations can not be told. Many very striking instances of physical healing which we have not space to speak of attended his ministry; but that these pages may reveal, if in no other light than the historical, that here is an example of true consecration, devotion, courage, diligence, humility, faith, patience, kindness, self-denial, and the Christian graces generally, that is worthy of being followed, is the earnest hope of

THE AUTHOR.
—ANDREW L. BYERS

Year 1921

CONTENTS

CHURCH OF GOD (WINEBRENNERIAN)

CHAPTER V

FIRST YEARS IN MINISTRY

CHAPTER VI

A NEBRASKA MISSION

CHAPTER VII

BACK IN OHIO FIELDS

CHAPTER VIII

THE HOLINESS AWAKENING

CHAPTER IX

A PREACHER OF HOLINESS

CHAPTER X

NORTHERN INDIANA ELDERSHIP

CHAPTER XI

EDITOR AND AUTHOR

CHAPTER XII

A SPIRITUAL SHAKING

CHAPTER XIII

A PROPHETIC TIME

CHAPTER XIV
THE GOSPEL TRUMPET

CHAPTER XV
THE CRISIS

CHAPTER XVI
EVANGELISTIC TOURS

CHAPTER XVII
THE MINISTRY OF SONG

CHAPTER XVIII
POETIC INSPIRATIONS

CHAPTER XIX
LAST YEARS

CHAPTER XX
AS OTHERS KNEW HIM

LIST OF ILLUSTRATIONS

Andrew L. Byers, Author of this Book.

Office Editor, Gospel Trumpet.

The Evening Light.

The Evening Light.

D. S. Warner.   (Zech. 14:7.)   H. R. Jeffrey.

1. Bright-er days are sweet-ly dawn-ing, Oh, the glo-ry looms in sight!
2. Mist-y fogs, so long con-ceal-ing All the hills of min-gled night,
3. Lo! the ran-somed are re-turn-ing, Robed in shin-ing crys-tal white,
4. Free from Ba-bel, in the Spir-it, Free to wor-ship God a-right,
5. Hal-le-lu-jah! saints are singing, Vic-t'ry in Je-ho-vah's might;

For the cloud-y day is wan-ing, And the eve-ning shall be light.
Van-ish, all their sin re-veal-ing, For the eve-ning shall be light.
Leap-ing shout-ing home to Zi-on, Hap-py in the eve-ning light.
Joy and glad-ness we're re-ceiv-ing, Oh, how sweet this eve-ning light!
Glo-ry! glo-ry! keep it ring-ing, We are saved in eve-ning light!

Chorus.

Oh, what gold-en glo-ry streaming! Pur-er light is com-ing fast;

Now in Christ we've found a free-dom Which e-ter-nal-ly shall last.

CHAPTER I

INTRODUCTION

A glance over Christian era—Early church divinely governed—Spiritual decline—A false church—Reformations—Sixteenth century
reformation—Human rule—Characteristics of true church—A
final reformation—Evil of sects—Protestantism in Revelation—
Wondrous times upon us—God's call to his people—D. S. Warner
a reformer—The correct attitude—Counterfeit movements.

The life and labors of D. S. Warner are so closely associated with a religious movement that any attempt at his biography becomes in part necessarily a history of that movement. I have therefore chosen the term, Birth of a Reformation, as a part of the title of this book. Brother Warner (to use an appellation in keeping with the idea of universal Christian brotherhood) was doubtless chosen of God as an instrument for accomplishing a particular work. What that work was, why it may be called a reformation, and why, in particular, it may be considered the last reformation, a few words of explanation by way of introduction are offered the inquiring reader.

It will be necessary to take a brief glance over the Christian era and review some of the important events and conditions. We note the characteristics of the church in the days of the apostles, which, by reason of its recent founding and organization by the Holy Spirit, is naturally regarded as exemplary and ideal. It had no creed but the Scriptures and no government but that administered by the Holy Spirit, who 'set the members in the body as it pleased him'—apostles, prophets, teachers, evangelists, pastors, etc. Thus subject to the Spirit, the early church was flexible, capable of expansion and of walking in all the truth and of adjusting itself to all conditions. It was in very essence *the* church, the whole, and not a section or part. The apostles and early believers did not restrict themselves and become a Jewish Christian sect or any other kind of sect. Peter's way of thinking would have thus limited him, for as a Jew he declined any particular interest in Gentile converts; but the Lord through a vision changed his mind and advanced his understanding to include the universality of the Christian kingdom. The Holy Spirit in the heart was necessary, of course, to the successful government of the church by the Spirit, otherwise he could not have been understood. There were no dividing lines, for it was the will of the Lord particularly that there be "one fold and one shepherd." Jesus had prayed in behalf of the disciples "that they all may be one; as thou, Father, art in me, and I in thee, that they also may be one in us: that the world may believe that thou hast sent me" (John 17:21). These conditions of being subject to the word and Spirit, of leaving an open door through which greater light and truth might enter as was necessary, and of possessing the love and unity of spirit that cemented the believers together and carried them through all their persecution, constituted the ideal and normal status of God's church on earth as he gave it beginning, of which it was ordained that there should be but one, only one, as long as the world should endure. "There is one body, and one Spirit, even as ye are called in one hope of your calling" (Eph. 4:4).

SPIRITUAL DECLINE

It was possible, of course, for the church to decline from her state of purity and thereby to forfeit her standing as the church. So long as her conflict with paganism lasted and the various forms of persecution tended to bring into exercise those principles and qualities which distinguished her from the world, she practically kept her first estate. When, however, the tide turned, persecutions ceased and Christianity came into favor and to be made the state religion of the Roman Empire, there were presented conditions favorable to every form of spiritual decline. Christians, instead of being longer persecuted, were protected, and to profess Christianity became popular and easy. The divine features of the church, by which she had been known for more than two hundred years, were lost. Every form of corruption came in. Human rule supplanted the divine, Holy Spirit, rule almost universally, both in the East and the West. The bishop of Rome, in particular, rose in prominence until he was made supreme head—pope—of the Holy Roman church. The reader of church history knows of the long eclipse of Christianity that followed, of the darkness and ignorance that reigned and gave to that period the name, Dark Ages. The true church, impossible of representation by such a colossal counterfeit as then appeared in her place and became in turn a persecuting power, could continue only in fragmentary form, in obscure places in the wilderness of the Roman Empire. She could not be manifest in her evangelizing capacity, but was persecuted. Millions of God's people, who refused allegiance to this false system of Christianity, were slain as heretics during this period. Thus, in the historical foreground we see, not the pure woman representing the church of God, but we see an apostate woman seated "upon a scarlet-colored beast," the Roman state.

"And the woman was arrayed in purple and scarlet color, and decked with gold and precious stones and pearls, having a golden cup in her hand full of abominations and filthiness of her fornication: and upon her forehead was a name written, *Mystery, Babylon the Great, the Mother of Harlots and Abominations of the Earth.* And I saw the woman drunken with the blood of the saints, and with the blood of the martyrs of Jesus" (Rev. 17:4-6).

The Word and the Spirit, the two divine authorities, were set aside. In the place of the former were the traditions of the Roman Church, and for the latter was substituted human rule and authority. These two divine witnesses prophesied in sackcloth during those long centuries, until such time as they should again function in their proper sphere in the church—I say *until such time:* for we are not to assume that in the design of God this state of affairs should always continue. True Christianity was not to perish from the earth. The book of Daniel prophesies of the papacy, "And he shall speak great words against the Most High, and shall wear out the saints of the Most High, and think to change times and laws: and they shall be given into his hand until a time and times and the dividing of time" (Dan. 7:25). (See the time-periods of the various epochs of the Christian era in our chapter A Prophetic Time.) For this vast agency of unrighteousness the time should come when the cup of iniquity should be full and the judgments of God should be executed and his people delivered. When Christ comes, his bride will have made herself ready, which implies that God's people will have been gathered out of spiritual captivity and brought again to Zion. Light and truth and the Holy Spirit rule will have been restored as at the beginning.

REFORMATIONS

Now the rise out of apostasy was expressed by a series of reformations, not by gradual ascent corresponding to the decline. The "mystery of iniquity," which crystallized in the blasphemous "man of sin," had already begun to *work* in Paul's day, and the drift into spiritual darkness on the part of the professing church was without specific opposition. But, on the other hand, to break away from conditions apostate always means war with infernal powers. The wrong is endured until a rising sentiment of protest breaks out with stern denunciation. God raises up instruments for this purpose. John Wyclif, in the fourteenth century, denounced the errors of the so-called church and the conduct of the monks and also had sufficient light to see the papacy as the "man of sin" foretold by the apostle Paul. His reform efforts, however, centered mostly in the translation of the Bible into English, which work, in spite of the attempt by Rome to destroy it, God graciously caused to be preserved.

John Huss, a little later, took Wyclif's attitude against the corruptions of the church and was burned at the stake as a heretic. His martyrdom furnished the occasion for him to utter this prophecy: "You are now going to burn a goose [Huss meaning goose in the Bohemian language], but in one hundred years there will arise a swan whom you can neither roast nor boil." True to this prophecy, in one hundred years came the intrepid Luther, under whose leadership history records the great reformation of the sixteenth century. Church and state were at this time united, which gave this reformation a political prominence, as it resulted in the change to Protestantism of two strong nations, Germany and England. What the sixteenth century reformation accomplished spiritually was, among other things, the bringing to light of the Scriptural doctrine of justification by faith in Christ instead of by priestly absolution.

It could not have been expected that all the Scriptural truths and principles should at any time or by any one reformer be recovered from the rubbish under which they had been buried for a thousand years. There have been numerous reforms, bringing out various truths that had been obscured by the apostasy. Thus Truth in her progress upward to the Scriptural level, has arisen only by successive steps, God having to use human instrumentalities that were limited by the prevailing tendencies and beliefs of the times. Each reformer naturally dealt with conditions that were most conspicuous from his view-point and was exercised in questions of truth that applied only to such conditions. His reform work was not final in character, inasmuch as it left some errors still uncorrected. Hence the progress upward was by a succession of reforms, each, as a general thing, springing from a higher level of truth and spiritual attainment than those preceding. With the great decline into apostasy now in the past, the church of God was disposed to rise out of confusion, her destiny being the attainment of her original standing, when it could be said that her sun should "no more go down."

HUMAN RULE INSTEAD OF DIVINE

The apostasy of the church, as one writer has expressed it, came by "ecclesiastical ambition and degeneracy." The human element got in the way where there should have been only the divine. There is necessarily the human element in the work of God, for Christian work is God and man working together; but in the true relation man is God's instrumentality and is altogether in subjection to the divine Head, who rules over all. When the human element supplants, gets in the way of, or acts in the place of, the divine, we have a fundamental error that always results in apostasy. This human ecclesiasticism, always more or less intolerant, reached its autocratic perfection in the hierarchy of the Roman Catholic Church and constituted the "man of sin" who opposeth and exalteth himself above all that is called God, or that is worshiped; so that he as God "sitteth in the temple of God, showing himself that he is God" (2 Thess. 2:3,4).

The spirit of human government in church affairs has shown itself in, or has followed in the wake of, every reform movement of the past. The Spirit of God worked in the movement to accomplish good, but was always checked by this baleful element. Luther meant well but was himself dogmatic and intolerant. He held to many doctrines of Catholicism whose wrongs he could not see. He did not make proper allowance that others besides himself might be right, or at least have some truth. Neither did he or his associates or followers leave the way open for God to lead into more truth, much less the whole truth. Thus the reformation of the sixteenth century, while it recovered from the debris of apostasy the doctrine of justification by faith, became the occasion for Protestant sects, human-ruled institutions, and these were succeeded by other sects. Some of these have been as intolerant, inflexible, and as unlike primitive Christianity as the Roman Catholic Church itself.

Church government, as humanized in the sects, has taken forms other than the hierarchic. We have the episcopal, or rule by bishops; the presbyterian, or rule by presbyters; the congregational, or rule by the local brotherhood. Our object here is, not to discuss which of these forms most nearly resembles or is most different from the Scriptural, but merely to show that man rule has manifested itself in various ways.

CHARACTERISTICS OF TRUE CHURCH

The true church of God, comprising all Christians, has in her normal state under her divine head certain essential characteristics which make her exclusively the church, the whole and not a part. These might be expressed as follows:

1. Possession of divine spiritual life. If the church does not possess this she is not Christ's body and therefore not the church. She must know the Spirit of God.

2. Disposition to obey all Scripture and to let the Spirit have his way and rule. This constitutes her safety in matters of doctrine and government.

3. An attitude receptive to any further truth and light. This safeguards against dogmatism and a spirit of infallibility and intolerance, against interpreting Christianity in the light of traditions and old ideas.

4. Acknowledgment of good wherever found and the placing of no barrier that would exclude any who might be Christians. This makes salvation, a holy life, and a Christian spirit the only test of fellowship, and disapproves all human standards of church membership and fellowship.

We repeat that these constitute the Scriptural standard of the church and characterize her in her unity and integrity. It is by lacking in one or more of these essentials that a sect is a sect. In the rise of the church out of apostasy any reformation that does not develop to the full the essentials that characterize the church in her wholeness and completeness must necessarily fall short of being the final reformation and must leave a cause for further reformation. This is the explanation of the existence of the so-called Christian sects, viewing them in the most charitable light. The Wesleys and their early associates sought for deeper personal spirituality as well as better spiritual association than was afforded in the state church of England. They brought to light and gave particular prominence to the doctrine of sanctification by faith and the witness of the Holy Spirit. Their work was a reform; but as in that day the question of division among Christians was not prominent, nor was the question of the one true church understood or appreciated, their work took definite form in a body humanly organized and called Methodist. The Campbells had considerable light on the unity of the church, and proposed the Scriptures alone as a basis on which all Christians could unite. But they blindly shut themselves in on a point of doctrine by associating entrance into the kingdom or church with the act of immersion in such manner as to make a wall between them and other Christians who should give evidence of having received salvation and therefore church membership, otherwise than through baptism. Thus they made themselves a sect. John Winebrenner had the correct idea of the church as comprising all the saved, and his work was on an unsectarian basis. Lacking, however, in the quality of letting the Spirit of God rule, eldership organizations were soon set up, a man rule came in, and they also became a sect. Inflexible as to doctrine, they closed the door of progress on themselves, rejected the truth on holiness, and became one of the most narrow of sects, though bearing the Scriptural name, Church of God.

A FINAL REFORMATION

It must follow, and the assumption is already established, that a reformation which takes in full the characteristics defining the church in her wholeness must thereby reach the New Testament standard and therefore be the last, or final, reformation. No reformation can make good such claim if it does not proceed on whole-church lines or principles. If a reform does progress on those universal principles, we need look no farther for, nor await future years to reveal, the final reformation resulting in the restoration of all things to the Scriptural ideal.

The errors of the religious world are, and have been, the failure to so preach salvation truth that people may obtain and enjoy full deliverance from sin; failure to conform to the divine standard on all lines; the human ecclesiastical system, which hinders Holy Spirit organization and government; and separation of God's people into parties, thus making true church relation impossible. A movement that comprehends a correction of all these, and meets the Scriptural standard, must therefore fill the measure of reform.

Reader, it is claimed for the movement represented in the teaching and labors of D. S. Warner, that it possesses these elements of finality, that by it God is bringing his people "out of all places where they have been scattered in the cloudy and dark day" of Protestant sectism, and is restoring Zion as at first. It is not assumed that Brother Warner was right on every point of doctrine or in every application of a Scriptural text, but that the movement, in addition to being based on correct Scriptural principles otherwise, possesses that flexibility and spirit of progress by which it adjusts itself as God gives light.

1. It teaches the Scriptural process of salvation, by which people may obtain a real deliverance from sin and have the Holy Spirit as a witness to their salvation.

2. The truth only, and obedience thereto, is its motto; and it recognizes the rule of the Holy Spirit in the organization and government of the church.

3. It does not assume to possess all the truth, but stands committed thereto, holding an open door to the entrance of any further light and truth.

4. The spirit of the movement is to acknowledge good wherever found and to regard no door into the church other than salvation and no test of fellowship other than true Christianity possessed within the heart.

Thus its basis is as narrow as the New Testament on the one hand, and as broad as the New Testament on the other. May it ever go forward on this line in the spread of the truth to all the world.

ANOTHER VIEW OF SECTS

In order to a clearer understanding of the reformation which took definite form in the work of D. S. Warner, as well as why he denounced the sectarian spirit in such scathing terms, let us take further notice of the evil of sect institutions.

In the first place, sects are confusing in that, while necessarily bad as factions, they are *associated* more or less with good. Many of them in their origin followed reform movements which apparently had divine sanction and were progressive in Christianity, and many of them have upheld truth which when preached was productive of good and brought salvation results. But here it should be noted, that whatever of salvation work has been accomplished has been directly by the Spirit of God in individuals, quite apart from any sectarian agency. It must be said, too, that whatever has resulted from Christian endeavor or influence and expenditure of means, whether in home or foreign lands, would have been in greater degree had the church back of these efforts been one spiritual whole instead of many sectarian divisions. So, when we come to apply analysis to this question of sects, we find that they are in no sense good. That they are called churches is but the part of confusion, for in the popular mind and in actual practise it tends to identify sects with the divine church, whereas in Scripture church always means something other than sects. Bodies that are differentiated by the isms of men are not, and never can be, Scripturally churches, for except in the local geographical sense the church takes no plural form. There is a distinction between the true people of God as constituting the divine church and the human institutions called churches that have divided them and placed them in unnatural and unscriptural relations. The true church of God, by virtue of comprising all the saved and therefore being a unit, places sects in comparison only as false churches. A commentator truthfully remarks, "False Christendom divided into very many sects is truly Babylon, that is, confusion." (Jamieson, Fausset, and Brown's Commentary.) Thus sects, because they are a hindrance to proper Christian activity and because they present a spectacle of religious confusion, professing to be churches when they can only be false, are bad.

This is no disparagement of the many noble men and women of God who have been connected with sects and have gone on to their heavenly reward, whose accomplished good was from the divine source and not from the sectarian. They may have honestly loved their sect, but in this they were honestly misplacing their love. It was the religious association with their fellow Christians that they loved, and this, had they only known it, was not enhanced but rather hindered by the sectarian distinction. They will not find these distinctions in heaven. If they really loved the sect, they had to leave that love behind, for it could not be included with such Christian excellence as entitled them to heaven. Thus our good parents and grandparents and the long line of reformers and Christian worthies receive their heavenly reward quite independent of the sectarian institutions that divided them here.

EVIL OF SECTS IN POSITIVE LIGHT

We have shown why sects are bad in rather a negative light, as being confusion and therefore a hindrance to proper Christian representation in the world. They are evil in a more positive sense, and it was because of this that God prompted Brother Warner and others in the reform to utter such sharp judgment against them. Any body of Christian people that arises and fails to qualify on all principles that mark the church of God as a whole, that proceeds to human organization and rule instead of recognizing only Holy Spirit organization and government, at once limits itself and becomes thereby a sect, a false representation of the church. As a false church it is soon a corrupt institution in which human pride and every element contrary to God may exist and become active. The human will, intended for the rule of our bodies and things terrestrial, things which belong to man's province, becomes sadly out of place when exercised in any sphere or capacity that belongs to God. In such sphere it becomes a rival of God, a monster evil of great proportions, a distinctive satanic spirit, always opposing the true work of God.

BEASTLY CHARACTER IN PROPHECY

This man rule in a province to which God alone has rightful claim (for indeed it exercises the prerogative of God when it presumes to direct God's work and people) has characterized all Protestant sectism just as it did Roman Catholicism, only in milder aspect. Man rule is represented in prophetic symbols by beastly character, whether it applies to political or ecclesiastical government. Thus in the 7th chapter of Daniel we have the symbols of four great beasts, representing in their respective order four universal kingdoms, as follows: Babylonia, Medo-Persia, Greece, and Rome. These were temporal powers that ruled the world. When a mere temporal power is indicated the prophetic symbol used is a dumb beast. If a beast or any part of such symbol is represented as speaking or exercising human propensities, then the thing indicated is also an ecclesiastical power. Thus the fourth beast in Daniel 7, which represents the Roman Empire, exercises first as a dumb animal; but directly a particular horn appears among the horns of this beast, and is given eyes to see and a mouth to speak great things, which indicates ecclesiastical exercise, so that we have here Rome first as a heathen power, and then as a so-called Christian power speaking great things, making war against the saints, etc.

In Revelation 13 we find this same Roman Catholic power represented by a beast to whom was given "a mouth speaking great things and blasphemies" and power "to make war with the saints and to overcome them." These anthropomorphic qualities given to a beast indicate man rule in ecclesiastical matters, a thing which is at once blasphemy in God's sight, utterly obnoxious and foreign to him.

PROTESTANTISM IN REVELATION 13

Beginning with the 11th verse of Revelations 13, directly after the prophecy of the Roman Catholic hierarchic power, we have the spectacle of a second beast, having two horns like a lamb but speaking as a dragon. The fact that he speaks gives him the quality of ecclesiastical rule. In this beast we have man rule in the form of Protestantism. He has a lamb-like aspect instead of the vicious, threatening character of Rome in the days of her power; but he has the voice of a dragon, which betrays his diabolical spirit. He exercises as much power in the world as Roman Catholicism did before him. He deceives by doing "great wonders," displaying spiritual manifestations. He causes people to worship the first beast (Catholicism) by copying its standards and doing reverence to a human ecclesiastical system; and an image to the first beast is made whenever a sect is organized. He causes the image to "speak" (exercise man rule) and to persecute those who, instead of bowing to the sect image, are disposed to exercise in their spiritual freedom and give allegiance alone to God.

Thus we see so-called Protestantism as a particular form of beast religion, a distinctive spirit that animates and dominates the sectarian system. The beast element is the man rule. We are not speaking merely of human instrumentality, which God certainly uses in his church when the will is wholly submitted to him and susceptible to his Spirit, but of that exercise and dominance in ecclesiastical matters which, as apart from God, is distinctly human. Such prevails more or less as a system in all sects, gives occasion for jealousy, pride, and emulation, wants to be let alone, and opposes any reform that threatens it. This is the element which naturally becomes disturbed at the preaching of the truth that exposes it, and which became a persecuting power against Brother Warner and all who executed the divine judgment against false religion. In this deceptive form of evil covering almost four hundred years Satan has had his seat. When the present reformation shall have resulted in bringing God's people out of sectarian divisions and placing them on the whole-church basis, Satan, driven to some new project, will muster the Gog and Magog forces in a last conflict against the saints, which shall end with the utter destruction of those forces by the judgment fires.

We have, then, Protestantism represented in two aspects: 1. As a period during which truth by a succession of reform movements has to a considerable extent been recovered from apostasy and restored to God's people. 2. As a system of false religion, a form of spiritual Babylon that is pervaded by a satanic spirit that deceives the world and opposes any effort to restore the church of God to her Scriptural unity, since such effort naturally threatens the ecclesiastical element lying at the base of organized sectarianism.

A DISPENSATION OF GOD

We apprehend, then, that wondrous times have come upon us. Great ecclesiastical systems are crumbling and are being left destitute as God's people make their escape. This movement proceeds with no show of prominence in the world. It causes no political disturbance, but works only in the province of genuine Christianity, silently, effectively, as the leaven in the meal. It is altogether a spiritual movement and its discernment can therefore only be spiritual. It may appear outwardly as only one religious body among many; for it is only when judged by the spiritual standard of God's word that its character is seen. It is a call to those who are willing to be led of God.

The dispensations of God are in their beginning often insignificant and despised in man's eyes. God chooses things that are not, to bring to naught things that are. The fact that Brother Warner's work was done in comparative obscurity counts for nothing against its being the work of God. It is quality that counts. Brother Warner had the right spiritual quality, the secret of which was letting God have his way. His entire abandonment to God in a complete consecration, together with his adaptable temperament and gifts, made him suitable for God's use in this great work, and God chose him. The time was at hand. Others, contemporary with him and leaders in the holiness movement, saw the evils of sects and deplored them, but when it came to renouncing their sectarian affiliations and coming out of the spiritual Babylon in obedience to God's call, "Come out of her, my people, that ye be not partakers of her sins, and that ye receive not of her plagues," they drew back. This point of leaving the sects, abiding in Christ alone and allowing God to reestablish his church on the primitive basis, was the real test. They longed for the time when God's people should all be one, but chose to believe that the time was not yet. And so they have been believing for forty years, and are today in the greater confusion. They lacked the spiritual equipment. One of Brother Warner's special endowments was that of considerable light on the prophecies. He saw that the sectarian denominations were of the true spiritual Babylon in which God's people were being held captive. He also had in the Spirit the prospective vision of the pure church unruled by man. His contemporary leaders who opposed him were too blind spiritually to have such a vision; or, if they had it, were disobedient to it.

But there were those, the humble ones, who were willing to let God have his way. At the sound of the trumpet, which God was giving through Brother Warner, thousands have rallied to the standard of truth, and through them the truth has been and is being vindicated. If God has his way all Christians will be led out of sects, all justified believers will be led into sanctification, the church will be perfectly organized and governed by the Holy Spirit, the whole truth will be preached uncompromisingly, full salvation will be held out to the world, and all will be led to cooperate and do their part. This is the full measure of Christianity today, and is God's design with his people. Here is true Christian unity. Such unity can come only by absolute abandonment to God, for *he* must be the one-making agent. Men may attempt a unity through some Interchurch World Movement or other plan, but no plan can represent the true Scriptural unity unless God does the work himself. He must have the full right of way in human hearts.

Brother Warner's mission was strictly that of a reformer. It was his part to venture boldly with the truth God had given him, with a willingness to run the gauntlet of persecutions that were sure to greet him on the right and left. His severe denunciation of all things sectarian was consistent with his pioneer position. There first had to be an awakening, a breaking up of old conditions, particularly of the recognition (into which the minds of people generally had settled) of the sects as being the church of God. His work was the initial, or birth, stage of the reform.

Following the initial stage has come the constructive, which comprehends the reformation in the local sense, the sense in which the Christian life and true ideal of the church must be exemplified in the community as something more than theory, something that will appeal as being better than what is represented in the sects. The constructive stage calls not so much for continual denunciation of sects as for manifesting those essential principles that characterize the church in her unity and entirety. The responsibility is to make good the claim, and this means much. Any tendency to establish traditions, or to regard a past course as giving direction in all respects for the future, or to become self-centered and manifest a "we are it" spirit and bar the door of progress against the entrance of further light and truth, or in any way to refuse fellowship with any others who may be Christians, would itself be sectarian, altogether unlike the true reformation, which, if it be final, must necessarily be a *restoration* and possess universal characteristics.

For proper representation everything depends upon the understanding of, and the attitude toward, this great movement. For any body of people to hold that the reformation is entrusted to them, or that they have become the standard for the world, is a self-centered attitude, vastly different from that which regards the reformation as something prophetically due, as having come independent of man, and as being greater than the people who have been favored with its light, and that it is their part to conform to *it* in principle, doctrine, and everything. The great movement is in the world, and any attempt to "corner" it or to limit it to a particular body of people could only result in making that body a sect, or faction, while the movement itself would proceed independently.

The true spirit of the reformation will be, however, with those who measure to its standard, whether they be few or many, and God will manifest himself accordingly. Satan has tried to becloud and defeat the movement by counterfeit factions—bodies of people who profess to be on the reformation line, but who misrepresent the truth by denying some part of it, as, for instance, the doctrine of entire sanctification in this life, or of the Christian ordinances, or who misrepresent it by advancing erroneous doctrine, such as the continuation of the Old Testmental law and Sabbath, or the speaking in tongues as a necessary evidence of having received the Holy Ghost. Many are the counterfeit movements today. One must ignore every influence of man and then rely on the witness of both the Word and the Spirit in order to be guided aright.

Brother Warner was a remarkable example of a man possessing the Christian spirit and the Christian graces wonderfully developed. While he could rebuke evil and deceptive influences in the strongest terms, he was one of the meekest and kindest of men. Christ-like, he loved all men, even his persecutors. As a husband, father, Christian brother and friend his love and respect were genuine and reached to the very soul. And yet the responsibility of his calling as a Christian and as a minister of God's truth as it applied to his time, he held more dear than all else, and to it he was wholly devoted. Not with any object of exalting the man, but to illustrate what God can accomplish in and through one who is so devoted, we introduce him to our readers.

CHAPTER II

ANCESTRY AND EARLY LIFE

Emigration westward—Settlement in Ohio—David Warner family—
Born a weakling—Paternal and maternal influences—Tributes to
mother—Location in Crawford County—A chosen vessel—His
boyhood character—Removal to Williams County—A school
teacher.

Among those who fought in the second war against Great Britain was one
Adam Warner, who was born in Virginia, and whose father was Christofel Warner. In this period of our national history a great tide of emigration from the Atlan-
tic States was spreading itself over what is now the Middle West. Adam Warner
seemed to catch the spirit of the times, and accordingly, in 1815, he set out with his
family for the new country beyond the Alleghanies. He settled in Stark County,
Ohio, where, about the year 1845, he died, at ninety-three years of age (a history of
Williams County, Ohio, says ninety-eight, and that he had a sister who lived to the
advanced age of one hundred and three). It is probable that before moving west
Adam Warner lived for a while in Frederick County, Md., for there is where his
son David was born, June 6, 1803.

David Warner, after moving to Stark County, was married, in 1823, to Leah Di-
erdorf, who was born in York County, Pa., Feb. 6, 1805. In 1830 he moved to Wayne
County, Ohio, and a little later to Portage County, then back to Wayne County in
1836, to a place then called Bristol, where he kept a tavern for eight years. Of the
parentage of David and Leah Warner, at their humble abode at Bristol, on June 25,
1842, amid the environment of tavern life, was born Daniel S. Warner, destined
to be one of the principal instruments in God's hands to produce a shaking in the
ranks of spiritual Israel, and to lead the hosts of the Lord back to Zion from their
wanderings in the wilderness of denominationalism.

The children of David and Leah, in order, were as follows: Adam, Lewis, Joseph, John, Daniel, and Samantha. John died at the age of twenty, leaving but the
five children. All are now deceased. A granddaughter says that the family was
Pennsylvania German. Evidently the mother was. The father, as already noted,
was a Virginian.

It was the misfortune of Daniel S. to be frail, sickly, and to a great extent unap-
preciated, from his very birth. His lungs were weak and he was denied that stock
of vitality with which every child has the right to begin life. Intoxicants were freely
used in those days, and David Warner had fallen an easy prey to intemperance. If

the affliction of this infant may not be ascribed to paternal indiscreetness, possibly inebriety, it is not because such instances were uncommon. Into how many homes has the demon of strong drink entered to bring sorrow to the wife and mother and to curse the unborn with the blight of its baneful effects! In this case, at any rate, the father was rough, and inconsiderate of his offspring. While he exercised toward his family a degree of temporal care, it seemed that the very frailty of this child, which should have awakened compassion, met only his frown and disfavor. In later years Daniel, in reflecting on the circumstances attending his birth and childhood, wrote the following lines, which are a part of his poem on Innocence:

> Conceived in sin, to sorrow born,
> Unwelcome here on earth,
> The shadows of a life forlorn
> Hung gloomy o'er my birth.
>
> A mother's heart oppressed with grief,
> A father's wicked spleen,
> Who cursed my faint and gasping breath,
> Combine to paint the scene.
>
> But life held on its tender thread,
> Days unexpected grew
> To weeks, and still he lived—
> Why, Heaven only knew.
>
> He lived, though life was bitter gain,
> His youth a flood of tears,
> His body doomed to cruel pain,
> His mind to nervous fears.

In contrast with this paternal attitude, however, was the constancy of a true-hearted mother. Blessed with this and endowed with indelible memories of a mother's devotion, what child growing up to cope with life's obstacles may not, after all, hold a chance of succeeding, however handicapped otherwise? If ever any planting bears fruit in the human breast, or becomes a latent force tending to guide one steadily through life's dangerous rapids, it is that of a mother's love. Especially is this true of the love of a *Christian* mother, coupled with her prayers.

Mrs. Warner was an excellent woman. Her patient and gentle bearing under disturbing conditions, her disposition to make the best of disappointment and discouragement, left an impress, not only upon the family, but upon the neighborhood. Her kindness is referred to in two other stanzas of the poem Innocence:

> If angels blessed his thorny path,
> It may be said in truth,
> But two e'er showed their smiling face
> In all his suffering youth.
>
> One was his mother, ever kind,
> A blessed providence;
> The other, pure and lovely friend,

Was angel Innocence.

It has been true generally that great men have first had great mothers. But what is a mother's greatness, after all, but simple, unalloyed, Christian motherliness?

"I should have become an atheist but for one recollection, and that was the memory of the time when my departed mother used to take my little hand in hers and cause me on my knees to say, 'Our Father, who art in heaven.'" —*John Randolph.*

Parents of D. S. Warner. The father holds a whisky-glass.

Mother of D. S. Warner.

"All I am, all I hope to be, I owe to my angel mother—blessings on her memory! I remember my mother's prayers. They have always followed me. They have clung to me all my life." — *Lincoln.*

"If my mother could rise in the dead of the night and pray for my recovery from sickness, my life must be worth something. I then and there resolved to prove myself worthy of my mother's prayers." — *Garfield.*

"It is to my mother that I owe everything. If I am thy child, O my God, it is because thou gavest me such a mother. If I prefer the truth to all things, it is the fruit of my mother's teachings. If I did not perish long ago in sin and misery, it is because of the long and faithful years which she pleaded for me. What comparison is there between the honor I paid her and her slavery for me?" — *St. Augustine.*

One more tribute. In his book Bible Proofs of the Second Work of Grace, published in 1880, Daniel S. Warner places the following dedicatory note: "To the sacred memory of my sainted mother, whose tender affections were the only solace in my suffering childhood, and whose never-failing love, and whose pure and innocent life were the only stars that shone in the darkness of my youth, this volume is respectfully dedicated by the author."

From Wayne County, David Warner brought his family, in 1843, to a farm of 140 acres near New Washington, Crawford County, Ohio. The house, built partly of logs, stood three fourths of a mile southwest of the village. It was here that Daniel spent his childhood. Of this period he writes:

> It seemed the special pleasure of
> Another certain one
> To quite demolish everything
> He set his heart upon;
>
> To chafe his spirit and extort
> The flow of bitter tears
> Out of a soft and pensive heart,
> Through all his tender years.
>
> He never knew that "Father" was
> A sweet, endearing name;
> Its very mention was a dread,
> His life's most deadly bane.
>
> The demon of intemp'rance there
> Infused the wrath of hell,
> And most upon this sickly head
> The storm of fury fell.
>
> Like chickens when the mother bird
> Gives signal of a foe,
> The little peeps are quickly hushed,
> All chicks are lying low,
>
> So, when returning from the town,
> The dreaded steps we heard,
> All ran and quickly settled down,
> And not a lip was stirred.
>
> O horrors of the liquor fiend!
> We've seen thy hell on earth.
> Thy serpent coils around us twined,
> The moment of our birth.
>
> O Rum! thy red infernal flame—
> I witness to the truth—
> Filled all my mother's cup with pain,
> And swallowed up my youth.

The Warner family, though clever, straightforward, and strictly honest, were but a simple rural folk and not inclined to religion. That such a bright spiritual light as was afterward exhibited in Daniel could come from such a family, is one of the puzzling questions of blood relation. Was it that in the family blood there was latent quality which in his case only was near enough to the surface to be called into action and developed by higher influence? or should it be said that he represents a variation in the strain, such as is sometimes seen in biological observation? If the latter, the mystery remains; for why do such things occur? Aside from natural phenomena, we believe that Brother Warner was a "chosen vessel" unto the Lord. He possessed such a combination of qualities as made him capable of high development in the divine graces. He was a Christian than whom perhaps none other ever lived who was more reverent, spiritual, and devoted; and God had a special work for him.

BOYHOOD CHARACTERISTICS

In his boyhood Daniel early displayed a gift of entertainment and of public speaking. The school in his district was ungraded. On occasions of entertainment, such as the last day of school, after the younger children had spoken their "pieces" and the program began to grow monotonous, a call would be made for Dan Warner. Then he would take the floor and soon would have them convulsing with merriment. Mischievousness and clownishness were traits. The trouble he sometimes caused the teacher was frequently such that the latter could not locate it nor determine just who was to blame. When he would be stood on the floor he would soon have others with him. On one occasion he did something for which he was sentenced to a scourging. When he appeared at school the next morning he was prepared for this contingency by having on two or three coats. He was, however, bright in his studies and in a general way sociable and well liked.

The community in which he lived was strongly democratic in politics. His father, a staunch democrat, actually had a degree of pride in his boy when the latter would make stump speeches during a campaign. It was natural for Dan to mount a storebox on the street or anywhere and address a crowd on the issues of the day. In later years, however, when he became a minister and his oratorical abilities were directed in the channel of preaching the gospel, his father was not pleased.

Among the sports in which he indulged was coon hunting. On finding a coon tree at night he and his companion would cover themselves with a coon robe and lie under the tree until morning. He got to be rather wild, and took particular delight in the dance, but never indulged in the lowest forms of sin.

These are but brevities of his boyhood career. It is difficult to prepare an account of this part of his life that would be to any considerable degree full. One accident, by which he was maimed for life, should here be noted. He attempted to remove a bunch of grass that had clogged the sickle of a mowing-machine. As he was in this act the team started and the ends of two of his fingers, the middle ones of the left hand, were suddenly clipped off. Fortunately the loss of these members did not hinder him in writing nor was it a disfigurement usually noticed in his preaching.

There was one more move for the David Warner family, and this was to Williams County, Ohio, the northwest corner of the State, where, in Bridgewater Township, about four miles north of the town of Montpelier, farm life was resumed. Here the parents spent the rest of their lives. The removal to this place was made in 1863, during the Civil War. Joseph Warner was drafted for the army. Being a man of a family, he desired to arrange for a substitute. For this Daniel offered himself, and accordingly became a private in Company C, 195th Regiment, Ohio Infantry. Little is known of his army experience. It is said that he found favor with the Captain and was made his clerk, or secretary. At the close of his term he was honorably discharged.

While living in Williams County, the occupation of teaching school appealed to him, and for several terms he was an instructor of the young in matters of common-school education. He was now in his early twenties. But here we shall close this chapter, and introduce him in our next in a different aspect.

CHAPTER III

CONVERSION, COLLEGE, AND CALLING

The question of religion—A Catholic and Lutheran community—Tries to be an infidel—Conviction by the Spirit—Attends dances—Conversion—Attends Oberlin College—Preparation for ministry.

It is natural that the question of religion should present itself to a young man or woman when approaching maturity. It is then that life is full of prospects, when one plans and builds for the future. It is then that opinions are formed, and there is an inclination to reach some kind of decision, for the time being at least, regarding every issue. One reaches this parting of the ways and the question comes, "Which road shall I take?" The answer, so far as religion is concerned, depends to some extent on what one has observed in those who make a profession, though it is true that the influence of the Holy Spirit alone—that monitor who makes his appeal to the inner consciousness—sometimes decides the question.

The community at New Washington, where the Warner family lived, was strongly Catholic and Lutheran. There was too much whisky and tobacco and too little of genuine Christianity for a convincing testimony in favor of the latter. As for Dan Warner, he thought to decide the question of religion by trying to be an infidel. But of course he had not considered that God might speak to him and convince him against his will. He naturally possessed a tender conscience, a capacity to exalt righteousness and a susceptibility to right spiritual influence.

And so we find him on reaching the age of maturity trying to believe there was nothing in Christianity; but at this his success was poor. There were certain persons within his field of acquaintance whose Christian piety made its impression. Then again, there was the influence of song. He had a good voice and found enjoyment in engaging in song with the young people. On a Sunday afternoon, at a neighbor's, where a number were gathered and were singing gospel hymns, he became greatly affected. God spoke to his conscience. His conviction was so strong as to cause him for several months to lose his love for the dance and to reflect seriously on his course of life. It was his turning-point so far as infidelity was concerned.[1]

But after a few months, when the conviction had worn away somewhat, he

---

[1] The use of tobacco, was very common among the professors in his community. It is related that he received an impression of the evil of this habit when on attendance at a prayer-meeting he saw one of those present attempt to take a chew secretly, by hiding his face behind a chair.

began to renew his attendance at dances and apparently to be more reckless than ever regarding his spiritual well-being. His heart, however, was yet tender from the wound made by the spirit of conviction. One night during a severe illness of his sister he attended a dance. After he had returned home at two o'clock in the morning, his mother went to his room and expostulated with her boy regarding his sinful career. Here again is where a mother's part played effectively. As she reasoned with him on his wrong conduct, his going to a dance while his sister—his only sister—lay at the point of death, and his offence against a just God, before whom he must one day stand in judgment, the depths of his heart were broken up and he fell on his knees and called for mercy.

From that time he was deeply convicted though to his companions he gave no evidence of a changed life, as he had not received the new birth. With some young friends he began to attend a protracted meeting in a schoolhouse not far from his home. The meeting was one of power, and sinners were made to reflect on the question of their souls' salvation. On their way home one night his companions were expressing their opinions as to religion, what it was, etc. One of them, addressing Dan, said, "What do *you* think it is?" He replied, "I am going to find out." Knowing him to be prankish the others supposed he meant to play some trick, and as they separated wondered to themselves what Dan could have up his sleeve. Not until he had gone forward to the altar the next evening and they had seen him rise a changed young man with the peace of God in his countenance did they take his words and actions seriously.

The date of this, his conversion, was February, 1865. He refers to the event some years later as follows: "Passed once more the old schoolhouse where I gave my heart to God (February, 1865). Thank God for that step! Oh, how glad I am it was ever my lot to become a Christian!"

Another item of interest relating to this time was his engagement to Frances Stocking, reference to which in his diary for June 11, 1874, the reader will find on another page.

One quality that was manifest in Brother Warner's early religious life as well as throughout his entire career was earnestness. He was sincere and intense in his devotion and his Christian work. We shall find as we read the notes from his diary that his words breathe a spirit of love and devotion, evincing a deep spirituality. When he yielded to God, he meant it as the decision of his very soul, and his conversion was for him an actual change for time and eternity. Old things were passed away. New propositions and prospects arose to occupy his thoughts.

ATTENDS OBERLIN COLLEGE

What ideals and plans were his immediately after his conversion we do not know. It was not long, however, until he decided that a more advanced education was needful. Nothing will give a young person nobler ambitions and greater desire to rise to all that is good and associated with usefulness than Christianity. On the 5th of September of the same year of his conversion he started to school at Oberlin College and enrolled for an English preparatory course. The details of his study at Oberlin and just how long he remained have not been learned. An old memorandum of his accounts indicates that he attended there only two months at first, and then taught school through the winter at Corunna, Ind., returning to Oberlin in the spring, and that he started again with the new school year in September, 1866. It is known, however, that his excellency of character shone while he was at school and was the subject of remark.

D. S. Warner, a student at Oberlin College.

He did not attend college as long as he had expected to; for it was while he was there that he began to feel God's hand upon him for the ministry. When he saw how long it would take to complete his college work and the need of laboring in the Lord's harvest while it was day, he felt impressed that God wanted him to cut short his college course and to prepare at once for the ministry. He accordingly went home, arranged for a room in his father's house, and spent one season there in applying himself to prayer, Bible-study, and those other things which he believed were directly necessary to his ministerial preparation.

Preparation for the ministry is more successful when, along with it, there can be more or less of actual practise. We can believe that Brother Warner was spiritual enough to keep in touch with God and to discern the divine leading in the important matter to which he had committed himself. At any rate, in connection with his work of preparation he began to engage in ministering the gospel. He preached his first sermon on Easter night, 1867, in a Methodist Episcopal protracted meeting in the Cogswell Schoolhouse, not far from where he lived. Text, Acts 3:18—"But those things, which God before had showed by the mouth of all his prophets, that Christ should suffer, he hath so fulfilled."

CHAPTER IV

CHURCH OF GOD (WINEBRENNERIAN)

The Scriptural name—Winebrenner's view of the church—Organization of Elderships—Growth and extent westward—Winebrenner's failure.

At the time of his first effort in the ministry, which occurred more than two years after his conversion, Brother Warner had not as yet given his name to any religious society. To join a sectarian denomination is never by divine prompting, but is urged from human source. A young convert possessing the spirit of Christ is naturally at home in the Lord and with Christians anywhere. It is foreign to that spirit for one to limit oneself by subscribing to any particular creed of men. Accordingly, our young brother was only "acting natural" when he manifested no particular anxiety to "join the church." Representatives of the denominations in his neighborhood proposed to him and presented their articles of faith. The fact that he referred the great question to the Scriptures and could see no authority for joining anything not recognized in the Scriptures shows that he was already poor material for sectarian construction, at least so far as the common arguments for sects go.

There was one society, however, by which he was persuaded. The followers of John Winebrenner called themselves the Church of God. As they professed to hold to no creed but the Bible, repudiated sectarianism, baptized by immersion, and observed as an ordinance the washing of feet in conjunction with the Lord's Supper, all of which seemed good to him, and especially as they had the exact New Testament name for the true church, he was constrained to unite with that body. The mark of fellowship which differentiated them from other Christians and constituted them a sect, was not apparent to him, and so, even during the many years of his earlier ministerial career, he identified this body with the true church. He said in later years that he had more liberty as a minister before he took that step than he had during the years he belonged to the denomination, which after all was but a sect.

The Church of God, spelled with a capital C, and more fully denominated General Eldership of the Churches of God in North America, was founded by John Winebrenner, in 1830. Winebrenner had been baptized and confirmed in the German Reformed Church (now the Reformed Church in the United States), and was given the pastorate at Harrisburg. He was a good man and the work of the ministry became the uppermost desire of his heart. He sought to raise the standard of true piety. His earnest preaching resulted in a revival in which he opposed theaters, dancing, gambling, lotteries, and racing. Revivals of religion were new experiences in the churches of that region, so that his ministry awakened strong opposition, which resulted in official charges against him. He severed his relations with the Reformed Church but continued his ministry, extensive revivals following.

Dr. C. H. Forney, in his History of the Churches of God, says,

> Winebrenner did not entertain the purpose of founding a new denomination. These bodies he stigmatized as sects. Professor Nevin called the United Brethren and like bodies "rolling balls," and accused Winebrenner with "putting in motion a similar ball, which continues rolling to this hour (1842), not without abundance of noise." Winebrenner denounced this as gross misrepresentation. "But, sir, I did not retire for the ignoble purpose, as you have intimated, of putting another sectarian ball in motion. No, not at all. I had seen, through mercy, the great evil of these rolling balls, put in motion and kept in motion by the cunning craftiness of men and devils, and how by their repeated and unhappy collusions they hindered and marred the work of God in the earth; and, therefore, I resolved to fall back upon original grounds—to stand aloof from all these sectarian balls, and to do the work of an evangelist and minister of Christ by building up the church of God (the only true church) according to the plan and pattern as shown us in the New Testament. This is the high and firm ground we take. Our ball, therefore, is not like your ball, nor similar to other human balls. Ours is the Lord's ball. It was not cut out of the Romish Church by the hands of Calvin and others as was yours. But it was 'cut out of the mountain without hands.' The ball commenced rolling upwards of eighteen hundred years ago, and it continues rolling to this hour; yea, and it will never cease rolling till every other man-made ball shall be either crushed or rolled up by it, and until the sound of it shall be 'like the sound of many waters, and as the voice of great thunder.'"

On the subject of organization the same writer continues,

> Winebrenner was indisposed to begin the organization of churches. The uniform testimony of his contemporaries is that he "had not at the beginning the remotest idea of organizing a distinct or separate body of people." But driven out of the pulpit by the Reformed Church, ostracised and persecuted, he was led to a closer personal investigation of church polity. He went to the highest source for light. He applied himself with singleness of purpose to the study of the Word of God. The result was a material modification of his former views on ecclesiology. As he himself testified later: "As the writer's views had by this time materially changed as to the true nature of a Scriptural organization of churches, he adopted the apostolic plan, as taught in the New Testament, and

established spiritual, free, and independent churches, consisting of believers or Christians only, without any human name or creed or ordinances or laws." The local church was the unit. It possessed perfect autonomy. It was wholly independent of every other unit. Each such unit "possesses in its organized state," as Winebrenner expressed it in 1829, "sufficient power to perform all acts of religious worship and everything relating to ecclesiastic government and discipline. Every individual church is strictly independent of all others as it respects religious worship and the general government of its own affairs." Fellowship between these "free and independent" units there would be, but no higher organization was then recognized by Winebrenner which could limit the powers of the local church. Each of these local organizations would accept no human name, creed, nor ordinances; but would adopt the divine name and creed and ordinances. In his broad platform he saw a basis of the union of all Christians and churches. And so the imperative duty of cultivating union between all believers was strongly urged. These views prepared the way for Winebrenner to fall in with the growing demand for local church organization. For the multitudes of converts had "conceived the idea of, and began to talk about, organizing themselves into churches founded on Bible doctrines and principles even before Winebrenner had determined in his own mind to do so."

Thus there were independent local churches organized in and around Harrisburg, which Winebrenner denominated simply Churches of God. Each assumed the name of "Church of God at — —." The members of these churches had equal rights, and elected and licensed men to preach.

ORGANIZATION OF ELDERSHIPS

There was as yet no common bonds, no general organization or directing authority. In order to effect this and adopt a regular system of cooperation, a meeting was held at Harrisburg in October, 1830, attended by six of the licensed ministers. Of this meeting Winebrenner writes, "Thus originated the Church of God, properly so called, in the United States of America, and thus also originated the first Eldership." This organized body assumed no other name than Eldership, though later the term General Eldership was used to distinguish this body from the eldership of the local church. The term General Eldership was, however, applied at first only to the presbyteries or Elderships of sections or States, which held their sessions annually. In October, 1844, Winebrenner proposed a General Eldership for the transaction of all business of a general nature affecting the various annual Elderships. It was provided that this General Eldership should hold its meetings triennially for the first twenty years and after that every five years. Thus we see that by this time Winebrenner's views of church government were still further modified.

The work continued to grow and spread to adjoining counties and to Maryland, western Pennsylvania, and Ohio, where Elderships were organized.

D. S. Warner and wife (Tamzen Kerr).

Each local church elects its own elders and deacons, who with the pastor constitute the church council and are the governing power, having charge of the admission of members and the general care of the church work. The churches within a given district are associated together for cooperation in general work. The pastors and other ordained ministers within a district, together with an equal number of lay members, constitute the Annual Eldership, which appoints the ministers of the various charges. Each local church votes for a pastor, but the Annual Eldership makes the appointments within its own boundaries. These Annual Elderships elect an equal number of ministerial and lay delegates, who constitute the General Eldership.

The Churches of God, as already stated, have no written creed but assume to accept the Word of God as their only rule of faith and practise. They hold the doctrine of the Trinity, believe in human depravity, the atonement of Christ, justification by faith, the resurrection, future punishment, and are, in general, orthodox. Through these articles of their faith, and the fact that they took the Scriptural name, Church of God, the followers of Winebrenner made their appeal to D. S. Warner. But they were lacking in some very important particulars, without which they could not possibly be, as was claimed, identical with the New Testament church. Winebrenner started out well, but on the subject of Holy Spirit organization and government he was not sufficiently illumined to avoid more or less of the human ecclesiastical authority which crept into the body of his followers and constituted them a sect. When holiness came they repudiated it, thereby revealing their position as outside the Holy Spirit control of believers. However, their teaching on the church question was correct as far as it went, and it took years of actual practise of obeying the lead of the Spirit to discover to Brother Warner and others the clash between the Holy Spirit rule and the rule of human authority.

CHAPTER V

FIRST YEARS IN MINISTRY

Gifted as an evangelist—Marriage—Death of wife and children—His physical description—New Washington revival—Diary accounts—Prejudice against sanctification—Meeting at Basswood—A presentiment of death—Standing committee—Rebukes youthful tobacco-user—Converses with infidel—Reflections at end of year—Appointed to Nebraska mission—Lessons on the church—A farewell meeting.

Brother Warner had the right view of ministerial qualification. He realized that in order to succeed he must have the spiritual anointing, and that since it was God's work it was needful that he be in that divine relation by which it would be God in him accomplishing the result. He held education to be very useful and it was his endeavor throughout his life to add to his knowledge; but he regarded the spiritual qualification as paramount. He soon proved to be gifted as an evangelist and engaged much in evangelistic work.

Before proceeding far in active ministerial work he was married, on the 5th of September, 1867, to Tamzen Ann Kerr. It is probable that he became acquainted with this young woman while he was teaching school in the vicinity of her home, which was near West Unity, Williams County. She lived to enjoy his companionship and to share his labors only about four and one half years. Early in 1872 she gave birth to triplets, which lived only a few hours. Nor did the mother long survive the ordeal, as she died on May 26, after a succession of spasms. A family record in an old Bible shows also the birth of a son, on Dec. 29, 1868, but fails to record his death. Brother Warner refers to this son once in his diary.

He was granted a license by the West Ohio Eldership,[2] which met in its eleventh annual session at Findlay in October, 1867. His reference to this event in his diary is given in another part of this book. In this chapter as well as in some of the succeeding chapters, the copious extracts from Brother Warner's diary will give the reader a better understanding of his character, his temperament, his spirituality and devotion, and his work, than would description by another. Unfortunately these journal records for the first five years of his ministry (for it is assumed that he kept such records), which no doubt would be very interesting, are not available.

---

[2] Dr. Forney, in the account of the Eleventh West Ohio Eldership in his History of the Churches of God, refers to D. S. Warner as being "later the leader in Ohio and westward of a body of people who gave the brotherhood considerable trouble."

All the information to be obtained covering this period is from those still living who had personal knowledge of the events, and from references to this period in his later records. In one of these he says he began traveling in 1868. In another he refers to having labored the first year in Hancock County, at Blanchard Bethel, in connection with Findlay.

During the first six years of his ministry his activities covered practically all of northwestern Ohio and a small portion of Indiana. Persons now living who were present in some of his revivals during this period state that they were remarkable for manifestations of God's power. Hard-hearted sinners, some of whom had not attended a meeting for years, would get under conviction and cry audibly for mercy. He ranked high as an evangelist—above the average of his day. In physical appearance he was slightly above average in height, rather slender and frail in build. His temperament was sanguine-nervous, eyes blue, hair brown—a fine sensitive organization. He wore a full beard, which in later years he kept shortly trimmed. He had the perfect bearing of a minister of the gospel, and his speech and conduct were fully consistent. His mentality was keen. His lungs were weak, but he wore well as a speaker. His voice was musical and possessed good carrying quality. One of his earliest revivals was held at New Washington, Crawford County, the home of his boyhood. He refers to it under date of Nov. 24, 1872, as follows:

> This town had ever been abandoned to the mercies of Catholics, Old Lutherans, and saloons, all of which were equally destructive of all moral good. No protracted effort had ever been made in the place. No conversions had ever been heard of. In the fall of 1870 I was put upon the Seneca circuit, of which New Washington was nearly in the center, and knowing the debauchery and ignorance of the people in general, I determined to lift up the standard of King Immanuel in that place. Accordingly I settled in the place and rented a vacant building that used to contain a drug store and saloon. The owner had speculative motives, having asked quite a dear rent for the room. But during the winter I and companion made special prayer to God for his conversion.

> The meeting was begun on the 17th of February, 1871. The night before the owner slept not for deep conviction. As soon as I arose in the morning he came to me in tears and confessed his sins and asked my prayers. I directed him to look to Christ for immediate pardon and deliverance. I gave him some of the great promises of Christ. And there, standing in his own stable, he looked to Christ and experienced a full pardon of all his sins. This settled the rent for the house. The third night six came to the altar. The meeting was attended with great power and produced a great stir among the people, many of whom had never seen the like. Fifty-six were converted, forty-six baptized, and forty-six fellowshiped into the organization.

Among these converts were a number of his school-mates, old acquaintances, and neighbors. George Pratt, of Nappanee, Ind., an old schoolmate and a former resident of New Washington, makes this statement concerning this meeting: "The meeting was held in my father's drug-store building. Brother Warner held the meeting unaided. He stood there alone and preached while others threatened. There were bad elements that rose in opposition, the Lutheran being the worst and the Catholic next. My father protected him. It was a wonderful meeting and many were saved."

The earliest of his diary records so far available begin in November, 1872, as follows, when he was on the Seneca circuit and had his home with a Brother Wright, in Crawford County, Ohio:

> **8.** Brother P. Wright brought me to Bucyrus. Staid all night with Bro. J. G. Wirt. The Methodists had a festival. I and a few members of the same church (who repudiated these follies and inconsistencies) met for prayer and the Lord was with us. These brethren were much dissatisfied with their church relation.

> **9.** Left Bucyrus at 7 A. M. Reached Lima at nine. Stopped at the Burnet House till 1:20 P. M. Wrote a letter to my brother and one to brother-in-law, L. W. Guiss.

> **10.** Sabbath. A. M., prayer-meeting at Brother Dague's, P. M., heard a Lutheran minister in Milton. Evening, preached from Isa. 28:16,17. I occupied the Presbyterian house. I preached here some in the schoolhouse in 1868, the first year I traveled.

> **11.** Took the train at 7:30 A. M. for Tontogany, with the design of finding where God wishes me to labor as a missionary. 0 Lord, guide thy servant to the place thou canst best use him! Walked from Tontogany to Brother Hardee's. Evening, went to Evangelical meeting. Brother W — — preached. Heard a great noise, but to the congregation it appeared as a tinkling cymbal and sounding brass, evidently having no effect. Nearly all blew loudly the horn of sanctification but manifested little of its fruits, such as travail of soul for the sinner and sympathy for the one soul at the altar, to whom none gave a word of encouragement, but each in turn arose and boasted of his holiness. Oh the delusions of Satan! How manifold they are!

In the entry just quoted the reader will notice his prejudice, existing at that time, against the doctrine of holiness, or sanctification. How strange it seems to those who knew him afterward to be a whole-souled advocate of the doctrine of holiness, that he should thus speak! It was altogether a matter of light and understanding. His heart was consecrated and he certainly was not unacquainted with the Holy Spirit during his early ministry. But as a definite experience to be believed for and testified to, he knew nothing about sanctification as yet. Also, it is possible that in its advocates whom he had met thus far, the doctrine and experience had not been rightly represented.

It will be observed also from these quotations from his journal that he meant to stand, and believed he was standing, free from sectarianism. He had considerable light on the church question and spiritual Babylon.

The place referred to in the following entry was near Holland, Lucas County.

13. Visited Father and Brother John McNut and Brother Irvin. Eve, preached in the brick schoolhouse, on Jas. 1:27. Here the Church of God had long been slandered and persecuted, principally by the United Brethren Church. One of the epithets they had for years called us is, "Johnny Cake Church." Bro. Henry S. McNut lives here nearly alone. He and his wife and their ancestors for generations past belonged to the United Brethren, but in the fall of 1870, after a hard spell of sickness in which he feared that he should die and be lost for not obeying the truth, he came to the West Ohio Eldership and received a license and began to preach amidst a storm of persecution from the United Brethren Church. Even his own companion, though an amiable woman, had been so poisoned against the Church of God that she joined in to oppose him. But he was firm and now commands the position. Every foe had fled and all that truly fear God join in to encourage the truth. Some will doubtless soon cut loose from sectarian bondage. Those that were the bitterest enemies now confess that we are right and they are wrong.

The Church of God, as we have seen, repudiated sectarianism, and the assumption by that church that it was the Scriptural one was a strong underlying principle. In some respects it held the correct idea of the Scriptural church. To some extent, therefore, Brother Warner's membership in that denomination afforded him light that naturally led to the full Scriptural standard which he afterward taught. His affiliation with that denomination in the first place was, as we have seen, because of a disposition to be Scripturally right on this point.

14. Brother McNut and I went to Toledo to look for a place in which to open a mission in that city.

15. Walked nearly all day in search of a place to open a mission. No success. May God soon open the way for the establishment of his church in this place.

In his diary Brother Warner recorded something for each day. Every time he preached it was noted and numbered and the text was given. The Eldership required each minister to give a report of his work. It is not necessary to quote all the shorter entries and items from his diary, which are much the same and generally speak of his visiting some one, making some trip, reading, writing, preaching, praying, fasting, baptizing, etc. Only the more interesting items, or such as are the most representative, will be given.

22. Returned to Auburn. Meeting at Basswood still in progress. The young men who made a start the last night I was there have all found Jesus their Savior. Preached from Mal. 3:8. A deep seriousness pervaded the minds of all. The feeling of that night shall not soon be forgotten. It was as solemn as the grave. A sen-

sation of dark and fearful forebodings of some approaching calamity ran through every mind. Bro. H. Caldwell arose and said
he had a matter revealed to him that he felt impressed to relate,
and that was that before tomorrow's sun should set some one in
this community would suddenly be killed. At his request we arose
and pledged ourselves to offer one more fervent prayer that night
in behalf of poor sinners.

23. Spent the day at home in reading, meditation and prayer.
Brother Jenner preached in the evening. I labored hard to bring
penitents to the altar. Three came out, two of whom were old
acquaintances of mine, for whom I had felt a deep interest. One
found peace.

After meeting was dismissed we heard that Ezekiel R— —,
an old man eighty-two or eighty-three years of age, who lived
one mile and a quarter east of the schoolhouse, had that day been
killed by the cars in crossing the track at Shelby. I knew the man
from my boyhood; he bought out my father in that country in
1853. He was very wealthy. God had blessed him with long life,
prosperity, and good health. But he had no thanks to offer to his
divine Benefactor, having set his whole heart upon the god of
this world. There was no place for Christ in his heart. He leaned
toward Universalism, because congenial to the carnal mind. He
was filled with skepticism and was always in the habit of speaking lightly of preachers and professors of religion. I visited him
twice during the meeting at Auburn last winter and conversed
with him on the subject of religion. He acknowledged that there
is one thing in the Bible that caused him to study a good deal, and
that is the new birth, which he said, was perfectly dark to him. He
told of having once gone to hear one of the greatest champions
of Universalism preach on the subject. "But," said he, "I received
no light whatever." His case was a clear fulfilment of 1 John 2:11,
"Darkness hath blinded his eyes," and 2 Cor. 4:4, "The God of
this world hath blinded the minds of them which believe not."
He had a very large development of brain, of which firmness was
the largest developed organ. What a pity that the devil perverted
these faculties!

I was informed that he was going that day to close a mortgage
and take a widow's farm from her. His last words to his wife,
who cautioned him to beware of the cars at the crossing, were, "I
was not made to be killed by the cars." This is like one who said
to his soul, "Thou hast much laid up for many days; eat, drink,
and be merry." But God said "Thou fool! this night shall thy soul
be required of thee." He said "I was not made to be killed by the
cars." But God said, "Thou fool! this day shalt thou be killed by
the cars." His brains were dashed out and strewn along the road.

His body was much mangled. But his poor soul has gone with all its guilt to where another rich man opened his eyes in torment.

The entry for the 24th, which was Sunday, records his preaching a farewell sermon to the congregation at New Washington, and also his reference to the revival held there in February, 1871. He had had the care of the congregation there.

25. I and Bro. S. Kline came to Conlay's, near Annapolis, Crawford County, Ohio, and began my first protracted effort in the name of Christ. Preached from Psa. 85:6,7. A good interest was manifested. Oh that God would visit the place in power, save many precious souls, and raise up a people for his name!

27. Started early for Bucyrus on our way to the Standing Committee at Rock Run. Took train at 10 A. M., arrived there at noon. I was chosen to fill a vacancy on the committee. Upon us devolved the solemn and responsible duty of trying and dis-fellowshiping Elder L. E— — for immoral conduct. Oh, what a pity! May the Lord have mercy upon him and help him to repent and be restored to the confidence of the people. May he be saved in the day of wrath. Oh, how careful the man of God, especially the minister of the gospel, should conduct himself in this wicked world! Lord, deliver us from temptation.

The meetings referred to in the next few entries were a protracted effort at the Conlay Bethel, near Annapolis, now called Sulphur Springs, Crawford County, Ohio.

Dec. 4, 1872. Visited a sick saint, J. McEntire, who has been afflicted for many years. He was near his last. Oh, what a happy soul. The night before he was almost gone. Said he, "I saw a convoy of angels around my bed waiting to carry my spirit home. I thought I was going home. Here I am yet lingering on the shores of time." Then a brother came in, to whom he remarked, "Sister Polly has gone home. I thought I would beat her, but I am left behind. All summer I and Cousin Patrick and Aunt Polly have had a hard race, but they have both crossed over and I am left to struggle on; but every gale wafts my little ship nearer the shining shore." "Oh!" said he, "It is all bright ahead, not a cloud do I see." After a little rest he remarked, "Oh! Brother, I know that my spirit will not go down into forgetfulness until the resurrection; but I am going to Jesus, which is far better. Oh, how sweet the name of Jesus!" I spent the day with this brother, sang and prayed with him. Eve, preached from Acts 3:19.

9. Spent the day in fasting and in much wrestling and prayer for poor souls under the guilt of sin. Preached from Luke 13:6-9. One young lady came to the altar.

10. Under much discouragement during the day. Evening, while singing the opening hymn I was greatly refreshed at the coming in of Bro. William Burchard, from Auburn, who was converted under my labors and baptized by me last winter. He was a very wild, wicked man, but has become a model of piety and earnest devotion. He has a brilliant intellect and has already made great proficiency in preaching. Thank God for such men of holy zeal. He being tired with the walk of eleven miles, I preached, from Ezek. 33:11. The penitent of the previous night came out and soon the good news went to heaven that another soul was saved by grace. It was a glorious meeting. One sister shouted. I got a great victory and was very happy. Likewise testified the convert and all the rest who spoke.

17. Good day meeting. Rebuked a boy for trying to pollute the house of God by spitting tobacco juice and quids on the floor. I said nothing to him, knowing that I should be insulted in return. But being filled with the Spirit I tried to encourage the three little mourners (girls who had come to the altar) and then addressed the brethren upon the importance of laboring for the early conversion of children, stating that it is enough to make the angels in heaven weep to see how the devil is leading even the children to wallow in sin and "glory in their shame." "Now, look at that poor boy," said I, pointing to him. "Ever since he came in here he has been doing his best to defile the house of God with his filthy tobacco. It was once said that 'He that doeth evil cometh not to the light lest his deeds be reproved,' but the devil has so polluted poor souls that even children in broad day-light do not blush to do such evil and dirty work for the devil as that. Christ said, 'That which cometh out of the mouth defileth the heart.' How defiled that heart must be, all that stench having come out of his mouth! A few nights ago a dog was accidentally shut in here and remained until the next evening, but did not pollute the house one half as much as that boy has done in half an hour." At this he grabbed his hat and, "being convicted in his own conscience, went out." God pity that boy and help older people to take a hint.

18. A. M., wrote most of the time. P. M., visited Brother McEntire. Found him much cast down and depressed, being overanxious to be absent from the body, in which 'tabernacle we groan, being burdened.' I told him that he ought to wait patiently till his "change cometh," knowing when he got home once he would have long time to stay there, even through all eternity; and the longer he should be tossed about upon the dark and tempestuous sea of this troublesome life the greater would be his joy when at last he should land in the peaceful harbor of the great city of God. After reading and singing and praying with him, he had great peace and perfect resignation to God.

25. Another Christmas is here. O thou Child of Bethlehem, may we this day bring the offering of a grateful heart! May every tongue on earth and all the angels in heaven join together to spread the glory of Jesus' name! Dear Lord, we thank thee for the unspeakable gift of thy Son to man. Oh, may every heart prepare him room! Dear Savior, draw poor sinners to thee. Show them thy bleeding hands, temples, and side. Oh that the star of hope would this day guide many poor wandering souls to thee!

28. Came to the place of meeting. Distance thirteen miles. Schoolhouse was full. Good attention. Went to Solomon B— —'s, an infidel. Talked till twelve at night.

29. Sabbath. Talked with Mr. B. until 10:30 A. M. He is a very smart man. Has his excellent memory stored with the writings of almost every wretch that ever dared to attack God and his holy religion. He is one of the best readers I ever met. What a pity that this noble intellect should be so basely employed! His horrid utterances are enough to chill the blood and heart of man and cause the angels of heaven to weep. He claims to be "a smarter man than Christ." "The devil is a gentleman compared with God." "Your God is not fit to be worshiped by a dog." "All professors are either hypocrites or fools." Oh, that God would pity that poor wretch who in the blindness of his depraved heart dares to rush with violence upon the Almighty!

30. Spent the day in reading, writing, and prayer, at Brother Conlay's. Eve, preached from Rom. 2:4. Good congregation. Saw some omens of good.

31. This is the last day of another year. How swift the years roll around and each brings us nearer eternity! Lord, help us to redeem the time and so "number our days, that we may apply our hearts unto wisdom," that at last it may not be said of us that "we spend our years as a tale that is told." Oh that each hour of my short life may bring some good account at last, when life's conflict is o'er! Great and many have been the changes of the last year. Yea,

> "What countless millions of mankind
> Have left this fleeting world!
> They're gone, but where? oh, pause and see,
> Gone to a long eternity!"

One there was, the dearest of my earthly friends, who a year ago stood by my side, the joy of my life, the sweet, innocent object of my fervent love. But she is gone, that dear companion upon whose rosy cheek and harmless lips I used to impress the kiss of burning, never-dying love. O Tamzen! thy heart and life, as pure as the white and fleecy snow that this morning covers thy peaceful resting-place, has reared an everlasting monument in the hearts of all that knew thee on earth.

I have now seen thirty years pass into eternity. Not quite eight years have been devoted to God. The year has been one of God's goodness to me, notwithstanding the loss of my blessed wife, which is her gain and God's glory, and therefore I am willing to travel on a lone pilgrim in search of souls for Jesus' sake.

'Twas very stormy. Wrote and read. Preached from Psa. 90:9, "We spend our years as a tale that is told." Tried to show the folly of living in sin.

Jan, 1, 1873. This is the first day of the year. O my soul, set out afresh for heaven! Lord help me to spend the year all to thy glory if we live to the end. But if it is said of me, "This year thou shall die," may I be ready to enter into rest.

7. Preached from Rom. 6:1. Told my dream, the subject of which I thought was in the way of a score of souls.

8. Fasted today. Very solemn meeting at Brother Crim's. All wept for poor sinners. O Lord, hear the prayers and groans and bottle up the tears of thy children and bring thy salvation nigh! Preached from Heb. 2:3. The meeting has received a great backset. I fear the whole work is killed. Before I came here I had a peculiar dream in which I saw a face that was strange to me. There was much confusion in those features, as in the midst of a council it stood out conspicuous, and there was something in the position of the person that pierced my heart. Last night I announced that I had recognized these features since I came here. Mr. B., the infidel, arose and asked whether he were the man. I said no. Tonight Esq. K., a poor blind Lutheran, came to meeting, and before I closed he arose and enquired if he were the man. While I was talking, I was powerfully baptized by the Spirit of God and replied, "Thou art the man." He was daunted, but stammered out a denial; but before I had time to ask a question he confessed that he had forbidden his family to come out to the altar. They are five young men and one daughter, three of them were under deep conviction and others serious. One of the boys is married and his wife and all their associates were serious and some anxious to come out, but all were prevented from coming to Christ by this poor wretch, whose form of religion fitted him to do this work for the devil.

In this attack I realized the fulfilment of the promise of Christ. 'In that same hour it shall be given you what ye shall answer, for it shall not be you but the Spirit that speaketh.' I warned him of the fearful account he would have to give at the judgment-bar of God.

9. Meeting at Samuel Shell's. We were all cast down and felt the Spirit of God had been grieved out of the community. Eve, preached from Jer. 28:16. Gave a farewell address and closed the meeting because, first, the work was so stagnated that nothing could be expected to be accomplished without a longer effort than I could devote to the place and, second, because it was highly probable that as soon as the work should break out again Satan would stir up trouble again from some source. I gained many warm friends and sowed seed which I trust will bring fruit to God. Some of the young men that desired religion I think will not give up the struggle. They sent me some money and word that if I would hold a meeting somewhere in reach that they would attend and seek religion, but there they had not the heart to come out.

25. Visited Brother and Sister Chapman. She is an excellent saint. Found her much afflicted. Brother C. had for many years been a skeptic and Universalist, but a year ago he came out at a meeting held by Bro. T. James and me. He is a faithful brother. A neighbor of his by name of L— —, who was the means of breaking up the fore-mentioned meeting, dropped dead in his tracks a few months ago.

Feb. 28, 1873. Good day meeting at Brother McClintock's. [near Larue, Marion County]. Eve, preached from Eph. 2:2. Four came to the altar and were blessed, one of whom had been an avowed Universalist. Others doubtless would have come out but the house was so densely filled that we could not crowd the people back to get more room for penitents.

Mar. 1, 1873. Spent the day at Mother Melvin's. Wrote an article for the Advocate. Brother Burchard preached. Four at the altar. All were blessed, I think. House crowded and many outside.

2. Sabbath. Speaking at ten. Preached on Church of God, Acts 20:28. Eve, the house was packed and all the windows were crowded on the outside. Preached, Jer. 13:16. By hard work we got a little space at the altar and four presented themselves for prayer.

5. Meeting at Brother Deen's. Fellowshiped twelve. P. M., because of the immense crowd that thronged the schoolhouse we divided the meeting. I preached at Windfall, from Job 22:15-17. Several rose for prayers. Brother Burchard preached at the Ellen Schoolhouse, one and one half miles north.

9. Sabbath. Brother Small and I went to the Shertzer Schoolhouse, where he preached at 11 A. M. on church matters, after which we received in fellowship eleven members, most by letter from the Methodist Episcopal and Presbyterian Churches. After taking a hasty dinner we mounted our steeds and rode four miles, partly through a woods, in the midst of a rain and severe storm. Reached Windfall at 2:30 P. M. Eve, preached on Acts 26:18. One at the altar.

10. Prepared a dam to baptize. Eve, Num. 10:28.

11. A. M., preached on sisters' right to speak and pray in meeting, after which we had a speaking-meeting. Fellowshiped fourteen members. House crowded and many on the outside. One brother who was always opposed to women's speaking arose and confessed his error. We then proceeded to the water, where I baptized twenty-two converts in eleven minutes. It was a glorious and beautiful baptismal service. All came out shouting and praising God. Eve, preached on Luke 13:6-9. Several rose for prayers, some of whom were old in sin. We had a speaking-meeting. All that had been immersed said that it had been a happy day for them and that they had turned a new and brighter page in the history of their pilgrimage. Oh how good it is to obey God! A good part of the number had been sprinkled, some after making a profession of religion in adult years. Great God, what a pity that the world is cursed by an unholy sectarian ministry "who teach for doctrine the commandments of men!"

12. Eve, preached on barren fig-tree. Matt. 21:18-22. Four came to the altar, one blessed. Went home with Mr. William Riser, who brought a horse for me to ride. It was a beautiful light night, and a ride of some two miles winding through the woods was somewhat pleasant. Did not retire until twelve o'clock.

13. This morning I spent an hour rambling far out in the dense, rolling forest to breath the pure air and to hold communion with my God. At ten William Riser's house was filled with brethren and sisters. We had a glorious meeting. All were happy, many shouted. It was something very strange to have a meeting in this house. All remarked that it was something they had never expected to see. Mr. R. is a man of nearly fifty years and a great sinner. His wife has been converted and I think the Lord is striving with his heart and his brother's, who is still older. Oh that God would raise them up as monuments of his mercy! Eve, Luke 19:10. Two at the altar.

14. A. M., meeting at schoolhouse. P. M., just before preaching I met with a few brethren who had been at variance, and helped to form a reconciliation, which was a perfect success. Preached on Matt. 22:21.

16. Sabbath. Preached one and three fourths hours on Ezek. 43:10,11, after which we fellowshiped and then baptized three. Eve, Brother Crawford, Baptist minister preached. Closed the meeting. Result, thirty-five converted, twenty-five immersed, church formed of thirty-three members. Expect more additions soon.

20. Eve, met the church at Windfall. Decided to build a meeting-house. Preached on church officers. Elders and deacons elected.

Apr. 3, 1873. Came to New Haven [Huron County]. Eve, met a number of my dear spiritual children in prayer-meeting. Had a good time and they exhorted me to meet them in heaven.

4. Beautiful day. How bright the sun shines! How the heart is gladdened at the return of warm and sunny days after such a long and hard winter as we have passed through! Oh, how I appreciate the Savior's beautiful metaphor in the Song of Solomon, where the present state of the church is represented by the winter with its dark clouds and howling winds, fierce with cold and hunger and hardship! But glory to God, the spring will come; already the fig-tree is putting forth her leaves, the turtle dove is heard in the land, and soon we shall hear the voice of the bridegroom calling, "Rise up, my beloved, my fair one, and come away; for the winter is past, and behold, thy beloved has come for thee." What a happy time that will be when, rising from the grave, we shall meet our dear friends and our Savior!

I am writing these lines in the beautiful cemetery near New Haven, Ohio. Before me is the little mound which shows the resting-place of my three little infants who a little over a year ago passed in a few hours through this vale of tears, and their little spirits are forever at rest with Jesus; and in one little box their bodies await the Savior's coming. What a glorious morning when all these graves shall burst open and the bodies shall come forth! they that have done good to the resurrection of life and glory, and they that have done evil to the resurrection of shame. Oh, may I be among the former class! Lord, make me a good man and keep me pure in heart. Farewell, sacred spot. Farewell, little tomb, with thy three-fold treasure.

16. Went to Bryan [Williams County] and ordered a tombstone for my wife's grave. The one selected cost fifty dollars, has a Bible lying on it, and I gave the following epitaph:

> How sweet and pure in social life,
> As daughter, sister, friend, and wife!
> Now done with cares below the sun,
> She shines before the snow-white throne.

18. Came home. Found Father and Mother and Brother well.

23. Commenced an editorial on Islamism.

24. Wrote and studied phrenology alternately.

26. Sent my article on Islamism. Brother Cassel and other preachers in Illinois send an urgent invitation for me to come to that State.

27. Sabbath. Preached today from 2 Pet. 1:10 in the Cogswell

Schoolhouse [near his father's home], where I made my first effort to preach the gospel, on Easter night, 1867. 'Twas in a Methodist Episcopal protracted meeting. The text was Acts 3:18. Never preached there since. In those six years I have preached all over northwest Ohio and some in two counties in Indiana, in all 1241 sermons. The number of converts 508, about the same number fellowshiped, some less baptized. Thanks be to God for his blessings and his presence! Though always of weak lungs, thought oft to be consumptive, yet my health has been better since in the ministry than ever before. Bless God for his goodness! I have never missed but one appointment on account of health. The years have swiftly passed, but, thank the Lord, I have enjoyed great peace and many rich blessings from the Lord.

May 13, 1873. Visited Tamzen's grave. Disappointed in not finding the monument up. Visited D. W. Dustin, one of my scholars. Exhorted him to give his heart to Christ.

15. Prepared a sermon on the evidence of the divine origin of the Bible.

16. Argument with Mr. Butler on the soul.

He attended, from the 21st to the 23rd, the meeting of the Board of Missions. He does not indicate where this meeting was held, but says in connection that he "preached in the Smithville Bethel" and "had very poor liberty, owing perhaps to the presence of many eastern ministers." It was at this meeting of the Board of Missions that he received his appointment to the mission in Nebraska, of which he thus speaks:

23. Beautiful day. Business finished up at 5 P. M. Brother Small was appointed to Chicago, I to Seward mission, Nebraska. Again I lay all upon the altar of God. It is very hard for me to leave my dearly beloved brethren of West Ohio. Thank God, for the great Head of the church is with them and his cause is greatly prospering here, and I must go help the cause in the far West. We parted with tears and many farewells.

24. Brother Small and I took train at 7:14 A. M., he for Marion, I for Larue, which I reached at 12 M. Received a letter from my beloved brother Sol. Kline. All our dear spiritual children are yet doing well on Seneca circuit. Wrote two letters. Preached at Windfall, 2 Pet. 1:13. Great row after meeting.

28. These days I have been low spirited and much cast down. It is the first anniversary of the death and burial of my blessed companion. How lonely I feel! My bereavement comes with all its weight upon me. Lord, be thou my comforter in all my loneliness. In eve, preached in Larue on the Church of God. Text, Eph. 1:10. I treated it as follows:

1. Notice the purpose of God.

2. "One" church.

3. Extent—heaven and earth.

4. Provisions for oneness:
    (a) One church typified.
    (b) One, bought, sanctified, made, built.
    (c) One faith.
    (d) One spirit to animate it.
    (e) One head, Christ.
    (f) One name, Church of God.
    (g) One law to govern it.

5. Standard of oneness—"As I and the Father are one."

6. Time of this oneness.

7. To be visible, "That the world may believe," etc.

8. Object of oneness.

9. Apostasy and restoration of the church.

10. Illustrations:
    (a) Paths, Jer. 6:16.
    (b) River.
    (c) House.
    (d) Corner stone.

The Lord gave me great liberty and boldness. Thank his holy name!

29. Staid last night with Bro. L. Orr. Sister O. is afflicted; prayed to the Lord for her recovery. Preached in Larue, eve, Ezek. 43:10,11.

30. It had been announced in the Larue Citizen that I would speak on the Church of God. This brought out quite a large congregation. Both nights I spoke plainly and boldly against the evil of sectarianism and other abominations. Many were ill at ease. Some preachers were present. The Lord gave me good liberty. Last night I diagramed my subject with chalk upon the blackboard. 2 P. M., took train for Pentecost meeting at Pleasant Hill.

Brother Warner became a strong exponent of the prophecies. Note his reference to some reform near at hand. This meeting was held at West Auburn, Crawford County, after his return from Pleasant Hill.

June 8, 1873. Sabbath. Thank God for life and health and this beautiful day! Behold the throngs pressing toward the house of God! Speaking-meeting was to begin at half past nine. Ere the time the house was filled. Others kept coming in continually, much to the detriment of the interest of the meeting. After all were seated that could be and the aisles were filled, there were numbers yet without. The house had been purchased by the Church of God from the Methodist Episcopal Church and repaired in good style. At eleven, preaching began. Text, Haggai 2:9, "The glory of this latter house shall be greater than the former, saith the Lord of hosts."...

I then took up the text used in the forenoon and showed that the destruction of the Temple and the Babylon captivity typified the dark age. The different attempts to rebuild typified the different reformations. Its final completion, i. e., all the so-called churches arising in and growing out of the Dark Age, including the sects, in which are many of God's people, who are, however, commanded of God to "come out of her." Further showed that according to the type and other Scriptures the church of God must arise to a glory excelling that of the first age, and that, owing to the fact that the world is near its end (of which we gave some Scripture evidence), some great revolution must be near at hand to bring about this prophesied glory of the church.

Some remarks were made on the ordinances, after which we engaged in the ordinances. Had a glorious time. A great many brethren and sisters were present to engage in following the Lord. Oh how I love those dear people! What a host of true hearts! God bless them.

14. Traveled by buggy to the grove-meeting at Windfall, four miles south of Larue. Brother Burchard preached an excellent sermon.

17. Received letters from Brother Bolton requesting me to come soon to my mission [in Nebraska] and one from Brother Shoemaker requesting me to stop and preach over Sabbath in Chicago.

19. Wrote out the record of the Church of God at New Washington. Eve, preached at Union. Here the church have a peculiar attachment to me. All wept much at my departure. A more true and faithful band is hard to find. God bless them. They are very dear to me. About half of the church are my converts.

20. Visited Brother E— — and Sister P— —. They embraced religion under my labors, and I joined them in marriage. Came home and packed for my journey.

21. Finished matters up to start. Received a letter from a **kind friend**. Went to New Haven in the evening. Farewell meeting at New Haven.

22. Sabbath. Thank God for a beautiful day. Many brethren came in from Union, New Washington, Auburn, and Liberty, and

Brother Mitchell and others from east Ohio. We had a glorious meeting. I preached on Luke 13:29, "They shall come from the east, and from the west, and from the north, and from the south, and shall sit down in the kingdom of God."

After preaching, Brother Jenner baptized four souls, two of whom had been converted here at New Haven, the other two were from elsewhere. Thus out of eight souls converted only two were baptized. This is the result of deferring to baptize for six months. Evening, preached on John 6:66-68. Had a good time in observing the ordinances. With many tears and farewell greetings, we gave each other the parting hand. Oh what friends are these! It tries the heart-strings to leave them. What a glorious thing that there is a meeting that knows no parting! What must it be to be there! May we all meet at last, when the storms of life are over.

Before leaving for the West, a correspondence was arranged with Sarah A. Keller, of Upper Sandusky. She is doubtless the "kind friend" just referred to with emphasis. Out of this correspondence there soon sprang a glowing flame of love, the beginning of a companionship that meant for him so much of both weal and woe.

CHAPTER VI

A NEBRASKA MISSION

The Nebraska field—The journey—Nebraska scenes—Reflections on his bride-to-be—Builds house—Returns to Ohio—Marriage—Resumes Nebraska work—All night in dugout—Outlook temporarily reversed—Long trips over prairie—Wife lonely—Visit to Indian camp—Fast in snow-drift—Birth of a daughter—Break in diary account.

The denomination known as the Church of God, founded by John Winebrenner in Pennsylvania in 1830, soon spread over western Pennsylvania and Ohio and gradually extended its missionary effort into the States farther west. Brother Warner's field of labor in Nebraska covered more or less the counties of Seward, York, Polk, Hamilton, and Fillmore. We shall again let him speak for himself.

June 25, 1873. This is my birthday. Thirty-one years of my hasty life have passed away. They have gone to eternity. Their record has all been entered upon the book by the Scribe of heaven. O Lord, whatever has not been set down to thy glory, for Jesus' sake blot out in the blood of Christ! Only eight years have been devoted to God and they crowded with many imperfections. Great God, I thank thee that we have an advocate to plead our cause and secure our pardon. Wash me, Lord, and make me clean. Oh, keep me pure in heart, that the remainder of life may all be given to God!

Took train at Upper Sandusky for Chicago. Ate dinner in Fort Wayne. Stopped off at Warsaw and went to New Paris to visit my brother-in-law. Found him and family well, thank the Lord. Eve, heard Dr. Everitt lecture on phrenology.

26. Was examined by Everitt and received a chart of character and instruction. I heard him deliver a course of lectures in my schoolroom in Corunna, Ind. the fall of 1865. He lectured in the evening on temperaments. Took notes.

28. Put in the day viewing the great city of Chicago. Nearly all the burnt district is built again with enormous buildings. It is wonderful to think that for miles we can walk streets built up on either side with magnificent buildings of brick, stone, and marble, from three to nine stories high, iron fronts, etc., all built since the fire. It inspires the heart with wonder and admiration to behold externally and internally the enormous hotels Sherman, Palmer, Tremont, and Pacific, of which the latter is the largest. It covers one half block and is nine stories high. Passed through under Chicago River. Chicago is one of the wonders of the world, a great city. Visited one of the parks. I was much interested with all we saw.

29. Sabbath. I preached in the evening from these words: "What do ye more than others?" Matt. 5:47. The day was pleasantly spent. Brother Shoemaker has spent nine years in trying to build up a Church of God here. Though the membership is yet small, we have a good church property and some good brethren here. I had the pleasure of seeing the wife, two sons, and one daughter of Elder John Winebrenner, who are members of the church here.

30. Took train at 10 A. M. on Chicago, Burlington, and Quincy Railroad to Nebraska City. Crossed the Mississippi River.

July 1, 1873. In A. M. took train for Danville, distance thirteen miles. Stopped at Bro. R. H. Bolton's. Found all well.

2. Enjoyed my visit very much with this lovely family. Received many useful hints from Brother B. concerning the West and the great missionary work.

3. Daylight found us at Creston. From there to Red Oak the country is a beautiful rolling prairie. Very little is cultivated, all grass. At Red Oak took branch road southwest to Nebraska City through a beautiful prairie valley. Beautiful corn. At Hamburg, eleven miles from Nebraska City, we came to a peculiarly formed bluff, high and sharp, from which we can see the city. Crossed the Missouri River at Nebraska City on the steamer Lizzie Campbell. The river was high and ran swiftly.

4. This is a proud day for Americans, the anniversary of American independence. There was quite an interesting celebration in Nebraska City. Free dinner, band, thirty-seven young ladies dressed in white with badges bearing the names of the thirty-seven states, also the goddess of liberty. Judge Kinney delivered a good speech on the occasion. A great crowd of people were in attendance. The whole matter displayed skill and ingenuity in its design and execution. Arrived at Seward at 9:30 P. M. Walked out through the prairie two miles to Bro. William Anderson's.

5. Visited Brother James Anderson. Walked across the country. How sublime and beautiful the rolling prairie! There is a strong breeze here nearly all the time, which makes the summer pleasant and agreeable. The wind is from the east; a good part of the time it is from the southeast.

6. Sabbath. At 4 P. M. I preached my first sermon in Nebraska, in the Anderson Schoolhouse. Text, Isa. 62:6.

Here we have to pass over a period of eight months. It is unfortunate that we do not have all of the books, forming a continuous diary account. His notes written during his first winter on the Western plain would have been interesting. As it is, we have to pass over the fall and winter of 1873 and begin again in March, 1874.[3] By this time it seems that he had taken up a claim at Wayland, Polk County. The Advocate he refers to was the church paper, published at Harrisburg, of which he was a correspondent. This chapter includes a temporary absence from the State, occasioned by his marriage and visit in Ohio, after which he returns with his help-meet to his Western field. His reference to Sarah, his bride-to-be, are, of course, full of tenderness. We shall give but brevities from the diary, omitting many of the details of sermons and texts, number converted, etc. The meetings first mentioned were held near Seward.

Mar. 14, 1874. This is a rainy day, the first of any account since the 22nd of November. Wrote two articles for the Advocate and some letters.

15. Sabbath. Preached at eleven on the second advent of Christ, two hours. Eve. Brother Robotham preached. 'Twas dry and dead enough to take all the life out of a meeting. I tried to exhort the people. Jesse Horton found peace to his soul. Thank God for the salvation of the old gray-headed sinner. Sister Anderson left her husband who sat by her side, and came to the altar in much earnest, seeking the Lord. This is a noble example. God bless the woman. I think her husband will follow.

16. The air was damp today. Read Nelson on Infidelity. Prayed and meditated. Eve, had some headache, but thank God it did not grow worse and prevent my preaching, as it sometimes does. The night was dark and damp. The congregation was much smaller than usual. Had good liberty. A number of young people were present, about all of whom were serious.

17. Had prayer-meeting at schoolhouse. Came home and wrote a letter to my darling Sarah, then went to Seward. Received a letter from Brother Shuler, treasurer, with post-office order for fifty dollars.

19. Day meeting at half past ten. P. M., mounted a horse and rode in company with Brother Figard to Mr. Pense's, two miles. Talked to them on the important subject of their souls' salvation.

---

[3] Dr. Forney, in his History of the Churches of God, says of D. S. Warner's mission work in Nebraska, that in February, 1874, he organized a church at Fairmount, Fillmore County, of twenty-four members. Also one at Cropsey, one at Evergreen, one in the Anderson community, Seward County, of sixteen members, and one other. He had fourteen preaching places.

Returned with some headache. Was disappointed in not having some one else there to preach, as Brother Combs, of the Methodist Episcopal Church, had promised to be there for the last two nights. Thank God, my headache abated and I spake with liberty on the text, "My Spirit shall not always strive with man."

21. Started for Fillmore County. Stopped a few minutes at a store at Nickleville. Heard some poor sinners swearing horrible oaths. Oh, how my heart was pained to hear them thus insult the Author and Giver of all their blessings! Came to Brother Witter's. Found all well and faithful to their Savior. They were much joyed at my coming. The church has grown in grace and influence.

22. Sabbath. Beautiful morn. Met at 10:30 A. M., heard a number of the brethren and sisters speak. Went to Indian Creek, where I had the pleasure of immersing the following [names nine persons]. It was a glorious time. All were happy. We felt that we were near heaven. At 3 P. M. started over to Brother Moffit's. Passed a pond of some ten acres on which were all of a thousand brants, a species of wild goose; they are white, except a black streak across their wings. Reached destination. Here are good prospects for gathering a church.

23. Quite cold this morn; 1 have to drive about thirty-five miles against the wind. It was a hard day's ride. Came on to the meeting and found that the work had not progressed in my absence. I could not have remained, but now I have only two nights and we must if possible see some poor sinners saved before I leave. O God! in mercy hear us and bless our efforts.

27. Had to go forty miles today to an appointment. Called on some of the brethren at Wayland. The day was cold.

30. Last night I had a precious dream of meeting my angel love, Sarah. Oh, how happy I was to return to that kind family and my precious companion, from whom I have been so long separated, and with whom my soul longs to be! Now are only seven Sabbaths until I start. Oh, how our hearts yearn to be together! Lord, speed the time. Never did woman have purer and stronger love for man than that of my dearest Sarah for me—yes, even me. O Lord, what a blessing thou hast here bestowed on thy unworthy servant! What a bliss to me, that I should thus be loved, and that, too, by the very creature that I would rather have love me than any fair female in all the world! O Lord! this is thy doing and it is wonderful in our eyes. How happy I would be this morning were my beautiful, virtuous, and loving companion by my side! How hard it is to stay apart so long! God give grace and strength of mind to endure this torture of separation.

Apr. 3, 1874. What a bright and beautiful morn! I am surrounded by beautiful scenery. The family live right on the bank of a stream, tributary to the Blue. The house sits on the edge of a bank about twenty feet on the north; on the south the stream making a loop comes around just far enough from the south side to make a nice little yard. To the east is a beautiful large yard. To the west is quite a picturesque scene; the stream, running very crooked, doubles around with but narrow, high banks between, and all covered with timber, some of the largest trees I have seen in the State, some oaks four feet across, yet not one of them enough to make a rail cut, branching out a few feet from the ground. The whole presents a romantic scene. Brother Querry settled here five years ago, when there were only a few families in the country. The settling up of the country has far surpassed in rapidity the wildest imagination. Bro. George Fellows and I went out on a hunt for prairie-chickens and wild geese. We went in the buggy, by which we can approach nearer to the chickens than otherwise. Had a few shots at wild geese but killed nothing.

5. Sabbath. Easter. Bright, warm, and beautiful morning. Preached at eleven on the Church of God, diagramed on blackboard. The truth was well received. There is a fine prospect for the Church of God. Dr. Stone who is no professor of religion but a thorough student of the Bible, and one whom I think will soon give himself to the Lord, is one with us in sentiment. Another good old Methodist Episcopal brother who preaches some sanctioned my sermon all through, even my strongest denunciation of creeds, sects, etc. Brother Stoner, a Disciple, was well pleased with the church but took exceptions to feet-washing, reception of the Spirit by faith before baptism, and the divine call to the ministry. He invited me home with him and we talked over the matter and he conceded my position on all these points. His companion before held with us on all these points.

7. Came to Brother Hoffer's. Selected a place for my house and staked off a yard, etc.

10. Wrote some letters. This was a warm and beautiful day. Oh, how lovely the spring after the long, cold winter; emblem of the time of the Lord's coming, the time of singing of birds! The turtle-dove is heard in the land, all to remind us of the Lord's coming.

The approach of summer also gladdens my heart because it is bringing us near the happy time when I shall be joined in holy matrimony with the pure and warm-hearted Sarah, whose constant and ardent love is worth more to me than all the treasures and honor of earth. Could I hold converse with that bright luminary whose beams and gentle rays fall so graciously upon the earth today, I would ask if the revolving earth brought another creature under his shining light so pure, fair, and lovely as my own blessed Sarah.

13. This morn is rainy. Drove to Wayland, fifteen miles, and then worked all day at my house. Bros. H. and M. Hoffer and Brother Berry had just got the lumber [hauled from Seward] on the ground and begun the work. We worked through the damp weather and got it finished, a stove up, and a bed by 10 P. M., when the brethren left, and I retired to sleep, the first night in my life in my own house and on my own land. Thank God for these blessings! May God help me to use it as not abusing it.

14. Returned to my house and made a stand. P. M., went to Barber's, where I preached at night on the signs of the coming of Christ. Had a house full of very attentive hearers. Spoke two hours. All seemed highly interested.

15. In the eve drove about seven miles over into York County and preached to a crowded house in the Parker Schoolhouse.

16. Went to Mr. Mahaffey's and had a good visit. He is a lawyer, a smart man, well informed in the Bible. Agrees with me on doctrine. He promised that he would give his heart to Jesus. Wishes to borrow some of my books to inform himself for the service of God. I pray God that he may be soundly converted and become useful. I had left no appointment, but several came together and begged me to leave another appointment before going east. I never saw people more eager for the gospel than here. Many have fallen in love with the Church of God and desire me to form a church here. P. M., went home and worked some at my house.

28. Drove to Bro. J. A. Mark's. The day passed off very pleasantly. Spent the time in meditation and singing praise to God. Drove about forty-five miles and reached destination about 6 P. M. There seemed to be no fatigue to me nor to my steed, Mattie Blaze. The roads were beautiful and the day delightful. How balmy the air! There perhaps never was another such delightful country to travel in. Found no one at home at Brother Mark's. Put up Mattie Blaze, compromised with the big dog, Watch, and took possession of the house. Ere long the family came home, having been at a neighbor's. They were well and glad to see me.

May 1, 1874. Came to Grand Island, in Hall County, about fifteen miles northwest of Brother Mark's. Found Bro. John Kramer and family well. They are a very fine people, firm in the principles of the Church of God. They have a beautiful place one and one fourth miles from the city. All that is wanting is a Church of God here. I feel sorry that they can not be supplied. But this is a hard place to do anything unless we have a house of worship. Brother K. could find no place in the city to have an appointment, so he has an appointment in his own house for Lord's day. Sectarian bigotry abounds here in the West; each sect, fearing the rottenness of its own foundation, is not willing to have it tried by the gospel.

2. Wrote, read, meditated, and prayed in a pleasant room at Brother K's. How pleasant it is to have a place of solitary retirement, so seldom enjoyed in the small sod houses of this frontier country! This afternoon there was a good deal of excitement in Grand Island on the occasion of breaking ground for a new railroad, the St. Joseph and Grand Island Railroad. It is now in operation from St. Joseph to Hastings. Grand Island is beautifully situated on the Union Pacific Railroad and on the north side of Platte River. It has a bright prospect for a large city and important railroad center.

3. Sabbath. Rainy in A. M., hence no preaching. Spent the day pleasantly with the kind Kramer family singing and talking on Scripture.

5. Started this beautiful morn to Fillmore County. Took my dinner and fed Mattie Blaze on Sec. 12, Twp. 9, Range 6 W. Two miles east is the nicest railroad section I ever saw. I crossed the South Blue River in a beautiful grove, which was quite green. The place was so beautiful that I could not resist the temptation to stop in the shade by the cool stream. I wondered if I should ever have the pleasure of crossing through this beautiful grove with my lovely Sadie, who of course is always brought to my mind when I meet anything that is lovely and beautiful, for she is the fairest and most lovely piece of God's creation.

Two graceful ducks were swimming in the water. This as well as the cooing dove near by brought forcibly to my mind my beloved, who is far away. The dove's cooing was an index to my heart, that longed to be with her, so dear to me. Even the beautiful stream suggested to me our two beings that were soon to blend fully into one to follow on in everlasting love, like two streams of water that mingle together and flow on in the same channel.

These lines are being penned in this beautiful grove while many feathered songsters are singing their sweet songs over my head. Thank God for the beauties of nature and all that they have brought to my mind.

6. Received a letter from Bro. J. A. Shuler, treasurer, with an order in my favor for fifty dollars. Thank the kind Lord and all who gave to this fund.

8. Came to Indian Creek. Found all well and anxious for my coming. All seemed faithful.

10. Sabbath. Sabbath-school at ten. Preached on Gen. 28:12,13.

A strange brother arose and said he would like to speak a few words. He remarked that for some time he had been searching for the truth and the old paths and that he precisely agreed with me that there is but one church, i. e., the church of God, so named by the mouth of the Lord, governed alone by the Word of God, including all who have the Spirit of Christ, by which they are baptized into the body, the church. The brother talks some to the people and accepted an invitation to preach in two weeks. Thank God for more laborers to contend for the truth.

After this went to Indian Creek, where I had the great pleasure of immersing [names seven persons]. At last baptizing Brother Winters told me that he had been baptized by his parents when a child, and now they were dead and gone, and out of respect for them he would never be baptized again. I told him to read his Bible and see whether that satisfied the demands of God upon him. I further reminded him that religion was a personal matter. He acted upon these suggestions and the result was he was anxious to obey God. Oh how the commands of God are made void by the traditions of men! The baptizing was one of great interest. All were happy. Eve, had a good speaking-meeting. Some said it was the happiest day of their lives. Preached on the ordinances and had a heavenly time in observing them. Bade the brethren and sisters farewell.

13. Was to have a breaking bee, but it rained all forenoon. P. M., worked on my claim. Eve, preached from Acts 20:32. We got lost going home with Brother Hoffer. Got home by eleven. It was raining and very dark.

18. Went to Seward in the morning. Spent the day preparing for my journey. Eve, preached in Seward and returned home.

19. The happy time has come at last that I start back to my beloved Sarah. May God's kind care be over me by the way. Took train at half-past nine at Seward. This is the morning I have been thinking about so long. The hard labor of another year is over. Since last July 4 preached one hundred and fifty-five sermons.

20. Nebraska City. Visited a beautiful orchard of eighty acres. Am enjoying my visit much with Bro. John F. Kimmel and family. Took a pleasant ride.

21. Today the Board of Missions meets in Chicago. Wish I could be there to report in person; but I sent out my report yesterday. At 7:20 P. M. started on my journey. Came via Hamburg, St. Joseph, and Kansas City, where I arrived at early daylight.

22. Took the Missouri Pacific through the State of Missouri.

Train stopped for dinner at Jefferson City. Ran through tunnels, under rocks. Many places the rocks stood a perpendicular wall one hundred feet on one side of the cars and on the other the Missouri River. Missouri in some parts seems to be a beautiful State; but taking it altogether it falls far short of Nebraska as an agricultural state. It is rather rough. Had three fourths of an hour in St. Louis. Purchased a suit for thirty-five dollars, also a small present for my beloved Sarah, a collar, $1.50, and cravat, $1.50. Took train on Toledo, Wabash, and Western at 7 P. M. Crossed the Mississippi on a transfer boat near the great iron bridge, which is a wonderful structure. Took sleeping-car and lay down with a heart full of gratitude to God for his protection through the dangers of the day and humbly entreating his care through the night.

23. Reached Fort Wayne at 7 A. M. Staid over till 12:30 P. M. Then came on with a light heart. Arrived at Upper Sandusky at 4:50 P. M. Rode out to Brother Keller's with Brother Hoffman. And now the long contemplated time of meeting my beloved Sarah has come at last. Thank the kind Lord for his care and protection over us through these eleven long months that we have been so far, far apart.

This eve went to see Father Shriner, who is nearing the other shore to dwell with the spirits made perfect. Had a season of prayer. Returned with Brother Keller.

25. Father Shriner died at 4 A. M. yesterday, and at 11 A. M. today Brother Small preached the funeral, followed by Brother Updike and me. It was a very large funeral. Father S. was an upright and godly man, firmly devoted to truth and right. Well do I remember words that fell from his lips some four years ago when, during his report, he remarked: "Brethren, I have always tried to maintain a ministerial character." These words, backed up by his exemplary life, had a great meaning and made a deep impression on my mind. They inspired me with new determination to live out the same character by the grace of God.

26. Spent the day pleasantly at Brother Keller's. Oh, how happy I am to have the blessed company of my dearly beloved Sadie! Surely I should be a happy and grateful man, having such a rich treasure.

28. Took train for Crestline, where I am now writing these lines, waiting for the train to Shelby. But here it comes! Twelve o'clock, aboard the train. Oh, how convenient to the great cause of God is the railroad! Reached Daniel Baker's, at Shelby, at 1 P. M. We were happy to meet again.

Nearly one year has passed since my last visit here in company with Bro. J. L. Jenner, who is now in eternity. Poor fellow, he became insane last April and on the 25th cut his throat and abdomen, from the effects of which he died some days later. From the best information I could get his mind was overcome by an unwillingness to preach the whole gospel of God, through a desire to gain the applause of man. As ministers of God we should take warning and fill our high calling in the fear of God.

29. Came to W. Auburn, where I met many of the dear brethren beloved as children. Preached from Psa. 144:15. How happy and grateful I am to meet with these beloved people!

30. This morn I went up into my old room at Bro. Peter Wright's and looked over all my mementos of my dear departed companion and sonny.

31. Sabbath. Had a good speaking-meeting. Preached on the signs of the coming of Christ. The house was crowded. Eve, Brother Awkerman preached on the ordinances, after which we had a happy time in obeying them. Human language can not express my joy.

June 3, 1874. Yesterday and today the women were busily engaged in preparations for our wedding.

4. This is the happy day to which my mind has so often soared ahead of time to embrace in sweet anticipation. Thank God that the onward flight of time has brought the day in which my angel Sarah and I shall be joined in holy wedlock. I was out early to breathe the balmy air. At the rising of the sun there was a heavy fog which all disappeared in a very short time, leaving the morning bright and lovely. All nature seemed cheerful. Never have I heard the birds sing so sweet and melodious as this morn in the woods over the way from Father Keller's brick farmer's home. It seemed that the dear little feathered songsters were congratulating me for the rich fortune the day brings to me. Went to Upper Sandusky in the morning. Weather hot. [Here he mentions a list of the guests from Auburn, Tiffin, and elsewhere.] At four the ceremony was performed, Brother Burchard officiating. Brother and Sister Tomlinson groomsman and groomsmaid. All passed off pleasantly. Received many warm congratulations, after which we proceeded to partake of the rich preparations in the dining room.

The evening was pleasantly spent sitting in the cool shade on the east of the house. Now a new leaf is turned, a new era begun, in the history of my life. O Lord, how can I thank thee enough for the great gift of my own pure, amiable, fair, and lovely Sarah! May God assist me to make her life happy as far as it is in the power of man to do so. God bless our union and make us together happy and useful.

5. This morning still bright and clear. We started for Brother Wright's. Stopped at noon at Bucyrus. Reached my old home at

W——'s about four. Our arrival was greeted with ringing bells and cheers from the boys. A rich infare supper was prepared. The evening was pleasantly spent singing and with music from two violins by Brothers Alvin Burch and Burchard.

Sarah (Keller) Warner.

7. Sabbath. Good speaking-meeting in the grove [near New Washington]. Preached on baptism. After speaking one hour a small storm arose, which threw the congregation into confusion. We dismissed the people to meet at three by the side of the Maumee River. There being a grove there I proceeded to finish my discourse and spake about an hour, after which I baptized the following ten [names omitted]. Eve, I spoke on the washing of

the saints' feet, after which observed the same. This was a good meeting. About a thousand people were present.

8. Took train for Bryan, where we were met by my brother, who conveyed us to my parents, in Bridgewater township, Williams Co. Thank God for a safe return to my parents once more.

11. Visited Brother Joseph. Eve, we took a walk to a beautiful cemetery on my brother's place. A new grave was there that awoke a train of interesting thoughts to my mind. It was the resting-place of Frances Stocking. She was the object of my affections and attentions at the time I gave my heart to God (February, 1865). She was handsome and accomplished, having a very strong mind and good education. Her father was skeptical, and the dire disease was transmitted to Frank and I think the whole family. Having talked matrimony together and supposing she and I had the proper affections, I supposed it my duty to marry her notwithstanding her infidelity and her rapidly failing health. Out of sympathy for her suffering, which she claimed would be removed by marriage, I pledged her my heart and hand. But I asked to defer our marriage until I pursued my studies a few years. Ere many months had passed I began to doubt the existence of the proper elements of union in our case. I took the matter to the Lord and was soon confirmed in the belief that our marriage was not ordained of God. Our attachments grew weaker and soon correspondence ceased and she became married to a rough young man by the name of Baker. They moved to the West, ere long parted, and she came back a year ago. When at home I learned that she was a spiritualist and by spells was crazy, in which condition she was hurried to the grave, a poor wreck, morally, mentally, and physically.

17. Passed once more the old schoolhouse where I gave my heart to God (February, 1865). Thank God for that step. Oh how glad I am that it was ever my lot to become a Christian! A beautiful house of worship stands near the place, belonging to the Church of God.

25. This is my birthday. Thirty-two years have passed over my head. How the time has flown! Oh God! blot out of my past years all that is wrong and help me give all that remain to thee and thy cause.

July 8, 1874. This is my dear Sarah's birthday. She is nineteen years of age.

24. Bro. Lewis Williams took us and our goods to New Washington. Had a good talk at the depot with Brother A— —. He seemed very much dissatisfied with my having organized a church in Upper Sandusky. Intimated that it would make me trouble. Oh that God would save his preachers from envy and vindictive cruelty in biting and devouring each other! Whatever the Eldership may do in my case, I am certain that I did what I have done through pure motives to the glory of God, for the good of his cause, and I believe with his approbation.

30. This morn went to West Unity, thence to Father John Kerr's in Fulton County. Eve, went to prayer-meeting. Heard a good number of my scholars testify for Jesus, thank God. Meeting was led by Bro. G. W. Dustin, who is a noble young man. Since he attended my school, I have felt impressed that God desired to make a minister out of him. I pray that God may lead him into all truth.

August 11, 1874. Father, Mother and Brother Joseph brought us to Bryan. Bade farewell to the friends once again. Reached Goshen about four. Found Mr. Guiss, my brother-in-law. Reached his home in New Paris about dusk. My sister's health is poor.

15. Preached in New Paris from Matt. 24:3. Four young brethren and two sisters were there from Syracuse.

16. Brother Keller came after us early this morning to convey us out to Syracuse, where I preached at 10:30 A. M.; Psa. 144:15. Went home with Charles Strombeck, whose companion is sick. Prayed for her. She seemed strengthened. Four brethren each put a dollar into my hand. Returned to town. Eve, preached on Ezek. 43:10,11. Diagramed on the board. House full. A collection was taken up for me. Never did I find such overabundant kind and benevolent people. They seem as near to me as though I had preached for years in their midst. God will surely bless them and greatly reward their kind liberality.

17. Took train at 10:20 A. M., reached Elkhart at eleven, laid over until 4:13 P. M. Reached Chicago 8 P. M.; Brother Shoemaker met us at the train and conducted us to his house.

18. In company with Brother S., visited the scene of the late fire. Visited the great water-works, also the exposition building, the largest building I was ever in. Walked through the tunnel and visited the Union, Michigan, and Jefferson Parks, where was much of interest. Traveled by street-car and on foot about ten miles. Took train on the Burlington at 10 P. M.

19. Reached Red Oak, Iowa, 7 P. M. Put up at the Tremont House. A lady was shot in the place tonight by one whom she had opposed as a suitor for her daughter. Four balls were fired, some of which took effect in the neck. She may possibly recover. The assassin was arrested and confined.

20. Took train for Nebraska City. Western Iowa is beautiful; Sarah much admires it. Reached the Missouri River at ten, and Brother Kimmel's in Nebraska City at eleven. Took train for Seward. The country looks beautiful. One thing strikes the mind as different from Iowa and Illinois, and that is the great abundance of wheat on this side of the Missouri River. Corn is raised in abundance in those States; but little proportionately is raised here, and will be almost an entire failure this year owing to the drought and grasshoppers. As soon as we crossed the Missouri we landed among swarms of those insects. Landed safely at Seward at 10 P. M. Thank God for his kind care over us, permitting us safely to return to my field of labor.

21. This morning Sarah and I walked over the prairie two miles to Bro. William Anderson's.

22. P. M., we went out to visit a colony of prairie-dogs. Eve, preached from 2 Pet. 1:3.

24. Went to Seward, Wife and I and Bro. J. W. K——. He leaves on the train this morn for Ohio to take a wife, a dear sister, Eliza T——, who was converted under my labors and is a special friend of mine. About a year ago I introduced them to each other, since which time they have corresponded and now have pledged themselves to live in unison for life. I pray God that their union may result in unbroken happiness and usefulness.

26. Wife and I came to Polk County. Wife is pleased with the home, but fears we shall not be able to build. I pray God he may send help from some source.

29. Drove about twenty-three miles, to Fillmore. Preached in the old sod schoolhouse. The brethren and sisters were glad to see me, as I also was to see them. Brother Grigg has been preaching for them during my absence. He does well and is sound in the Scriptures. I am glad that I found him out before I left.

31. At 3 P. M. started for Seward County, thirty-eight miles. At sunset stopped and ate our supper by the way. Turned out Mattie Blaze to pick grass. Then came on. The curtains of night were soon thrown about us. It was cloudy, and not being able to see my guiding stars we lost our way. When I discovered the north star we traveled some distance by it with no road at all. We went several miles out of our way and landed at Bro. J. Anderson's after twelve.

Sept 4, 1874. Drove twenty-six miles to Polk County.

5. Went over to our house and found our goods; Brother Fox had brought them from Seward. Found everything all right. Read in the Testament. Finished it today. Had finished and re-commenced it last Thanksgiving Day. Oh, that I had more time, and would better improve in the future what I have, to read the precious Bible!

10. Started to York Center. Rained. Turned in to Bro. Samuel Marble's. No one at home. Soon he came. Left us in search of his wife. Did not find her till between three and four. We spent the time pleasantly in his old dugout. Instead of being lonesome it was pleasant to be found alone—even in an old wet dugout and on a dreary day. It appeared like a small taste of the bliss that a home of our own would yield us. The greatest difficulty was something to eat. Plums were plentiful, else we could find nothing. When they returned they felt very bad that they happened to be away from home. They spared no pains to make us welcome and comfortable. Supper was served, after which the rain and darkening shades of night prevented our return.

12. Sabbath. Started early for Polk County. Received some letters, one from Father and Mother Keller. All are well but seem to have no sympathy for us here on the frontier, not even a disposition to do justice by us. Lord, forgive them. We will suffer all things for thy sake. O God, my heart is bruised and crushed! We seem to meet with no sympathy from friends or brethren. Many have grown cold. Brothers H—— and O—— would not go to meeting. Went on to the Bense Schoolhouse. Preaching time, but no one there. Two neighbors came, no member of the Church of God. O Lord, the waves are rolling over me! All things against us. Some are offended because we will not recognize the devil's secret gods with which they have been polluted. Others are backslidden. Lord, the troubles of my heart are enlarged! It is more than I can bear. I can not restrain my grief for the desolation of Zion. The people are now gathering, but my tears prevent the reading of a hymn. Companion and a few brothers and sisters shed their tears with me.

14. Wrote for Advocate.

15. Sister Berry, Sarah, and I went to Lincoln Creek. Got tub of plums.

18. Tried to get lumber on time, but could not. Felt very much cast down. No money yet from the Board. Friends in the East have no sympathy for us. Brethren here have no means. Winter is coming on soon and no home for my dear Sarah and me! With a heavy heart we started out to Bro. J. H. Anderson's. Heard he was not at home. Went on to Brother Green's. As soon as he found I could not build they kindly invited us to move into their north room, which is a pleasant room with bed-room above and cellar privileges. Thanks be unto God! Behind a frowning providence, he hides a smiling face.

19. Sabbath. Eve, preached at the Osborne Schoolhouse, up Lincoln Creek, a new point. Stayed at Mr. O——'s, who is a Campbellite. Had some talk, but a few Scriptures silenced his doctrine.

20. Gathered some grapes for Sarah. Came home to Brother Green's.

21. Sarah and I went to Polk County.

22. Spent in our house preparing to take things back to Brother Green's, Seward County. Sarah and I slept in our house all night.

23. Staid all day again at house. Bro. J. W. Figard came to take our things.

27. Came to Seward County, Brother Green's. Stopped at noon in the timber of the Blue River.

Oct. 1, 1874. Eldership meets in West Ohio. May God bless their deliberations. Worked till noon. At 3:15 P. M. started for York County, twenty-six miles. Could not reach it. Stopped at Brother Everett's.

3. About this time the West Ohio Eldership has passed through another session. I now begin another year's work.

5. Drove home. Found my dear companion well. How happy we are to be alone this eve in our little home! How sweet the home where love reigns! Oh the love that unites our hearts! How pure and strong, and still increasing! How happy I am! How blessed and favored!

6. Worked at cupboard and helped my dear wash.

7. Provided and arranged things for wife. Dear creature wept this morn that I had to be away again so soon and long.

9. Came to Brother Berry's [Polk County]. P. M., in my house. Wrote some letters. Preached in the Bense Schoolhouse, 2 Pet. 2:11-14. Staid in my house tonight.

10. Visited and talked with nearly all the members of the church. Many are cold and indifferent. Many have strife and bickerings. Oh shame! Great God, save this church, of whose piety and devotion I have so often boasted. Some are spiteful at me because I touched the god of this world. Brother Mc—— raved and foamed over at me. God pity and forgive the poor graceless man. Thank God for grace to endure unruffled his abuse. Staid all night in my house.

12. Started for home, anxious to see my blessed wife. This is the longest we have been apart since our marriage—five days. How long the time seems to me, notwithstanding I have been very busy! How lonely she must be! God bless her. Came by way of Seward. Dear Sarah had been way out on the prairie waiting for me.

20. Started for the Oliver Schoolhouse, about twelve and one half miles to the northwest. Dear wife felt so bad to see me leave. The dear creature wept bitterly. Oh, how it pained my heart to leave her feeling so sad! Green's folks were absent, which made it more lonely. O God, must I tear myself away from the dear wife bathed in tears? But 'tis the cause of Christ and I must go. O Lord, comfort her loving heart.

24. Started for Fillmore County. Drove against a very heavy wind.

25. Sabbath. At 11 A. M. preached, Psa. 48:14. The old sod was full of hearers.

26. Drove to Brothers ... and gathered quite a good load of vegetables and feed that these good brethren gave us. Came to Brother Weeter's, where the donation was increased and Brother W. having business at Seward hauled it over for us. God bless these kind people. I fed and ate my dinner on the Blue River. Reached home 3 P. M., found dear wife well.

31. Spent the day at Brothers M— — and B— —'s. Busy studying sermon. Eve, preached on Isa. 9:6,7. Studied till twelve at night on sermon for Sabbath eve.

Nov. 1, 1874. Sabbath. This morn arose early and prepared a sermon on the subject of the Sabbath.

2. At three started home. Arrived at dark. Dear wife was very lonesome and almost despaired of my coming home that day. Thank God, we are blessed with a home and a thousand domestic comforts. Oh what a blessing is home when illuminated with the pure love of an affectionate companion!

3. Went to Seward, where were two barrels of apples sent to me by a kind friend in Ohio. May the Lord bless his soul and reward him. He not only donated the apples but paid one dollar for the barrels and $1.25 freight to Chicago. The cost here was $4.20. Not having the money to lift them we let Brother Anderson have one barrel to lift them for us.

6. At 11 A. M., started for Crete. Stopped in a deep draw at 1 P. M. to feed Mattie Blaze and eat our dinner. Sarah and I ate a whole chicken, some bread and butter, and finished off with an apple apiece. Went via Milford and Camden. Passed through a very large colony of prairie-dogs. Enjoyed a leisure visit among this brisk and numerous little folk.

7. Was glad to meet our dear and esteemed old Brother Moore, of whom I had heard so much. He is a very intelligent old pilgrim, greatly in love with the doctrines of the Church of God. It was through his earnest appeals that missionaries were sent to this part of Nebraska. At 4 P. M. we met in the Bethel to take the preliminary steps to the formation of an Eldership in Nebraska. Organized by the election of Bro. K. A. Moore speaker and Brother McElwee and myself clerks.

9. Met at 9 A. M. for business. The day was passed off very pleasantly. Love seasoned all our deliberations. According to committee on program, I delivered a discourse on church polity. Missionaries reported, and other business transacted. Closed by a touching speech from Brother Moore and prayer by me. The meeting was very edifying to us all and greatly strengthened the brotherly ties.

10. Met early this morning in the Bethel for a social meeting. Good time. Brother Moore left us for home. God bless the old pilgrim and spare his life yet many years to bless his cause. Brother McE. and I spent the day in transcribing the minutes of the Eldership.

I preached in the Bethel, 1 Chron. 29:5. God blessed my soul. This afternoon I had a special season of secret prayer and communion with my God. Oh how near he came to his poor servant! This eve I was unusually blessed in presenting the thoughts he had given me on the text, "And who then is willing to consecrate his service this day to the Lord?" A deep interest prevailed. A Mr. B— — living six miles from town went home with an arrow in his heart. I expect to hear of his early conversion.

13. Made out program for Ministerial Association to be held next spring in Seward.

14. Came home. Pretty cold. Captured a wild duck which had its wing broken that day by some hunter. Reached home at nearly dusk.

15. ... This was an earnest day's work. I pray God that it may bring forth fruit to his glory.

Dec. 25, 1874. This is Christmas. At eleven preached on the incarnation of Christ. Returned to Bro. M. Hoffer's, where the kindred, companion, and I partook of a good feast. Roasted fowls. All passed off pleasantly and in a Christian manner. I was solemn and meditative. We sang some. Eve, spoke on John 14:23. With solemn and feeling hearts and minds performed the ordinances of feet-washing and the Lord's Supper.

27. Sabbath. I preached about two hours on the immortality of man. Read twenty-three Scriptures speaking of the Spirit and twelve of the soul, all positively declaring the spirituality of man's nature. Also several places proving that the soul came forth from the body at death and is as much more important than the body as the man is than the tent in which he lives. Proved also the conscious existence of a soul in an intermediate state. When through, Mr. K— —, a poor silly Adventist, harangued some moments. How confused the wretched Adventist doctrine!

Jan. 1, 1875. Another year has rolled into eternity. God is still favoring us with his kind care and preservation. Oh, how many souls are in eternity today who with light hearts enjoyed friendly greetings and sumptuous festivities a year ago today! Some, alas, we fear, have been "cut down out of time," who had no Christ in the soul. Oh, what a mockery are all the pleasures of the wicked! True and warm hearts wished them a happy New Year one year ago today; but alas, their sins have made it the year of their doom to eternal misery. O God! give us grace to enable us to spend our years to thy glory. Companion and I spent the day very pleasantly in Seward with.... The two ladies are sisters, and old friends and acquaintances of Ohio. They had a sumptuous feast. We sang a few hymns, read a chapter, and knelt in prayer to our Father in heaven. Then came home.

2. Took Sarah to Brother Anderson's and started to visit the church in Fillmore County, a distance of about thirty miles. Stopped in Nickleville and fed Mattie Blaze. Warmed and ate my dinner in a store. Reached Brother Weeter's a little after dark. The brother was gone and I was so cold I could hardly put my pony away. Sister W. soon got me some supper, and after eating hastily I set out afoot one and one half miles to the schoolhouse. Found three brethren there. No light. Gave them a short discourse from Heb. 10:35.

3. Sabbath. Some brethren tried for two hours to get the old sod schoolhouse warm, but the stove was so poor they failed. They then came up to Brother Horton's, where I spoke to a little band of brethren and sisters from Heb. 9:16,17. Started for Brother Moffitt's. Quite cold and stormy. Stopped at Bro. P. H. Griggs. Talked till a late hour on Scripture. The brother is troubled with the no-organization doctrine advocated by Johnson, editor of the Stumbling Stone. The brother confessed that elders and deacons are authorized in the New Testament as the completion of the local organizations, and in short the polity of the Church of God is Bible.

5. Went to Seward. Got coal and a box sent by Father and Mother Keller.

7. Helped Wife wash. Read Moral Philosophy.

8. Made apple butter of the frozen apples in the box sent by father-in-law.

9. Very stormy and cold. Improved the time in mental and religious improvement.

10. Sabbath. Strange to find myself at home with no appointment. Meditated what to do. Having appointments here a week from today, I concluded not to go this week to York County, but hoping we would be favored with good weather I dispatched Brother Green to circulate appointments for tonight and during the week at Occidental. Eve, pretty good turnout.

18. Helped Wife wash. Read and wrote. Devotion was sweet and precious this morn.

19. At 12:45 P. M. started for York County, about twenty-six miles. Reached destination at 6 P. M. Small turnout.

21. This morn realized a precious nearness of Christ in family worship. Spent two hours in private room reading Testament and in prayer and meditation. It was a precious season.

25. Praise God for the great triumphs in his cause! I am spending many hours on my knees praising God and imploring mercy for sinners. What a glorious work!

27. Started for home. Dear Wife was much cast down owing to my stay being longer than I had intended. Dear affectionate creature! My absence seems to rob her of all the happiness of life. It would be none the less the case with me were it not for the absorbing cause of God during my absence.

29. Strong wind from the west, and not feeling well I did not go to York County. Read and wrote.

30. Quite stormy. Can not go to the meeting today. Spent the day in reading and writing, prayer and meditation.

Feb. 12, 1875. Wife, I and [names several others] went to visit about two hundred Omahas, camped on the Blue two miles from Seward. They were on their return from their winter's hunt. Were well-laden with robes and furs. It was an interesting visit. The squaws were busily engaged in dressing and tanning buffalo robes; the men stood and looked on. Poor creatures! They seemed to be but servants for the men. How wrong and cruel such a custom! We went into their wigwams; but few could, or at least would, speak English. The little papooses were amusing themselves by loading each other down with bundles of weeds, etc., in imitation of their pack-ponies. They also had a tent constructed out of blankets. One girl about twelve had a little papoose but a few weeks old tied on a board and hung on her back. Sometimes she would lay it down face up in the sun, other times she had it on her back engaged in play with other children. I could see a marked improvement in the rising generation in the moral and intellectual organs. Their more frequent contact with white people and a general tendency to improvement in the tribe renders the children far superior to their parents. Some I noticed were as well constituted as many white children. One boy of about thirteen could spell quite well. May the kind providence of God yet elevate this poor distressed people to a higher plane of intellectual, moral, and religious enjoyment. The Omahas are among our most honorable and refined tribes. Bought a fine robe for ten dollars. Cost in Ohio about nineteen.

16. Brother Mc. and I came to the Oliver Schoolhouse. It was nearly enough to break my blessed wife's heart to have me leave her. Oh Lord, comfort her heart! Were it not that "necessity is laid upon me," I could not leave her. House nearly full. Psa. 85:6-8. Came home with friend Mitchel. Turned cold.

17. The house being a small shell, I suffered much last night with cold. Arose and got overcoat. Fared some better but ached much and slept little. Spent the day till 4 P. M. at Mr. M's. Talked much on religion. He acknowledged that he always read the Bible to condemn religion till I preached here last fall. He is not convicted. Hope he will soon yield to God.

18. I find that I have taken a severe cold from my cold night's lodging. After dinner examined Brother Hibbard's head. A meeting two and one half miles south has been in progress some over two weeks and for a few nights there has been some interest, hence I must go there.

21. Sabbath. Had good speaking-meeting. Preached on Jer. 6:16. Was sent for to visit a sin-sick soul one and one half miles south. Brother Oliver and I went, found him, Bro. John Cowan, scarcely able to be up, in great distress of mind. We read the Word, talked, sang, and prayed until God blessed his soul, and we all rejoiced. His mother shouted and anon praised God for "Winebrennerian religion," declaring it was the old kind and as good as Methodist Episcopal or any other. It was amusing to see them all come down from deep-rooted prejudices. The brother's feet and ankle-bones having received strength, and he having eaten some, came with us to meeting.

22. Had family prayer-meeting at 11 A. M. Examined Brother Mitchell and gave him a phrenological chart.

23. Stormy. A few of us met for prayer. Staid all day at Brother Hibbard's. No meeting. Oh how I longed to be with blessed companion this dreary day and night! Through the night I spent hours listening to the muttering storm. Recalled all the draws between there and home, wondered if any were filled so as to be impassable. Determined to go home the next day if the driving snow would allow me to see three rods.

24. Morning came and the storm nearly subsided. Started for home. Mattie Blaze got into a snow drift in which she could not reach the ground. Could not go through. Had to get out and get her loose from the buggy. Took her to Brother Hafer's, near-by. Warmed myself, then drew the buggy back, hitched up, and drove out another way. Got home all right. Saw Sarah's smiling face. Thank God, the dear creature is well.

March. 2, 1875. We had a glorious day meeting. How my heart leaped with joy to see my beloved Brother Anderson reclaimed again! He has been a special object of my prayers. He is a brother I dearly love.

5. Good day meeting. Brother Briggs related how his little step-daughter was blessed here yesterday. "She told her mother that she felt the Spirit of God knocking at her heart. Then Brother Warner came and took her by the hand and said, 'Give your heart to Jesus,' and she said to Jesus, 'Take my heart.' Then she felt so happy. She got up and spoke like a little soldier." Sister Anderson also told of her little girl's singing Good News Gone to Canaan last eve and she got happy and clapped her hands for joy.

9. Went home with Bro. James A — —. Tried to show the domestic duties of religion. It is a delicate task, but the shepherd often finds families that need plain talk on duties to each other and to God in the family. Religion should find its most sacred altar in the family circle. There should its holy affections glow with the greatest warmth. If religion in all its tender affections and holy fruits does not burn on the family altar, the world will fail to see its light. God bless this family.

10. Last night and today a terrible cloud rested on us all. We felt as though the devil had triumphed somewhere.

11. Staid at home. Read and prayed. Felt much depressed. Something is wrong. Satan has a victory somewhere.

12. The dark cloud, thank God, is passing. Find what the difficulty has been. Some of the young men who have been at the altar have been loafing and visiting saloons. Last night after meeting Sister Rebecca Anderson told them of their inconsistency, which I think has broken the devil's chain, hence we had a good meeting today.

14. Sabbath. Preaching at 11:30 A. M. Eph. 3:14,15. Proved the oneness of Christians; the fact that this oneness is not manifest to the world; that it should be; and how. After preaching Brother S— — got up and harangued in favor of sects. He said I had doubt of my sincerity. He believed I was a true Christian if there was one in the world, but what I had preached got him down in the heels. He made no attempt to prove nor even assert that I had preached anything false. In fact, he never called up the question whether I had preached truth or not, only that my preaching made him and others feel bad. I told him that I had no doubt of it, for Paul had told us long ago that the time would come when men would not endure sound doctrine. Told him that I sympathized very much with him, that I had been in the same dread dilemma when I was not willing to accept the whole truth; it always hurt me to hear it. In answer to questions I made him acknowledge to the truth of all that I had preached before the congregation. After meeting, Brother B— —, another poor sectarianized soul, pitched into me. The people crowded around. I made him confess that Paul forbade Christians at Corinth to divide into sects. Brother Riley, a fine man recently converted, seemed highly elated to hear the glorious doctrine of the Word defended. He will soon come into fellowship with the church.

Bro. Lewis Anderson, who has enjoyed the meeting very much, staid away today and tonight. How fearful is a disturbed conscience! Brother Hafer, who is a good man filled with the Spirit, remarked a few days ago to Brother Houck that we were having a good meeting but he feared Brother Warner would spoil the good feeling by preaching on the church. Brother H. told him that he need have no fears. If Brother W. preached the truth, it should not hurt a Christian; if error, it is too weak to hurt anything. He advised him to come and hear for himself. He did so, sat with his head down, doubtless felt the force of truth but was too honest to trifle with it; confessed that I had preached nothing but Bible. Oh that the world were freed from the curse of human creeds, that men could be at liberty to obey God! We had a good and pleasant meeting. My heart flowed with peace.

18. Dear Sarah very sick most of the afternoon. [Confinement]. I too felt nearly overcome at her suffering. Had a season of prayer and was much comforted. Had the assurance that she would get along well from this time. She was no more so sick. At 6 P. M. the Lord delivered her of a large daughter, 8 pounds. Thank God for his goodness!

And now, O Lord! another sacred charge is committed to our trust. This day we acknowledge new responsibilities laid upon us. Thou hast committed to our care a pure and spotless soul. Give us grace and wisdom that we may bring up this dear child sound in body and mind, pure and innocent in heart and life, that thou, O God, its Maker, may be honored and glorified by its life and career on earth. O God! thou author of its being, this night I bow before thy throne and consecrate this precious household gem to thee. Thou hast given it to us, and we wait not for one sun to pass over its head until we lay it upon the altar of consecration to God, that all its days may be thine. O God! we solemnly vow to rear this child for thee. Shouldst thou see fit to leave it to grow up under our care, we shall bless thee for its angelic society; and shouldst thou rather choose to take it to thyself in the dewy time of youth, O Lord! we can not murmur; for thine it is and only entrusted to our care till it seemeth good for thee to commit it to wiser and more worthy care in a more congenial abode than this dreary, sinful earth. God bless the dear little creature!

19. Took care of dear Wife.

20. After taking care of Wife and child, went to Seward. When starting home Mattie Blaze stumbled, fell, and broke one of the shafts. Took buggy back to shop, left it, and rode home. Eve, preached at Occidental, returned at eleven greatly exhausted. Great weakness of back from stooping continually over the bed taking care of dear Wife and babe.

23. Sarah feeling rather worse. P. M., went to Seward. Have taken a bad cold, being up so much of nights.

25. Am constantly taking care of dear Wife and child. They are getting along fine, thank God. Quite warm. Birds are singing. Summer appears; nature is awakening from her long winter slumbers.

27. For some days I have had a severe conflict in my mind concerning my leaving to fill appointments in Fillmore County. 'Twas hard to think of leaving dear Wife yet confined to her bed, as our girl has made no attempts to take care of her or child because I preferred to do it and she had no experience. Hard as it seemed for dear Wife, duty seemed all along to say I should go. I determined to do so. Preparations were made to go, but when the moment was at hand Wife wept, and fearing a want of care and too much anxiety might bring on a relapse I felt it my solemn duty to stay and take care of her. P. M., went to Seward and tried to get a place to preach Sabbath eve, feeling that I dare not spend the Lord's day without doing something for Christ; but I failed to get a place to preach.

28. This is Easter Day. Spent the day in solitude with dear Wife and daughter. Wife feeling pretty well; sat up much of the day for the first except a short time yesterday. Think this is the second Sabbath in eight years that I have not preached the Word of God. The day was mostly spent in reading and meditation. Felt ill at ease that I could not be preaching somewhere.

31. Terrible storm all day. About five inches of snow fell.

Drifted much.

Apr. 2, 1875. Sister Sarah Anderson, our girl, became home-sick and would stay no longer. Could not leave to fill appointments in York and Polk Counties. Deeply regretted that I could not be with the dear brethren, but could get no one to take care of Wife and child; besides, the roads were almost impassable.

3. Pitched into housework as usual. Did the cooking and washed dishes. Sarah quite sick this A. M.

4. Sabbath. Did up the work this morn, and though late I started for prayer-meeting, thinking I could get there in time to have at least one prayer with the dear brethren. Found they had just closed their prayer-meeting. I read a chapter, talked some, and sang and prayed with them. My heart was full. Having been kept at home from public worship for some weeks, I felt as a bird set at liberty. Bless God for the privilege of appearing in his courts to offer our sacrifice of praise! Returned home. Found dear Wife and child asleep, both feeling very well. The little creature slept right on till night. Sarah and I spent the time pleasantly reading and talking of our blessed hope of glory. My heart was light and happy. Bro. David Figard today kindly invited me to move into his house. Thank God for this kindness. The brethren know that we have not a very pleasant place to live, yet I have no room for complaints, but much occasion for thanks.

7. P. M., heavy rains. About a mile to the southeast of Seward there was a great waterspout extending from a black cloud to the earth. It was a grand and sublime sight. As it followed a high ridge on the opposite side of the Blue River valley from us we had a beautiful view of it. We could see the water strike the ground and a dense spray arise around it resembling smoke. I have learned that it tore one house and a wagon to pieces.

9. Drove to Brother Figard's via Seward. Our ride of about seven miles was the first for our dear little Levilla Modest.

12. About one last night I took quite sick with, I suppose, cholera morbus. Sick all day. Sorry I could not go to Polk County, but it is necessary that blessings disguised in affliction come at times as well as the almost constant blessing of health. Tonight, I think, is the third appointment in eight years that I have missed through my physical disability.

13. Drove to York County. Called at Father Fenton's, a United Brethren preacher, who is poorly. Found also another aged pilgrim in the family, who desired me to bring him some good books to read. Being anxious to bestow some kindness on this good old Methodist father, I left a book with him that I was taking home, having had it lent for some time. Had a season of prayer and then some conversation on the hope of the saints.

14. Found that my appointment which I had failed to reach had proved a blessing after all, for they had a good prayer-meeting. Appointed another for the following Sabbath eve, which was a success also and resulted in the organization of a Sabbath-school, which is under the officership of those who hold with the church of God. Prospects are good here. A railroad-station is expected close by. P. M., drove to Fillmore County. How beautiful and pleasing, yea, charming, even to making happy, the day and the landscape!

17. Brothers Figard and J. H. Anderson moved us today to Brother F's.

20. Drove to Polk County. Distance, twenty-eight miles. Found the brotherhood well and hungry for the gospel.

23. Wife and I drove to Indian Creek, Fillmore County, distance, thirty-four miles.

26. Wife and I went to Seward. Asked for the Presbyterian meeting-house for Ministerial Association in case we are refused the Methodist Episcopal house. Found the latter wished to reserve some of the time hence accepted the Presbyterian house. Had programs printed.

27. Drove to Polk County and planted fruit trees.

28. Planted trees, potatoes, and garden seeds until after 4 P. M. At five minutes past five started for Wilson schoolhouse, about fifteen and one half miles. Reached in time. 1 Pet. 1:13. This is a new point, with good prospects. 'Tis only a half mile from where it is said there will be a station on the Midland Pacific, which is now being extended to York Center.

May 2, 1875. Sabbath. Stormy. Went home with Brother Price, it being handy and the weather bad. Several came there to spend the afternoon. The time passed off very pleasantly singing, and I lectured some on moral and mental culture. Examined some heads.

4. A. M., wrote letters. P. M., went to Seward. Completed arrangements for Ministerial Association.

5. Sarah and I drove over to the Blue. Had a pleasant time fishing. Caught a mess.

8. Visited Brother Mitchell's. Left Wife there and drove over to visit Brother Lichty. He was one of our seekers when I closed the meeting last winter. I was anxious to see him; but he being from home, I was disappointed. Found them quite poor. Large family of children. Live in dugout. Mrs. Lichty quite unwell, which added to the distressful appearance of things. Talked to the woman and children about Jesus and heaven. Read, prayed, and sang with them. Distributed fifty cents among the children.

13. Studied for Ministerial Association.

14. Ministerial Association began. Went early to town. Glad to meet ..., but was very much disappointed to learn that ... could not be with us.

15. I discoursed on the polity of the Church of God in lieu of Brother Howard.

16. Sabbath. This is Pentecost day. Thank God for the beautiful weather. All nature seems to be waking from its long winter slumber to praise God. The beautiful prairie is green with grain and pastures. The valleys are dotted with herds of cattle, which, as well as they on a thousand hills, are the Lord's. The beautiful streams are lined with plum-bushes all in bloom. The groves are preparing to cheer the heart of the prairie inhabitants with their pleasant shady foliage.

At eleven Brother Aller preached in the Methodist Episcopal house and I preached the Pentecostal sermon in the Presbyterian house. Acts 2:1-4. At 3 P. M. Brother Aller preached a glorious and lovely sermon on the brotherhood of the saints. Deep and lasting impressions were made. How powerfully this dear brother preached for the unity of the saints of God, with the eloquence of tears and overflowing love!

We parted with brotherly greetings at a quite late hour to meet at Crete second Tuesday in September.

17. Went to Brother Green's. While there Brother S—— came in. We were just ready to engage in prayer. The Lord wonderfully blessed me in prayer. I prayed fervently for him, though he has been acting the part of an open enemy to me and the cause I represent. Went to Seward. Received fifty dollars from the Board. Called on Bro. J. W. Figard, who is applying himself vigorously to the pursuit of an education. Hope the Lord will raise him up for an effectual minister of the gospel.

21. Made out report to the General Eldership.

23. Sabbath. This was a glorious and happy day's work in the vineyard of the Lord. The Master was very near me all day. Oh what liberty in speaking! what peace in my soul!

26. Up at daylight. Brothers Figard and Anderson moved our things to homestead. We arrived about 1 P. M., they in the eve. Unloaded, took supper, and staid all night in our house.

Here the record of Brother Warner's labors in the Western field must end abruptly, as the succeeding portion was in a separate book that has not been found. We leave him with his little family just moved into their own house in Polk County, having spent the winter near Seward. Our next of the diary accounts begins in the following December and finds him back in Ohio fields, whither, probably by decision of the Board of Missions or Eldership he was called to labor again. The daily accounts which have been omitted for want of space show him always active—traveling, preaching, visiting, praying, etc. The selections that are given from his diary are chosen in order to display the various sides and aspects of his life and character. We have noticed his great zeal for the work of preaching the gospel and caring for those under his charge. The widely separated flocks meant much traveling and exposure in that new country.[4]

We note his attitude and teaching on the church question. In a large measure he had light on the true Bible church, and he supposed he was not a member of any sect when, as a matter of fact, he was. The benefits of his knowledge and teachings of the one church were directed in the interest of the so-called church of God, which he was ignorantly laboring to build up. It was not until he received the experience of perfect holiness and began to teach the truth on the subject that he was made to feel his limitations to human ecclesiasticism and thus discover the pen he was in.[5] His teachings and applications of the Scriptural church (there is but one) was possible only among the followers of John Winebrenner or in some similar body supposing themselves to be that one true church. It is an interesting fact that upon the fulness of time for God's people to throw off all human ecclesiastical bondage and sever themselves from spiritual Babylon, the lead was taken principally by those who had belonged to the Winebrennerian following. Thus this denominational body may be regarded as a sort of preparatory medium, or half-way step, for the reformation which is now an established thing. At any rate God had in Brother Warner raised up a man particularly disposed to emphasize the church question, and the denomination mentioned seemed to be the only one he could affiliate with till more advanced light and truth forbade his remaining longer with them.

---

[4] Dr. Forney says that in June, 1875, Brother Warner organized a church in York County of thirty-one members, and further says of his work in Nebraska that "to such an extent were the ministers and churches encouraged that, they conferred together on the advisability of organizing an Eldership in Nebraska." Brother Warner notes in his diary account for Nov. 7, 1874, that a Preliminary Eldership was organized at Crete, in Saline County. Application was made to the General Eldership, which assembled in Ohio in May, 1875, and an Eldership of the Church of God in Nebraska was chartered. The first meeting of the Nebraska Eldership was held at Cropsey, Oct. 1, 1875. Among the fifteen names enrolled Brother Warner's does not appear, hence we conclude that by that time he had left Nebraska.

[5] That his disposition to be freely led of God made him poor material for a human ecclesiastical machine is evinced in the account by Dr. Forney of the Eighteenth West Ohio Eldership, for the year ending Sept. 30, 1874. He says: "The beginning of trouble between D. S. Warner and the Eldership is foreshadowed in an action on the adoption of his report, which stated that he had 'organized a church in Upper Sandusky contrary to the Rules of Cooperation,' and regarding this as a 'schismatic movement,' highly disapproved of his course in organizing said church."

CHAPTER VII

BACK IN OHIO FIELDS

On Ashland circuit—News of mother's death—Visits penitentiary—A course of studies at Vermillion College—Embraces the cause of holiness—Seeks and obtains the experience.

In his resumption of the work in Ohio we find Brother Warner in charge, it seems, of the Ashland circuit, with his home at Hayesville, Ashland County. Here, as was characteristic of him everywhere, he was wholly absorbed in spiritual labor, the salvation of sinners and the general spiritual welfare of people everywhere within his reach. In his diary for Dec. 21, 1875, he says:

> Went out visiting and talking to the people. My soul was so happy all day that I could hardly refrain from shouting. Oh, how sweet it was to talk to sinners about Jesus and his love! Found in shops and houses a number of precious souls that were serious. I admonished them to repent. Some gave much hope of a start.

The closing moments of the year 1875 were devoted to a renewal of consecration of himself and others.

> A few minutes before twelve we all bowed down and to the service of God consecrated ourselves and vowed fidelity. God accepted the offering and sealed our vows to him by the gift of his Spirit. After affectionate New Year greetings and congratulations, we went to our homes to rest.

Into his congregation at Shenandoah an Elder L—— had come and was poisoning the minds of the converts by teaching the Campbellite doctrine of baptism as an essential condition to the pardon of sin. He afterward held a public discussion with this preacher.[6]

---

[6] Brother Warner was one of the principal debaters of the Church of God. Dr. Forney mentions his debates as follows: In August, 1871 with the Reverend Mr. Baker, of the Disciple Church, the proposition being, "The Church of God of which I am a member is the only church of divine origin." In June, 1872, with Leonard Parker, Methodist Episcopal Church, on the old subject of baptism. On May 15, 1874, near Orton, Nebr., he defended the perpetuity and public observance of feet-washing as an ordinance against E. Evans, of the Disciple Church. At the Osborne Schoolhouse, near Seward, Nebr., with C. L. Boyd, Adventist. The proposition discussed was, "The first day of the week has been set apart by divine authority as Sabbath or Lord's day." The discussion was the outcome of a series of addresses by Boyd on the seventh day Sabbath. So well did Warner defend the proposition, says Forney, that

Feb. 19, 1876. Drove to Shenandoah. Found Elder L—— having a good time deluding and baptizing sinners. Found the converts greatly strengthened by the wind of doctrine that had been assailing them. However, a few had been corrupted by the false doctrine and were inclined to go from the Church of God, being carried by the wind of doctrine. With a mean, sneaking look they applied for letters. I told them that I had not taken them into the Church of God and could not dismiss them from it, and there was only one way to get out and that was through sin. This they could not deny, nor could they give a reason for their course.

About this time he gradually came into the knowledge of the truth respecting divine healing, and we find in his accounts an occasional reference to his praying for the sick and of their recovery.

He was sent for by his father-in-law to come to Upper Sandusky, where sectarians were making inroads among the converts.

April 2, 1876. The sectarians are making a stampede this morning. They have been after about every convert to go to their church and now this morning they have their conclave outside and every convert is stopped and asked to join the Methodists. An excitement is raised and the people's minds are bewildered, and some who had said they would stick to the Church of God are now standing back. Before closing, an old bigot, belonging to the Methodists, took the liberty to get up and call for all to raise their hands who wanted to go to Methodism. Some responded. O Sectarianism! thou abomination of the earth, thou bane of the cause of God, when will thy corrupt and wicked walls fall to earth and cease to curse men to hell?

June 4, 1876. This is the second anniversary of our marriage. Thank God for connubial and domestic happiness. May God continue to bless us with love, peace, and sacred union.

July 18, 1876. Received the sad and startling news of the death of my dear mother. She died July 13. The days of her pilgrimage were seventy-one years, five months, and seven days. Hers was a life of trouble and care. But, thank God, she has gone to her sweet rest in heaven. Oh, how sacred the memory of thy pure and virtuous life! "patient in tribulation," constant and untiring in thy kindness and care for all under thy roof. Oh, what love like a mother's! What mother like my own dear, sainted mother? In all the ordeal of life thy calm and peaceful spirit has never known a ruffle. Thy love has never once failed. Thy sorely tried patience never was exhausted.

Dearest mother, in childhood and youth thou wast my all.

---

at the close of the debate the congregation present voted thirty-six to sixteen that he had established it. The debate continued three evenings.

And when maturer years had launched my bark in the midst of awful breakers, dark clouds, and tempestuous seas of corrupt society, thy pure life was my only star of hope. Thank God, thou shalt be honored in heaven with the salvation of one poor, wayward son by thy holy influence. Praise the Lord for a good and holy mother!

She was always strongly inclined to piety, the fear and reverence of God. In October, 1870, she was fellowshiped by the Church of God at South Bridgewater and the same day immersed by me in the St. Joseph River. Though she was feeble and the weather cold and the distance over three miles from home, she chose to go home before changing clothes. She was a happy soul, and the next day seemed quite improved in health. Now she is gone. One of the dearest ties that bound me to earth now attracts me to heaven. I can not lament her departure. I only grieve that I was not informed of her affliction that I could have been there to cheer her while approaching the river. Or, had I only been apprized of her death that I could have seen once more the face of my own dear mother before she was laid in the tomb! But I shall see her not again until the heavens are no more and the Son of God shall come to call the saints from the dust of the earth. Farewell, dear mother. We soon shall meet again.

July 29. We visited the penitentiary [in Columbus]. Over 1,300 prisoners. All at work manufacturing nearly everything in use. The extensive work was interesting, but the study of the heads and faces of the workmen was much more so. One striking characteristic was, almost invariably, great firmness. This being perverted enabled them to execute their dark crimes. Conscientiousness was low in every head. This left them without moral restraint. Some I observed were very deficient in the social group, especially was inhabitiveness almost entirely deficient. This gave a rambling disposition, hence irresponsible and exposed to bad society. A large majority exhibited a very good intellect, many even above mediocrity. These intellectual powers, which had they been sanctified to God would have been very useful, being perverted were used only to devise crime.

Oct. 1, 1876. Eldership meeting at Findlay. I was much overcome with emotion as I tried to speak of my meeting with the Eldership for the first time in that house nine years ago. Never shall I forget the solemn feelings I experienced at that time. I had not expected a license; but how I trembled with fear and dread when I learned that a license and a field of labor were given me! I thought it all a mistake of the Eldership. I repaired to the stable of Brother F——, where I poured out my heart to God in prayer. Bless God, he heard me and comforted my agonizing heart. I then received the assurance that he was directing my way. My soul was unburdened and my peace flowed like a river. And now my laboring soul and inmost heart would give thanks to God who has upheld me in the arduous labors of the past nine years. Having begun an invalid, supposed by many to be a consumptive, my strength has gradually increased through God's blessings and mercies.

30. Gathered some chestnuts this morning. Had a season of prayer in the woods.

Nov. 30, 1876. This is Thanksgiving Day. Oh, that the whole nation would indeed thank God for his goodness and mercy! Brother Oliver and I each made a short discourse on the occasion. P. M., read O. S. Fowler's Physiology, Animal and Mental. O God, forgive me of the sin this book has convicted me of. By the grace of God, from this day forth I will reform in quantity, etc., of food as much as my irregular mode of life will allow. How much I can improve the vigor of the mind and the fervor of devotion! Thank God for this volume! Oh, that every one had it who is suffering for want of its instruction!

Dec. 31, 1876. Sabbath. Arose early to go to my appointments. Levilla ill. Mother Keller very sick with headache, unable to be up. Was compelled to stay at home. Oh, what distress of mind I was in this day through the fearful conflict of duty to family and duty to the cause! How wretched I felt all day! The day was pleasant and I know there were crowded houses to hear the gospel. How I longed to preach to them!

January 7, 1877. Went to visit Mr. S— —, who is suffering awful distress. Was met by a young man who was coming after us. We went with the hope that the poor, dying man was eager to hear of Christ and his salvation; but oh, horror of horrors! When we approached the house we heard the poor soul hollowing out in wild strains: "I can't die; I can't die." I asked him if we should pray for him. He hollowed out "No!" But I thought he was delirious and concluded to sing and pray with him, which I did with all my heart. After prayer I talked with the family and learned that he had said he was a lost sinner, that he could not be saved. I asked him if we should pray. He shook his head. I talked to him of how Christ died for sinners and how he loved and desired to save him; but there was a hideous look in his eyes. He looked frightful, yet he was conscious, answered every question we could ask him. I called for oil and said I would do as the New Testament directed. So I bowed down, anointed his forehead, and was about to anoint his breast when he seized his shirt and drew it together. I laid one hand on his head, the other on his body, and began to pray. He drew his head forward and tried to get it under the cover. He shoved my hand from under his head. I could pray but little. He told every one present that he did not want us to come back. He said he would die; was not prepared to die; did not believe that Christ died for him; did not love Christ and did not want to. He showed every appearance of being possessed by the devil. When we kept our distance he would turn and look at us with fiendish vengeance. When we approached he would turn his face to the wall. Poor soul! soon he will be in eternity, I presume, and yet raging mad against Christ and his people. I shall never forget the horrors of this day. When we entered the first room we met several women weeping. The old mother fainted away. He was crying loudly in the other room.

In 1877, while on the Ashland circuit Brother Warner arranged, in connection with ministerial duties, to take some selective studies at Vermillion College, located at Hayesville. This was a Presbyterian school of some note at the time, enrolling three hundred to four hundred students. It was founded in 1845. Dr. Sanders Diefendorf became its head in 1849. Brother Warner and his wife were invited to occupy rooms in the building, and they did so, as they found they could live much cheaper there than in Mansfield and would enjoy better privileges of study. They engaged five rooms for the summer of 1877, which cost them six dollars a month. Among Brother Warner's studies at this place were English Analysis, Greek, German, and studies in the New Testament. He took an active part in the literary society.

The year 1877 was a notable one in Brother Warner's life. Already accomplished as he was in deep spirituality and devotion, it would seem that these graces were multiplied or intensified tenfold by an attainment that from this year became his permanent possession. That attainment was the experience of entire sanctification as received definitely by faith and subsequent to regeneration. *He embraced the cause of holiness.*

He had been for some years honestly prejudiced against the doctrine; but he heard some truth by the holiness advocates that set him to thinking. It was doubtless largely through the influence of his father-in-law's family that he began to be won to the doctrine. They had become friends of the holiness cause and had received the experience. His wife also was sanctified, and the change in her was a test that he had no words to gainsay. A holiness band had been formed at Upper Sandusky, where his wife's people lived.

The one minister who perhaps more than any other led him into the experience of holiness, was C. R. Dunbar, a Baptist who was laboring in connection with the Holiness Alliance. Brother Warner says of him, "He is a very able man intellectually, but still more potent in faith and gospel, Holy Ghost power." He was the musical author of the song, now so common:

> "I'll live for him who died for me,
> How happy then my life shall be!
> I'll live for him who died for me,
> My Savior and my God."

The great holiness movement was sweeping over the country at this time. Brother Warner was too loyal to God and to the teaching of the Bible ever to be classed among those who should reject holiness when brought face to face with the issue. He and his wife gave their names to the holiness band at Upper Sandusky, and he quoted the words of the Psalmist: "I am a companion of all them that fear thee, and of them that keep thy precepts." At this time his impulsiveness led him to claim the blessing at once, but he soon found that it could not be picked up so readily; that for him, as well as for others, there was a consecration to make and self to be crucified.

A little anecdote in this connection is told by a brother who heard Brother Warner relate it of himself. He (Brother Warner) had been attending some meetings of the holiness people and had received some light. On returning to his charge he preached a sermon on holiness without having obtained the experience. Two sisters who had received the experience knew that he did not yet have it and urged that he get it before attempting to preach it. At the altar service that followed he got down as if to pray for others, but first prayed privately for his own sanctification. Then audibly he began, "Lord, sanctify us," whereupon one of the sisters said, "Brother Warner, do not pray, 'Lord, sanctify *us*'; but say, 'Lord, sanctify *me*.'" At this he wilted and came right out with "Lord, sanctify *me*."

We shall quote freely from his diary, as his experience at this time is best expressed by his own words.

> **April 13, 1877.** Had much talk with Brother Dunbar on sanctification. I have always believed in a full salvation, and agree that it is usually obtained after the justified state. This was my experience as well as that of all advocates of holiness; but I was inclined to attribute the deficiency of the justified state to infantile weakness, which through outward sinful influence, was not able to carry out the pure nature fully in practise. But he and all sanctificationists attribute it to the remaining depravity of nature.

> **16.** Since I arose this morning my constant prayer to God has been that he will lead me in all things. I pray God to take me like an old sack and shake me until entirely empty, and then fill me with the fulness of himself. O God! turn out every nook and corner of my heart and purge me, soul, body, spirit, and mind. I received a blessing about the time I entered the ministry that seemed to correspond with the experience of sanctified ones; but I have not always kept that state of perfect love, and my God knows that I need a fresh blessing of sanctification power.... Though I experienced sanctification ten years ago, when entering upon the work of the ministry, yet I want and need a renewal of God's power, that my testimony for God may be more effectual. Also, I know that I have not always lived in this glorious liberty. I have this day examined my heart carefully and feel assured that I accept the whole will of God and now stand by faith upon the promise of God. I leave myself and all my concerns in his hands. By faith I

say, "I am the Lord's, and he is mine."

Here Brother Warner quotes the poem, "Farther On." How appropriate this was to his life at this point! How much of his activity and accomplishment were enveloped in the "farther on"!

> "A soft, sweet voice from Eden stealing,
> Such as but the angels sing;
> Hope's cheering song is ever thrilling,
> It is better farther on.
>
> "I hear Hope singing, sweetly singing
> Softly in an undertone,
> And singing as if God had taught her,
> It is better farther on.
>
> "By night and day she sings the same song,
> Sings it while I sit alone;
> And sings it so the heart may hear it,
> It is better farther on.
>
> "She sits upon the grave and sings it,
> Sings it when the heart would groan;
> And sings it when the shadows darken,
> It is better farther on.
>
> "Still farther on, oh, how much farther?
> Count the milestones one by one;
> No, no! no counting, only trusting—
> It is better farther on."

April 25, 1877. I was dull today. Study was a drag. I prayed to God that if I am pursuing these studies for his glory he should quicken my mind. I was, as oft before, convinced that I ate too much, which stupefied my mind; hence resolved, as oft before, to quit gormandizing to gratify appetite. I resolved in God's name and in his strength to do this thing. I ate but a few spoonfuls of graham mush for supper. Felt cheered by God's presence in evening worship.

26. My mind was active today. Lessons were easily learned, spirits cheerful, recitations more successful. O Lord, keep me in the possession of a clear, active, and retentive mind, a pure heart, and a consecrated life, devoted to God's service.

May 19, 1877. Had a very interesting meeting in the Excelsior Society. M. J. Boyd and I conducted the main discussion on the following question: Do We Suffer More from Real Than Imaginary Evils? I affirmed.

27. Sabbath. Beautiful day. Arose early and, taking a testament with me, I took a long walk, enjoying the precious pure air, the beauties of nature, and communion with God through his

Word and Spirit. Read and meditated upon several chapters. Precious season in family worship. Just when we were through with breakfast the boy raised the cry that the house was on fire. We ran to the bedroom and found the curtains and clothing around the wall in a blaze. Great excitement prevailed. But soon by means of a few pails of water and by throwing some of the burning fabrics out, the fire was extinguished with the loss only of some clothing. The fire was started by a small child, who finding a match on the candlestick, struck it and then dropped it on the end of the curtain that reached to the floor.

June 1, 1877. Prepared and delivered a lecture before the Excelsior Society on the Interrelation between Mind and Body, and their Mutual Dependence.

7. Built steps over the fence to avoid having the gate left open, as much of my cabbage has already been destroyed. As a consideration, Professor agreed to give me more ground to garden.

8. Worked on an essay for the Society tonight, also on a composition for the Board, to be criticized. Eve, met with the Excelsior Society and entered upon the duties of secretary. There being few present, all other exercises were dispensed with but a general discussion on the subject, Is Force More Effectual in Government than Persuasion. I took the negative. Mr. W. Diefendorf also spoke on the negative. The vote was almost unanimous for the negative.

15. A. M., recitations as usual. P. M., prepared for Society. Rained all afternoon and evening. No Excelsior meeting. Visited the Philo Society. Participated in general discussion on the following question: Is the Fear of Punishment a Greater Incentive to Exertion than the Hope of Reward? Spoke on the negative. Large majority in our favor on the final vote.

July 5, 1877. Met at half-past nine in the Bethel. After a profitable season of prayer, reading the Word, testifying, etc., I presented myself at the altar to seek entire sanctification. I enjoyed that blessing ten years ago, but I had all this time repudiated the second work and accounted for the wonderful change that God had wrought in me at that time to my yielding to the call to preach the blessed gospel of Jesus, after being disobedient. I had often been disgusted, too, with the fanaticism I saw mixed with the professors of the second work; it had steeped me with prejudice through and through.

Though I could not deny that the experience of these people was in perfect harmony with my own, yet I strongly opposed their views, claiming that God does not do his work by piecemeal, but that he makes a full and complete finish of it at once. I attributed the second experience to the fact that after conversion we are weak infants and not able to carry into action the pure nature that God has given us until we grow to that degree of strength that we can successfully cope with outer temptation, and that holy nature given to us in regeneration reaches a degree of development in strength that it will no more be under subjection to sin in the world around us.

Thus, while I did not doubt the truthfulness of their testimony. I thought I comprehended the whole matter and saw the slight mistake, as I supposed, in the basis of their experience.

But God having let Father and Mother Keller and the whole family into this glorious experience, with my dear companion, I began to search the Scriptures anew to see if I might not be mistaken myself. I carefully reviewed my conversion and recollected that I sought and asked of God only pardon of my past sins and relief from my past guilt. That in ten years labor, in which some seven hundred souls came to Christ, I never knew one to seek for anything else but pardon for actual transgression; and it is a fact that we do not ask of God that which we have not apprehended the need of, and God does not give until we ask for a thing.

Moreover, it is claimed that justification is not a partial but complete work of itself, and sanctification, i. e., purification, another. Since seeing every day the change in my dear wife I thought I was beyond doubt of this second work. But, ah, the devil is rallying his forces against me. Am I making a fool of myself coming out here where I have invited and labored with sinners? My old arguments would come up and I had powerful temptations to settle back upon them and forever repudiate the second work. I obtained no light.

P. M. We met at half-past two and held meeting till nearly five. I labored at the altar. At night after Brother Burlison read a Scripture lesson and talked for some time on holiness, we all bowed around the altar; but I could do nothing, all was dark. I came here fully believing in a second work of God in the soul; but now, as I attempt to seek it, how thick the temptations of Satan come up before me! how all my old arguments and objections gather like rubbish, obstructing the light! Sometimes I was about to conclude that this was all foolishness. I was ashamed to bow at the altar and seek sanctification of "soul, body, and spirit" after I had invited sinners to and labored with them at the same altar.

6. Arose early this morning and searched the Scriptures and asked God for light. I noticed whenever I felt resigned to God and was willing to make any sacrifice to know the truth I was strongly impressed to seek sanctification.

This morn I was directed to 1 Pet. 5:10 and Eph. 3:14-20. Light is becoming brighter in the Word. Thank God. Met at half-past nine. The foundation of faith was now becoming strong in me. I arose and read some portions of the Word and boldly declared my faith in the second work, and that I was resting in the promises of God to my entire sanctification. Met again, at 2:30 P. M., having spent most of the interval in searching my heart, and truly I found that it has not been as good as I before supposed. Oh how much self there has been in all my past labors! God of power, kill and cast out all of self. I reviewed my observations of the past ten years' labor. About seven hundred souls I have observed seeking salvation, and I can not recall any who did not definitely seek for justification from past sins. It appears that the condemned sinner can think of nothing else and does not possess a capacity to grasp the idea that God is able to destroy all evil in depraved humanity. "God, forgive my past sins and help me in the future to keep from sin," is about as great a blessing as the mind beclouded by guilt can conceive and ask for. With a still more deep and fervent consecration I again sought the blessing of perfect holiness. Glory to God, I was able to claim the blessing by faith, though yet without the anointing of power. After meeting I spent most of the time talking holiness to several brethren, which I felt was pleasing to God.

Eve, Brother Burlison read 1 Corinthians 3, and talked a little; then, an invitation being given, a good many surrounded the altar, several of whom were seeking the blessing. Thank God, some professed to receive the blessing. I am still standing, yea, resting sweetly in the promise of God for entire and constant salvation through the blood of Jesus.

7. Today we fasted all day. Met in the Bethel at 9 A. M. and held meeting until after 4 P. M. without intermission. This day I was the least conscious of a physical nature and my relations with a corporeal world of any day in all my life. I seemed to be entirely unconscious of passing time. Only the spirit seemed to live, stir, feel, and take cognizance. Glory to the God of wonders! Is this really but the foot-stool of God?

Mother Keller, Sarah, and I went to Brother L— —'s for supper. She (Mrs. L.) very soon began to pour out her bitter railing against holiness and holy ones; but praise God, he kept our souls in perfect peace. After my communing with God in secret for some time, the Lord told me to go immediately to see a poor sick girl near by. Mother accompanied me. Found her barely able to sit up, having been suffering for nearly one year. She had exhausted in vain all available medical aid. We spoke of the Great Physician. She said she believed that he was able to heal her. We called for oil, anointed her in the name of the Lord and laid hands on, and prayed for her present restoration to health. We entreated God with all the faith and earnestness of our inmost soul and then left her in the hands of God, with a comfortable degree of faith that God would raise her up again.

Eve, met at a quarter to eight. Mighty power filled the house. The altar was filled from one side to the other. Several were seeking sanctification. Glory to God, this night he began to give me some of the evidences (besides my hitherto naked faith) that I had got out of the wilderness into Canaan. Jesus, my blessed Savior, just cut me off one bunch of the sweet grapes of this "land." Oh, glory to God, once more I was a little child! I felt the blood of Jesus flowing through my entire "soul, body, and spirit." Heaven on earth! Halleluiah, it is done!

8. Sabbath. At five this morning a goodly number met in the Bethel for prayers. The Spirit was with us. Returned to Brother Bell's; ate a piece for breakfast, as we all felt that bodily wants were simple and few while the soul was so dearly fed with the bread of heaven. Met at half-past nine, and after many clear testimonies were given in for Jesus Brother Dunbar preached the word of life with great power and sweetness. Text, "For God hath not called us unto uncleanness, but unto holiness." He read much of the First Epistle to the Thessalonians, where this glorious second work is brought out so clear and forcibly. My soul was never before so wonderfully fed by the gospel in any sermon I ever heard. Oh, how sweet and glorious the word of life came to my renovated heart!

Mother, Sarah, and I went to Brother Furman's for dinner. Returned to the two o'clock meeting. Among many clear witnesses I testified today to the blood that cleanses from all sin and also uncleanness of nature. The long altar was again crowded and several found sanctification in the blood. Some backsliders were restored. God is wonderfully at work. All glory to his name!

At six we met again in the Bethel, after spending a long time in the closet with God. The Spirit impressed me to talk to the people on the commands of Jesus, and in simplicity I did so, using John 14:15 as a text. I read the word of the Lord concerning the duty of washing the saints' feet. Then we proceeded to obey the Lord. God wonderfully blessed me in talking, but my soul leaped for joy as I saw the dear sanctified ones come promptly to the bench and joyfully obey Him whom they love. God wonderfully blessed them, as they all testified the next day. Many of them had never seen the holy ordinance of feet-washing observed before. The Church of God brethren had said that if these holiness people would obey these lowly commands then they would have confidence in them. Thank God, true holiness needs but to be tested to be proved genuine.

10. This morn had to miss prayer-meeting in order to take Mother Keller and our dear Levilla to the train, as they go to Upper Sandusky this morn. We will go by buggy at the close of meeting. Sister Bell and Sarah went to the country today to get berries. I wrote and prayed most of the forenoon. Then, feeling very empty and destitute of the stirrings of the Spirit, I sought God earnestly in secret and then started out to work for him. Visited and prayed with two families, but still felt destitute of the Comforter. Met at 2:30 P. M. at the house of God. Several observed that I was being much tried. But I was eager to defeat the enemy of my soul by testifying to the sanctifying power of the blood of Jesus. I did so, declaring that the blood of Jesus had washed from all sin. While I was talking, the Lord showed me that I had now entered upon the path of perfect trust in Jesus, and that as faith was eternal and unchangeable, I had forever abandoned the up-and-down road of feeling. I also (in an absent-minded manner) made the remark that I had been cheated out of the morning prayer-meeting. But quick as thought I saw that it was wrong, for it was either complaining of or speaking lightly of God's providence. This remark furnished a subject of meditation through the afternoon. I see how entirely loyal to God's providence I now was. I felt that the above remark and all similar ones, so common and admissible in my past state, were not only wrong, but could not be true, as I have given myself, all I have, to God, surrendered all my ways, time, talents, means, influence, name, reputation, and everything with which I am connected—wife, child, friends, my destiny—all into the hands of God. I glorify in the blessed truth that no being in the whole universe can cheat me out of anything or do me the least harm. Glory to God forever! How happy I am in accepting all the will and providence of God! From the time of my testimony I realized the glorious river of life flowing through my entire being. What a sweet sense of perfect purity filled my mind and heart! Holiness was written everywhere. My very body seemed sacred and pure, a temple for the holy God. Glory to the cleansing power of the blood of Jesus!

> "Precious Jesus, thou hast saved me,
> Thine and only thine I am.
> Oh, the precious blood has reached me!
> Glory, glory to the Lamb!
>
> "Long my yearning heart was trying
> To enjoy this perfect rest;
> But I gave all trying over,
> Simply trusting I was blessed.
>
> "Glory to the blood that bought me,

Glory to its cleansing power,
Glory to the blood that keeps me,
Glory, glory evermore!

"Yes, I will stand up for Jesus;
He has sweetly saved my soul,
Cleansed me from inbred corruption,
Sanctified and made me whole.

"Oh, I can no longer doubt it,
Halleluiah, I am free!
Jesus saves me, soul and body,
And he sweetly dwells in me."

CHAPTER VIII

THE HOLINESS AWAKENING

Doctrine of sanctification—Widespread interest in the subject—Prominent leaders—Holiness bands—Doctrine opposed—Its advocates recede on the church question—A remnant who walk in the light—Holiness editors—Jacksonville convention.

The decades of the sixties, seventies, and eighties of the last century witnessed a special revival of the doctrine of holiness, or sanctification. Sanctification was held as being a work of God's grace wrought in the heart subsequent to pardon, and accomplishing for the individual, through consecration and faith in Christ, (1) restoration of the soul from innate depravity and uncleanness, the destruction of that carnal element which antagonizes the godly purpose of the soul, and (2) the infilling and indwelling of the Holy Spirit. In short, it was the doctrine of Christian perfection, the state of loving God supremely and of living victorious over every form of sin.

This doctrine was nothing more nor less than one of the great Scriptural truths that had been obscured by the apostasy. It had been taught by the Wesleys, but through the denomination-building zeal of their followers it had become to a great extent a dead letter in their articles of faith. The bright spiritual lights of the world throughout the gospel dispensation were generally individual men and women who believed in and possessed the experience of sanctification; but now the time came, in the unfolding of God's plan, for holiness to be given specific attention on a scale amounting to a general awakening in religious circles. The various Protestant sects had about reached the heyday of their deplorable rivalry, and it was but natural that the unifying influence of holiness, appearing in striking contrast to such rivalry, should appeal to all true Christians. The movement did indeed, as a rule, enlist the most spiritual members of the so-called churches.

This holiness awakening was a movement that should introduce a prophetic day. It was of God. It was not planned by human agency. Individuals here and there of the more earnest and spiritual class of Christians were led into the deeper experience altogether independent of each other. For some reason they felt impelled to give special emphasis to the doctrine of holiness. These tiny flames were by some unseen hand fanned into a great conflagration destined to sweep the country.

A few paragraphs from M. L. Haney's Inheritance Restored, published in 1880, are on this point.

A number of Christian farmers feel strangely moved to aid in the salvation of the perishing, and they plan a laymen's camp-meeting, in which the fires of holiness break out. This leads to the organization of a Laymen's Holiness Association, and results in bringing many hundreds to the joys of pardoned sin and the experience of holiness. Three or four ministers are mutually impressed with the necessity of holding a holiness camp-meeting. The seal of God's approval of the service is so manifest that they are compelled to go farther. An association is formed for the purpose of holding a number of camp-meetings for the promotion of holiness. The work enlarges till many earnest inquirers look to them for specific instruction on the subject of holiness. To meet this demand, and remain true to God, they are compelled to furnish these thirsting thousands with specific holiness literature. Thus the unexpected springing up of a monthly magazine, with books and tracts, all teaching the way of Christ's cleansing blood.

One minister, comparatively illiterate, stands alone for years. He preaches, and prays, and testifies, and sings, and shouts, as here and there a soul is bloodwashed through his ministry. He mourns the downward tendency, as the sympathy of his brethren seems ofttimes withdrawn; but at last God brings one of them to stand by his side. Another, and yet another is added, till God has bound three or four souls in bonds of perfect love. The obligation to disseminate the gospel of holiness among the people of God in all the churches leads them, after much prayer on the subject, to publish a paper which shall be the medium of instruction on the special doctrine of holiness. Without a dollar, or a subscription list, with nothing at the base but unshrinking faith in the God who leads, they launch a weekly paper. But God touches the heart of a wealthy layman, and gives him no peace till he pledges three thousand dollars for the support of that paper....

"God works in a mysterious way, his wonders to perform." When God determined to break the chains of slavery he revealed to no man the time or methods of its accomplishment. In like manner, in the holiness movement, his faithful servants have gone "out, not knowing whither they went." The way has been so rugged at times that many have turned aside; but God has put two in the place of each faltering one, and the ranks of the holiness army are steadily increasing.

We call attention to the remarkable fact that the holiness work has sprung up simultaneously in different parts of the earth; in the east, in the west, in the north, and the south; in the old world, and in the new; among Arminians, and among Calvinists; in cities, in towns, and in country places; indicating an unseen hand and guiding power.

A mechanic, in Pennsylvania, receives a call from the chaplain of King William's court to come to Germany and teach the church of Martin Luther the way of holiness, and four hundred learned ministers sit at the feet of a Presbyterian layman to learn of holiness in the city of Berlin. A young minister, whom God hath baptized with the Holy Ghost and with fire, completely girds the earth with holy song, as he travels to regain his failing health.

One of Wesley's mightiest sons, is sent to the other side of the globe to receive this blessed experience, under the instruction of a Presbyterian minister. Suddenly an organized army springs up in Europe to spread holiness, and the power of Satan is broken by its advancing legions.

A number of holy men and women are compelled by their convictions to make the circuit of the earth, and are invited to preach, and sing, and testify to holiness in the shadow of the Vatican. Reader, who do you think has planned, and whose hand is guiding, this movement?

The truth is, the holiness movement was a movement prophetically due at this time as the introduction to the great reformation (restoration) that now succeeds it, in which God's people are not only embracing holiness, but are taking their stand free and complete in Christ, distinct from all humanly organized bodies called churches. The reader of church history will observe that the progress of Christianity has not been by gradual, steady increase of light and truth, but by reformation after reformation in which some special truth is emphasized and men's hearts are stirred.

Among the early leaders of the movement in this country were Dr. W. C. and Phoebe Palmer, of New York. Mrs. Palmer, especially, was prominent in this respect. She wrote a number of books on holiness and with her husband held meetings in various openings in the East and was otherwise very active in the cause. William Macdonald, John S. Inskip, Daniel Steele, and J. A. Wood were others who, both by preaching and the press, gave prominence to the doctrine of entire sanctification as a second, distinct work of grace. Holiness societies sprung up, books were written on the subject, periodicals were started, and holiness bands began to canvass the country. Well does the writer remember of seeing when a boy these holiness bands travel about the country in covered wagons. They carried a spiritual fire that caught in the hearts of the more fervent ones who, on the barren plains of sect religion, were seeking for a higher and better Christian experience. The activity on this line was not on the part of the various denominations, as such, but on the part of earnest Christians within the denominations.

Leaders, Authors and Editors, prominent in the Holiness Movement Forty to Fifty years ago, Contemporaries of D. S. Warner.

(1) W. C. Palmer; (2) J. S. Inskip; (3) Wm. Macdonald; (4) Daniel Steele; (5) Geo. Hughes, of the Guide to Holiness; (6) Isaiah Reid, of The Highway; (7) T. K. Doty, of the Christian Harvester; (8) L. B. Kent, of the Banner of Holiness

Holiness, it must be remembered, is Scriptural, a part of God's will to his children, and the movement must not be regarded as being something new, but as a revival of truth intended for man. Since the attainment of this distinct higher experience requires a perfect consecration, an entire abandonment, to God, it was but natural that the doctrine should be opposed by the pleasure-loving church members, those who were Christians only in name and did not care for any advancement or improvement of their spiritual status. These, of course, were greatly in the majority. The holiness advocates were at once opposed and often persecuted; but silently and surely, as leaven works in the meal, the holiness agitation increased and spread throughout the country. It was a very unwelcome and disturbing element among the cold professors. They said that sinlessness was not to be attained in this life; that we could not be sanctified till death; etc. But when shown by the Scriptures that it is indeed God's will for Christians in this life, they would declare that it is attained by growth, or perhaps would say they had received it in conversion. They were opposed to having any further spiritual obligation placed upon them.

But it was not alone the advocacy of an advanced Christian attainment that might well make the holiness movement distasteful to sect devotees. Holiness is unifying. It makes Christians one, in accordance with our Savior's prayer: "That they all may be one; as thou, Father, art in me, and I in thee, that they also may be one in us: that the world may believe that thou hast sent me" (John 17:21). True holiness is destructive of divisional elements. That is why the advocates of holiness in the different denominations lost to a great extent their sectarian bigotry and could join together in holiness associations independent of their denominations. As a general thing the holiness editors and teachers spoke against sectarian divisions.

This brings us to the critical point. Would those espousing holiness dissolve their sect relations? Here is where many in the holiness movement compromised and would not follow in the onward march of truth out of all denominational confusion and into complete oneness in Christ. Instead, holiness associations urged and even required their members to maintain also a sect membership. They seemed to believe sects were a necessary evil and they opposed the idea of coming out of sects. This is as far as the majority in the holiness movement would go. They deplored sects, but seemed to think that to be outside of all sects would be to have no church relation at all. Had they walked in the light they would have comprehended the true body of Christ and been led out of sectarian entanglements; but failing to follow the true leading of God, they receded, and their holiness degenerated into what was mere sect holiness. To this day they have their holiness associations and their conventions, but fellowshiping as they do the sects and factions of almost every description, they are left to grope in their own darkness and confusion, still making an effort but accomplishing nothing toward Christian unity.

Their confusion on the church question is illustrated by the following quotation from the salutary address adopted by the General Holiness Assembly held in Chicago in May, 1901:

> In respect to the matter of church fellowship we observe that

the church is the institution of Christ, having many members in one body, himself being the living Head. He has redeemed it with his blood, and engraven it upon the palms of his hands. Membership therein is a precious privilege, and always to be highly esteemed. Wherever practical, every saved man and woman should be connected with some church.

The first two statements are clear in their reference to the true Christian church as the one body of saved people everywhere, redeemed by Christ's blood. But when in the next breath they urge that "every saved man and woman should be connected with some church," as if such were not already in the church through redemption by Christ's blood, they are talking about something else, not the body of Christ. They perhaps do not realize their own blindness; but to the one who spiritually discerns the true church and its sufficiency for all the people of God, their confusion is very apparent.

The writer had an interview not long since with one of the holiness leaders who used to know D. S. Warner and who still labors to bring about the unity of Christians through a holiness that respects sectarian divisions. This man was asked about the prospects for unity after so many years of effort. His reply, in which he complained of the bigotry existing among the denominations, was anything but encouraging. He seemed to have no knowledge of a way out of the trouble, and regarded the present true church movement as only a sect, or faction, saying that "a sect is any body of Christians joined together in the same belief," etc. "But suppose a number of persons come out from and leave the sects with which they have been connected, and stand only on the Bible, independent of sects—suppose they assemble together in a body; would they be a sect?" he was asked. "Yes," was his reply. "Then what about the body of Christ itself, the whole, of which sects are regarded as cut-off factions—is that a sect?" "Yes," was his answer. And then, as if he could know nothing but sects, he referred to Paul as calling the Christians in his day a sect, and assumed to quote him thus: "For as concerning this sect, we know that everywhere it is spoken against" (Acts 28:22). He was told that these words were not spoken by Paul, but by his opposers. "Well," said he, "I will look that up."

Thus his conception of the subject makes the true church impossible. When men have been forty years in the ministry and in the holiness movement, and are just as far from discerning the church as when they started, and even suppose that Paul called the Christians a sect, how blinding and confusing must be the darkness in which they grope! Having failed to follow in God's way when came the call, "Come out of her, my people," they have been building with wood, hay, and stubble a structure that only awaits the consumption at the last day.

But not so all who were engaged in the holiness movement. God had a remnant whom he was leading entirely out of spiritual Babylon, who were returning to Zion over the highway of holiness, with singing and everlasting joy in their hearts. Holiness led them to the threshold of a brighter day, and they did not stop, but passed over. Keeping in the light they retained true holiness and all that God had given them. Thus, coming out of the holiness movement and embodying its true elements, is a movement that not only upholds holiness, but repudiates sectarianism and represents the true Christian unity that Christ prayed for. It holds and knows Christ as the only head of the body, and as complete, in all things, to the church.

It was through the workers in the holiness movement that Bro. D. S. Warner was made to face squarely the issue of holiness. His rejection of holiness in his earlier ministry may have been because of its poor representation on the part of professors; or, in other words, because his introduction to it was not such as would cause him to think seriously of its claims. When he comprehended that it was the line on which God was particularly working, he was not slow in being led into the light and experience and becoming an ardent advocate of the doctrine. Meeting with opposition from the so-called church of God, to which he belonged, and finally being expelled from the West Ohio Eldership, his associations were to a great extent with the holiness bands and societies. Among these he stood prominent.

Of the holiness editors who were contemporary with Brother Warner were John P. Brooks, of the Banner of Holiness, Bloomington, Ill.; George Hughes, of the Guide to Holiness, New York; Isaiah Reid, of the Highway, Nevada, Iowa; and T. K. Doty, of the Christian Harvester, Cleveland. There were also a number of others. Brother Warner himself came to be an editor and to have an acquaintance with nearly all the editors and prominent workers of his day.

As a delegate from Rome City, Ind., he attended the Western Union Holiness Convention, held at Jacksonville, Ill., Dec. 15-19, 1880. George D. Watson, who was a prominent holiness leader and author, was president of the convention. Brother Warner was appointed to the committee on program, serving with four others. He was slated for and delivered an address on the subject, The Kind of Power Needed to Carry the Holiness Work.

At the close of the convention he was placed on a committee of seven to confer and decide relative to the calling of a future convention of holiness workers in the West, with authority to issue a call for such a meeting, if they deemed it necessary. Thus he stood prominent in the holiness movement.

I Ought to Love My Savior.

I Ought to Love My Savior.

D. S. Warner.　　J. C. Fisher.

1. I ought to love my Sav-ior, He loved me long a-go,
2. I ought to love my Sav-ior, He bore my sin and shame;
3. I ought to love my Sav-ior, Up-on the cross he died;
4. I ought to love my Sav-ior, He par-doned all my sin,

Looked on my soul with fa-vor, When deep in guilt and woe;
From glo-ry to the man-ger, On wings of love he came;
Be-hold the world's Cre-a-tor, "My God! my God!" he cried.
Then sanc-ti-fied my na-ture, And keeps me pure with-in;

And though my sin had grieved him, His Father's law had crossed,
He trod this earth in sor-row, En-dured the pains of hell,
Oh, lis-ten to these ac-cents Of love di-vine so free;
He fills me with his glo-ry, And bears my soul a-bove;

Love drew him down from heav-en, To seek and save the lost;
That I should not be ban-ished, But in his glo-ry dwell;
"'Tis fin-ished" — my sal-va-tion; Thine shall the glo-ry be;
This world, oh, won-drous sto-ry, 'Tis love, re-deem-ing love;

Love drew him down from heav-en, To seek and save the lost.
That I should not be ban-ished, But in his glo-ry dwell.
"'Tis fin-ished" — my sal-va-tion; Thine shall the glo-ry be.
This world, oh won-drous sto-ry, 'Tis love, re-deem-ing love.

CHAPTER IX

A PREACHER OF HOLINESS

A rather new field of activity—Writes for publication—Meets with opposition—Tirade and charges by fellow minister—Canton camp-meeting—Eldership meeting at Smithville, faces charges—Assigned to Stark circuit—Visits father and place of conversion—Locates at Canton—Writes covenant with God—Return to Upper Sandusky—Revival at Findlay—Reflections on New Year's Day—Expulsion from West Ohio Eldership—Meetings at Dunkirk—Increasing vision of apostolic church—A peculiar test—Work opens in Indiana—Death of father and daughter—Attends Ohio Holiness Camp-Meeting—Brought low with affliction.

The attainment of the experience of perfect holiness led Brother Warner into a new and enlarged field of ministerial activity. Since the time had come for a reformation along the line of holiness, when it was the divine plan that the subject be made prominent, we should expect Brother Warner, as one of God's ministers, to make sanctification his principal theme and at once to begin preaching it. He began writing articles on sanctification for the Church Advocate, the denominational organ. Also he began writing with a view of publishing a tract or booklet on the subject of sanctification. He was thus placed in a new field, with a new issue to defend. New lines were drawn in his ministerial relations, as there was opposition from many along a line that had not existed before.[7]

As his diary covers the events of his life at this point we will let him again speak for himself. The reader will remember, of course, that these are but selections, as he wrote something for every day and the accounts are too full to quote in their entirety. He was at this time on the Ashland circuit, with his home in the Vermillion College building, near Hayesville. He had been taking a special course of study at the College, but as he beheld the need of the evangelistic field in greater proportion than ever, he felt it his duty thereafter to give less attention to study and more to his ministerial calling.

July 14, 1877. Wrote, meditated, and prayed most all day with only the Lord present. Commenced article for the Advocate on

[7] His profession of holiness soon brought him to conflict with the leaders in the church. Speaking of the period of 1875–80, Dr. Forney says in his History of the Church of God: "During several of these years the Eldership was contending against inroads of heresies advocated by D. S. Warner. It had finally to resort to the old remedy of excision in order to prevent the spread of the disease and restore the body to good health."

sanctification.

15. Quite sick this morn. As the holiness meeting [near Upper Sandusky] was interrupted by an appointment by a Dunker preacher this A. M., we all went to Rock Run to hear Brother Smith, but he absolutely required of me that I preach for him. I was very weak; but thinking it was of the Lord I committed all to God and expected his aid. Text: "They shall not hurt nor destroy in all my holy mountain, saith the Lord" (Isaiah 65). The Lord helped me to show the dear people some of the Scripture and reasons for the second work of grace, and that as soon as we merged up into the holy mountain, love, union, and peace prevailed without alloy. May God bless the truth. There was great attention. Some questions were asked at the close of discourse, all pleasantly, however. Oh, that God would lead the dear people on to perfection!

20. The Ohio State Holiness Convention met last night in Marion on the fair ground. Will continue several days. I should be happy to attend, but the Spirit seems to direct us to return and lift up the banner of holiness on our field of labor. Hence we started this morn for home, the weather pleasant. Having brought feed and dinner we stopped under a shade tree and ate our dinner and enjoyed a pleasant rest and communion with God.

25. [At Hayesville.] School begins today. Busy at domestic duties.

26. Wrote, read, and communed with the Lord.

27. Still writing on sanctification. The Lord is giving me much light. Praise his name! Met with the Excelsior Society. Read a lecture on pneumatics.

28. Finished my second article on sanctification.

29. Sabbath. Arose as soon as daylight. Spent some time with the Lord. Started about seven for Mansfield. Met a few hungry souls. The Lord wonderfully baptized my soul from the time I entered his house. Glory! glory! glory! Oceans of love flow through my soul. Oh, how inexpressibly sweet and joyful! Read part of Acts 21. After giving myself anew into the hands of God I proceeded to talk from Acts 21:14. The Lord so greatly led me out on his work **in us** that I did not get to the last two points, namely, his will done **with us**, and his will done **by us**. Praise the Lord, he so abundantly fills my mouth with holiness that I can not get to anything else to say.

Had a long talk with a sister of the Church of God who was mortified over my going to the altar to seek sanctification. She thought I must have been backslidden or something. I told her that something was wanting, but I knew very well what ailed me.

I had been in need of the sanctifying power of God and, glory to Jesus, I have found it. She thought that she was fully sanctified when she was converted. I replied that if that were so her experience differed from that of the first converts to Christ, as well as that of the Corinthians, the Ephesians, the Thessalonians, etc. To this she could make no reply but that it was to be attained by growth, but I reminded her that God was to do the work.

Aug. 3, 1877. This morn went into the Lord's camp. Dr. Steele, from New York, was reading his interesting Bible lessons, giving the benefit of the Greek and Dean Alford. Very instructive. Was happy to meet several brethren of my acquaintance from Crawford County and elsewhere. Thank God, they are on the holiness line.

4. Went out to camp at 5:30 A. M. Prayer-meeting in the tabernacle. Stayed all day on the ground, or until afternoon preaching by Brother Rice, who (probably unknown to the Methodist Episcopal ministers) had his license taken from him two days before by the Northwest Ohio Conference for preaching holiness. He gave us a straight, close-hewing sermon on sanctification. He did not preach holiness for the glory of Methodism, as some others seemed somewhat inclined to do. Some were much displeased at his exposure of the opposition to holiness in the Methodist Episcopal Church. Came home this eve. Found dear Wife and child well.

8. Sister Ella Snyder called on us. She was visiting at Brother McKey's, who, by the way, is a strong opposer of entire sanctification. Ella soon began talking on the subject and talking somewhat differently from what she did on last Sabbath. We think it probable that she had just been receiving the teaching of some one outside of the second work. She treated the subject with much lightness. Before she left we bowed in prayer, at the close of which she fell powerless on the floor. I raised her head, asked her if she was sick. She said not. Looked strange and confounded. Prayed some and confessed that the hand of God was upon her. Wife asked her if she was now sanctified. She replied that she knew not where she was. She grasped my hand very firmly. I raised her up, asked Sarah to support her; but she would not loosen her hold. As I endeavored to give her over to Wife, she gripped my hand the harder. We raised her up but she could not stand. We dropped her into a rocking-chair and soon kneeled again in prayer. She prayed constantly to God for a "clean heart," "sanctification," etc. Her full consciousness had hardly recovered when she said she had to go, as her party were waiting on her. Sarah accompanied her a piece and left her looking very solemn. I pray God to lead her to the cleansing fountain.

12. Sabbath. Beautiful morn. Was up early and in counsel with the Lord. Soon received my text, 1 Thess. 5:24. Observed that this text forever took away all excuse of inability; that it laid down a principle which converted all the commands of God into promises; that every thing unto which the Lord called us he would work in us. Applying the subject, as the apostle did, to entire sanctification, I defended the distinct work by experience, reason, and "thus saith the Lord." The Lord powerfuly blessed the testimony of my dear wife before preaching, and I believe that seed of truth has been sown in the hearts of the people. Went home with Bro. Jacob Freed, Brother and Sister Long, and others. We talked some on holiness. Brother Long opposed it by denying inherited depravity, which he did after my discourse today in the pulpit. Much of the afternoon was spent in the closet and private walks with the Lord. Oh, how much I prefer the company of the Lord to any other!

16. [At Eldership convention. Place not stated.] Met at half-past eight. Half hour devotion. Topic: Proper Home Influence; Duty of Parents to Their Children. The Spirit of the Lord deeply impressed this subject upon the minds of all. Hearts were melted. Tears flowed for unsaved children of ministers and members. Unconverted souls and backsliders were deeply affected. The Lord converted the convention wholly into an effort to save souls. Fervent prayers were offered, exhortations and tears, invitation hymns were sung (the organ was forgotten), and all the congregation was deeply stirred. A few souls arose and asked prayers. The unconverted children of Brothers ... were especially prayed for. Oh, how I praised God that the dear brethren were willing to let the Spirit lead the meeting! The whole forenoon was given to devotion.

18. Spent the day in writing, reading, and prayer. P. M., long talk with Brother Mitchell and Sister Shriner on sanctification. Brother M. talks reasonably; Sister S. is hostile to the blessed truth, but of course it is through ignorance. She thought I should leave the Church of God at once and not destroy it by my doctrine of holiness, having actual fears of holiness. Oh, I hope and pray to God to lead my dear brethren on to this heart-perfection. Would to God they understood this blessed full salvation! Nothing but wrong notions of perfect holiness or an evil spirit can oppose entire sanctification, as it does not in the least disturb or conflict with any doctrine of the church. It allows all that the Bible or any man attributes to regeneration. Instead of depreciating, it has greatly magnified justification.

19. Sabbath. At ten a funeral procession arrived from Rome, bringing a sweet little angel form, Bertha Estella Curtis, the only child of Z. H. Curtis, of Van Wert County. As their parents reside at Rome, they brought the child back there for burial. Brother Wilson preached an impressive discourse from Job: "Man that is born of woman is of few days and full of trouble." We laid the little form away and tried to comfort the young parents and friends.

Came to Shenandoah. Brother Burchard preached from: "Christ has left us an example that we should follow his steps." With his usual earnestness he urged all to live a whole-hearted Christian life. I wish the dear brother would learn to bring dear souls to the blood that cleanses from all sin, instead of infusing strength and zeal to fight inbred corruption. Recently I talked with this brother on the subject of sanctification. I had a conviction of mind that he knew something about it. He confessed that after seeking for mercy for three days the load of guilt and condemnation fell from his heart and he testified to the pardon of his sins. (This I remember myself.) But soon he found himself wanting before God. Then began another struggle for deliverance from something (he knew not what, as he felt no more guilt) that greatly disturbed his peace and shut out the smiles of God's face. After one week's prayer, and dedication of self and all he had to God, he "sank down in all the depth of humility and nothingness that was possible for him to conceive of." God wonderfully blessed him with perfect light, peace, and love. What was this but entire sanctification? But for want of being better taught he calls this his conversion. Strange confused theology. The idea of pardon one week before conversion! I pray God to show this brother his mistake and renew him in the blessing of perfect holiness.

21. Sent out about twenty-five cards of invitation in the mail. People began to come in to the reunion here at the College.

22. College yard filled. Some good speakers, but about all chaff and vainglory, ministers and lawyers alike using their brains to evolve some trashy nonsense to tickle the ears of the foolish. I was quite unwell. Eve, much reduced, but went out to Vermillion, where I met a few precious souls and preached that men should "trust in the Lord," and in trying to do so myself I was blessed with strength to preach about forty minutes.

26. Sabbath. The Lord helped me to set forth his great power to save from all sin in this life. Went home with Bro. David Donelson's. Conversed on holiness, spent much time in secret prayer. Was impressed to preach on holiness, yet felt sure that the church did not want to hear it; but I knew there was some hungry soul there that did want it.... The church here is quite strong numerically and there is much good material. Oh, that all these vessels of the Lord would be purged, sanctified, made fit for the Master's use, prepared unto every good work! Drove home, arriving at nearly one o'clock.

27. Arose in good time, feeling greatly refreshed in the Lord. Helped to get ready to go to Shenandoah.

28. Sister Shriner is boiling over with railing toward God's pure little ones. Glory to God! he has "saved me from the strife of tongues." Christ kept me, in imitation of his own example, from answering a word. It were folly indeed to try to talk holiness where there is no appetite but for carnal contention. Thank the Lord for this wisdom.

29. Fasted and prayed today. Father N— — seems very cold and unsociable toward us. Probably the enemy has put something in his heart. I sank very deep down in the great ocean of God's love and goodness this morning. Had inexpressible conceptions of the wonders of salvation. Visited at Brother Kline's. I spent about all the time on my knees in prayer, which I love most to do.

30. Sold my mare and colt to Mother Wolf for $130.

Sept. 1, 1877. Elmer Wolf took me part of the way to Mansfield. I gave up the faithful Mattie and little Billy to him. Walked a few miles and was overtaken by a kind man who took me in his buggy to town. Called at a few places. Spent much of the time in prayer. Eve, preached the gospel of perfect salvation.

2. Met in a holiness prayer-meeting at 5:30 A. M. Took some breakfast. Stayed much on my knees before God. At 10:30 A. M. met, and tried to talk to the people from Eph. 3:20. Then we went to a small stream at the west side of the city and had the happy privilege of immersing.... They all enjoy entire sanctification. Never before did I feel the solemnity of the ordinance as now. How unworthy I regarded myself to imitate my blessed Master, especially in immersing those whom he had led far out into the ocean of his perfect love! We sang a hymn, then knelt down upon the green sod and called upon the Lord, who was so very sensibly near to us. The day had been very dark and dreary, the sun not having shone through the clouds since early morn. But now the gentle hand of God brushed the clouds aside and sent down upon us the most glorious and brilliant streams of light that I ever witnessed. Sister F— — was the last of the three. She has been walking with God upon the strait highway of holiness for some years and her whole life is swallowed up in God alone. Though the sun was shining brilliantly, yet as she arose from the water I was impressed that a light shone upon us "above the brightness of the sun." She stood calmly gazing upward for a moment, with the light of God beaming from her face. I gave way to the impression that the occasion and circumstances had made on my mind and spoke of the heavenly light, which I still supposed was natural;

but she afterward informed me that it was more than sunshine—rays of glory. The whole assembly was awed into reverence, and a strange feeling of sacredness pervaded all our minds. How applicable the words of the prophet: "Arise, shine, for thy light has come and the glory of the Lord is risen upon thee"!

3. Took train for Perryville to begin a holiness meeting at the Brubaker Bethel. A pretty good crowd assembled. I tried to teach them their rights in the gospel, taking special pains to admonish the brethren and sisters not to allow the enemy of their souls to stir up bitterness and hatred in their hearts against the way of perfect holiness, assuring them that this way was so hated by the devil that if possible he would overthrow the best of Christians and set them foaming and raging mad against the pure in heart and true holiness. I was surprized to learn that since my last visit here the enemy had already begun to work, fearing the destruction of his kingdom.

6. Meeting nearly all day. Satan still angry. Small stones were thrown into the house from the door and windows. Two brethren ventured to speak. The first took occasion to unload his mind of many grievous objections and charges against the holiness work, and sat down much humiliated when he saw that his harsh speeches only elicited pleasant smiles and kind words from the sanctified. The second said he did not endorse what his brother had said, but still could not see this second work. Both asked for "thus saith the Lord."...

7. Fasted and worshiped God all day. Met at 10 A. M. and continued until 4 P. M. Just before closing we engaged in prayer to God for my perfect healing. I was wonderfully strengthened both in body and faith. Walked about one mile over hills to find places for God's little ones, then drove to Loudonville and Brother L—— and I ate some refreshment, about 5 P. M., at the baker's, I not having eaten anything since the day before at noon. Glory to God, I felt no weakness.

8. Drove back to the Ridge. Found God's little ones there at noon and no food, and no encouragement to go anywhere for dinner. We sent to Perryville and got some provisions, but before it came we had begun afternoon meeting, and cared but little for the bread that perisheth.

9. Sabbath. In the saving strength of the Lord, Wife, child, and I walked to Vermillion. Went the two and one half miles with scarcely any fatigue. Now began the eruption of a volcano in the form of a preacher, even my beloved colleague [W. H. Oliver]. The red-hot lava of scorn, scoff, and persecution, yea, words of slang fit only for the worldly rabble, poured forth about two hours, all against those whom the blood had washed whiter than snow. Glory to God, I only added that I thanked my holy Savior I was counted worthy to suffer persecution and reproach for his name's sake. Praise God, he keeps me in a storm as well as in the calm. We came to Brother Ford's. Sister Ella Snyder came along, and after she and Sarah had a good talk, we had prayer together, and, praise the Lord, he sanctified her soul and body.

I came to Hayesville, where an appointment had been announced for me at 3 P. M. By the help of the Lord I talked from 1 Thess. 5:24. Glory to God, the truth went home to the heart. Rode most of the way back with Father McQ— —. Poor old man tried to pick a quarrel with me on baptism. I finally calmed his nerves by singing The Precious Blood Has Reached Me. Shut myself up with God until meeting. Found the church mostly displeased with the harangue of the forenoon. Good speaking-meeting. Wife testified boldly to the second work and admonished the church. Sister Snyder, whom the Lord smote down in my room some time ago, and who entered into rest this day, also testified to her entire sanctification. I talked to the people about twenty minutes from Acts 5:28-39. Oh, how sweetly the Spirit led me and talked through me! Some shouting.

10. My soul was very happy today. It appears that I only begin to realize the glorious work that God has done for me. I do thank God for the test of yesterday. O Lord, try me in every way and see if there is any evil way in me! I do praise the Lord that I can not feel the slightest ill will in my heart against the persecutor. May the Lord enlighten, humble, and save him. I suppose he really thinks like Paul, the persecutor, did, that he is doing God service.

13. I walked over to Sister Smith's and called to invite her to the meeting. Had a season of prayer with her and family. As I was about to start she asked if I did not wish to sell my buggy. I told her I did. So she gave me a beast to ride to Shenandoah and bring the buggy back on my return. Thank the Lord, this is his kind dealing with me. Eve, abstained from supper, as I commonly do when I have services. Good full house. Delivered my farewell discourse to the people of Shenandoah. Acts 20. Brother Oliver was present, and was so much annoyed when I addressed the few little ones whom the Lord has perfected in love that he could not compose himself and sit in one position three seconds. God pity any one thus mad against the work of God.

14. Met a Brother and Sister Daily, from Morrow County. I enquired of that country as a missionary field and heard of some destitute localities, where the Lord may send me to win souls for Jesus. Came to Shenandoah, thence to Brother M. Bell's, south of town. Visited until 5 P. M. Poor man thinks it impossible to get rid of the Adamic nature while we live. So "because of unbelief they entered not in." Had a season of prayer with the family and twice interviewed the Lord in the pleasant woods near by. Glory to Jesus, he is near, yea, reigning in me most preciously today. Came over to Paul's. Found that they had been in expectation of me all day. Prayed with and encouraged them to stedfastness.

15. Ate some breakfast this morn with the design of fasting the rest of the day. Desired much to visit some, but felt the importance of shutting myself up with the Lord, so I did, and was greatly blessed. At 2 P. M. we met in the grove and had a profitable little meeting. Brother Oliver, by my request, again preached.

16. Sabbath. Early this morn I went to the beautiful grove prepared for services. Spent a long time upon my knees there in prayer and reading His Word. At ten people convened. Had a good speaking-meeting. Then Brother Oliver preached on Eph. 3:14,15. Preached over an hour on Christian union. I am sick of hearing union thrown at the people with the sling of depravity. Might as well go into a drove of sheep and expect to get them all into a solid mass by pounding them around with a club. It can but scatter more.

I took dinner with Brother and Sister Ferguson on the ground, then went off into the woods nearly a half mile and stayed with the Lord alone until 2:30 P. M., the time for preaching. The Spirit directed me to read and talk upon 1 Corinthians 13. Though I said scarcely anything but what every true Christian can endorse, yet Brother Oliver took occasion to put in about a half hour opposing holiness as a distinct work of God. Poor soul, he is greatly disturbed with the subject of perfect love. Went home with Brother and Sister Tomlinson and Brother and Sister Crum. They were anxious to learn of the way of holiness. Had prayer together and some supper. I walked to the Bethel, found it full and Brother Oliver preaching.

Brother O. took me in hand on holiness; asked me many questions, made grievous charges, and wanted me to leave what he termed "my theory." Asked me if I was going to continue preaching as I have for the past months. I told him that I would continue to teach all the light I had received and as much more as the Lord would give. I patiently heard his long heckling and thanked him. As he finished he drew from his pocket a paper and handed it to me. My first impression was that it was a note that someone had sent to me, but as soon as I took it I felt the Spirit of God go through my whole being and I knew that it was something from which God would bring great good to my soul and his cause. I thanked him and put it in my pocket. Came to Brother Stoner's and got my beast and buggy and drove to Brother Wolfe's. Stopping for some things there I took a moment to read the portentous paper I had received. I read as follows:

September 15, 1877.

The following charges are preferred against Elder D. S. Warner:

First. For inviting a sect of fanatics calling themselves the Holy Alliance Band to hold meetings in the local Churches of God without consulting the elders or trustees or myself.

Second. For joining in with these said band and bidding them God speed and thereby bringing schism and division among those churches.

Third. For the accommodation of this professed holy band that he invited to hold a meeting of ten days in the Church of God chapel in Mansfield. Elder D. S. Warner did on the evening of the 8th of July in less than one hour hold the ordinances of washing the saints' feet and the Lord's Supper attended to.

Fourth. For stating publicly in Shenandoah, about the 26th of August, that he had been preaching his own doctrine prior to seeking his so called holiness.

W. H. Oliver.

I thanked God and put the paper away without saying a word. Bid all farewell, including Della Oliver, whom I invited to come and visit us. I drove to Sister Smith's, twelve miles. The night was beautiful and light, and my soul was happy. I praised God all the way and was too happy to sleep when I retired about 12 o'clock. Of these charges I feel as Joseph told his brethren: "Ye thought evil in your hearts, but God meant it all for good, for you see how much people he hath saved from death by the famine."

To the first charge I say: Thank God that calling people hard names does not make them such, but only shows the depravity of the accuser. No band was invited, but simply persons from different localities who enjoyed holiness.

Second. The charge of schism is without the least shadow of foundation. Through the mercy of God a few souls have been sanctified from their pride, etc., and qualified to be useful in the church.

[The answer to the third charge is omitted from the journal. Perhaps an oversight.]

Fourth. This is a mistake. I simply said that on sanctification I used to preach what I believed, but now I am able to testify that I know.

21. [At Canton camp-meeting.] A. M., Brother Oliver tried to preach, being very hoarse. After preaching a brother presented a call for money for Brother Oliver's horse. I joyfully took a paper and solicited for him with his paper of charges in my pocket. Thank God for entire sanctification. P. M., I addressed the people from 1 Thess. 4:1. By the help of God a portion of the discourse was given to testifying and teaching entire sanctification. Brother Petra followed in German with a cross-fire. Brother James followed him with his mixed talk, part of the time seeming to endorse me and the other Brother P. Oh, how much waste of time for the want of seeking a definite experience and then being able to "give the trumpet a certain sound!" Brother James announced that in the evening he would preach from, "This is the will of God, even your sanctification." I prayed God to keep him from opposing the truth and, thank His name, he talked only to sinners and said little on the text.

24. [Canton camp-meeting.] I thank God that I came to this meeting. I have never in all my life met so much good, old-fashioned, plain, humble, Holy Ghost religion. What a kind-hearted people! God bless them. After long time was spent in sobs and farewell greetings around a large assembly of people who were solemnly touched by the deepness of the feeling, we marched around in single file again singing, "We are traveling to the New Jerusalem." Then we gathered in front of the stand, and as we stood singing, the Holy Spirit came upon us and there was wonderful shouting in the camp by sisters, about all young, single ones, who were carried entirely off in the Spirit. We did not get away from the sacred altar until about 2 o'clock at night, so greatly did the Spirit rest on the camp of the dear saints.

25. Arose greatly refreshed. Went to the camp for breakfast once more, after we all bowed in the tent to worship God. Had a precious stroll and season of prayer out on the camp-ground. Returning, met Bro. Milton S— —, a very faithful young man. I read in his face some very unfortunate misgivings, and told him the same, to his surprize. I gave him nearly an hour's lecture on the evils of violating and perverting physical laws, also on self-culture and mental improvement. The dear brother was lost for language to thank me for the favor. He was wonderfully teachable, and urged me never to miss an opportunity to instruct and admonish persons in his condition.

Brother James and I started for Middle Branch, where I had an appointment. We stopped with Sister Lucy, ate a dish of peaches and cream, and had a season of prayer. Rather small congregation, and they rather sleepy from having been up so late last night at camp-meeting.

On the 27th Brother Warner went to attend the Eldership meeting at Smithville. He says that on account of insufficient pure air in the house he did not remain in much of the time. He also says, on the 28th, that "Brother James was taken into the ecclesiastical mill today." On the third day of the session Brother Warner was called upon for his report of the year's work. He reported 203 sermons, 68 converts, 66 accessions, 40 immersed. There were 164 members in good standing, whereas there were 75 when he took charge two years previous. Proceeding in his journal, for the 29th he says:

> Reported that God had fully saved and sanctified me, and that I was under the necessity to preach that precious truth to the glory of Jesus; that I desired to cooperate with the Church of God; could not exchange truth for truth but must walk in all the light of God. The Holy Spirit rested on me in power, and tears flowed freely all over the congregation. Praise God for his power and presence! Brother Oliver then arose and made known to the body that he had charges against me. The speaker appointed ... a committee to investigate my case. Brother O. subpenæd a large number of witnesses, many of whom knew absolutely nothing about the case. I told the body that I had never informed but three persons about the charges against me, had asked no witnesses but had committed my whole case to God; however, if anyone felt directed by the Spirit to appear in defense of the cause of God and holiness they should meet with us. We went at once to Brother Z——'s office and began the investigation.

> I felt greatly impressed with the need of prayer and hoped these dear old saints would not begin such a solemn work without invoking the Holy Spirit's guidance. But I was disappointed, as they opened the business at once. Even after investigation began I felt that I must go to God on my knees; but I did not, as I had no control of business. Yet I did wrong in not demanding the right of prayer. I also lost power to conduct myself with that calmness and sweetness that I had been so ardently wishing from the Lord, though I felt no such thing as a roiled temper for one second for all the hard aspersions and carnal accusations thrown at me. Yet I did sometimes speak when I should have kept silent, as my blessed Master did.

> What was my astonishment when Elder O. read letters from Vermillion and Brubaker's signed by about all the church, charging me with insanity whenever I touched on sanctification, also with causing division and schism in the churches and every evil work imaginable! As I heard the names of the dear brethren read over that were appended to those letters I had strange feelings. I truly felt myself in a queer world. Never in my life did my reasoning powers receive such a dreadful shock. I felt myself sinking, then looked to Jesus and all was calm and peaceful again.

I asked Brother O. who had got up those letters. "They are headed respectively from the Vermillion and Brubaker churches to the Eldership, Please tell the Committee whether the elders have written them or who." Brother O. looked very much confused and refused to answer. I demanded an answer. The Committee sustained me. Then with shame and confusion he confessed that they were both written by him. I told him that it was all right and thanked him for his trouble.

Brother Roller, elder from Vermillion, who confessed to me that at the ordinance-meeting he was ashamed of Elder O's two-hour harangue of abuse against the work of "perfecting the saints," being present, was then called to the witness-stand. After he stated in direct examination that I was insane on sanctification, I asked him to inform the Committee what the manifestations of my insanity were. He gave the following three points, which I record to his shame:

First. "You hesitated to proceed to preach once at Vermillion, stating that you wished to be led by the Spirit in the selection of a subject and that if the Spirit wished you not to preach you would read the Word, talk experience, or be silent, as the Spirit directed."

Second. "You do not act as you used to. At our ordinance-meeting you sat back, and I believe Brother Oliver had to invite you forward." Brother O. concurred in this remark. But I then appealed to them if it was not a fact that I came down from the pulpit immediately after closing my remarks and led In the preparation and observance of feet-washing. Then he remarked that it was at the Brick, on Brother Lynn's charge, and Brother O. was not there at all, and that it was after feet-washing Brother Lynn stepped to me and asked me to assist in the Lord's Supper (which was perfectly proper for me—to wait for an invitation).

Third. "You do not preach as loud on sanctification as you used to preach, but you are more low and calm."

These were his only reasons for the assertion of my insanity.

Brother Mitchell only stated that some young people asked him "what ails Brother Warner, he does not preach as heretofore," hence concluded that I was partly insane. Brother O. said all he could to taint the character of the holiness workers. Many of his aspersions were never answered. It is of no use to give particulars, only this, that I was grateful to God for these fiery ordeals, and though the Lord kept me from an evil thought, yet I was conscious of great weakness and must say to my shame that I did not keep that perfect calmness and sweetness in the midst of the storm of unexpected accusation. However, I came out with another perfect evidence that 'the very God of peace had sanctified me wholly.'

I was entirely free from the least hard feelings against any of my brethren. Glory to God, I felt good toward them all. Looked upon their efforts to condemn me and the holiness cause as springing entirely from ignorance, sin within, and a blind zeal to protect the church. I went to my room a happy soul. Related a few points of the many wonderful things developed before the committee and then we concluded that it did not minister grace to talk about them, hence we had a sweet season of worship and lay down and slept sweetly until morn.

30. Sabbath. Arose early and sought the Lord. Spent about all my time with God and my Bible until 10 A. M., then went up to the Bethel to speaking-meeting, and heard Elder T. Hickernel make a long speech of caution to brethren who seemed to have been flinging at sanctified ones. He made this sensible remark: "You who claim to have been fully sanctified at conversion, be careful that you do not prove your claims false by picking and persecuting those who have the second experience." At half-past ten went to the Methodist Episcopal house of worship, where a large congregation had assembled to hear me speak on perfect holiness. I felt more like keeping quiet in some small corner. A number of the brethren were present, some to sit back and try to criticize. Yea, these were preachers, and about all of them left before the sermon closed. But there were several others who came to learn and who gave close attention and were compelled to sanction the truth. The Lord wonderfully baptized my soul and all the lovers of truth and holiness. I believe I never before spoke with such power and liberty. Glory to God, he so freely poured his Spirit upon us that it filled the whole house. After services. Brother Oliver's daughter came forward and told us that she enjoyed the blessing of entire sanctification. She said she was wonderfully strengthened and wished that her father were fully saved.

We went to Brother Baker's for dinner. Brother Torbet, the Methodist minister, was also with us. We enjoyed a good season in reading some good holiness works, such as Dr. Steele's Love Enthroned, and prayer, then came to meet at the Bethel at 2:30 P. M. Went to the home of Brother Oliver's daughter. Her father was to come also, but seeing us go there, or for some other cause, went elsewhere. The poor woman is very unfortunately married, but Christ is her only true companion. Eve, Brother Updike preached with all his might (his usual style) on Christ a teacher. We then observed the ordinances.

Oct. 1, 1877. Committee on my case reported "charges sustained," but recommended me favorably to the body for license with this restriction only, that I do not bring holiness workers or any outside elements to hold a meeting anywhere in the Churches of God without their consent. This I readily consented to, as a meeting thus appointed could do no good, or but little. I also, unsolicited, apologized for the appointment of some meetings in the past which to my surprize proved offensive to the churches.

The report was adopted and my license renewed. Thank the Lord! However, I had perfect peace on the whole matter, and had my license been withheld I would equally have given God thanks. Glory to Jesus!

Was out much of the day talking with brethren on perfect love, etc. The brethren from Stark circuit again called me out and consulted me about taking their circuit. I told them if they could stand perfect holiness and all the counsel of God preached, they might apply for me, and I would leave it all with the Lord and the Eldership. This eve I gave a concise account of my experience of justification and sanctification. At a late hour the Eldership closed with a report of the Stationing Committee. I was assigned to the Stark circuit, consisting of Canton, New Berlin, Middle Creek, and Stump's Bethel. Thank the Lord! His ways are not our ways. I had built much on free missionary work, but he knows best. I committed it all to him, besought him to prevent my appointment to a circuit if he did not wish me to take one, even by cutting off my license if no other way; and now I receive this appointment of the Lord, and by his blessing and power I hope he will make his Word to run and be glorified in the salvation of hundreds of souls.

Following this decision of the Stationing Committee, Brother and Sister Warner had the task of changing their place of abode, which in their work they had so many times to do. Their belongings were certainly not many, nevertheless the work of packing and the obtaining of some means of conveying their goods to the station was left generally for them to attend to. His literary society about this time gave an entertainment at the College, but he with Sister Warner preferred to attend a holiness meeting about four miles distant. Of this meeting he thus speaks:

3. Met Brother Ackers, from Bucyrus, whom I had not met before. He is a wonderful specimen of God's great salvation, raised from the delirium tremens to perfect holiness and mighty faith.

7. Brother Ackers testified for God that the happiest moment he ever saw was when he found he had lost all his property and had not a dollar left, though he had been a wealthy merchant in Bucyrus. I was led to testify how the Lord had taken me through some storms in great calmness. Eve, the church and the large schoolhouse on the same corners were both filled. I delivered a short sermon in the former on perfection, then went over to the other house and gave an exhortation to sinners.

Before leaving for Canton, Brother and Sister Warner decided to visit the latter's former home near Upper Sandusky. From that place he went to visit his father, at Bridgewater, Williams County.

11. This morning arose before daylight, started quite early to Loudonville. Brother Eyer came to the station and brought a quilt for us and a small one for Levilla, which the sisters of the Brubaker Church had got up for us. I spent some hours in packing things more securely to ship. Took train at 2:16 P. M. for Upper Sandusky. Reached there after seven. Walked out to Father Keller's. They had about given me up and were engaged in family worship. With reverence and admiration I stood at the window and looked in at that dear, affectionate family, all "made perfect through the blood of the everlasting covenant," while bowed together in evening devotion. Father was praying with a beaming face toward me. It appeared that the whole house was illuminated with the presence of God. My heart was made to burn with love and the Holy Ghost. When through with prayer, I entered, and then we had a moment of joyful greeting in the name of the Lord Jesus. My full heart then suggested that we bow again in praise and thanksgiving to God, which we all did. Oh how my poor heart tried to find utterance for its weight of gratitude to our God of wondrous love and salvation! Until quite late we talked of the kind dealings of God to our souls. I praise thee, O my God and Father, that thou hast ever connected me with this family. Through thy blessings, we have been wonderful helps to each other.

13. I took train at about half-past five for my father's in Williams County. Lay over about an hour at Toledo. Reached Bryan about half-past one. Went up in the town and soon found a man by the name of Faith, who could take me within one and three fourths miles from Father's. Talked with the poor man about his soul; but he had taken an oath to stick to the Lutheran Church as long as he lived, and that oath must be kept if he violates every obligation to Christ and loses his soul. Called at Brother Dean's. Found the poor man much cast down over the death of his dear wife. He wept as I alluded to her. Came on home. Found Father pretty well and happy to see me.

As I came from Brother Dean's, I passed the old schoolhouse where I surrendered to Jesus. It is no more used. I revered the sacred spot. Approached the door and found that it was not locked. I entered and kneeled as near as I could where I bowed at the altar a penitent sinner twelve years ago last February. I poured out my full heart of gratitude to the Father of mercies that he ever sent his spirit to convict me of my sins and show me my awful doom if I continued in sin. I truly thanked God that he had there prevailed upon me to repent of all my sin. I praised the great Shepherd of my soul that his grace had kept me those years from the power of an enraged foe. My thanks ascended to God for all the good he had done through this lump of unworthy clay. There I reconsecrated to God, after a careful examination of myself before him.

After some talk with Father, we bowed down together and I earnestly prayed God to save my poor father from the dreadful end of the wicked. For some time I have been unusually burdened in heart for my poor old father. I trust God in his infinite mercy will yet save him ere he goes to his long home. Before retiring, in my bedchamber I continued long in prayer with my blessed Savior.

14. Sabbath. Bro. Joseph Neil and I went to Madison Bethel, where Brother Coblen (recently from the German Baptists) had an appointment to preach. Brother C. spoke about thirty minutes on Heb. 2:2. Did well. I then talked over thirty minutes, mostly on the perfect escape from sin.

The church here are living in a high state of justification and spirituality. They all sanctioned entire sanctification. We then had a good speaking-meeting, when some of them acknowledged their need of full salvation. Oh, what a pity this church could not be led into the blessed land of perfect rest! But perhaps the next preacher that comes along will try to turn them against the truth. What a dreadful thing is an unsanctified minister! O Lord! make haste to "purge the sons of Levi." Took dinner with Brother Troxel. As soon as we arrived, Brother Neil began to entertain some young people on the porch with stories, while the disgraceful pipe protruded from his unsanctified lips. I withdrew at once to the room, read a few chapters, then to the bedroom and communed with my God until dinner was about ready. After eating, the pipe presented itself again. The Lord led me to rebuke such filthiness of the flesh. I told them that the use of tobacco was positively a sin: First, because it was the gratification of an unnatural and unholy appetite; second, it was offensive to all who were not therewith corrupted; third, it was a sinful appropriation of the Lord's means; fourth, it disqualified for refined and pure society by its extreme filthiness. Brother Neil then hitched up his beast, drove to the front, and called for me. I told him to come in. I read a portion of God's Word and then engaged in prayer. The Spirit led me into some very solemn requests for my brethren, and I trust they will hereafter have a more sacred conception of what it is to be holy in life, heart, and "all manner of conversation." Came to Father's. Had a long season of prayer in the chamber where I dwelt so much with God at the beginning of my ministration of the Word. Then for exercise and meditation I chose to walk to the meeting-house, about one and one half miles. The house was densely crowded. I was astonished that the word had spread so rapidly to such a great distance in every direction. The Lord gave me glorious liberty and power. 1 Thess. 4:1. Touched on sanctification, and I saw in a moment that I had some hearers who were in the land and others seeking the crossing, all members of the Church of God. The Lord gave me a very solemn appeal to the sinner. Many wept. My father was greatly melted down.

15. Father and I drove to Brother Joseph's. I walked to the cemetery and communed with God beside the grave of my beloved and revered mother. I knelt down there and thanked God for having been brought into the world by such a pure and beloved mother; for her tender and never-failing care for me when in sickly childhood and youth; for the hallowed influence of her constant life of love and patience and humble trust in God in the midst of constant wickedness in this world; for her triumphant death and the hope of meeting her in heaven. Though I began in secret I soon forgot my surroundings and called loudly upon my blessed Jesus, not only in thanksgiving, but for the salvation of Father, Brother and friends.

16. Arose early. Communed with the Lord. Bathed, as my custom is each alternate morning. Read a little tract on Joshua's stopping the sun and moon, written by D. M. Bennett. While reading the little bit of corruption the Lord gave me wonderful light to expose it to my father. These facts flashed across my mind: 1. The world was lost in ignorance of God and debased in sin. 2. The first thing necessary in human salvation was for God to make man sensible of His existence and power. 3. He had to take mankind in the condition sin had placed him. 4. Man, possessing very little mental and less moral elevation and energy, would not have been impressed with awe and reverence before God had he manifested his perfections of wisdom and holiness, any more than a base society would entertain peculiar respect for a man who appeared among them with superior intellect and morals. 5. As man's chief ideal of greatness consisted in valor, heroism, and physical achievements, it is a fact that on this low plane only could man be led to recognize the true greatness and actual existence of God, by the manifestations of his power in the manner he used in destroying those idolatrous nations.

P. M., Father and I drove to Montpelier on a little business. Father gave me five dollars, and one dollar in silver for Levilla. He also gave me a small package of some of my revered mother's clothes. How blessed her memory! Eve, Mr. Frisby (married to my niece), my brother, and a large wagon-load accompanied me to Madison, where I spoke to a full house. About the whole church received the light of holiness.

On the 19th he took train on his journey toward Canton. He stopped at Loudonville and visited the church. Arrived at Canton on the 20th and proceeded immediately to visit congregations on the circuit. Sister Warner and child arrived on the 23d. The search for a house in which to live extended over a period of several days. There were good, faithful brethren who assisted them with provisions, but yet to a considerable extent they were left to provide the necessaries of life themselves. Of his effort to procure wood and hay we observe, for November 6:

> Cold. Snowed some last night for the first. Went to hunt wood and hay. Found no wood or hay to spare. It seems hard that a poor messenger of God must expose himself to drive about sixteen miles through mud and very raw air to hunt those necessaries. It seems a light thing nowadays to sow to the people spiritual things, but a heavy thing to reap a few temporal things, even when we try to live more simple and cheap than our poor. Oh, how good it would have been for me to have had this day in the warm with the Lord in my library! But glory to Jesus, we still joy in sustaining sacrifice for his sake and feel content with our lot. Only, dear Lord, give us a good supply of the spirit of love, zeal, wisdom, and power.

Meetings in town were held from house to house until a permanent place of worship could be opened. It was not long, however, until they both felt the Lord leading them to resign the circuit. Brother Warner had accepted with submission and good grace the charge given him (which, after all, was of man's appointment), but as a preacher of holiness with an ever increasing interest in a wider field, he doubtless felt that God wanted him to be free to go and do as the Spirit directed. The following is his entry for November 23:

> This morn before daylight, when having morning devotion, the Spirit of God spoke to both Sarah and me to fast today. Thank God for such a precious Leader. Who would not obey such a wise Counselor? Spent most of the day in reading the Word, singing, and prayer. At ten A. M. we were both before the Lord in silent prayer when we were both directed by the Spirit to resign this circuit. Still on our knees, we made known the orders received. We could but say amen, and the refreshings from the presence of the Lord came upon our hungry souls. We engaged in prayer and praise, when I was directed to proceed at once to write my resignation.

> This tried me, as I had never before been thrown among such very kind brethren and sisters. It seemed hard that I must throw up the circuit without as much as consulting them. But we dared not disobey God, as some hesitancy to obey in the past had cost me much power and sweet rest in God. Praise God, our hearts were much lightened and we felt that we had now got back at the beginning of the highway of holiness, which we had to some extent missed. We could now sing, "He leadeth us." Eve, went up to the office and received a card earnestly calling for our services at Columbiana. Of this call I had an impression before I went to the

office, and believe it of the Lord. Glory to God! My way has been hedged up ever since we came on the circuit.

At Columbiana he found a number whose hearts were open to sanctification. His work there resulted in ten persons receiving the experience and one sinner being converted. Returning to his house in Canton on December 6, he became impressed with the idea of writing out in somewhat itemized form the solemn covenant that constituted his consecration to God.

8. I fasted today. Remained up with the Lord until after 11 o'clock at night. I was led by the Spirit to a deep self-examination. I found myself utterly nothing in the sight of God. I read with great interest the experience of Bro. R. Yeakel, in the Living Epistles of 1873. As I read over the solemn written covenant that this holy man entered into with God, I was much impressed to do likewise, but feared that my impressions came from a wish to imitate one of God's holy men rather than to follow the Spirit.

Went to the office this eve and received a letter from Brother Chambers, chairman of the Ohio Holiness Alliance. As soon as I saw his name on the envelope the conviction of last Sabbath that I should give myself up to be a holiness evangelist came strongly to my mind, and as I walked home I promised God that I would not lie down until I had reported myself to Brother Chambers for this work. The Lord helped me to do so, and as I wrote down my convictions and surrendered to the Lord, the Holy Ghost graciously fell upon my soul.

13. The day was mild and fair. Took a walk in the woods to commune with God. Thought much of the words of God, "I will make a new covenant with the house of Israel" (Jer. 31:31). In Hebrews 8 and 10 I read that this covenant related to the new dispensation, and the apostle, in Hebrews 10, actually connects it with sanctification. I felt like entering more personally and formally into this covenant with the Almighty. But I thought, Can such a worm enter into an everlasting covenant with the Holy God of the universe? God makes the proposition, and with solemn reverence I venture to step out upon it. And this I do in the name of the Lord Jesus, my only righteousness.

A covenant is an agreement of two parties in which both voluntarily bind themselves to fill certain conditions and receive certain benefits. God is the party of the first part of the contract, and has bound himself.

1. "I will put my laws into their minds and write them in their hearts."

2. "And I will be their God."

3. They "shall know me from the least to the greatest."

4. "I will be merciful to their unrighteousness."

5. "Their sins and their iniquities will I remember no more."

O thou Most High God, thou hast left this covenant in thy Holy Book, saying, "If any man will take hold of my covenant."

Now, therefore, in holy fear and reverence I present myself as the party of the second part and subscribe my name to the holy article of agreement, and following thy example will here and now write down the conditions on my part.

"They shall be my people." Jer. 31:33. Amen, Lord, **I am forever thine**.

> The vow is passed beyond repeal,
> Now will I set the solemn seal.

Lord, thou hast been true to thy covenant, though I have been most unfaithful and am now altogether unworthy to take hold of thy most gracious covenant. But knowing that thou hast bound thyself in thy own free offer to "be merciful to their unrighteousness," I take courage to approach thee and would most earnestly beseech thee to fulfil thy wonderful offer to BE MY GOD; and I do most joyfully yield myself entirely TO BE THINE.

Therefore this soul which thou hast made in thine own image is placed wholly in thy hands to do with it as seemeth good.

This mind shall think only for thy glory and the promotion of thy cause.

This will is thy will, O God!

The spirit within this body is now thine; do with it as thou wilt, in life and death.

This body is thy temple forevermore.

These hands shall work only for thee.

These eyes to see thy adorable works and thy holy law.

This tongue and these lips to speak only holiness unto the Lord.

These ears to hear thy voice alone.

These feet to walk only in thy ways.

And all my being is now and forever thine.

In signing my name to this solemn covenant I am aware that I bind myself to live, act, speak, think, move, sit, stand up, lie down, eat, drink, hear, see, feel, and whatsoever I do all the days and nights of my life to do all continually and exclusively to the glory of God. I must henceforth wear nothing but what honors God. I must have nothing in my possession or under my control but such as I can consistently write upon, "Holiness unto the Lord." The place where I live must be wholly dedicated to God. Every item of goods or property that is under my control is hereby conveyed fully over into the hands of God to be used by him as he will and to be taken from my stewardship whenever the great Owner wishes, and it is not my business at all.

She whom I call my wife belongs forevermore to God. Use her as thou wilt and where thou wilt, and leave her with me, or take her from me, just as seemeth good to thee and to thy glory. Amen.

Levilla Modest, whom we love as a dear child bestowed upon us by thy infinite goodness, is hereby returned to thee. If thou wilt leave us to care for her and teach her of her true Father and Owner, we will do the best we can by thy aid to make her profitable unto thee. But if thou deemest us unfit to properly rear her or wouldst have her in thy more immediate presence, behold, she is thine, take her. Amen and amen.

And now, great and merciful Father, thou to whom I belong, with all that pertains to me, and thou who art mine with all that pertains to thy fulness and richness, all this offering which I have made would be but foolishness and waste of time were it not for what I have in thee obtained to confirm the solemn contract. For were it not that thou art my God, my promises would be but idle words. I could fulfil nothing which my mouth has uttered and my pen has written. But since thou, Almighty, Omniscient, Omnipresent, and Eternal God, art mine, I have a thousandfold assurance that all shall be fulfilled through thy fulness.

My ignorance is fully supplied by thy own infinite wisdom. My utter weakness and inability to preserve myself from sin is abundantly supplied by thy omnipotence, to thy everlasting praise.

Glory to thy holy name! Though I have solemnly pledged all things to thee, yet, as thou art my "all and in all," I have nothing to fear. Now, O Father! my God and Savior, I humbly pray thee so to keep me that all my powers of soul, body, and spirit, my time, talents, will, influence, words, and works, shall continually, exclusively, and eternally glorify thy holy name through Jesus Christ, my Lord and Savior. Amen and amen.

In covenant with the God of all grace and mercy, who has become my salvation, my all, and whose I am forever, to the praise of his glory. Amen.

Entered into by the direction of the Holy Spirit and signed this Thirteenth day of December, in the year of our Lord Eighteen Hundred and Seventy-Seven.

DANIEL SIDNEY WARNER.

I realized much strength by obeying the impressions of the Spirit in writing out the foregoing covenant. God seemed present as though I was making an agreement with a person whom I could see by my side.

Eve, Romans 12. The Lord was there to make truth effectual, and after preaching succeeded in getting about all the members in the altar, and we had a solemn, heart-searching time. Then we had speaking meeting. I urged the brethren and sisters to confess what they felt to be their true condition and their wants. About all confessed: "I have an evil nature within me which I would like to get rid of if that can be." "I confess I have sin in me." "Have carnality yet in me." Glory to God, this brought the Lord very near. My soul seemed in heaven. Everything seemed melting down before God and yielding to his constraining love and sinners were serious.

16. Sabbath. Preached on Hebrews. Had a talk with Bro. William Fuller on sanctification. He was critical and talked for argument. The Spirit bade me leave him, but I did not obey for some time, wishing to show my regards for the young brother. I have learned, however, never again to disobey God out of deference to man. When God says cease an argument, the cause of holiness can only suffer by disobedience. I finally withdrew to the closet and confessed my disobedience to the Spirit. After coming out, Mr. W— —, a poor sinner, attacked me, using some insulting language. I read a little Scripture and left him.

Eve, read 1 Thessalonians and 1 John on perfect love. The Lord's Spirit was there to melt hearts. Opposition began to give way. Brother Fuller, after meeting, confessed that his eyes were being opened to the truth; hoped I would return. Bro. Abraham Whitmire confessed his convictions that unless this community accepted holiness the cause of religion would greatly suffer here. Others with tears asked our prayers. Glory to God, good seed is sown here which will bring forth in the future.

On the 19th Brother and Sister Warner began packing their goods to move to Upper Sandusky, the home of the latter's parents. They had received word that a holiness revival was desired in Findlay, where the seed had already been sown. On arriving at Upper Sandusky they found that they were already engaged for Findlay and were to go there the following Monday. Of their work in Findlay, in which they were assisted by Father and Mother Keller, a few selected notes from the diary will give a sufficient account.

24. Reached the Bethel in Findlay before preaching. Found that God was wondrously at work here. Twenty-three sanctified. Some of the old members fighting the work. The Lord blessed me in preaching full salvation. His power rested on the people and some came to the altar. Father and I went home with Father Sherick. He had been opposed to holiness but, thank God, he is now yielding and begins to confess his need of full salvation. He is eighty years old and probably fifty years a Christian—but has never grown out of depravity.

25. Today we celebrate the birth of Christ. Arose before daylight, as usual, and after my daily bath Father and I had a precious season of prayer and praises. Met at ten at the Bethel. Had a prayer- and general experience-meeting. The "little ones" testified straight and strong. Eve, house full. Was asked to preach again. Felt much straightened. The elders were to let us know about our having the Bethel for a holiness meeting, and it was expected that tonight the meeting should be conducted for sinners; but last night God showed me after preaching that this must be a holiness meeting. So I was hedged up by the church on one side and God on the other. Tried to preach some time to sinners, but was absolutely abandoned to myself. Oh, how empty and hollow all I said! I saw that this would not do, so I proceeded to full salvation for believers. Glory to God, I had some unction then, but felt the displeasure of some of the church. Two mourners and three believers presented themselves at the altar. One soul sanctified. After meeting a very intelligent and pleasant sister came forward and said, "God gave me the wonderful Christmas gift of entire sanctification while you were preaching." Glory to God forever! We announced meetings in the future on the holiness line.

26. Up before the family, bathed and prayed. A. M., wrote, occasionally talked holiness to persons coming in seeking light. All the city is in an uproar on holiness. Halleluiah! At half-past two met at the Bethel. Brother Linsey led the meeting. Satan made a dreadful rally today. All the old cold members got in the back part of the house. Bro. Samuel Ferguson acted as spokesman for the devil. He set out in a raging storm. Called this work the judgment of the whore, the abomination that maketh desolate. Called God to rebuke it, to smite it in the mouth until the blood should fly out. He hollowed and stamped and foamed like a madman. Glory to God, who kept his little ones in perfect peace. God gave me great peace, and I could but say thank God for the trial of his holy cause. I proceeded in a calm spirit to show the people some of God's sacred truth that they were rejecting. Brother Wilson arose on the opposition side and asked some questions, threatening a call of the Standing Committee. May the Lord help him to seek the cleansing blood.

A young man, member of the church, by the name of Teams stepped out in the aisle and began to yell and stamp and walk to-and-fro. He consumed about fifteen minutes in silly harangue against perfect holiness by the blood of Christ. There was no reason, sense, Bible, or even apparent civilization in his aspersions. All the little ones were kept in perfect peace. Eve, Brother Updike preached his farewell sermon to the church. He felt so directed because of the recent abuses of his wife by some of the church and because of the wicked opposition of the leaders of the church to holiness. He declared his withdrawal from this charge. The old and formal part of the church were aroused most furiously. I followed by some remarks. A few came out to seek purity.

27. Had meeting at 2 P. M. in the court-house, whither we have moved because of the constant disturbance in the Bethel. Eve, tried to preach to a good congregation at the court-house. The Lord was with us in sweet peace and power. We felt we were in a purer spiritual atmosphere.

30. Sabbath. Met at ten. Heb. 13:20,21. The Lord helped me to show the people that perfection is commanded and attained **now**; what it is and is not; that it is not attained in conversion, but by a second work. At 2:30 P. M. met in the court-house in a temperance meeting. Brothers Linsey and Ackers both glorified God by testifying to their wonderful salvation from drink and tobacco, both having had delirium tremens several times. Brother A. called the tobacco habit a twin sister to strong drink and claimed that it was the cause of his becoming a drunkard. After they spoke, a Lutheran minister arose and deprecated the springing of tobacco in the meeting and palliated this abomination as consistent with perfect consecration to God and piety. Shame! Shame!

A brother asked concerning our holiness. So we bowed together and had a season of prayer, and as we afterward began to talk he constantly interrupted me, would not let me finish a point or connect the Scripture proofs of the two works. We bowed again in prayer and he led. He asked God to purify his heart and take all the evil nature out of him. After arising I remarked that as he would interrupt all my efforts to give him instruction I would now ask him some questions and learn. I asked him what things we were allowed of God. Answer, "Such things as he promises." Do you always pray for such only? "Yes." Do you receive them? "Yes." Then you have just now been sanctified, made pure, is it not so? "Yes." Then you should hereafter not ask God to do what he has done! But he contended that he should keep on making the same prayer. Brother Larcomb suggested the equal propriety of continuing to pray to God to convert him. Oh what confusion and ignorance! Still they thought we had gone astray.

31. A. M., wrote. Eve, met at seven and continued the meeting until after twelve. The house was crowded, the isles standing full of people to the close of the meeting. Pretty good order for the throng. Brother Updike preached. After some altar work, we had good testimony-meeting. I then preached a short discourse on Eph. 4:22-24. A few minutes before twelve the altar was again filled with seekers and little ones. I read the Christian consecration, and all said amen. The power of God came upon us. Many shouts. A Mother Goodwin, of the M. E. Church, was the subject of a wonderful work of grace tonight. For eighteen years she had sought for this experience. She had a dreadful death, turned perfectly white and shook like a leaf. She hesitated to believe through the temptation of unworthiness. I asked her if Christ was not worthy. Told her to believe for the glory of his name. Then she took hold. She soon fully overcame by the blood of the Lamb and the word of her testimony. It was a wonderful work wrought by the power of God in one of the most intelligent and pious ladies of Findlay, of about fifty years of age. She was filled with wonder at the great change and testified with a halo of glory beaming from her countenance. How can such a marked work be doubted? What a reproach upon the ministry that this dear saint should be kept eighteen years in the wilderness longing for some Joshua to lead her over to the land of perfect rest of soul from all sin!

Jan. 1, 1878. Praise God for the mercies of the past year. I am so thankful that the old year witnessed the final death of the old man in me, and now for the first time I enter upon the New Year all renewed in the image of God. Glory to his name in the highest! I am redeemed and washed in the blood of the Lamb. O Canaan, sweet Canaan, surely here flows milk and honey! God is my everlasting all, my satisfying portion. Oh, wonders of redeeming love! Can it be that through the precious blood of Christ I have "entered into the holiest" and am forever shut in with God, and dead to the world! O God, I feel that I can stand in thy holy presence! I tremble with awe and reverence. O my God and Redeemer! keep me on thine altar and in spotless purity lest I offend thy Holiness and die. I shall forever dwell with thee, and through the riches of thy boundless grace my whole being, every thought, word, feeling, emotion, appetite, desire, wish, purpose, and action, yea my whole life, shall be a continual offering to God, in the flames of his love. Amen. Almighty, All-wise, and ever present God, fulfil this thy pleasure in me. I am in thy hands. Amen and amen.

A. M., wrote some. Met at 10 A. M. and held meetings until 4 P. M.; the power of God rested upon us. Four, I believe, were sanctified. The Lord gave me much light on the sanctuary as setting forth the different degrees of grace (Heb. 10:19,22). In chapter 8 the apostle compares the sanctuary and the temple service with the present spiritual house or church. 9:9 shows that the former temple service was typical of the church, also 10:11. Now, as the temple all through the Bible typifies the church, so also the tabernacle. We must make some application of its departments. This the apostle does for us. The court represents penitence or approach to the church, the sanctuary or "holy." From this we have access into the "holiest." In the sanctuary they are "brethren" and (v. 22) have "their hearts sprinkled from an evil conscience." Were justified when they came into the holy, and now are invited into the holiest, not into heaven but into a state of purity through the blood of Christ.

2. Wrote some. Brother Doty came today. Thank the Lord. Eve. Brother Doty preached on the difference between justification and entire sanctification. (1) Inbred sin is not cognizable to our consciousness when actual sin and guilt crowd the conscience. (2) We need not lack wisdom, for such is Christ to us; but may greatly lack knowledge. (3) Entire sanctification takes away all vain curiosity. (4) Makes us simple in giving, etc. (5) Leaves natural appetites the same, but removes unnatural.

Two were most gloriously sanctified, one an old mother over eighty years of age. Oh, how wonderfully God blessed her! She ran around as spritely as a young girl. The house, as usual, was greatly crowded, the space on the floor about all occupied by standers. The whole city is stirred. All the protracted efforts in the place are without interest. All the elements are attracted here. Sinners want this kind of religion that saves from all sin. Glory to God forever! Some of the county officials, I presume, are getting uneasy, hence concluded that we could no longer have the courthouse. Received the promise of the Reform house, at least for the next evening.

3. God's power was with us. Three souls were sweetly sanctified, one of whom, a sister Miller, was converted to God from Catholicism last winter. They say her conversion was among the most bright of the 150 converts and her life has been true. Oh how calm and clearly she came out! Her testimony was sublime and more than human. It was spoken by the Spirit. Praise God! Another meeting was held in East Findlay. The Lord was also there in power. A brother in the Church of God who had rashly denounced holiness was sanctified at this meeting.

Eve, the promised house was not opened. The little ones were scattered each not knowing where to meet the rest, and yet we felt a great desire to be together. One company gathered and we went to a United Brethren Church. As we passed along, crowds gathered after us and asked where we were going to have meeting. The people were much disappointed. Brother Engle, the pastor, preached an earnest sermon to sinners from, "The way of the transgressor is hard." I felt that the church was an iceberg between this sanctified preacher and the sinners. We all prayed fervently for the efficacy of the word. Some twelve arose for prayer, among the number was Sister Wert's son, a very intelligent young man with whom I called today. When I asked him concerning his soul's interests, he said that he did not "go much on religion." I calmly replied that I presumed he had none to go on. I added that I did not go on religion either before I had any to go on. This was God-sent, and he knew not how to express himself again. I waited a few seconds then proposed prayer. We all kneeled and I presented him to the mercy of God. After holding his hand and giving him a few words I left him, praying to God to bring him down to the cross. Praise God, I saw him rise in the congregation.

Brother Linsey and I stayed up all night in prayer to God for Findlay. God rolled upon our hearts a dreadful agony for souls and gave us an awful sight of the wicked apostasy of the churches. Like the old prophets, we groaned and cried to God for salvation to come out of Zion.

27. Sabbath. Met at the United Brethren Church. Good testimony-meeting. One sister said, "I do not believe in a second work; would as leave you would hit me in the face as to speak of it; it is like a dart to my heart to hear it." Just so the "pure testimony put forth in the Spirit cuts," etc. Brother Engle read a very interesting chapter of United Brethren history showing the holiness revival in that church. Otterbein, Bishop Edwards, Wilson, and many others of the most eminent ministers professed and taught holiness as a distinct work.

At this point in his diary Brother Warner tells of his expulsion from the West Ohio Eldership, and gives the subject a special heading.

TRIAL AND EXPULSION FROM THE WEST OHIO ELDERSHIP OF THE CHURCH OF GOD FOR PREACHING FULL SALVATION; FOR FOLLOWING THE HOLY SPIRIT; FOR HELPING TO SAVE OVER 150 SOULS IN THIS PLACE

30. Standing Committee met in Findlay today. Principal business to attend to was charges prefered by Bro. G. W. Wilson against Bro. J. V. Updike and me—against him for maladministration of the church here, deserting it, and turning church interests over to the Holiness Alliance, etc.; against me for (1) transcending the restrictions of the Eldership, (2) violating rules of cooperation, (3) participating in dividing the church.

As to the first, it relates to an action of the body last Eldership in which I was prohibited from springing the holiness meeting on any church where they did not wish it. This charge was not sustained by a single proof. The facts are as follows: Father Keller was led by the Spirit to go to Findlay to procure a place for a holiness meeting. He found a meeting in progress in the Church of God, tried to get the house to begin as soon as they were through, but they refused. He then engaged the Reformed house, but left an offer still with the Church of God to occupy their house if they concluded to let us have it. When we received word that the meeting was about to close we went up and found it still in progress, and as the holiness workers were there, we wished to begin a meeting on the holiness line. We gave the church the first offer to use their house, and they consented to our using the house. However, this I think they did because they knew that if we went to another house we would carry all the interests from their house. And when the whole counsel of God was presented they could not stand it, but gathered in the back end of the house with wicked men and fought the work of God, so that we soon saw that nothing could be done there, hence we removed to the court-house. I had nothing at all to do with the appointment of the meeting there and only did some of the preaching after Father Keller and Brothers Ackers and Linsey had got the use of the house from the elders and trustees, or a majority of them.

Second charge, "Violation of rules of cooperation." The rule cited was like this: No person shall go upon another's field of labor to hold meetings, etc, without the consent of preacher and church. When we announced meeting at the court-house, one of the elders announced preaching there at the Bethel the next night. Brother Wilson filled the pulpit and continued some four or five nights with no success and small congregations. Now, because I assisted in the meeting at the court-house while these church services were continued in the same town, I am thus charged, when these meetings were really appointed after and in opposition to the real work of the Lord, where souls were daily being saved.

Third charge, "Dividing the church." I showed that the only results of the holiness meeting were fifty-three sinners converted and 118 believers sanctified, and that all the division and confusion was caused by the carnal and wicked opposition on the part of the rest of the church, just like the envious Jews stirred up the people at Thessalonica and Berea (Acts 17) and interrupted the apostles in their peaceable work of leading souls to Jesus, as well as disturbed the peace of the city. The apostles, of course, had to bear the blame, and like everywhere else they went, bonds and prisons awaited them; and I, too, was ready to suffer affliction with the people of God for the sake of Christ. All Adam became aroused, so that I was stopped from reading other Scriptures. [He had been reading and speaking from Isa. 32:15.] When for the sake of the dear people calling themselves the Church of God I was studying how to compromise the two elements in the church here, the Lord gave me this text, and the Spirit led me to preach it straight, although it conflicted with what I had cherished, that is, a hope of fraternizing the sanctified and the unsanctified.

Eve, Brother Updike's case was adjusted by the Committee, the elders, and himself. They tried hard to bind him down to abandon holiness as a definite work and to have no communion with holiness workers. He agreed to some restrictions about preaching holiness where it was not wanted. Received his license and was placed on McComb circuit. Evidently they have some hopes of leading him to a recantation. May the mercy and grace of God keep him from coming down from the highway! Brother Chambers was at our meeting in North Findlay this eve.

31. Was brought to the depot this morn in sled. Heavy snow falling. After I had been riding some time in the train with him in conversation, Brother Cassel, one of the Committee, seeing that I was not enough concerned to ask him what disposition they had made of my case, informed me that the Committee had decided that the charges were sustained, and that they had withheld my license.[8] I thanked him for their decision and assured him that if I were to look upon the matter from the mere human standpoint and consider my attachment to the Church of God and her principles, I should regard their action a dreadful calamity and intolerable to bear; but that I had now that charity which "believeth all things" and "endureth all things," and therefore I calmly rested in the promise of God that "all things work together for good" to me, and the sweet assurance that my dear Father, to whom I belonged, would turn this and everything else (as long as I stay on the altar) to my good and his glory. Praise his holy name! Reached home about 2 P. M.

Up to the time of leaving Findlay there were 53 converted, 118 believers sanctified, including about all the 53 converts. Many of them were sanctified at the next meeting after converted, and a few the same meeting. Glory to God for full salvation!

Following the effort at Findlay, a series of holiness meetings was held at Upper Sandusky in the early part of February. Brother Dunbar and others assisted. On the 9th, Brother Warner was called to spend Sunday at Dunkirk, and was kept there for several days. While at Dunkirk he was impressed by the Spirit to announce that if any sick in the town would send for him he would go in faith to

---

[8] This trouble came up at the Eldership meeting the following September. "The Warner case was indirectly revived when the Committee on Resolutions adopted the following: 'That any minister of this body that may presume to preach the dogma of a second work for sanctification shall be deemed unsound in the theology of the Church of God, and should not hold an ecclesiastical relation as a minister in this Eldership.'" — From Dr. Forney's History of the Church of God.

pray for them to recover. A sister who had been afflicted for years with catarrh in the head, which had spread to the throat and lungs so that she was consumptive, thought much about being healed. She had strong faith and came to meeting the next day, and in answer to prayer was gloriously healed, perfectly sound. Another, a blacksmith in Dunkirk, was impressed to go and pray for the healing of a young colored sister on the verge of death from consumption. She was wonderfully benefited, as for six weeks she had to be lifted from her bed but now was able to arise and, assisted by the hand of a sister, walk across the floor. She had been able only to whisper, but now could sing praises to God.

Brother Warner felt that he should return to Upper Sandusky to assist in the meetings that were being held there. In a day or two after returning he was called back to Dunkirk to preach the funeral of the young colored sister. The brother who had prayed for her and a sister who had strong faith believed that God would raise the departed sister from the dead in answer to their prayers. Brother Warner announced the funeral for 10 A. M., if the Lord did not direct matters otherwise. He prayed and examined the scriptures relative to miracles and found that (1) Christ aroused and inspired faith and admiration in the people by miracles, (2) the final commission teaches miracles, (3) they were the means of the success of the apostles, (4) the gift is set in the church. Hence, he concluded that miracles were to be a permanent factor in the system of salvation. He does not say that he was particularly impressed that God was going to work a miracle in this case. He rather fell in with the idea as urged by the sister who felt so impressed. At her home she and her husband and Brother Warner waited in prayer for some time, then went to the house where the corpse lay. The two brethren kneeled in prayer while the sister uncovered the body and commanded the departed to arise in the name of Jesus. Their faith for some time was wonderfully strong and they confidently expected to see her arise. They held on with unwavering faith for half an hour, when they all felt relieved and that the will of the Lord had been done. Brother Warner preached the funeral the next day. He writes that this incident seemed only to increase their faith and that he believed that God was well pleased with the effort to exert this faith; that if not through them, God would through some one else revive this element of apostolic power.

There was a report, intended to ridicule, and published by some who opposed Brother Warner, that he with others tried to bring a dead body to life by standing it on its feet and commanding it to walk, etc. This of course was untrue.

Remaining in Dunkirk for a few days, he held meetings which resulted in about twenty conversions. He found himself much attached to the brethren and sisters here. They had come out of the United Brethren and Methodist Episcopal denominations and had formed themselves into a Wesleyan body. Many of them, however, were not satisfied with a human church and creed and there was a strong tendency to come to the apostolic faith. Returning to Upper Sandusky he assisted in the meetings there. In company with Father and Mother Keller he visited the jail and prayed with the convicts. One of those, by name, John Bristol, was gloriously converted. Bristol said he did not care a cent to get out of jail so long as Jesus stayed with him. He had been badly abandoned and had followed shows, drinking, balloon ascensions, etc. He once fell sixty feet from a balloon, breaking an arm, a leg, splitting a hip socket, etc. The sparing of his life was only by the mercy of God.

For the 7th of March 1878 we quote the following:

> Fellowshiped some fourteen souls in the Church of God formed on a congregational basis, with holiness the principal foundation-stone. On the 31st of last January the Lord showed me that holiness could never prosper upon sectarian soil encumbered by human creeds and party names, and he gave me a new commission to join holiness and all truth together and build up the apostolic church of the living God. Praise his name! I will obey him.

In March an evangelistic effort was made in Tiffin, but with difficulty. The denominational houses seemed to be closed to holiness. A few meetings were held in a private house and in a rented room. He states that at this place Sister Warner was called to go to Mansfield to assist in a holiness meeting. This was a peculiar test and he thus speaks of it:

> **23.** Sarah left today. The Lord tested our loyalty by requiring us to labor apart. At first I disbelieved that it was the order of God and was decidedly opposed to her going. So were Father and Mother Keller. I thought it would give place to the devil and hurt the sacred cause and endanger our domestic happiness. But this morn I arose early and consulted the Lord. I laid down all my understanding and the many seemingly plain reasons for her not going and besought God to direct the matter, and to my astonishment the Holy Spirit confirmed Sarah's call by reminding me of my solemn covenant with God, that there I had laid her on the altar and given her back to God to use her where and as he saw fit. At the same time all unwillingness vanished from my mind. In fact, a desire was at once created within me for her to go.
>
> O God, thy ways are not our ways, but we will walk in thy ways all the days of our life. Season sad. Here she is greatly needed; there is a strong old band. How would it look for me to work for God here and she whom the Lord had joined to me go elsewhere? Were I at home, not at all in a meeting, then there could be no appearance of evil in her going. But ah! I now see there would then be no test, which is just the thing God intended. Abraham's faith would not have been half so much tried and proved had not Isaac been the heir of the promise. Father and Mother still strongly opposed her going, so that doubtless she would have shrunk with a burdened heart from the call had not God raised help in me.

On the 4th of April he received a letter from her stating that the meeting at Mansfield was excellent for the establishing and strengthening of God's little ones, and that she had gone home.

During this time Brother Warner was getting much light on the Scriptures concerning holiness and was writing with the view of publishing a tract on the subject. The matter he was accumulating, however, proved to be enough for a book, which, as we shall see, was published two years later. Also, he speaks of an effort at this time to obtain more of the manifestation of God in his soul.

25. I set out this day to seek a more full and conscious manifestation of the Father, Son, and the Holy Ghost in my heart. Spent much time in the closet. Visited and prayed with a few families.

30. Prayed much for a more perfect, full, constant, and conscious manifestation of God in my soul. Had a glorious victory. Yesterday Brother Lee was about to start to walk home to Nevada, twenty-two miles. I thought it was too hard a task with such muddy roads. How I wished for the means to send him home by railroad! Recently, being without means to send a letter, I took it to the Lord, and before I had the letter written a kind sister gave me fifty cents. I had a quarter left and I thought of giving it to Brother Lee if others would make up the remainder. But then the tempter said, "You are dependent yourself and should not give to others that which the Lord has sent to meet your wants." I took it to the Lord and the Spirit said, "Give and it shall be given." I gave the quarter to Brother Lee. The dollar needed by him was soon made, and he was able to stay until this morn. Praise God, this morn a kind sister called and said the Lord had sent her to give me a dollar. The Spirit kept his promise and gave four-fold.

Apr. 3, 1878. God is daily giving me more of his great fulness and conforming me more and more to his glorious image. This is because I am earnestly endeavoring to consecrate more perfectly every moment of my time to him and because I spend more time with God alone in the closet. I have on several occasions besought God to conform me more perfectly to his nature, and without any particular emotions that might indicate the answer I claimed the desire of my heart and by faith thanked Father that he had granted my petitions. To the glory of God I can say that as I went on my way I found from hour to hour that as my faith was so was it meted out to me. Oh, how sweet it is to go to our heavenly Father for all our heart's and soul's need, and in the name of Jesus ask for it rejoicing that we know we have the desire of our heart! Surely "happy are the people that are in such a case; yea, happy are the people whose God is the Lord."

On his return to Upper Sandusky on April 9 he found some urgent calls to go to Indiana, and he felt that the Lord was in it. On Sunday the 14th, he conducted the services in Upper Sandusky. The theme in the evening was, Salvation from Church, using 1 Pet. 1:18,19 and 2 Pet. 1:3,4—deliverance from all that is human and the reception of all that is of divine origin.

The Lord blessed me and greatly awakened my own mind and I think opened the eyes of others to the importance of abandoning all human and party creeds, party names, party spirit, and party interests in order to maintain a life of perfect holiness, as well as to the duty of returning to the "faith once delivered to the saints" in its entirety.

It is interesting to note that at this time, coincident to his receiving the call to Indiana, there came to his mind the idea of using the printing-press as a means of publishing the gospel truth he was so burdened to promulgate.

Recently I asked my heavenly Father to send means to meet our wants, pay debts, and as soon as I was ready to print my work on holiness, to furnish the means. I received gracious answers by the Spirit, and the following night while lying in meditation how I could better honor God in publishing full salvation, the Lord opened a new field for me. The Spirit suggested that my heavenly Father would provide me with a small hand printing-press by means of which I could print my book myself and scatter many holiness tracts as leaves of salvation.

Praise God, today I received a most cheering letter from Eld. W. W. Roberts, of Missouri. He is in the land of Canaan, and having seen my articles and the Standing Committee's action in the Advocate he writes to encourage me in the good work; and though he knows nothing of my circumstances he offers to furnish me some money if I need it. Praise God, who is faithful and always heareth his poor and needy little ones that cry unto him.

Returning to Tiffin with his father-in-law, Keller, he found the little ones in good spirits. All testified definitely and boldly. He held three services there on the following Sunday. He found there had come to be a wonderful awakening in Tiffin among the denominational churches on the subject of perfect holiness.

On the 22nd he took train for New Washington, the place of his childhood home. Here seven years previous he labored alone in a revival that resulted in the salvation of about fifty souls. For one year they did well. A good house of worship was built and twice a week it was filled at prayer-meetings that were very lively and interesting. But adversity came and there now remained but a small force of faithful ones to tell the story of salvation. Elder Oliver, who had preferred charges against him for the preaching of holiness, was in charge of the work here and of course had greatly prejudiced the people against holiness. Two of the flock, however, had received the experience.

At this place, through his brother Lewis, who lived in the vicinity, he learned that his father was very poorly and he at once became much burdened for his father's soul.

May 5, 1878. Sabbath. Met about 10 A. M. All the little ones testified boldly in the Spirit to sanctification. Brother Oliver and wife were much annoyed at the same. Brother O. preached from

Rev. 21:27. A good text to enforce holiness, but alas, the time and opportunity were wasted in attacks upon the Lord's work of full salvation. How my heart was grieved that the dear brother was not led by the Spirit of God! What a favorable opportunity and text to set forth the necessity of holiness and the all-cleansing blood! But alas, how few unsanctified preachers know what spirit they are of! Oh, how little they value the worth of souls! How indifferent to the solemn responsibilities of the ministry!

16. [At Upper Sandusky.] Preached the funeral of a poor sinner who was accidentally shot dead with a revolver. He died in fifteen minutes, calling upon God for mercy. He was married one week ago today. Life is but a vapor.

On the 16th he left for Indiana. He reached Silver Lake, Kosciusko County, the next day and was met by Bro. F. Krause and conveyed seven miles through a heavy rain to Beaver Dam. In spite of bad weather a fair congregation assembled that evening to hear him preach. About all manifested their desire for sanctification by rising to their feet. In his sermon on Sunday he identified the inheritance in sanctification with the promise made to Abraham. At the afternoon service about fifteen were at the altar seeking full salvation.

In this section of the country Brother Warner found many warm hearts. They had read his articles on holiness in the Church Advocate, and had doubtless heard of his rejection by the Ohio Eldership. He held meetings at Beaver Dam, Yellow Lake, and Silver Lake. His diary gives the following account for Sunday, May 26, at Yellow Lake.

Sabbath. This day was put in for God. From my waking moments this morn I began to plead with God for the salvation of the people. Had gracious answers to prayer. Was sure God would save a number of souls. We had announced a fast all day, and meeting to begin at 10 A. M. and continue until 4 P. M. The house was filled. Had a lively testimony-meeting. Preached on the tabernacle (Hebrews). Several at the altar. But there seemed to be a dulness. None grasped the blessings. We had speaking-meeting, but the interest seemed to be moderate. I was impressed that the dear little ones were hungry, and Satan said we had better close. But, glory to God, I knew that God would yet come and save souls, as he impressed me in the morning, hence I held on to him. Preached a short discourse on faith and gave another invitation. Several came to the altar for sanctification and soon the holy fire fell on us from heaven, and all were sanctified. Some that were not at the altar received the blessing. The Holy Ghost filled the house, and there was great rejoicing. A fellowship-meeting resulted from following the Spirit; and as the dear ones went about shaking hands many, yea, about all in the house, were melted to tears. I gave another invitation and then friend Yocum came out, also Brother Bear's daughter, and another young lady for sanctification. She soon received a glorious baptism, and Sister Bear was converted. Came home with Brother Bear. We did not get to close until nearly five o'clock. Spent much of the time until eve on my knees.

Eve, house crowded. People were there from a distance of six and eight miles. I preached mainly to sinners. I had announced a few nights ago that I had an impression to preach to the unconverted, but I now see my mistake. I should have made no such announcement. The Spirit seemed to be baffled in giving me a subject. I did more preaching myself tonight than I have for a long time, was conscious that Christ Jesus was not preaching as much as usual. Thank the Lord for the lesson learned. Three at the altar. Brother Yocum was greatly smitten down by the Spirit; all physical strength was gone. About 9:30 P. M. we dismissed the congregation, but Brother Y. would not leave the altar. Several of us stayed until after eleven. He was measurably blessed. He has been a very good moral, benevolent, and honorable man, and thought heretofore that he had but little sin and could easily get salvation when he once came for it; but he found himself a great sinner under the searching light of the Spirit.

Glory to God for this day's work! It was a high day for my soul. Among the fourteen sanctified were two very fine young men by the name of Smith. They are brothers, both school-teachers, and I pray that God will make them both very useful.

He found a wide-spread awakening for holiness in this part of Indiana. The time for the annual Eldership Meeting of the Church was at hand, and he asked the Lord whether he might not stay and attend the meetings instead of going to the Eldership. As there were others who could continue the meetings the Spirit seemed to relieve his mind of all burden for that place, and he felt it his duty to attend the Eldership.

June 1, 1878. Came home today. Found family well. At the General Eldership I found that the leaven of full salvation was working. Had many private talks. Found some in the experience, but rather mute. Strengthened them. Many spoke of my articles in the Advocate and said they were seeking light. But the Eldership possesses little of the power of godliness. The first night it made me mourn for Jerusalem. Here were assembled the best elements of the whole church, and yet I could feel no God in her. There was no spirit of devotion, no communion with God. Pride and nearly every other manifestation of carnality were manifest. God save the Church. Thank God for the blessing of home and family. Dear Wife met me at the train.

9. Sabbath [at Findlay]. Awoke before day. Was much pressed in spirit for Brother Burchard. Arose early and had a gracious season of prayer. Was led out much for Brother B. At 10:30 A. M.

heard him preach. A dreadful death reigned over the congregation. He spoke with a good deal of energy, according to his pathetic temperament, but he surely had not help by the Spirit. But I think he is honest, and if he had the cloud of prejudice removed from his mind he would want full salvation and would be useful. Oh, that God would lead him into the light!

Feeling that he should visit his father, in Williams County, he took train for Bryan, Ohio, on the 10th, arriving there late in the evening. The account of the death of his father and of the events that followed are here given.

June 11. Arose early. After devotion and my usual morning bath, I paid for lodging, went to the baker's and got a loaf of graham bread, and started on my way. Got to ride about five miles and footed the rest. Reached Father's about half-past ten. Found him very weak, and failing. He was overcome by emotion when I came in. His breathing is difficult. I soon sought a private room and poured out my heart for his salvation. Brother Joseph is staying with him all the time. Father can not last long. Oh that God would be pleased to have mercy upon his poor soul!

14. Father still failing.

15. Brother Lewis reached here about 5 P. M. Eve, went to the Cogswell Schoolhouse to hear Bro. Henry Barckley, but he having gone from home did not appear. I was asked to improve the time. After prayer I began to look to the Lord for a message, but nothing came to hand. Soon young Brother Wallace came in. He came by request to fill the appointment. He had only once before tried to preach. He was indisposed to go ahead; but I told him that I thought it was the order of the Lord. He consented. Did well enough, but needs the special unction of the Holy Ghost. I talked some.

16. Sabbath. L. W. Guiss came at four o'clock this morning. Father failing very fast this morning. At 10:30 A. M. met a congregation at the Cogswell Schoolhouse. Heb. 7:25. God blessed his precious word. Mr. Guiss, my brother-in-law, who has become a bold infidel, was much affected by God's truth. Some wept for clean hearts. I asked all who knew they were children of God to hold up their hands. A good number responded. I then asked all who could testify to perfect salvation from all sin to hold up their hands, but there was no response. But when I asked all who wished to be wholly the Lord's to hold up their hands, a number responded, some with tears. Time would not permit altar exercise.

Took dinner at Brother Joseph's and came back. Found Father declining very fast. Poor man, he is near his end, yet unsaved. O my God, must my poor father go into eternity bearing all the sins of his past life! Oh the death of an immortal soul! Since God has converted my soul and called me into the ministry, I have often seen Father's heart touched by divine truth and the Holy Spirit. Tears flowed freely, but he would not yield. When I began to preach, twelve years ago, I spent a summer at home, and he afterward told Mrs. Rang that my constant praying gave him much trouble and that he was glad I was gone. I marked the deep convictions that followed him all that summer and hoped he would soon be brought to God, but he wore them away. Two years ago this coming July my beloved mother passed away gloriously saved. She held his hand and exhorted him until he trembled. Not long after, I came home and spoke in the Dean Church, when he was greatly melted down. I gave an invitation to come to God, but again he refused Christ. Since his last illness, I have daily implored the mercy of God upon his poor soul. Since I have been with him I have talked to him about his soul, but do not see that he was awakened to his condition. I felt that all depended upon the blessed Holy Ghost to discover to him his sin and awful danger. He asked my prayers and songs of salvation. He shed tears over the wicked infidelity of G., my brother-in-law; but when he made any reference to his hope he based it all upon his principles of honesty and doing right and that he had favored a good many persons in his life, etc. He confessed some misgivings of conscience for not having been confirmed in the Lutheran Church as he had promised his parents he would when married; but said he, "I always felt some way that I could not get religion." When conscious of much distress he would wish he might die. Once he feared that he might have to lie a long time, and when on a certain occasion his throat seemed to be closed against food, he said, "I just believe that it is my doom to lie here and waste away; that there is nothing grown for me to eat any more." Frequently he expressed a strong desire to get well; but I never heard him say that if he did he would live a different life.

I went alone into the woods where so often I sought God and his grace when a young convert. I had a long and precious communion with God. Returned. Father is very rapidly approaching his end. He can not live through another night. Once while I was wetting his lips he looked very pitifully at me and said, "If you could only give me something that would make me well!"

O my God, how hard it is to close a life that was not given to thee! But it is appointed unto man once to die, and after this the judgment. Joseph feels this stroke very much. I thought it best not to go to the schoolhouse this eve.

9:30 P. M. Father is gone. He passed off with no struggles or convulsions. His spirit has left the body. Probation is ended, and a lifeless corpse only remains. I sensibly feel the cords of love that bind my heart to my last earthly parent, but the gentle breathings of the Spirit of God seemed so graciously to sustain me that all was calm within. I felt a perfect loyalty to God and all his providence that so sweetly over all prevailed and gave me such perfect peace that I could not even weep. Oh, how tranquilizing to my soul was the deep assurance that God doeth all things well!

17. Brother Joseph is almost down sick with sorrow and loss of rest. Poor father lies a corpse. Two brothers, L. W. Guiss, and I wore away the long melancholy day as best we could.

18. Last night at twelve o'clock Mr. Double awoke me and said there were some gentlemen without that had a telegram for me. I arose and dressed, feeling a very calm peace keeping me. The Holy Spirit brought these words to me: "He shall not be afraid of evil tidings." The following was the dispatch: "Come home, your child is very sick. L. W. Keller." I came in, examined the papers and my railroad guide. Found that a train left Bryan at 8 A. M. that made connection at Toledo, bringing me to Upper Sandusky at 1 P. M., but if I waited for a later train I should not reach home until late at night. What shall I do? Here lay my father cold in death, to be buried this A. M., and should I stay or not? I had a season of communion with the Lord, and the Spirit seemed to say go. I took my usual morning bath, packed my valise, and started to my brother Joseph's, bidding adieu to my brother Lewis and my lifeless father, the latter of course to see no more until the heavens cease to be and the earth shall flee away before the approach of the great Judge of the human family.

I was conveyed to Bryan by David Warner, my nephew. Improved the time in meditation and prayer. I recalled the feeling that had rested upon me for some days, a deep solicitude for my family. Both on Sabbath and yesterday I went out into the woods where I used to seek the Lord when a convert and besought God to preserve my dear family. I also felt led to ask God to try us in any way he wished to. I felt the need of some trial of our faith and loyalty to God.

In my deep meditation and fervent prayer to God the time passed off swiftly with the fast gliding train, and at 1 P. M. we reached Upper Sandusky. Leaving my valise, I walked out at once and found the dear child very sick, having first taken down with a sick stomach and then with the affliction developing in the brain. The precious creature recognized me and made an effort to embrace me with her loving little arms. Her sweet little lips could responsively receive a father's kiss, but they were silent for want of sufficient strength to articulate, A good number of kind neighbors were in attendance, and I at once saw what was threatening the very life of the poor little sufferer. She was exquisitely fine in the texture of brain and her head measured nineteen inches in circumference around her forehead, and she had a very sensitive nervous temperament. Hence it was extremely important that the most perfect silence should be maintained in her presence, and with this strong nervous action, with any sickness or weakness, much talk and noise would necessarily draw the disease to the brain. I had her removed from the room where the family mostly stayed and everybody came in, to a more retired room; demanded silence and forbade more than two at a time to be in the room. Sarah had seen the necessity of such regulations, but many dear good old sisters, not knowing their importance, were much inclined to sit around the lounge and talk, and not being in her own house she had not been able to enforce them.

19. Dear Levilla still low, but I had good hopes of her recovery. Spent as much time as I could with the Lord. Left all with him.

20. Dear child still dangerous, but we trust some better.

21. The doctor could see no improvement.

22. Wife and I thought Levilla better and still clung to the Lord for her life if it be his will to restore her; but all others had given up hope. We thought it impossible that we should do without the company of this sweet little creature.

23. Sabbath. The doctor did not come as usual this morning. I presume from the report last eve he supposed she was dead; but all day she seemed better. P. M., sent for doctor. He thought she had some symptoms for the better, which raised our hopes. Eve, a number came in and despite our efforts to keep them away they would crowd around the dear child. She grew worse. She had had very light spasms all day but they did not seem to hurt her; but now she began to fail fast. Phlegm began to accumulate in her little throat, making it difficult to breathe.

24. Toward morning the poor little sufferer was compelled to struggle hard to get her breath, and it became apparent that unless God miraculously interposed, her suffering must soon end in death. While we sorrowed for her suffering, we felt a calm and sweet resignation to the will of God, to whom the dear child belonged. We could say in truth, "Thy will be done." At five o'clock in the morning her redeemed spirit was freed from its earthly abode and taken away to be with Jesus and holy angels.

Now remained only the poor little emaciated body. As we recalled the large, active, plump, and rosy-cheeked Levilla, we could scarcely help but exclaim as we looked upon the reduced and colorless form, "Is this Levilla? Can it be that this is our child?" Since my return I had anxiously cherished a hope that ere long I should hear those sweet lips utter words again; but they are now silent in death, or rather the sweet and dreamless sleep that shall pass off when the Lord comes to call us forth from our earthly repose.

25. ... Brother Leay conducted services. We looked for the last time upon our beloved child, whose sweet and innocent little form was robed in its little white dress and skirts, with a beautiful little bouquet of flowers protruding from her little hands folded upon her heart. As my dear wife was deeply afflicted with her departure, her sweet little face seemed to speak forth from its little white coffin and say, "Weep not, dear mother, for though your loss seems to be great, my gain is infinitely greater. I have gone to the better land, where sickness, sorrow, pain, and death never, never come."

We laid the dear and only child in the Mission Cemetery at Upper Sandusky, near the road at the west side, between two evergreens. There with sad, yet resigned, hearts we left her to sleep beneath the angels' care until called forth at the last day.

Levilla Modest was born Mar. 18, 1875, near Seward, Nebr. She passed from suffering to the society of angels June 24, 1878, and was therefore three years, three months, and six days of age. She was a child of more than ordinary mental ability. Her organic quality was the very finest. Her temperaments were sanguine and mental. Her brain measured nineteen inches. Though of such great nervous activity, we had by careful diet imparted to her a good, large physical structure. She measured three feet five inches. She was very knowing about all kinds of work, and ever eager to assist. For some months past she would stand upon a chair beside her mother and wipe knives, forks, spoons, saucers, etc., with the utmost care and perfection. She would do the most of her dressing and undressing, and never failed to hang up or put away every garment and everything she handled. She seemed to have very fine taste and perfect order. Her causality was wonderfully developed for a child.... She daily astonished us with questions concerning everything she saw, and her remarkable ability to anticipate what next was wanted, and with what eagerness those little feet ran errands for mother and father, and grandmother and grandfather. Since eighteen months old she would sing parts of familiar tunes and hymns. I believe her first was Happy Day. For some time past she would tread the organ with one foot, place her little fingers upon the keys, and sing loudly, "Halleluiah, 'tis done," "I am washed in the blood of the Lamb," etc. She had a remarkable tendency to imitate all that was pure and religious. She often had her little prayer-meetings by herself, and would teach older children to engage with her in her childish prayers and songs. After attending an ordinance where she paid marked attention to the saints' washing feet, the next day she called for a washbowl of water and washed her feet, then took off her mother's shoes and stockings and washed and wiped her feet and gave her a kiss. Every evening she kneeled at her mother's knee and said her little prayer. At the sight of the picture with raised hands she was sure to say, "Man lift up hands and praise the Lord." In her sickness she would sometimes sigh out, "O, praise the Lord!"... She excelled all other peculiarities in the wonderful depth and fervency of her affections. Her love seemed to possess the purity and strength of one fully renewed in the image of God and yet the innocence and simplicity of a child. As she placed those precious little arms around our necks and gave the warm kiss, we could not help but feel that this was real and not mere child's play; and those embraces were free for all who sought them.... This is my birthday; a sad one: but still in the midst of all the Lord supports me and comforts. Though we can not understand this bereavement, yet God knows all about it and will doubtless bring our highest good and his own glory out of it. The Lord giveth and the Lord taketh away. Blessed is the name of the Lord.

26, 27. Spent the time largely in communing with God. Wrote some letters.

29. Wife and I drove to Tiffin. When about one mile from the city our beast, that we thought very safe and quiet, began to make efforts to run off. I held her, when she began to kick desperately. I turned her to the side of the way and got her stopped. Before this I was out. I told Sarah to get out behind if she could. We had a top-buggy. The curtain was rolled up, but she could not get out. The beast was loose from the buggy all but the holdbacks. Sarah got out and stood a moment, when she found that she was hurt. Some friends came up just then. I gave the mare to one to hold and I helped Sarah to the fence, where she sat upon a stone. We found that she had been hit upon both limbs. On one the mare's hoof (she had no shoes) cut through linen duster, dress, skirt, and stocking, and cut a small wound to the bone. She had much pain. Three or four men kindly tendered all the help they could. They took us in a one-horse wagon to Tiffin, having fastened our buggy behind, and one led the mare. We came to Sister Lewis'. A small congregation gathered and I preached a short discourse, of course on holiness.

July 2, 1878. Got a crutch for Sarah. She concluded that she could go home by railroad. Took her to the train and committed her to the care of the Lord. I drove the mare and buggy, trusting in God for his protection from all harm by the way. The Lord preserved me from harm. Found dear Wife had safely made the trip.

4. Spent much of the day picking berries all alone with the

Lord. Meditated upon the goodness of God in continuing our national blessings.

6. Spent the day in prayer, meditation, and reading. Impressed with the duty of preaching against the enormous sin and galling yoke of sectarianism.

7. Sabbath. God helped me and blessed me in exposing the yokes of Satan by which God's children are brought under bondage.

On the 12th of July, 1878, Brother Warner, accompanied by his wife, made a second trip to Indiana. He stopped in Goshen with Mr. Guiss, his brother-in-law, on the 18th. As the latter was a bold and reckless infidel, he did not enjoy his visit there. He felt that he was staying where the Savior was excluded and that he could be admitted only apart from him.

He reached Yellow Lake on the 20th, and found that the meetings had been carried on for a few evenings after he left in May. Several had been saved. On the 23rd his wife returned home to Ohio, while he went on to Auburn, to Brother Lowman's, whom he found firmly established in holiness. When he and Brother Lowman began to open their minds to each other he found that both had been impressed with the idea of together printing a holiness and church paper, Brother Warner to edit the former and Brother Lowman the latter department.

After discussing the publishing project with Lowman he returned to Ohio, to Wood County, where he held a number of meetings and assisted in a camp-meeting near Rising Sun, and also attended a United Brethren camp-meeting at Portage. He speaks thus of a manifestation in his meetings at Rising Sun:

Aug. 22, 1878. Mr. Gay, a spiritualist, or rather a mesmerist who possesses a superior mind and is believed to be possessed by evil spirits, was present. He has attended for some time and has at different times attempted to mesmerize me while preaching. At a few of the last meetings his wife has been seeking sanctification, and he has made some good speeches in favor of the gospel. Today from the beginning of the meeting he began to maneuver his spiritism. He made many strange motions; walked the floor once and tried to dance. It is probable that this was all involuntary on his part. But we all kept our minds on Jesus and God through the Holy Spirit to take care of him. He began to show signs of distress, got upon the floor, wept and cried out. A stronger power than the indwelling one had taken hold of him. His suffering became more intense. His wife brought him water and he drank some. She fanned him for a long time, and he became speechless and seemed nearly suffocated.

In September, Brother Warner attended the Ohio Holiness Camp-meeting held on the fair-ground at Marion. Of his experience there he records the following:

Sept. 8, 1878. Sabbath. I began to fast on Friday. Ate but little yesterday and nothing this forenoon. The Lord came very near to me. Oh, how he let me down to nothingness! I saw and felt ashamed of the trouble the Lord has had with me. I sank down into the dust before him, and instead of wondering why God did not give the greater measure of power that the Spirit impressed me I should have I was led to wonder that he had intrusted me as much as he had. Oh, what shameful weakness and many errors were disclosed by the more perfect light that God has flashed into my soul! O God, let me be buried deeper and more perfectly hid away with thee.

12. Came home. An incident in this camp-meeting should be recorded to the glory of God. Brother Rudic took sick not long after he came here. After lying in camp a few days he was taken to Brother Kennedy's. Prayers were being offered for him, still he grew worse. Last Saturday night he sent word to camp that after meeting a few believers should get together and ask God in faith for his recovery. They did so, and great power and strong assurance came upon them. They claimed the answer to their prayer, and some of the number were able to praise God for the brother's restoration just as if he had been raised up before their eyes. Sister Lea, who had taken violently sick that eve, was also taken to the Lord with much assurance. The next morn both were in camp perfectly healed. Brother R. suffered so much during the night and was so reduced that he thought he surely must die, and made some arrangements for his departure. But early in the morning he began to look to God once more, when his faith joined that of the party in the camp at eleven in the night, and he arose, instantly made whole. All glory to God!

Following the part just quoted there is a gap in his diary until October 2, the entry for which will explain. In this, one observes his humility, his deep self-examination and his desire to exalt God alone.

Oct. 2, 1878. Today I resume my pen again, with an earnest endeavor to record some of the mercies and blessings of God upon my poor soul. After I returned from camp-meeting, the Lord saw fit in his tender love to suffer affliction to befall me. Yea, "I was brought very low, but he helped me." I had bilious remittent fever and an attack of hemorrhage of the lungs. Friends and even a physician were much alarmed and felt my work was done. As soon as taken down, I ordered cards sent to the "little ones" at different places to pray for me. I put my case in the hands of the Lord and wished only his will. Dear Wife was kept in great tranquility of mind through an unwavering faith in God that he would raise me up again. My rest in God was so deep and perfect that I hardly knew anything of my physical condition. I thought myself but slightly ill, when others despaired of my life. For a few days I talked only in a whisper, and when I began to recover I was astonished to find myself reduced to a mere frame and unable to stand.

During my afflictions, the Lord not only kept my mind in perfect peace, but also taught me many precious lessons of my littleness and his exalted greatness. Oh! let us praise and magnify the name of the Lord. I saw myself but a speck of dust resting upon an invisible grain of sand. Oh, how the eye of God scrutinized my past life and showed me yet more than at the camp-meeting my weakness and unworthiness! Oh, how vile I had been in the sight of God! How many times Satan had succeeded in resurrecting some self in me! The Spirit has plainly shown me that I should never speak of having prayed for certain persons in connection with their conversion, etc. Oh! I am so ashamed of my folly and weakness in often relating such things. I thought I was doing it all to the glory of God, but now I can see that there was some self in it. O Lord! save me in the future from such presumption and sin. I thank thee for this affliction, for I know it is all for the good of my soul. Thou hast also shown me that I have boasted too much of my health and ascribed it too generally to my knowledge of and prudence in observing natural laws. O God forgive me of this offense. I thank thee that thou hast such a constant supervision over all thy works that every good must be ascribed to thee and thanks be given to thee just the same as if no means were used at all to convey them to us. Blessed God, let me sink down forever out of self. I cried unto thee and thou hast healed me. Thou hast brought up my soul from the grave. Thou hast kept me alive that I should not go down to the pit. Sing unto the Lord, O ye saints of his, and give thanks at the remembrance of his holiness!

3. I have had a desire to attend the Northern Indiana Eldership, which convenes tomorrow eve. But Wife and friends all intreated that I should not venture from home in my present weak condition, so this morning I went to my study to write a letter to that body; but before doing so I consulted the Lord, when he gave me a strong baptism of the Spirit to go and a strong assurance that he would abundantly support me and strengthen me. I said: Lord, I will go in thy name. I firmly declared my intentions. Wife began to take the matter to the Lord and soon felt resigned. Oft through the day as I thought of going the Spirit would come upon me, and I increased in strength with wonderful rapidity.

On the morning of the 4th he was conveyed to town to take the train. The weather was unfavorable and there was some rain, but he felt he was carrying out the Lord's purpose and the Lord sustained him. From Ada, Ohio, to Fort Wayne, Ind., he had the company of Bros. S. Rice and C. E. Rowley, two prominent holiness evangelists. He reached Silver Lake in the evening and was conveyed to Beaver Dam, the place of the Eldership meeting.

CHAPTER X

NORTHERN INDIANA ELDERSHIP

Opposition to Freemasonry—New Eldership formed—Becomes an associate editor—Herald of Gospel Freedom.

The pagan system of Freemasonry began to make inroads in the body of Christians known as the Indiana Eldership of the Church of God. A storm of opposition arose from some who were of the more spiritual element of the Church when a number of the members became affiliated with the Masonic Lodge. It appears that the main body of the Eldership did not object to secret societies, and the result of the agitation was that a number of ministers who stood for the opposition and refused to fellowship Freemasons were expelled from the Eldership and were denied a renewal of their licenses. Others left the body of their own accord. In consequence a new Eldership was formed called the Northern Indiana Eldership.

Among those who constituted the original members of the new Eldership were Elders J. Martin, J. S. Shock, C. Clem, E. B. Bell, B. F. Bear, I. W. Lowman, and J. W. Ray. The new body came into possession of most of the church property and the best churches. They appointed a Board of Publication, which took steps to begin publishing a paper devoted to the interests of the cause for which they stood. Accordingly there appeared in January, 1878, the first number of the Herald of Gospel Freedom, a monthly periodical published from Wolcottville, Ind., at fifty cents a year. It stood for the promotion of gospel truth and freedom, opposition to all oathbound secret societies, Freemasonry in particular, and loyalty to God and conformity to his Word. I. W. Lowman was editor.

At the Eldership meeting which convened at Beaver Dam on Oct. 5, 1878, and which was the third annual session, Brother Warner was voted a member. In his diary for October 5 appears this account of the proceedings:

5. A good deal of time was given to prayer during the day. Much unnecessary business usually gone through within the various Elderships was dispensed with. All went off smoothly and with love. Not a grating word or discordant note in all that was

said and done. No one was called to order; no one was materially
out of order. The manner in which business was done and the
good degree of devotional spirit with which it was pervaded was
a great stride from the carnal and formal wranglings of Elderships
of the present to the simplicity and spirituality of an apostolic Eldership. Praise God, he is leading his children out into the glorious freedom of the gospel.

The most of the time was devoted to the publishing interests.
A very important measure was enacted—that of enlarging the
Herald, issuing it semi-monthly and devoting a part of it to the
promotion of Bible holiness. Praise God for this glorious movement. It is wonderful how he is controlling things for his glory.
Probably a large majority of the Eldership are not in the experience of full salvation, and of course some are disbelievers in it,
among whom are some of the preachers. Brother Shock, one of
the number, the present speaker, is probably our most talented
man. But all glory to the name of God, he controlled all these elements so that Satan could not move one to open his mouth against
this work of God, and this Eldership voted to support holiness as
a second experience. Trusting in God, I can see glorious results
from this project. It is bringing about what the Lord showed me
last winter; that is, a people straight before God in holiness and
truth. By this blessed little organ God is going to bring the true
church foundation and Bible truth into the hands of holiness people, and holiness doctrine into the hands of Church of God members, which must result in a divine union of truth and holiness.
And this is just what is wanted to save the world. Holiness, the
great lever of power, has since the Reformation been weakened
and encumbered by party names and creeds and human traditions; whereas the Church of God, though established upon eternal truth, has nevertheless been without strength to accomplish
her mission for the want of perfect holiness, the divinely appointed power to bring the world to God.

At this session of the Eldership, as Brother Warner says, special attention was
given to the Eldership's paper, the Herald of Gospel Freedom. During its first year
it had been a 10 by 15 four-column folio. It was now increased in size to a five-column 13 by 20. It was made a semi-monthly and its subscription price advanced to
seventy-five cents. Lowman was reelected editor and publisher and Brother Warner was elected associate editor to conduct a new holiness department. A number
of special contributors were chosen. A music department, already established and
conducted by Professor J. F. Kinsey, of Cincinnati, was to be continued. The best
exchanges were secured, and with this prospect the paper started on its second
year, 1879. A portion of the prospectus for that year is here given.

PROSPECTUS OF THE HERALD FOR 1879

This paper was started one year ago as the organ of the Northern Indiana Eldership of the Church of God, a body of Christian workers who were raised up through the following circumstances:

Several ministers of the Church of God in Indiana through a scrupulous regard for truth and righteousness refused to fellowship men who were yoked together in the dark leagues of secrecy. For thus reproving the works of darkness their licenses were withheld. Accordingly through the providence of God and the force of circumstances they formed themselves together as an independent body, recognizing God as the founder of his own Church and all true Christians as her real membership.

The Bible is their only creed, and Christian character their only test of fellowship.

The labors of this little band have been signally blessed of God, and their members increased.

The Herald, all things considered, has been a decided success. At the recent session of the Eldership Eld. I. W. Lowman was reelected Editor and Elder Warner was elected Associate Editor.

As heretofore, it shall be the aim of the Herald to "contend earnestly for the faith once delivered to the saints," not a part, but the whole faith of the gospel, ignoring the traditions of men, reproving the works of darkness and enforcing all the will of God.

It believes in raising men to the Bible standard of holy living by leading them into the Bible measure of grace.

It advocates a salvation that lifts men above the regions of mere duty and places them in such sweet and perfect harmony with God that they delight to do his will; a salvation that constrains to every good work by the infinite power of perfect love, and not by the lash of the law.

Viewed from a human standpoint the Herald may appear to possess two separate features; namely, that of an organ of the Church of God and an advocate of holiness. But viewed from a pure Bible standpoint these distinct features naturally blend into one effort to restore and propagate the pure religion of the Bible.

Church signifies "called out." The divinely given title, Church of God, therefore denotes the called out of God or separated unto God. Holiness means the same thing; that is, to be separated from all sin and wholly given up to God.

The editors of the Herald firmly believe that apostolic truths and Bible holiness can not be separated.

The work of holiness has been too long encumbered by human creeds and disintegrated parties among its friends.

Though holiness as a distinct experience is the most precious and important truth of the gospel, its wonderful triumphs have been much limited and rendered comparatively unstable for the want of being identified with all other Bible truths and divested of human systems.

Upon the other hand, the Church, ever accepting the only infallible and divinely authorized standard of discipline and wearing the only church title that was "given by the mouth of the Lord," is utterly disqualified to perform her appointed mission in bringing the world to God unless she be girded with the invincible power of perfect holiness and the full and distinct baptism of the Holy Ghost.

Truth is mighty; but holiness, being the fulness of God in man, is almighty. The union of these divine forces, we believe, will make a complete conquest of this world for God.

To restore the divine plan in the harmonious action and the spread of these elements of salvation is the primary object of the Herald.

A part of the paper will therefore be devoted especially to that doctrine and experience of entire sanctification, to be conducted by the Associate Editor, the Editor-in-Chief being also fully in line with holiness definitely through the blood.

With an unshaken trust in God, and confiding in the integrity of our cause and the support of all lovers of truth and Christian purity, we begin Vol. II of the Herald in the name of the Lord Jesus.

I. W. Lowman,
Editor and Publisher.
D. S. Warner,
Associate Editor.

An entry from the diary, dated October 7, contains an interesting item and will close this chapter.

As I arose this morning and approached the Lord I was led to ask my heavenly Father for some means, as I was entirely destitute, having been just able to pay my ticket fare here by the addition of a postage-stamp which through the kind providence of God I happened to have and the agent was kind enough to take. I came down, washed, and took my little morning walk for exercise and meditation, returned, and as soon as seated Father M. said, "I feel impressed that I should give this brother some money and I believe we all ought." He handed me a half dollar and the several brethren all followed with half dollars and quarters. Glory, honor, thanks, and praises be unto God our Savior forever and ever! Oh, bless the Lord, my soul, who supplieth all my needs according to his riches in glory in Christ Jesus!

CHAPTER XI

EDITOR AND AUTHOR

Locates at Rome City, Ind.—Writes book—Attends various camp-meetings—Mob at Upper Sandusky—Remarkable healings—Eldership seeks union with Mennonites—Close of diary account—Becomes editor of Herald.

The difficulties and privations incident to Brother Warner's years of faithfulness in the ministry, his persecutions on account of holiness culminating in his expulsion from the Ohio Eldership, his bereavements of some of his nearest relatives—all were serving to draw him only closer to the Divine and thereby fitting him for greater responsibilities and usefulness. As we become acquainted with his career and the mission to which God had chosen him, we discern the hand of Providence leading him to his appointed field.

On his return to Upper Sandusky from Tiffin on Apr. 9, 1878, he found some urgent calls to go to Indiana, and he said, "I think the Lord is in it; expect to go next week." At this time he became more fully awakened to the importance of abandoning all party names and creeds and returning to the "faith once delivered to the saints" in its entirety. At this time, also, he began to have some conception of the printing-press as an aid in publishing the truth. The manuscript for a tract on the subject of holiness, which he was writing, was growing to the proportions of a book, and he began to pray for means to have it published. He "received gracious answers by the Spirit," as he says, and the following night while he was lying awake in meditation, the Lord opened up to him the new field of publishing holiness by means of the printing-press.

Over the State line, in Wolcottville, Ind., the Lord had prepared the opportunity. The little paper Herald of Gospel Freedom, was in its first year, and its editor, I. W. Lowman, was favorable to holiness and had been impressed that Brother Warner should conduct a holiness department in the paper. The appointment was made at the Eldership meeting, as stated in our previous chapter. As usual when undertaking any responsibility, Brother Warner placed himself in entire dependence upon God. He thus speaks of the project:

> Oh, that God may endue us both with grace and wisdom to discharge this solemn and important calling! O my God, I cry unto thee for help! I am sure thou hast put me under this solemn and responsible charge. Now thou must qualify thy poor tool for the work. Be pleased, O Lord, to touch my heart and all my in-

tellect and religious powers afresh with the Holy Ghost. Be thou
thyself my qualification. I am so glad thou hast promised to be my
wisdom. Oh, give me also thy mind. Be thou the fountain of all
knowledge and goodness in me. Lord, I accept thee for my ALL.

His holiness articles contributed to the Church Advocate, the regular Church paper, had been effective and had won for him openings and warm hearts in various places. He possessed excellent gifts for writing as well as for speaking. His discourse was entertaining and instructive. He began his editorial duties in much physical weakness, as, it will be remembered, he was just recovering from a severe illness that laid low his naturally weak frame.

Oct. 16, 1878. Feeling bad. Much fever. Called upon the Lord.
Fasted most of the day. Applied water frequently to my head and
back of my neck. Was compelled to do some writing in order to be
in time with my continued article. This greatly increased my fever
and pain in the head.

17. Gathered some apples for myself. Feeling better. Praise
the Lord!

18. At twelve Brother Lowman and I started to Wolcottville.
Undertook to me the enormous task of walking to Waterloo, a distance of three and one half miles. The roads were muddy. I soon
felt that it was impossible for me to go through on my strength
and began to look to God. I took him for my strength. All glory
to God and the Lamb, when we reached the station I felt stronger
than when we started. Lay over some time in Kendallville. Visited
printing-offices, as we are contemplating the purchase of press
and type to run the Herald.

19. The Lord is opening the way for us to buy a whole printing-office here very cheap. Praise his name!

On the 24th he visited Rome City in view of finding a suitable place to reside. He felt directed to locate here, and wrote his wife to come. On the 26th of November they moved to their new location. He bought the south half of lots 103 and 104 for $213.

The entry for the new year, Jan. 1, 1879, is of interest.

Since the last account my time has been closely devoted to
writing for the Herald and on my little book. This seems to have
been the order of the Lord, and he has most wonderfully blessed me in the work. The Spirit is continually taking the things of
Christ and showing them to me. Glory to God for the new beauties and blessed unfoldings of divine truth under the clear light
of the "anointing that abideth and teacheth of all things." The lu-
minous heavens of revelation seen through the all-searching tele-
scope of the Holy Ghost raise many texts that were but dim and
of doubtful application to the definite purifying grace, to their

true magnitude of absolute authority; while one beautiful, blazing constellation of Bible truth after another is brought to view until the adoring soul sees no end to the divine evidences of the "second grace" save the end of revelation itself; and even there the Spirit takes up the eternal theme and writes it all over the soul, on the tablet of the heart and upon every fiber of our conscious being; yea, writes it upon the "merchandise" of the saints all over the entire universe of God's creation, on every surrounding object. Even "upon the bells of the horses shall there be HOLINESS UNTO THE LORD."

We can begin to see the effects under God of "praising the beauty of holiness" in this place in our prayer- and class-meetings. Many express a hunger for full salvation, and as we frequently present our dear neighbors to God in prayer, the Spirit seems to indicate a glorious harvest of souls in this place in the near future. All glory to God!

And now, my soul, another year of thy earthly career and time to work has passed away. Thank God, it was the first whole year of my life that I have dwelt in the Canaan of perfect love and sinless glory. All its events through God have indeed worked together for good to my soul.

11. Since last writing we have constantly shared the goodness of God. The time has been closely devoted to writing on my book and for the Herald. The Holy Spirit has greatly assisted. The weather has been very cold, as much as twenty-four degrees below zero. The first week of the new year was observed as a week of prayer. The weather being severe, but few attended our union prayer-meeting. Last night in the name of Jesus we began a meeting here in the Methodist church-house on the line of holiness.

The book he speaks of was the Bible Proofs of the Second Work of Grace. It was printed and bound the next year, 1880, at the E. U. Mennonite publishing house in Goshen. Two thousand copies were printed. It contained 493 pages and was, it would seem, an almost exhaustive treatise on sanctification as a second work of grace as shown by the Scriptures. It was counted an excellent book by the holiness people and leaders, and doubtless accomplished much good. Copies of the book may yet be found in individual libraries. This was the first book of which Brother Warner was the author. He became the author of a number of publications afterward.

27. Closed meeting tonight. A few souls have found Christ a perfect Savior. The leading elements in the M. E. Church did not come near during the meeting. Some did all they could against it. The preacher in charge a week ago made a very brave defense of sin in the flesh, justifying rather than condemning it. Oh, the shameful clamor for sin! the dead and godless condition of the

Church! Surely her glory has departed. Some who were longing for full salvation, when they saw the united influence of an
apostate church arrayed against this very fundamental doctrine
of their creed, were scared away from the good purposes of their
heart and away from the meeting. Poor souls! Having lost a good
conscience they can not look me in the face; and vainly they talk
of growing the remaining sin out of the heart. Oh, that God would
appoint salvation for this people!

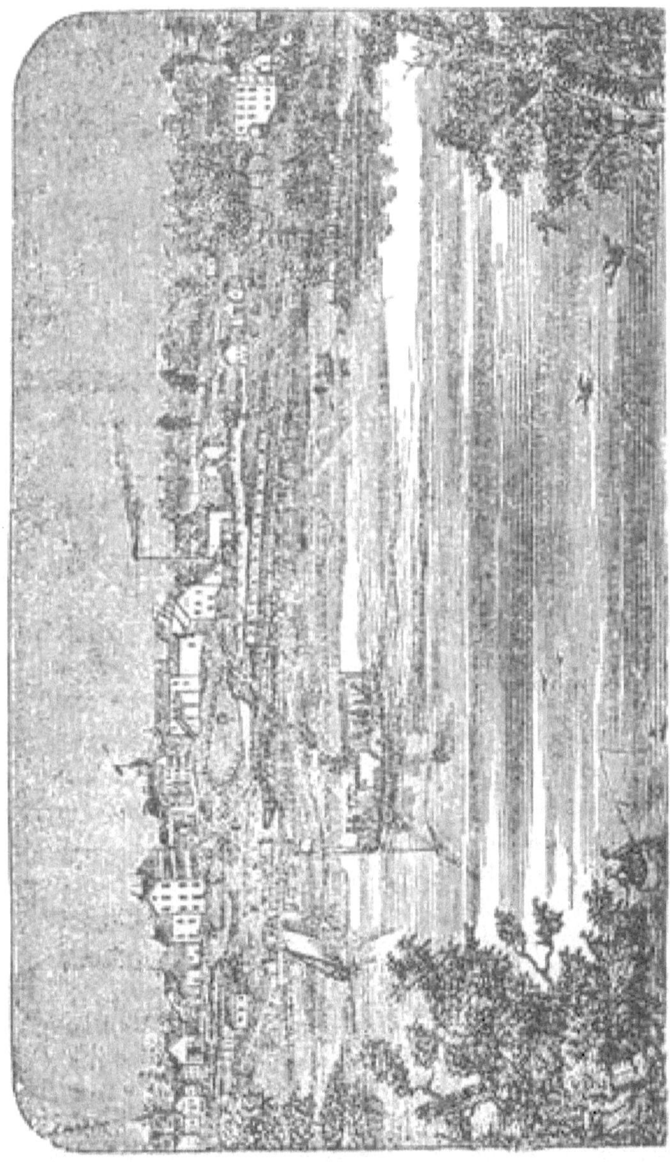

Rome City, Ind., in 1878. Birthplace of the Gospel Trumpet.

Feb. 2, 1879. Have been very busy writing during the past week. Brother Lowman moved the press here last Thursday. Praise the Lord! He showed me by the Spirit that I should locate here, and that the press would be located in this place, when nothing had been thought or said about it. Oh, I am so glad the Lord does lead his little ones! I can do much more for the paper now. Oh, that God would keep Brother Lowman and me straight on the line of holiness and continue to make the Herald a **real** herald of gospel freedom! Our circulation is increasing, thank the Lord!

10. It is wonderful how God takes care of his dependent little ones. When we came here, kind friends bade us farewell with some sadness, fearing that the holiness evangelistic work would not support us here, where we had no friends and acquaintances. But what a lesson our heavenly Father has taught us! He has abundantly provided for us, even at home. I must record some of his kindness.

Fuel is rather scarce here, wood quite high, and the weather being quite severe I could not well see from whence we should be supplied. But as we do not walk by sight I trusted all in the hands of the Lord. We have a neighbor who is a very wicked man, but no loving children of God could be more kind and benevolent to us than the whole family are. They tell us by word and action that we shall not want for any good thing while they have it. Another very wicked young man had bought twelve acres of timber about three miles from town. The best timber and most of the nicest cord-wood timber had been taken off. My kind neighbor asked him how much he would take for all that remained, and to his utter astonishment he said, "I will give it to **you** for five dollars." Neighbor and I had talked the matter over before and he agreed to take me in partnership if we could get the wood reasonable. He was true to this agreement, and we both have wood enough to do us for two or three years.

This is nothing else than the dealing of God. Oh, who would not trust thee, blessed Father of mercies! Thou art all love and boundless goodness. But thou art also perfect wisdom, therefore will we trust thee when thy providence **seems** to be against our wishes and inimical to our happiness; for we know that such can only be in appearance, because of our ignorance. Oh, we thank thee that we can rejoice in all thy righteous will; for as thou art thyself love, nothing but love can proceed from thee.

11. Bro. L. Spencer and Brother Kimmel brought me home, each bringing me a load of wood from my place of procuring fuel. When arriving home, I found wife well as usual. Arrived at one o'clock, and at two I was to preach the funeral of Miss Sigler. Poor girl, I visited and prayed with her last Saturday before leaving home. The family are not religious, the father is quite wicked and intemperate; but Mary gave me satisfactory evidence that God had forgiven her sins. However, when about to die she was left in great distress of mind. Brother Newton, residing near by, was sent for; he prayed for her. She obtained the victory and closed life in peace.

The temperance meeting that was in progress when I left continued with success until tonight. Over three hundred signed the pledge, and a permanent organization was effected.

23. Sabbath. A. M., preached in Albion on faith. P. M., led the holiness meeting and organized a holiness band of sixty-six members. Praise the Lord, they expect to work for the Master in spreading holiness.

On the 11th of March he and Elder Lowman drew up articles of agreement by which they were to be joint editors and publishers of the Herald and all other papers, books, etc., issued from their office. Brother Warner was to pay Lowman $250 for a half interest in the paper and office. Both were to bear half the expense of publishing the Herald and any other publications. Both were to share equally in all the income of the office except the job-work, which Lowman was to do with his own press and stock, and receive the proceeds. Brother Warner, however, was to realize fifteen per cent from all the job-work he should procure. All manuscripts written by or donated to either party after the date of their agreement were to be jointly published and owned, and all manuscripts written by or donated to either party before the date of agreement were to yield to the owner ten per cent more than one half the proceeds.

From this time the diary entries are rather scattered, until finally they cease altogether. This is owing to the fact, doubtless, that the events of his life were associated with evangelistic and editorial effort and went largely into the paper as news items.

May 4, 1879. Sabbath. Went to hear Brother Allison, United Brethren minister. He requested me to talk. I did so, with great liberty and power of the Spirit. Brother A., who had hitherto been an opposer of distinct holiness, was overwhelmed by the power of God and truth, and confessed that it was Bible doctrine. Another man, whose carnality was greatly stirred, turned pale, grew nervous, and finally interrupted me with questions and contradictions. Just then God sent an increased volume of sweet love to my heart. Glory to God! Burning coals were freely heaped upon his head, and soft words soon turned wrath away, and after meeting he humbly apologized.

17. Brother and Sister Shock brought me to Syracuse. Being late, Brothers Martin and Bell had left just a few moments before. Brother and Sister S. began to lament their disappointment. I began to praise God, for the Spirit seemed to say, "I want thee with me alone today." I said I expected a glorious time by the way. They looked astonished that I was so free from complaint and regrets. They suggested that I should go by the cars. I remarked that the conductor would probably put me off, as I had no money. I praised the Lord that he would be my strength to walk. They looked the more strangely as I started off with praises to the Lord. I hope that God may convince them of the blessedness of the rest of faith. Walked about sixteen miles to Warsaw, and God did most wonderfully bless my soul by the way. Reached Warsaw about 3 P. M., without fatigue or hunger. Called at Brother Barber's a few moments. Looked for a team that was going out south, but had to take the train, the Lord having told Brother Barber to give me fifty cents to pay fare. Brother Lowman was on the train. After reaching Silver Lake we had three miles more to walk to Gospel Hill. Praise God, he was my strength this day, even without food from early morning till late in the eve.

18. Sabbath. Brother Bear and many dear holy ones came from Yellow Lake and elsewhere. Glorious time in the Lord.

P. M., met at half-past two. I was urged again to lead the meeting. The Spirit of the Lord was wonderfully upon me; anointed me to preach the acceptable year of the Lord. Halleluiah! The deep prejudices began to give way; opposition ceased; God was triumphing.

Eve, Brother Lowman having the sore throat, Brother Martin not being well, and Brother Bear having left, I was much humbled before God in talking again to the people. I was brought low in the dust at the thought of being too prominent among the brethren in thus leading the meeting so much.

June 4, 1879. This is the fifth anniversary of our marriage. Took early train for home. Found dear Sarah quite ill; may the Lord bless the precious object of my strongest earthly love.

July 4, 1879. Sarah and I got a horse and buggy and went out three miles and picked a fine lot of raspberries, and thus escaped the throng and rabble that filled our little picturesque city. Oh, how much more sweet and comfortable to get away with the Lord alone!

6. Sabbath. At home. Unwell. The Lord sent a young man here today, that I might have something to do for Him. Some weeks ago I found the poor wayfarer at the lake, fishing. Having learned that he was a stranger and without money I brought him home for the night. He seems very teachable. I tried hard to get him to call upon the Lord and be saved. This is the second time he has been to see us, not having found us at home the former time. He is a very intelligent Swede. Has had some practise in type-setting, and has corresponded some for papers.

Aug. 6, 1879. Came to Warsaw camp-meeting. The Lord was at work, many being saved. About forty tents occupied. Bishops Weaver, William Taylor and a host of preachers present. Rejoiced to form the acquaintance of Brothers Lambert, Krupp, and Low, of the New Mennonite Church. They are gloriously saved and definite for Jesus. We found a wonderful affinity in our hearts. If the Lord will, I shall attend their conference. I pray God we may become one fold.

The Lord did not have his way fully in this meeting. Too much looking to men.

Sept. 3, 1879. Took train for Upper Sandusky. Found Wife and friends and many of the holiness workers already on the camp-ground.

10. Meeting closed tonight. A mob of two or three hundred of the baser sort were let loose by Satan upon us. They threatened everything to Bro. W. T. Ellis, against whom they were incensed by what appears to have been imprudent conduct of his own. We finally succeeded in escorting him through the surging, raging rabble to our quarters. Some eggs were fired upon us. This Brother E. is indeed to me a mystery. His conduct is very rough. He is truly a "new sharp threshing-instrument having teeth." Notwithstanding he provokes malice from the world and forfeits confidence of believers, he brings souls to God.

On Tuesday we had a faith meeting. Special faith and gifts of healing were considered. All who had infirmities which they believed the Lord desired them to be healed from presented themselves before the Lord, and several remarkable healings were performed. Sister Monnett, from Bucyrus, who walked upon crutches, was made whole, and used them no more. Another sister was healed by the Great Physician of a spinal affliction which she had had from her youth. The next day she was surprized to find that even the deformity had disappeared. Praise God!

22. Came home via the Baltimore and Ohio.

24. Went out to the Mennonite conference in the Hawpatch, about nine miles from here.

26. Bade these beloved brethren farewell, feeling that our hearts are wonderfully knit together in love. They appointed a delegate to our Eldership.

27. Met beloved companion this eve at our Eldership at Yellow Lake Bethel, she having come directly from Ohio.

29. Sessions very pleasant, even spiritual. After leaving the house, very strange feelings came over me. I felt sure that the powers of darkness were about to make a desperate rally. We stayed up at Brother Bear's and prayed until one o'clock. I then lay down and took a short sleep, when the Spirit bade me arise and go out in the woods. Oh, what wrestling and agony of soul! What burden of heart and cries unto God for the salvation of his cause in that lone place from about 4:30 till 6 A. M.! Received some relief and victory. An evil spirit seemed to be upon the session from the opening this morning. The foreseen darkness was there. Business did not pass off so pleasantly. At noon I spent all the time shut up with God, and received great relief from the mountain that seemed to crush my heart. This was a new and strange experience to my soul. Closed business at a late hour at night. The Eldership purchased the office from Brother Lowman and me.

Oct. 1, 1879. Sarah started home this morning. I felt led to go to see the brethren in the Cook neighborhood and Warsaw concerning the formation of a State Holiness Alliance.

14. Received an urgent call to go to Wakarusa. Was led to go. Asked God for the means, and in less than one hour a gentleman came and summoned me to affirm a small matter before the court, which any of my neighbors could have done as well.

21. [At Palestine.] Quite a good turn-out. Two quite zealous Christians who disbelieved the second work of grace—a father and son—both spoke. The first believed in sanctification as a gradual work after pardon and consummated at death. The latter testified that he received it in conversion. What incongruity in the two, but harmony in all who have the fulness!

Eve, read prophecies of the present holiness movement. Exhorted the many holy ones present to fill the Bible description of God's holy army, moving out in every direction, setting the wilderness on fire, invading every city, casting down every wall, staying and burying Gog, beating the mountains fine, and blowing the mass of chaff from the Lord's threshing-floor (Ezek. 38, 39).

23. Came home. Among the mail awaiting me was a card stating that obligations to the amount of $45 must be paid at once in Wolcottville. Blessed be the Lord, another letter contained the precise amount of $45, that had been due me nearly a year from Nebraska. Glory to God, he supplies all our needs. How perfectly he meets all our wants!

Nov. 16, 1879. Sabbath. A glorious meeting was in progress at Churubusko. Brother Wood, the leader, had taken sick and the little ones were praying to the Lord to send some one to proclaim the word of the Lord. We heard of the meeting and at once were moved to go. We found the Methodist Episcopal house crowded.

A good band of holiness witnesses and singers all had their eyes on the Lord to send a man to lead the host. Praise his name, he anointed me for the work and a glorious meeting ensued. Four or five fully saved.

17. This morning we found Brother Wood still quite sick. The doctor anticipated a severe attack of bilious pneumonia fever. We anointed him with oil and the Lord heard prayer in his behalf and raised him up at once.

18. Brother Wood quite well and able to work in the meetings. Held a special faith-meeting today. Prayed for the restoration of the boy who is perfectly deaf. We were not at all discouraged, but felt it our duty to continue in prayer from day to day just as we often have to do with those seeking pardon and purification.

19. After our day meeting a brother and sister and I formed one of the visiting committees. When nearly sundown we found a poor suffering "woman who was a sinner," and blind for some time, and afflicted with much pain. We told her that Jesus could wash away her sins and heal and open her eyes. The Spirit soon brought on conviction and new-birth labors. She was gloriously converted, and giving a shout she sat down, and after a few seconds composure said, "Glory to God, I can see! My eyes are healed!" She then embraced her child and husband, whom she had not seen for about two weeks. She had lost all power to move her eyes, and they were both turned upward in her head. She was very weak, having eaten but little for days, and she sat with her hands over her eyes to exclude the light. Now she had the lamp lit and proceeded at once to get supper. All glory to the Great Physician! Twenty-seven sanctified souls arose to join into a holiness band. Hallelujah! God is mustering his host to the battle.

The accounts immediately following, in which he speaks of consolidating the Eldership with the Mennonites, show that he had not as yet gotten away from the idea of an external union in addition to that which the bonds of salvation alone can afford. He had already made a trip to Goshen, and had met Brother Lambert and others of the Mennonite faith.

Dec. 5, 1879. Am pushing my book to completion. Today Sarah and I started for the joint meeting of our Standing Committee and the Mennonite Quarterly Conference at Hawpatch.

6. Drove eight miles this morning to the place of meeting. Was happy to meet with those beloved brethren once more. Had a joint convention. The subject of consolidation was warmly advocated from both sides, while our hearts glowed with the unifying glory of Jesus Christ. The following preamble and resolutions were adopted:

Whereas, the God of all grace has most emphatically taught

us in his Word that his church is one as the Father and Son are one, and that a manifestation of this unity is to be the world-saving salt of the church.

Therefore, we, as the professed sons of God and members of the United Mennonite Church and the Church of God assembled in the name of Jesus Christ in a joint meeting, do confess it our duty to put away from us every accursed thing that might in the least distract, divide, and alienate us in heart, or cause divergency in practise; and for the sake of securing an answer to the prayer of the adorable Savior, we do solemnly agree to abandon anything not warranted by the Word of God and accept any and everything it teaches. Therefore—

I. Resolved, That we joyfully consent to the will of our Lord and Savior Jesus Christ and agree to unite in one body as soon as in the providence of God the consolidation can be consummated, and

II. Resolved, That we recognize the Word of God as the only true basis of Christian union. Furthermore,

III. Resolved, That we believe that the truth as it is in Christ Jesus is within our reach, hence, can be ascertained on all points of difference, and that we are therefore morally bound to learn and abide its decision.

14. [At home.] Preached at the Wesleyan house at 1 P. M. on faith in relation to gifts of the Spirit. In the evening at the United Brethren house on the philosophy of faith.

16. Though very stormy, quite a company of dear brethren and young men turned out to chop and haul me wood. Oh, the goodness of God!

Jan. 1, 1880. Last night after a very successful and powerful meeting at Chambers' Schoolhouse we came to the watch-meeting at Albion. The Spirit greatly moved us to come. On reaching the house I dropped on my knees, when the Spirit gave me a searching message for the people. We kept up until after twelve. The old year passed away while we were on our knees in solemn consecration to God.

This is the last quotation which we make from his diary. By the first of the year he was given full charge of the Herald, and any further record of his life-events must be found in the papers which he was editing. Unfortunately, from Jan. 4, 1880, the date of the last entry in his diary, until the issue of the Herald for Nov. 7, 1880, is a gap over which we must bridge with silence, as I have no access to any copy of the Herald for that year other than the one mentioned, nor have I been supplied with information from any other source covering that period. In it is also announced that the following resolution was passed. "Resolved, That we are willing to consolidate the Herald with any other paper that advocates the same gospel principles."

In the number of the Herald referred to is printed the decision of the Board of Publication to make the following announcement: "Edited in the name of the Lord Jesus Christ, by D. S. Warner, Rome City, Ind. Dedicated to the God of the Bible and to the service of all saints who desire to love God with a pure heart fervently, and the holy Church he has established over eighteen hundred years ago."

From his book Bible Proofs we have drawn material for our next chapter.

CHAPTER XII

A SPIRITUAL SHAKING

Prophetic description of reformation movement—Old Testament figures—Shakings incident to divine visitations—New covenant complete in entire sanctification—Prophecies that apply to these times—Separation of wheat and chaff—Arguments against sects—Entire sanctification a remedy—Unity the hope of God's people.

In his book Bible Proofs of the Second Work of Grace, Brother Warner devotes three chapters to the prophetic description of the great work of restoration in the latter times, when, through the preaching of holiness and the upholding of the full Scriptural standard of truth, God should bring his people into unity again. This chapter is intended as an abridgement of the three chapters referred to.

I wish to say by way of introduction that many of the events in the history of ancient Israel are figures of and have their counterpart in things occurring in the Christian dispensation. And many of the utterances of the prophets, associated primarily with the events of those times, have their fulfilment as well in connection with the things foreshadowed. To regard these prophetic writings as referring only and finally to the literal affairs of the people of the Old Testament is to stop far short of their intention and use. The old dispensation was preparatory of the new. It was full of types and figures of things to be realized in the latter. Everything pointed forward in anticipation of the fulness of times when God should establish his new and better covenant with his people. Shall we say then that the prophecies did not share this anticipation; that they had to do only with the literal figures? Nay, it was the spirit of prophesy more than anything else that foretold of the times of the gospel dispensation, not only by direct reference, but also in many of those passages which touched first those immediate affairs in Israel's career and through them those greater things farther on. We note how the New Testament writers picked up the Old Testament prophecies and applied them, with such reference as "that it might be fulfilled which was spoken by the prophet," or, "as it is written," etc.

But let us not suppose that the applications of prophecy were to be confined to the days of Christ and the apostles. Many things were said of David and other Old Testament objects that had their extended and more important fulfilment in Christ or in the establishment of the church, but there were other utterances that had their final import in the later affairs of the New Testament kingdom. Those that cluster about the captivity of Israel in Babylon and their reestablishment in their own land and the rebuilding of Jerusalem are especially rich in secondary application to the corresponding crises in the history of the church.

It is thus that many of the prophecies have a two-fold application, not that they mean two different things, but that they apply to both the literal and spiritual phases of the same thing. A sufficient proof of this lies in the fact that in the Revelation, where their spiritual meaning is assumed, we find the same Old Testament figures. There is unity of purpose in God's system of types and figures and in his plan throughout, and hence many of the prophecies that pertained in the first place to events in the history of Israel are used by the Spirit today in connection with the antitypes of those events.

Great epochal events or changes in which God by some particular institution unfolds his plan, or in which there is involved the divine approach to man, whether for approval or for judgment, are attended more or less by violent manifestations in the earth or the elements. Thus on the occasion of the giving of the law at Mount Sinai the mountain shook and smoked and there were thunders and lightnings, and the people trembled. At the crucifixion of Christ, the central event in all history, the sun hid his face and the earth shook, the rocks were rent and graves were opened. The Pentecostal outpouring of the Holy Spirit was with the sound of "a rushing mighty wind." When the apostolic church prayed for the special endowment of divine power, "the place was shaken where they were assembled together, and they were all filled with the Holy Ghost." When the imprisoned Paul and Silas prayed and sang praises to God, the divine response came with a great earthquake which shook the foundations of the prison, opened all doors, and loosed every one's bands. On the day of final judgment the very earth will be moved out of her place and the elements will manifest the awful day of God.

The shaking of things, as accompanying the divine visitation, is also taken in the spiritual, or figurative, phase, and it is this application of the idea of shaking as used in the Scripture that Brother Warner employs in reference to the great spiritual movement of these latter times. As a key to the prophecies on this subject he uses Heb. 12:25-29, which reads as follows:

> "See that ye refuse not him that speaketh. For if they escaped not who refused him that spake on earth, much more shall not we escape, if we turn away from him that speaketh from heaven: whose voice then shook the earth: but now he hath promised, saying, Yet once more I shake not the earth only, but also heaven. And this word, Yet once more, signifieth the removing of those things that are shaken, as of things that are made, that those things which can not be shaken may remain. Wherefore we receiving a kingdom which can not be moved, let us have grace, whereby we may serve God acceptably with reverence and godly fear: for our God is a consuming fire."

We have here two distinct shakings. The first one, according to the apostle's words beginning with verse 18, plainly refers to the manifestation at Sinai when the first covenant was given to Israel (Exod. 19). The second shaking attends the voice which in this dispensation speaks from heaven. The former was a literal shaking, while the latter is of course spiritual, and attends the establishment of the new covenant. "See that ye refuse not him that speaketh" is in the present tense to this dispensation and is an injunction for *us*.

Now, the new covenant involves the very highest standard of relation between God and his people, a standard much superior to that of the old Sinaitic covenant. It is distinguished by the laws of God being written in our hearts and comprehends our perfect obedience to them. In this relation we become his people and he our God in the very closest sense (see Heb. 8:10, and 10:16). This relation is none other than entire sanctification, which to attain requires the complete crucifixion of the self-life, the destruction of every idol, and entire abandonment to God. It is a close-girding covenant and admits of no sin either in practise or in the heart. The words "yet once more" refer to the shaking as final and to the standard of truth as being perfect, *ne plus ultra*, and as therefore consisting only of things unshakable.

It is the voice calling to this holiness standard of the new covenant that produces the mighty shaking, causing both earth and heaven to tremble. Whenever this voice is heard, whether in the beginning of Christianity or in a movement that effects the reestablishment of the new covenant in the hearts of God's people today, the shaking occurs. Both sinners and professors are made to tremble at God's mighty truth and he who would obey the divine appeal must suffer the shaking loose and consequent loss of all things contrary to the divine will, however dear they may be in the selfish affections. God has through grace made it possible for one and all to measure to this standard, so that for him who refuses the voice that speaks thus from high heaven there is positively no escape.

Our quotation from Hebrews leads us back to the prophet Haggai, whose words in chapter 2, verse 6, are what the apostle doubtless refers to. This introduces us to that field of prophecies relating to the captivity and the return, so typical of the apostasy and of the final restoration of the true church in these last days. It should not be a thing incredible that the great spiritual events of these epoch-making times should be in accordance with prophetic utterance, nor that the Holy Spirit should lead Brother Warner, as he testifies to having been led, into these things as prophetic truth. Indeed the reader, if he be a seeker after truth, should not be surprised to find the Holy Spirit confirming to his own mind that these things have a prophetic illumination. Brother Warner's reference to these prophecies, and his comments, are here given. Of Heb. 12:25-29 he thus speaks:

> On the 30th of August, 1879, the Holy Spirit in a special manner gave me the foregoing scripture. I had never clearly comprehended its meaning and I felt impressed that the Lord was about to lead me into a new vein of truth. I shut myself up with God and the Bible, when "the Comforter, which is the Holy Ghost," took most of the things that are contained in what follows and showed them to me. Being fully assured that my mind had been led into the pure light of truth, we published it from the pulpit, much to the edification of the holy brethren. We feel confident

that the following chain of Scriptures, correlative with our text, will conduct every meek and candid reader into the same light it has your humble servant. We shall find the foregoing words of the inspired apostle a key to the prophetic description of the great work of holiness....

Let us examine the same declaration elsewhere in the Holy Book. Haggai 2:5-7: "According to the word that I covenanted with you when ye came out of Egypt, so my spirit remaineth among you: fear ye not. For thus saith the Lord of hosts; Yet once, it is a little while, and I will shake the heavens, and the earth, and the sea, and the dry land; and I will shake all nations, and the desire of all nations shall come: and I will fill this house with glory, saith the Lord of hosts." The rebuilding of the temple is the subject under consideration. This ancient abode of the great Shekinah was such a marked figure of the church of God that it is seldom spoken of by the holy seers but what the spirit of prophecy flashes forth in interspersed references to the "spiritual house." Says the prophet, "The glory of this latter house shall be greater than of the former, saith the Lord of hosts: and in this place will I give peace, saith the Lord of hosts" (v. 9). Is it not in the midst of his church where God speaks peace to thousands who seek his face? Let us also thank God for the gracious intimation that the glory of the restored, latter-day church shall exceed that which preceded the dark-age captivity.

It is quite evident that the words in verses 5-7 were in the mind of the apostle when he wrote the words of our text. And we find here additional evidence that the "once more shaking" relates to the triumphs of the gospel, because it is associated with the coming of Christ, not as Judge, but the "Desire [or Savior] of all nations."...

God never designed that we should

> "Roam through weary years
> Of inbred sin and doubts and fears,
> A bleak and toilsome wilderness."

If you have not passed through the Jordan, the death-convulsions of the "old man" of sin, to the Canaan rest, it is because you have either ignorantly or wilfully "refused him that speaketh," and "entered not in because of unbelief."...

"I will fill this house with glory." Here is the glory that Christ gives: "The Spirit of glory and of God," that fills and rests upon the church when inbred sin and all weights are shaken out. What is here associated with the "once more" shaking corresponds with entire sanctification.

The prophet Ezekiel gives us a very interesting chain of concurring prophesy. Who with his spiritual eyes open can fail to see the application of the 34th chapter of Ezekiel to the ministry, in general, of this age? They "eat up the good pasture"—fare sumptuously on fat salaries. 'Ye tread down the residue of your pastures' and 'foul the waters with your feet.' They are the real cause of spiritual famine instead of the means of refreshing the flock. "Ye eat the fat, and ye clothe you with the wool." Make a lucrative merchandise of your Christless sermons, instead of administering the free gospel of salvation. "Ye kill them that are fed: but ye feed not the flock." When any find their way to the true Shepherd and receive food, life, and holy fire in their souls, they annoy the dead and sleeping, who proceed at once to kill them. This is no idle fancy. It is an undeniable fact that in most of our present-day churches a real convert can scarcely maintain spiritual life. The few that are not killed are usually driven or thrown out. O ye shepherds, a crisis from the Almighty is coming upon you. As the Lord liveth, the fires from heaven shall sweep away your craft. "Howl, ye shepherds, and cry; and wallow yourselves in the ashes, ye principal of the flock: for the days of your slaughter and of your dispersions are accomplished" (Jer. 25:34). Their time of feasting upon and dispersing the Lord's flock will come to an end.

"I will deliver my flock from their mouth," and "they shall no more be a prey" (Ezek. 34:10,22). "I will seek out my sheep, and will deliver them out of all places [sectarian divisions] where they have been scattered [into several hundred parties] in the cloudy and dark day" (v. 12). We talk of the dark age as in the past; but the seer of God declares that we are yet under its lingering fogs, and shall be until holy fire from heaven shall sweep away every partition-wall, human creed, and party name, and purge out that infamous god, the sectarian spirit; the vile "image of jealousy" which sits in all the thresholds of Babylon.

"And I will bring them out from the people, and gather them from the countries, and will bring them to their own land, and feed them" (v. 13). Yea, "I will feed them in a good pasture, and upon the high mountains of Israel shall their fold be" (v. 14). "And I will set up one shepherd over them, and he shall feed them, even my servant David [Christ—David was already dead four hundred years]; he shall feed them, and shall be their shepherd" (v. 23).

The perfect reign of the Messiah, and his love in the soul, is to succeed the dark day of party confusion. The two are not compatible with each other. "And I will make with them a covenant of peace" (v. 25). Their own land, and this covenant-union with God, is simply entire sanctification. See Jer. 23....

In Ezekiel 35 we have the judgment of mount Seir. Seir—**rough, shaggy**—we presume is used [in the typical sense] to denote the Catholic power.

It was inhabited by the Edomites, the descendants of Esau, who were therefore brothers with Israel, the descendants of Jacob; but the Edomites had a deep-rooted and perpetual enmity against Israel, they harassed and distressed them by all possible means, (See A. Clark.) "Behold, O mount Seir, I am against thee, and I will stretch out mine hand against thee, and I will make thee most desolate ... because thou hast had a perpetual hatred, and hast shed the blood of the children of Israel by the force of the sword in the time of their calamity, in the time that their iniquity had an end." (vs. 3-5). Does not this look like the record of the "beast that sits upon the seven hills"? Martyrdom, it appears, is confined to such times when God's people have reached an "end of sin."

As the spirit of prophesy uses mount Seir to represent Catholicism in chapter 35, and the Caucasian mountains [Gog and Magog, see Bible dictionary] to represent sectism in chapters 38 and 39, so in chapter 36:1 the "mountains of Israel" are used to represent the true conscientious Christians. The Lord says, "Set thy face against mount Seir," "against Gog," and "prophesy against him;" but in reference to the mountains of Israel, the order is changed to "prophesy unto," showing that the former were rejected, but the latter accepted of the Lord; to these very precious promises are made. In the latter part of the chapter we have associated together salvation "from all uncleanness," the gift of the Holy Spirit, and "bringing into the land," i. e., the land of perfect holiness....

The spirit of prophesy now takes up another figure to set forth the holiness crisis and the glorious effect in those "that abide the day" of the Refiner's coming. "Moreover, thou son of man, take thee one stick, and write upon it, For Judah, and for the children of Israel, his companions: then take another stick, and write upon it, For Joseph, the stick of Ephraim, and for all the house of Israel his companions: and join them one to another into one stick; and they shall become one in thine hand. And when the children of thy people shall speak unto thee, saying, Wilt thou not shew us what thou meanest by these? Say unto them, Thus saith the Lord God; Behold, I will take the stick of Joseph, which is in the hand of Ephraim, and the tribes of Israel his fellows, and will put them with him, even with the stick of Judah, and make them one stick, and they shall be one in mine hand" (Ezek. 37:16-19).

Who does not know that this never was really fulfilled in the alienated sects of Jacob's literal seed? While it may apply to the formation of the church in the beginning of the reign of Christ, it was specially designed to typify the return of the church to God and the mount of holy union after the "falling away" or "cloudy and dark day." The figure does not properly suggest the formation of a new church state, but the gathering again of a divided and starved-out church under the pastorate of corrupt and self-aggrandizing shepherds. "I ... will gather them on every side, and bring them into their own land ... I will save them out of all their dwelling-places, wherein they have sinned, and will cleanse them, so shall they be my people and I will be their God. And David [Christ, "the root and offspring of David"] my servant shall be king over them; and they all shall have one shepherd" (vs. 21-24). Nothing but entire sanctification can unite the saints under the direct control, and headship of Christ, through the Comforter.

"And they shall dwell in the land that I have given unto Jacob my servant, wherein your fathers [in the day of the church's purity] have dwelt; and they shall dwell therein, even they, and their children, and their children's children forever: and my servant David shall be their prince [even Christ, for him hath God exalted to be a Prince and a Savior] forever. Moreover I will make a covenant of peace with them; ... and the heathen shall know that I the Lord do sanctify Israel, when my sanctuary shall be in the midst of them forevermore" (vs. 25-28). Here is the solution of the whole matter. The reception of the Spirit, uniting into one, placing in the land, cleansing, and the "covenant of peace" under the glorious reign of the "Prince of peace," is all summed up and consummated in the sanctification of the church through the indwelling of the Holy Trinity.

Instead of exterminating the idols and "Canaanites in the house of the Lord of hosts," the "shepherds of Israel" have catered to their unholy lusts. They have so long truckled to the world in the church, so long fawned and pampered sin under the cloak of religion, that a terrible conflict ensues whenever it is attacked by the sword of the Spirit. This crisis is described in the two following chapters, namely, Ezekiel 38, 39.

"Son of man, set thy face against Gog, the land of Magog, the chief prince of Meshech and Tubal, and prophesy against him, and say, Thus saith the Lord God; Behold, I am against thee, O Gog" (38:2,3). The Bible dictionary applies Gog and Magog to the Caucasian mountains, a chain that extends from the Black Sea to the Caspian. The Scythians of those regions were a fierce and warlike people. For many years they had made their name a terror to the whole Eastern world. They were finally conquered and driven out, B. C. 596, a few years before the time of Ezekiel's prophesy. These events being fresh in the mind of the ancient seer, the prophetic spirit employs Gog and Magog to represent the acrid and intolerable spirit of sectarianism and its final overthrow.

Meshech and Tubal, allies of Gog, are noticed in history as "the remotest and rudest nations of the world." David, it is probable, spoke prophetically of the same contentious, unsanctified zeal: "Woe is me, that I sojourn in Meshech.... My soul hath long dwelt with him that hateth peace. I am for peace, but when I speak, they are for war" (Psa. 120:5-7).

In applying the army of Gog and Magog to the false, deceived, and sectarian forces, the enemies of the Lord's true and holy church, I am clearly sustained in Revelation 20:8-10, where they are declared to have been deceived by the devil, therefore have a spurious religion—are professors. "They compass the saints on the breadth of the earth;" hence are diffused throughout all nations and everywhere arrayed against the holy; but shall be finally destroyed by fire from heaven. This vast army Ezekiel represents as 'coming from their place out of the north parts' (38:6,15; 39:2), indicative of a cold and heartless religion. The attack upon the "land" by Gog, shall be in the "latter years," "the latter days," (38:8,11). This language all through the prophets points to the last, or present, dispensation.

"In the latter years thou shall come into the land [the sanctified] that is brought back from the sword [saved from the carnal, sectarian "strife of tongues"], and is gathered out of many people, against the mountains of Israel, which have been always waste;" i. e., more or less destitute of the apostolic faith and power.

God sets the testimony of his anointed against the worldly churches. Gog in return makes war upon them. But being dead to sin, and having a resurrected life, they are an invulnerable army. "They shall dwell safely all of them" (v. 8).

"And it shall come to pass at the same time when Gog shall come against the land of Israel, saith the Lord God, that my fury shall come up in my face. For in my jealousy and in the fire of my wrath have I spoken. Surely in that day there shall be a great shaking in the land of Israel" (vs. 18, 19). When the sword of the Almighty is unsheathed against self-righteous orthodox sinners, there is soon war in the camp, and a general commotion in the heavens and the earth. The two-edged sword of definite testimony is now wielded in every church, which has never been the case in any of the past holiness reforms.... Amen! Let the battle rage, though the heavens and the earth be moved. Send down the fire, O Lord, send fire from heaven, and burn every Gog-schism out of the church! Yea, saith the Lord, "I will send a fire on Magog, and among them that dwell carelessly in the isles: and they shall know that I am the Lord."

The burning of the weapons and burying of Gog is described as the cleansing of the land—the church. Therefore it is the special work of sanctification, and the heavens and the earth are now shaken by the tread of God's holy army, who are 'severed out to continual employment, passing through the land to cleanse it.'

Let us now begin with 1 Pet. 4:17,18. "For the time is come that judgment must begin at the house of God: and if it first begin at us, what shall the end be of them that obey not the gospel of God? And if the righteous scarcely be saved, where shall the ungodly and the sinner appear?" Here is a trying ordeal, a judgmental shaking of the church parallel with that described in Hebrews. It is the execution of Christ's verdict of death to sin in the flesh. "The time is come." Scriptures thus introduced almost invariably refer to some previous prediction. In the prophecies of Isaiah we find what is doubtless the antecedent of Peter's words: "I will turn my hand upon thee, and purely purge away thy dross, and take away all thy tin: ... afterwards thou shalt be called, The city of righteousness, the faithful city. Zion shall be redeemed with judgment, and her converts with righteousness" (Isa. 1:25-27).

The judgment of Zion, the house of God, is her full redemption. It is the hand of the Almighty 'purely purging away the dross and all the tin' from his church, that it might be called the "city of righteousness." This experience is not for the sinner, nor is it confined to the aged and dying; but the "converts" in Zion, saith the Lord, shall be redeemed from sin, by the spirit of judgment and the spirit of burning. This purging is parallel with the removing of those things that are shaken.

"In that day shall the branch of the Lord be beautiful and glorious [i. e., 'sanctified and cleansed, a glorious church' (Eph. 5:26,27)], and the fruit of the earth shall be excellent and comely for them that are escaped of Israel [have 'escaped the corruption that is in the world']. And it shall come to pass, that he that is left in Zion, and he that remaineth in Jerusalem, shall be called holy, even every one that is written among the living in Jerusalem: when the Lord shall have washed away the filth of the daughters of Zion, and shall have purged the blood of Jerusalem from the midst thereof by the spirit of judgment, and by the spirit of burning" (Isa. 4:2-4). This explains the words of Peter very clearly; the judgment of the house of God is a divine washing and purging. The church, having passed through the spirit of judgment and of burning, all that are left therein "shall be called holy." Therefore, we understand the words of Peter as having reference to the sin-consuming flames of the Sanctifier, the baptism of the Holy Ghost, which corresponds with the shaking of the church, of which Paul speaks in Hebrews; for he concludes by saying, "Our God is a consuming fire."

If ever there was a time when Peter's words were pertinent, it is now. The hand of the Almighty is upon his church, and he will smite and humble it with his judgments; shake it with his voice from heaven, and consume it with the flames of his Spirit until every foul spirit is driven out and all the "works of the devil" destroyed; that nothing may remain but the pure, unalloyed elements of the divine "kingdom, which can not be shaken." No wonder the churches so often fear and dread the coming of God's holy bands; yea, "a fire burns before them," which quite frequently closes all meeting-houses and every other place where the sects can defeat their access. It is because they know that they are but a collection of ecclesiastical stubble, which can not abide the fire which accompanies the Lord's army of definite witnesses. Here we also see that the charge that insisting upon the definite experience of entire sanctification destroys the churches is true only so far as they are composed of "wood, hay, and stubble." Fire never destroys gold and silver....

In Joel we have the declaration: "The Lord also shall roar out of Zion, and utter his voice from Jerusalem [the holy church]; and the heavens and the earth shall shake" (3:16). A church that has no voice to shake sinners and professors, no voice that "turns the world upside down," that makes not the wicked flee, the devil howl, and persecution rage—that church may have "gods many," but has not the true God dwelling in her; for, following the foregoing the prophet says: "So shall ye know that I am the Lord your God dwelling in Zion, my holy mountain: then shall Jerusalem be holy, and there shall no strangers pass through her any more" (v. 17). The Lord wants his church so holy that no stranger to God will pass through her, much less dwell and carry on business in her....

Let us now trace the heaven- and earth-shaking hosts of the Almighty in the prophet Isaiah. "Cry out and shout, thou inhabitant of Zion: for great is the Holy One of Israel in the midst of thee" (Isa. 12:6). Here is the power that does the shaking. A church that has the great and Holy One in her midst always produces a commotion in the world....

But who are required to do these things? Thus saith the Lord, "I have commanded my sanctified ones, I have also called my mighty ones for mine anger, even them that rejoice in my highness" (chap. 13:3). The sanctified soul rejoices only in the exaltation and glory of God; there is no principle left in the heart that seeks self-aggrandizement. They even glory in being abased, if God is thereby honored. Glory to his name!

Now observe the effect of lifting high the banner of holiness: "The noise of a multitude in the mountains, like as of a great people; a tumultuous noise of the kingdoms of nations gathered together: the Lord of Hosts mustereth the host of the battle" (v. 4).

A commotion soon follows the definite testimony and "lifting up of holy hands in the sanctuary" of the Lord: an army springs into existence; God himself mustereth the host. Halleluiah!

"Howl ye; for the day of the Lord is at hand; it shall come as a destruction from the Almighty. Therefore shall all hands be faint, and every man's heart shall melt.... Behold, the day of the Lord cometh, cruel both with wrath and fierce anger, to lay the land desolate: and he shall destroy the sinners thereof out of it." (vs. 6, 7, 9). This conflagration from the Almighty sweeps, with a besom of destruction, all sinners from the land—out of the church. If, therefore, the holiness movement lays waste some churches in its course, it is simply because they are composed, in general, of sinners. This fact also proves that it is the very crisis we are here tracing in the Bible. It does not destroy true Christians nor spiritual churches; but, saith the Lord, "I will cause the arrogancy of the proud to cease, and will lay low the haughtiness of the terrible" (v. 11)....

SEPARATION OF THE WHEAT AND CHAFF

The great war for the extermination of sin out of the heart, or sinners out of the church is destined to sweep over all the nations of the earth. "The isles saw it, and feared; the ends of the earth were afraid, drew near, and came" (Isa. 41:5).

Thus saith the Lord: "Fear not, thou worm Jacob, and ye men of Israel; I will help thee, saith the Lord, and thy redeemer, the Holy One of Israel" (Isa. 41:14). When sin and self are all destroyed there is barely enough left of Jacob to constitute a small worm. But by thus reducing her to "naught," God has prepared the church to exhibit his power in shaking the heavens and the earth and bringing "to naught the things that are"—the great things of the world.

"Behold, I will make thee a new sharp threshing-instrument having teeth: thou shall thresh the mountains, and beat them small, and shall make the hills as chaff. Thou shall fan them, and the wind shall carry them away, and the whirlwind shall scatter them: and thou shalt rejoice in the Lord, and shalt glory in the Holy One of Israel" (Isa. 41:15,16). The characteristic of God's church here portrayed is nearly lost sight of at present. People think it is the business of the church to stand like a beggar at the door of the devil's kingdom and politely coax his subjects over; saying much about the duty and advantage of belonging to church and little about their sin and the duty of repentance, as though God were dependent, and the devil proprietor of the universe. Satan, having thus stolen the spikes out of the church—her power of execution—has distinguished himself in helping to run the empty machinery. But he that sitteth in the heavens will arise and bring to naught Satan's devices.

> "The time is soon coming, by the prophets foretold,
> When Zion in purity the world shall behold;
> When Jesus' pure testimony will gain the day —
> Denomination selfishness vanish away."

Already the Lord has begun to make Jacob new again; a sharp instrument, reset with the spikes of its primitive power, the "weapons of his indignation."

A church or ministry that is destitute of these teeth will hurt no flesh, awake no persecution, thresh out no wheat, please the devil, and give no glory to God. But spikes are not the only essential to a first-class thresher. Anciently grain was threshed with flails or trodden out by cattle and horses. Then a great improvement was secured by the invention of what is called the "old open machine." But, oh, the heaps of chaff that piled up, and filled the entire floor! Then came the dreadful task of cleaning up — of separating and removing the worthless heap.

Such have been the crafty open machines that have for years imposed heaps of trash upon the Lord's threshing-floor. They have not taken "forth the precious from the vile" (Jer 15:19). "Her priests have violated my law, and have profaned mine holy things: they have put no difference between the holy and profane, neither have they showed difference between the unclean and the clean" (Ezek. 22:26). "Ye have wearied the Lord with your words ... when ye say, Every one that doeth evil is good in the sight of the Lord, and he delighteth in them" (Mal. 2:17).

Is not this perfectly fulfilled at present by preachers who invite sinners into their folds without requiring a particle of saving grace, and who even flatter them that they are already pretty good, and need but to come and join the church? And how many of their poor, deluded victims remain in the church for years and never hear the gospel preached straight enough to convict them of their unregenerated hearts! The policy of these teachers has been to "gather of all kinds," but the next thing in order — to separate and "cast the bad away" — has been wholly omitted. But as the Lord liveth, he is going to clear away this ecclesiastical rubbish.

"Whose fan is in his hand, and he will thoroughly purge his floor, and gather his wheat into the garner; but he will burn up the chaff with unquenchable fire" (Matt. 3:12). Who would accept as a gift a few bushels of wheat scattered through a great heap of chaff and dirt? And think you that God will accept the church in her present condition? No, indeed; the gold must first be separated from the dross. The bride must dissolve her unholy friendship with the world, in which she is guilty of spiritual adultery in the sight of God (Jas. 4:4). She must put away all her rival gods, and adorn herself in robes of spotless white, before prepared as a bride for her husband. The Bible most assuredly teaches that God will separate the chaff from the wheat before he comes to garner home his church. To accomplish this he is converting Jacob from an open machine to a separator....

When the "rushing mighty wind" from heaven strikes the gathered heaps of stubble and chaff and begins to "scatter them," people think the church is being ruined; but this fan is in the hand of the Lord Jesus, and it will not carry a grain of wheat off his floor, and why fret about that which is not meet for the Master's use? "What is the chaff to the wheat? saith the Lord." Let the wind from heaven drive it, and the fire consume it, "and thou [even in this scatterment] shalt rejoice in the Lord, and shalt glory in the Holy One of Israel."

In the prophet Micah, chapter 4, and verses 1, 2, we have the mountain of the house of the Lord (the church) established, and the law going "forth of Zion, and the word of the Lord from Jerusalem." In the 10th verse we have recorded the captivity, or "falling away" of the church—"Thou shalt go even to Babylon." And, in order to restore her purity, the Lord commands the following severe measures in verse thirteen: "Arise and thresh, O daughter of Zion: for I will make thine horn iron, and I will make thy hoofs brass: and thou shalt beat in pieces many people: and I will consecrate their gain unto the Lord, and their substance unto the Lord of the whole earth."

Threshing and separating, purging and consuming is the order of God, in the day of the Refiner. Many think we must so temper the gospel as to preserve peace in the church, notwithstanding her sin and idols. But, "Suppose ye that I am come to give peace on earth [peace with sin]? I tell you, Nay; but rather division." So answers the Lord. His "fan is in his hand," and he would rather blow the church to atoms and secure a little clean wheat by itself than see it prosper in peace and multitudes and under mortgage to Satan, and bearing his brand mark, i. e., spots of sin. For this purpose, says Jesus, "I am come to send fire on the earth; and what will I, if it be already kindled? But I have a baptism to be baptized with; and how am I straightened till it be accomplished!" (Luke 12:49,50). Jesus intimates that the work of refining the church with the Holy Ghost fire could not begin until he himself had passed through the ordeal of suffering and death.

"For, behold, the Lord will come with fire, and with his chariots like a whirlwind, to render his anger with fury, and his rebuke with flames of fire. For by fire and by his sword will the Lord plead with all flesh: and the slain of the Lord shall be many" (Isa.

66:15,16). Here is the fire, sword, and division that Christ came to send on earth. Its shaking and purifying power was first manifest on the day of Pentecost. This light makes Israel see her condition and cry out, "My leanness, my leanness, woe unto me!" "Wherefore glorify ye the Lord in the fires, even the name of the Lord God of Israel in the isles of the sea." "When thus it shall be in the midst of the land among the people, there shall be as a shaking of an olive-tree, and as the gleaning grapes when the vintage is done" (Isa. 24:15,13). "And it shall come to pass, that he who fleeth from the noise of the fear shall fall into the pit" (v. 18). There is no escape from the sweeping fire of holiness but into the pit of sin; and all that can not "abide his coming" are "like chaff, which the wind driveth away."

But nowhere in the Bible is the line more clearly drawn between the wheat and the chaff, the gold and the dross, than in our key-note text to this entire subject. What shall remain after the "once more" shaking? Nothing but the divine elements of the "kingdom, which can not be moved," and which Paul represents as "righteousness, and peace, and joy in the Holy Ghost" (Rom. 14:17). These only remain in the heart that has passed through the crisis. Halleluiah! But what is thereby removed? Answer: All "things that are shaken" and that "are made." By the first class we understand everything that flinches and shakes before the searching light and sin-exterminating gospel of Christ; every vein of our nature, every motion "flesh and spirit," every temper of the mind and habit in life that does not perfectly harmonize with the "righteousness of God revealed" in the Bible, will naturally shake beneath the voice of the Holy One, and must, therefore, be removed. The second class—all "things that are made"—denotes every thing that is not original: every phase of our moral being that is not implanted by the hand of God. Or, in other words, everything adhering to us that was produced by Satan, sin, or the perversion of our moral being. As the Lord says, "Every plant that my Father has not planted, shall be rooted up." This includes inbred sin. We have all along assumed the existence of this besetting foe. Yet we are aware that a very few deny the fact. But we think David settles this matter in the 51st Psalm, where he declares that, as fallen creatures, our very being is "conceived" and "shapen" in the mold of sin and iniquity. Paul also avers that we are "by nature the children of wrath" (Eph. 2:3); and that we are "cut out of the olive-tree [Adamic root] which is wild by nature" (Rom. 11:24).

But why multiply texts? Observation must necessarily teach everybody that children are possessed with a perverse nature long before the knowledge of right and wrong is developed. Justified Christians almost uniformly confess this same inward trouble. The remaining question is, Can we get rid of it in this life? To decide this, we have but to ascertain whether it is original, or the result of the fall. That it formed no part of the likeness of God in the soul, is very certain. It is therefore the "works of the devil," and just what Christ "came to destroy." It shakes, flashes out and roils up when pierced by the sword of the Lord, and must, therefore, be removed from the soul.

But the words of Paul apply to the church, as well as to the individual. It is designed to assay and remove the dross of the whole body of Christ. Before the great holiness reform had shed its benign influence upon the Christian world, and to some extent raised the church out of the narrow rut of churchism into a deeper and broader loyalty to God and unselfish love for humanity, the idea of getting saved from "your church" would have been regarded as blasphemy. But, thanks to the Lord! a purer light and higher standard of truth now compel the trumpeters of God all along the line of holiness to insist on salvation from all "our churches." But it may be asked, What is it that we must be saved from in "our churches"? Surely there must be some way to discriminate between that which is pernicious and that which is of God. Now, I know of no corner from which to run off this line but the one that Paul points out: "Other foundation can no man lay than that is laid," and, "This word, Yet once more, signifieth the removing of those things that are shaken, as of things that are made." God has founded one body—one church, fold, or kingdom. In it he has placed every element that is essential to its work, its prosperity, and its perpetuity. His wisdom has adapted it to all ages of time and conditions of men. Its faith was delivered to the saints once for all. Its principles and precepts are the last testament, the final and immutable will of the eternal God. This divine organization is invested with such absolute symmetry and perfection that to attempt the slightest modification of its divine unity or polity is wicked presumption in the sight of its divine Founder, and incurs the curses and forfeits all the blessings of God's Holy Book. Now, since the work of entire sanctification is designed to elevate the church to her normal and perfect condition in the sight of God, it must shake out and purge away every existing element that was not originally implanted by the hand of the Lord. This test, I think, is one in which all true Christians agree. Indeed, if we were to untie from this moorage we should soon be driven to sea without compass or chart; we should virtually open the door for every tradition of Rome and invention of error.

Starting, then, from this corner-stone of divine truth, established at Jerusalem nearly nineteen hundred years ago, and with the Bible as our compass and field notes, let us run off a line.

1. Between the true and false spirits in the church—let us "try the spirits whether they are of God." "Now if any man have not the Spirit of Christ, he is none of his." But the party spirit, so prevalent in the churches, is not of Christ, hence must be removed, purged out of the heart. A zeal that springs from anything but pure, unmixed love for God and humanity, a spirit that would even promote holiness, or the conversion of sinners, partly to build up "our church," is badly mixed, is soon shaken and can not survive the Refiner's fire. It is only when the "eye is single" that the "whole body is full of light"—wholly sanctified.

A spirit which, out of deference to its own creed, wilfully disobeys the divine word, is not of God, and can not coexist with a pure heart. All these secondary motives, these mixed and unclean spirits, "shake" at the voice of the "mighty God," and are "removed" in the thorough work of entire sanctification.

2. The next thing I am compelled in the fear of God to speak of, as included in the catalog of the devil's shaky works, the foul smut and chaff of error, is the evil of sectarianism. This is the most destructive bane that God has ever suffered the devil to sow in his kingdom. It is the very mildew of hell, that spreads its blasting curse over nearly all the precious fruit of the Lord's vineyard. Here the words of Paul are an all-sweeping besom.

Oft the enlightened Christian's conscience inquires whether it is right for the church to be divided thus into a plurality of sects or denominations, with their respective human creeds and party names. In the light of truth we are compelled to answer, No. And for the simple reason that these parties are not of divine origin. Christ is the source of all true union among his disciples, and all divisions between them and the world; while the devil is the instigation of divisions in the church, and of all union between it and the world.

I quote the following from an editorial in the Christian Harvester.

"1. God has a church on earth. It is one and indivisible. It is made up of all and singular who are born of the Spirit.

"2. Individual (local) churches, or congregations, are as Scriptural as they are necessary.

"3. There is not one word in the Bible favorable to denominations or sects. The only sect among Christians that is spoken of in terms—the Nicolaitan—is severely condemned. There are indications of sectish belief, against which John is supposed to labor in the first chapter of his Gospel, and Paul withstood in the

Judaizing tendencies, even in a brother apostle. Denominations are directly or indirectly the result of sin remaining in the great body of professors. Thorough and wide-spread holiness would soon destroy denominations.

"4. But the evangelical denominations of today contain the mass of true Christians, with a multitude of mere professors. Because of differences sects can not yet be abolished; and an effort at abolition would result in a new one. Therefore sects are a present necessity, until holiness more generally prevails.

"5. The possessor of perfect love of necessity overleaps denominations in spirit, and so regards all the sanctified as perfectly his brethren."

We are personally acquainted with the editor of the Harvester, and believe him a holy man of God. We admire the frankness with which he acknowledges that "there is not one word in the Bible favorable to denominations or sects," and that "denominations are directly or indirectly the result of sin remaining in the great body of professors."

Such must be the honest verdict of every intelligent, God-fearing man. It is no pleasant thing, we know, to look upon and admit this monster evil, this fell destroyer of the purity, love, and power of the Lord's Zion. Says Wm. Starr, "My heart has groaned as, pen in hand, I have looked at this subject, arranged my thoughts to present them to you." But for the love of truth I am constrained to differ with the position that sects are a present necessity. They originated from sin in the church; and shall we admit that the fruit of sin is a necessity under any circumstances? "Shall we do evil that good may come? God forbid." Where the cause—sin in the church—is removed by full salvation, should not its effects also disappear? But it is thought that "because of differences sects can not yet be abolished." We might say, with equal propriety, because of sects differences can not be removed. They coexist and mutually support each other. These divergent views, and party shibboleths, may have had their root in carnality, but they are stereotyped and perpetuated by sectarian parties and their man-made creeds. Therefore we have no more right to palliate the sin of sects because of differences, than to excuse the latter because of the former. One of the great evils of sectarian divisions is, they prevent the return of the church to the "faith once delivered to the saints"; and shall we let the baneful tree stand until it ceases to bear its legitimate fruit?

Again, it is thought that "sects are a necessity until holiness more generally prevails." "Thorough and wide-spread holiness would soon destroy denominations." Sects and holiness are antagonistic to each other. This truth is clearly implied in the above remarks. The fire of true holiness burns up all the fences that Satan has placed between the saints. And shall we defeat this its real mission, by not lifting up the sword of the Lord against sects, and attempt to abolish the evil, until holiness prevails more extensively? That is the same as saying that we should make no attack on unholiness until holiness gains a certain degree of ascendancy. Yea, it provides that we should give place to the devil in the church to destroy holiness, until the church becomes more holy. These are no trifling words. It is a solemn fact that adherence in different denominations is the devil's wedge, whereby the unity of the Spirit, so perfectly procured in the grace of prefect love, is again destroyed. Party names, party creeds, and party spirits almost of necessity go together; and the natural return of this spirit, because of membership in a fragmentary church, takes more souls off of God's altar than do everything else together.

Let sects alone until holiness prevails! What a device of the enemy! How can we expect to bring forth permanent fruits into holiness, if we allow the plowshare of God's truth to slip over this fallow ground of sin? Sects are the devil's "high places" in the land, the groves of his own planting, and gods that he has set up to corrupt Israel, and "provoke God." How many of the kings Jehovah complains of because they did not, like Josiah, "purge Judah and Jerusalem from the high places and the groves" (2 Chron. 34:3)! Beware that we partake not of their sins. Of Azariah it is said that "he did that which was right in the sight of the Lord ... save that the high places were not removed.... And the Lord smote the king [Azariah] so that he was a leper unto the day of his death" (2 Kings 15:3-5).

Says W. H. Starr (a conscientious Presbyterian minister) after quoting 1 Cor. 1:10-13 in his Discourses on Sectarianism: "It would seem as if no man could read these words of the great apostle without vividly seeing that party divisions among the people of Christ were, in his view, a most astounding evil. 'Is Christ divided,' he says, that ye who are all his, and who have been 'baptized by one Spirit' should be sundered one from the other by party names?

"And he adjures them in the most solemn manner, he beseeches them by an appeal the most sacred that words could utter, even by the name of Christ, as it were for his sake, and for his bleeding cause, to forsake these pernicious ways, and to be perfectly joined together in the same mind."

Hear what this author thinks of promoting holiness over these "high places," or sect walls.

"The divisions of the Christian church, as they now exist, are a prominent cause of the low state of piety among believers; the greatest single obstacle which now exists to the spread and triumph of our religion in the world." "The moment you separate the church of Christ into distinct divisions, you set up the idol of party. Success or adversity will no longer affect the mind simply as they touch the cause of Christ, but they will be felt, also, as affecting 'our side' or 'our church.' It is not Christ and his cause to which their whole thoughts and desires are now turned; the idol of party has now been set up, and it claims, and receives, part of their regard. The man, I think, is almost more than human that can wholly avoid this influence, at least after he has been long identified with any branch of the church. It is an influence which is all the time at work. The idol has been set up to divide the heart from the blessed Savior and his holy service; and its influence is as ceaseless as the existence of the cause. And this party feeling is, as we have seen, the essence of all sin, so that sinful desire is blended continually in the heart with its love to Christ, and pollutes the worship which it offers him."

This is an honest and faithful description of this monster evil. The party feeling is very sin. Yea, says this God-fearing man, "It casts a millstone round the neck of those who are struggling upwards to the image of their Redeemer. It mingles poison with the streams of salvation that flow to the soul through the church, and casts a blight upon its budding fruit."

Again, "Sectarianism is the greatest foe to the exhibition of love which God has ever suffered Satan to beget. It hinders brotherly love among Christians, and regard for the souls of men. It is vain for brethren in Christ to talk about the duty of loving one another, and to try to feel love for one another, while they refuse to act as love dictates [by separating into parties]. Their actions will control their hearts, as men's acts always do in the end. The fences which they set up between them in fact will become fences in **feeling**. And that is now even so, every Christian knows.... The divisions of Christ's people beget and stimulate continually that opposite spirit of rivalry and contention, which is the spirit of the world.... Yes, I charge all this mischief, the existence of which you all know, upon the sectarian divisions of the people of Christ; and let him deny it who can. It is in fact their legitimate fruit."

The division of the church into parties not only destroys the power and holiness thereof, but is the greatest impediment to the conversion of the world to God. Again we will hear Brother Starr, and the blessed Redeemer himself. "Would that the church of Christ might pause long enough from its sectarian strife to hear the voice of its Redeemer and Lord pleading with God in prayer on that sorrowful night ere the traitor came—'Holy Father, keep through thine own name those whom thou hast given me, **that they may be one**, as we are.... Neither pray I for these alone, but for them also which shall believe on me through their word; that they all may be one; as thou, Father, art in me, and I in thee, that they also may be one in us; that the world may believe that thou hast sent me.' The prayers of Christ were not offered for a light matter, least of all that memorable petition which the pen of inspiration has recorded for the church in all ages to wonder and weep over, the prayer of its dying Lord. The desirableness of that visible union of his people for which Christ prayed as the means of impressing his truth on the world, and the evils of those divisions against which the apostle so earnestly exhorts, need to be better understood by the church.... May God grant you a disposition to look the evil fairly in the face."

Oh, the thousands of souls that are being lost to all eternity through the selfish, wicked, and carnal spirit of our churchism! God is dishonored, yea, robbed of the purchase of his Son's death, and infidelity stalks abroad; the result of a divided house.

It is said that "the possessor of perfect love of necessity overleaps denominations in spirit." Does not this love prove that they are in the way of the Spirit of Christ? And shall we compel the Lord to drag his children together over these cursed walls, only to have walls rise up again, and grieve away the Holy Spirit?

If it be true that "thorough holiness destroys denominations," then it follows that where they yet exist this genuine degree of holiness has not been attained by the people. But I have not quoted correctly: it is "thorough and wide-spread holiness." Ah! here is the sticking-point—a condition put in by the enemy of souls. It implies the following: "Though entire sanctification removes all sectarianism out of my heart, I will still adhere to my sect until people generally abandon their schismatic parties and creeds." The devil is perfectly easy over these principles. Now, if this evil is to be done away by popular sentiment, then it is not through holiness; but if by the latter it does not depend upon any foreign influence. The condition of the church in one State does not rob the Word and Spirit of God of their virtue in another. The power of holiness to destroy denominations in one community does not depend in the least upon another. Judah can burn down his groves and destroy his idols, whether Samaria and Ephraim do it or not. Therefore, we repeat, where the professed followers of Christ are divided into a plurality of sects, they have not yet become thoroughly sanctified to God.

Can it be said of professors of holiness that they have "one heart" and "one mind," while some have a mind to be Presbyterian, others Baptists, others United Brethren, and others have a mind to adhere to the several different sects of Methodism? Have they "one heart and one way" when they rise from the solemn altar in the holiness meeting and go, each one in his own way, to the synagog of his own sect?

Now, I must confess that I can not see the necessity of this, unless it be to please the devil, break the unity of the Spirit and grieve away the heavenly Dove, bring to naught the divided house of the Lord, and destroy the work of holiness as fast as it can be built up; to this end alone it is necessary.

But let us come still closer home. I would lay the responsibility of this enormous evil just where God places it and all other sin. We shall not be judged by sects, States, nor even by neighborhoods and towns, but "every one of us shall give account of himself to God."

A revival of holiness in a community is the result of personal consecration and faith; and its relapse will be in proportion to the number of individuals that remove the sacrifice from the sanctifying altar. There is no such thing as thorough holiness, except as wrought by the Sanctifier in individual hearts; and if, as has been said, and as I verily believe, thorough and widespread holiness destroys denominations—burns up sectarian distinctions—it must do it in your heart as an individual. And if this work is done, the fruits must exhibit the fact; you will be 'saved by the precious blood of Christ from all vain conversation, received by tradition from your fathers'; such as "Your church," "Our church," "Our preacher opened the doors of the church," "What branch of the church do you belong to?" "You ought to join some branch," "and if there be any other thing that is contrary to sound doctrine"— that grew out of a "perversion of the right ways of the Lord" and the gospel of Christ (Acts 13:10; Gal. 1:7). If the bitter root of sectism is entirely destroyed out of your heart, you will ignore all sectional lines and party fences, the dreadful curse of which Brother Starr has so honestly pointed out. If you are a true, intelligent Bible Christian, a holy, God-fearing man, you must cast off every human yoke, withdraw fellowship from and renounce every schismatic and humanly constituted party in the professed body of Christ. Instead of belonging to some branch you will simply belong to Christ and be a branch yourself in him, the true vine. Instead of remaining identified with any sect, i. e., cut-off party, "directly or indirectly the result of sin," you will claim membership in and fellowship with the "one and indivisible church that God has on earth, and that is made up of all and singular who are born of the Spirit." On this broad and divinely-established platform, and here only, can you stand clear of the sin of sectarianism and the blood of immortal souls that perish through its pernicious influence. Are you strictly loyal to God while you persist in adhering to a sect, notwithstanding he says "there should be no schism [sects] in the body" (1 Cor. 12:25)?

I am not advocating the no-church theory that we hear of in the West, but the one, holy church of the Bible, not bound together by rigid articles of faith, but perfectly united in love under the primitive glory of the Sanctifier, "continuing stedfastly in the apostle's doctrine and fellowship," and taking captive the world for Jesus.

But it is thought that we should not fight against sects nor attempt to abolish the evil at present, lest we thereby form another sect. This is virtually saying we should go on sinning, "lest a worse thing come upon us!"

An attempt to rally Israel under any of the many party names and creeds might indeed result in a new sect. But this is not what we contend for. Nay, but let us rather burn to ashes these high places of Israel's corruption, and, returning to Jerusalem, let us build "upon the foundation of the apostles and prophets, Jesus Christ himself being the chief corner-stone." Let us abandon the nonsense of ecclesiastical succession; cease to inflate our pride and vanity by parading the good and long-since departed, who innocently wore our party badges—the piety of our fathers will not atone for the worldliness of the church at present. Let us also quit flourishing our church creeds as though their excellency were an essential supplement to the wisdom of inspiration. Let us, we pray you, in the name of Jesus Christ, for the sake of our holy and divine religion and a world that is lost in sin—oh, let us put away these childish things, and return to Jerusalem, not to form a new sect, but as the 'servants of the God of heaven and earth let us build the house that was builded these many years ago, which a great King of Israel [Jesus Christ] builded and set up' (see Ezra 5:11).

Many say we need more union of hearts, but think a visible organic union unnecessary; but remember that it was a visible union that Jesus prayed for, such as the world could see and be thereby convinced and saved. We quote once more from W. H. Starr.

"They will say to me: Can not we have union of feeling without external union [that is, with external disunion]? I answer No, you can not, except in rare instances, and in an imperfect degree. It is vain to be beating off the leaves of the tree while you continually nourish its roots. And sectarianism is the "root of bitterness," whose acrid and legitimate fruit of divided hearts, and jealousy, and strife, doth continually grieve away the Spirit of our God and Savior, and leave our churches in a comparative poverty of grace and growth that methinks must make the very heavens groan with sorrow as they look down upon our dying world. Up, up! my brother, my sister in Christ, inquire of the Lord concerning this thing! Why slumber ye here while Satan has entered the fold of Christ, a wolf in sheep's clothing, and is rending the flock? Oh, cry to God that he will direct you and all the children of his grace, till the church of his holy Son shall be purified and saved. Alas! it is now 'a house divided against itself.' Oh, pray that the Lord would unite and build it up in the truth; and that he would show you your duty in the matter. The wants of the world require a holy and united Church."

From what has been said, and the uniform teaching of the Bible, the following facts are very evident:

1. The division of the church into sects is one of Satan's most effectual, if not the very greatest, means of destroying human souls.

2. Its enormous sin must be answered for by individual adherents to, and supporters of, sects.

3. The only remedy for this dreadful plague is thorough sanctification, and this is wrought only by a personal, individual contact with the blood of Christ through faith.

4. The union required by the Word of God is both a spiritual and visible union.

5. The divisions of the church are caused by elements that are foreign to it as a divinely constituted body, by deposits of the enemy, which exist in the hearts and practises of individual members, involving their responsibility and requiring their personal purgation.

These facts make your duty plain. What you and I want, dear reader, is "thorough and wide-spread holiness" in our individual souls to destroy denominationalism there. Holiness, ever so thorough and wide-spread around you, will not cleanse your heart; neither can the sin of division in the hearts and lives of others attach to you, unless you drink in their spirit and also become a partisan. You need not waste time in planning general union movements, or praying the Lord to restore the unity of his church, until you go down under the blood and have every bone of contention and cause of division purged out of your own heart; then you may do something to influence others to do the same.

You are praying and longing for the happy time when God's children shall all be one, but are you willing that the "once more" shaking shall have its designed effect **in your own case**? Do you, indeed, suffer the Holy Ghost fire to consume out of your own life, heart, religion, and conversation, all the shaky chaff and stubble the devil has made to divide the children of God? Do you, indeed, withdraw from and ignore all churches, so called, but the one Christ purchased "with his own blood" and founded nearly nineteen hundred years ago, and to which the "Lord added" you by regeneration (Acts 2:47)? Do you discard every church title but that "which the mouth of the Lord hath named" (Isa. 62:2), even the name of the Father, in which Christ and the apostles kept the church (John 17:6,11,12; Acts. 20:28; 1 Cor. 1:2; 1 Tim. 3:15)? Do you honor the divine head of the church by rejecting every creed but the one that "is given by inspiration of God;" every door that is opened and shut by men; and every spirit but the Sanctifier; and every motive but the love of God and humanity? If you, by the grace of God, die to all these prime causes of sectism and their concomitant sins, then, and not. until then, will the Lord have "thoroughly purged" so much of "his threshing floor" as you will have to answer for in the day of judgment. Where this is not accomplished, the grace of God is frustrated; holiness is not permitted to reach the Bible standard of thoroughness, nor spread its healing virtue to every part of the soul.

It may look foolish to many thus to blow the trumpet of the Lord around the high and massy walls of sectarian glory and selfishness, but the power of God with the faith and shouts of the "holy people" will surely bring them down. Though the heaps of sectarian chaff have reached the magnitude of mountains, God has some wheat scattered through them, and he will have it separated for his garner. Therefore he says to Jacob, "Fear not ... thou shalt thresh the mountains, and beat them small, and thou shalt make the hills as chaff. Thou shalt fan them, and the wind shall carry them away, and the whirlwind shall scatter them."

The pure elements of God's church possess a wonderful inherent attraction and cohesion; but the devil neutralizes the divine cement by mixing in his chaffy and sloughy trash, thereby effecting divisions; therefore, the Lord restores union by the "removing of those things that are shaken, as of things that are made" by the enemy, thus removing discord and schism. Glory to God! Little Jacob has barely commenced threshing and separating. Soon we shall see clouds of chaff driven by the "mighty rushing wind from heaven."

Says Bro. I. Reed, in his paper, The Highway: "The great holiness movement is shaking harder than ever. It is to be a real moral earthquake yet. We have nothing to fear in that direction. We have allied ourselves to the Power that does the shaking, and feel a kind of holy joy at the falling walls, reeling Babels and ecclesiastical fortifications that can not stand the grand holiness shock. In anticipation we enjoy the grand smash-up of things semi-religious—this half and half, linsey-woolsey type of 'Good God, Dear Mammon,' kind of fashionable moral froth, too often called 'religion'—that is coming some of these days. It is coming. We hear the tread of the mighty army."

Amen. Let the conflict come. God will have a pure church. He will shake the chaffy works of the devil out of his kingdom, though all hell be moved in rage; though Gog and Magog surround the camp of the saints on the breadth of the whole earth.

Dear reader, I am aware that I have here written things that will be unwelcome to many, truths that will assail and stir up many prejudices; but in doing so I have determined to cast from me the fear of man, and clear my conscience in the sight of God.

It is, indeed, my honest conviction that the great holiness reform can not go forward with the sweeping power and permanent triumph that God designs it should until the gospel be so preached and consecration become so thorough that the blood of Christ may reach and wash away every vestige of denominational distinction, and "perfect into one"—yea, one indeed and in truth—all the sanctified.

I am aware that this will elicit storms of persecution, but in the name of the Lord it must come. God will be glorified in the escape of his holy children from all human enclosures into the "one" and identical "fold of Jesus Christ." Oh! let us be honest before God in this matter.

Prophetic Truth.

Prophetic Truth.

D. S. Warner.   (Ezek. 34:12-14; Isa. 51:11.)   B. F. Bear.

1. 'Twas sung by the po-ets, fore-seen in the Spir-it, A time of re-
2. We stand in the glo-ry that Je-sus has giv-en, The moon, as the
3. Now filled with the Spir-it and clad in the ar-mor Of light, and om-
4. The proph-et's keen vi-sion, trans-pierc-ing the a-ges, Be-held us to
5. The fig-tree is bud-ding, the "eve-ning" is shin-ing, We wel-come the

fresh-ing is near; When creeds and di-vi-sions would fall to de-mer-it,
day-spring doth shine; The light of the sun is now e-qual to sev-en,
nip-o-tent truth; We'll tes-ti-fy ev-er, and Je-sus we'll hon-or,
Zi-on re-turn; We'll sing of our free-dom, tho' Ba-by-lon ra-ges,
won-der-ful light! We look for the Sav-ior, for time is de-clin-ing,

And saints in sweet un-ion ap-pear.
So bright is the glo-ry di-vine.
And stand from sin Ba-bel a-loof.
We'll shout as her cit-y doth burn.
E-ter-ni-ty's loom-ing in sight!

Chorus.

Oh, glo-ry to Je-sus! we

hail the bright day, And high on our ban-ner sal-va-tion dis-play,

The mists of con-fu-sion are pass-ing a-way.

CHAPTER XIII

A PROPHETIC TIME

Many world events foreshadowed in prophecy—God has a design
with man—Events of the world grouped in periods—The four
world empires—The fourth given particular attention—The little horn of Daniel 7—Time periods of Romanism and Protestantism—Corresponding prophecies in Revelation—What Babylon
is—God's people called out of her.

That many events of the world are foreshadowed in the prophecies of the Bible is something which perhaps the average reader does not pause much to reflect
upon. He rather inclines to regard the prophecies as a difficult portion of the Sacred Writings, and in consequence of their being passed by, ignorance generally
prevails concerning them. There is nothing inconsistent in the idea that events in
the world occur in accordance with prophetic utterance. It does not necessarily
give credence to the doctrine of fatalism—that everything which happens must
happen. The affairs in man's life are largely subject to his control. He has a scope
of freedom all his own. He can make his own choices and govern his own career.
He may do an act or he may not do it. An accident occurs which may have been
avoided had more care been exercised. Nevertheless, from this free volitionary
scope which belongs to man we may not exclude God's design; for he does exercise a controlling hand in the affairs of man.

It may be said, however, of the greater things that occur in the world, the trend
of public thought, the drift of conditions, the great political upheavals, things
which are rather beyond man's individual control, and which involve mankind
as a body and their destiny as a race—these more particularly belong to God and
are made the subject of prophetic forecast. God did not create the world and then
abandon its processes. He created all things according to design, and we may be
assured that he has design in the progress of things as well as in their first creation.
Nor will the grand play of the world's events reach its conclusion without the de-
cree of him whose prerogative it is to say, "It is enough; time shall no longer be."

Christ's coming into the world was freely prophesied hundreds of years in
advance of that event. This is so plain that no student of the Bible, unless he means
purposely to be infidelic, will dispute the fact. Likewise, the fulfilment of prophecies that went before concerning the Jews and their city Jerusalem is much in
evidence.

The events of the world naturally group themselves into periods, or epochs.

They are like panoramic scenes that unfold in the theater of the universe. Thus we have the two dispensations separated by the incarnation of Christ, the grandest event in all history. And thus we have, as divisions of the latter dispensation, the event of paganism giving place to the papacy and ushering in a dark day of apostasy, known in history as the Dark Ages; and the Renaissance and the Reformation of the sixteenth century, ushering in a period of Protestantism, which is also an age of letters and invention.

In the interests of his church and the progress of his truth God has shown in advance in prophetic vision the periods and epochal events covering not only the Christian dispensation, but also a considerable time previous to it. These are for the Bible-student, the minister of God, and for all Christians, to know and understand.

There is a prophecy in the 7th chapter of Daniel fore-shadowing the four successive world empires—the Babylonian, Medo Persian, Grecian, and Roman—and the papal power, that grew out of the Roman. The book of Revelation is but a series of panoramic displays of the events of the entire Christian dispensation and the end of the world.

And so we may expect that, inasmuch as the prophecies served primarily the interests of the church, or the New Testament kingdom, any marked advance for the church, such as the deliverance of the saints from spiritual Babylon, should have its foregleam in the utterance of the seer. In our preceding chapter, Brother Warner has already given quotations from the prophets relating to bringing out a pure church through the preaching of holiness. We wish to show by several other lines of prophecy that this state of the church, as being free from the bondage of human ecclesiasticism and enjoying her primitive glory, marks a distinct prophetic time or period in this evening of the dispensation.

Referring again to the 7th chapter of Daniel, where four successive world kingdoms are represented by the four beasts, we note that special attention is given to the description of the fourth beast, which is the Roman power in its pagan phase. It was a beast "dreadful and terrible, and strong exceedingly; and it had great iron teeth: it devoured and brake in pieces, and stamped the residue with the feet of it: and it was diverse from all the beasts that were before it; and it had ten horns. I considered the horns, and, behold, there came up among them another little horn, before whom there were three of the first horns plucked up by the roots: and, behold, in this horn were eyes like the eyes of man, and a mouth speaking great things" (vs. 7, 8).

Daniel wished to know the truth respecting the little horn that had eyes like the eyes of a man, and a mouth speaking great things. He beheld that the "same horn made war with the saints, and prevailed against them; until the Ancient of days came, and judgment was given to the saints of the Most High; and the time came that the saints possessed the kingdom" (vs. 21, 22). Now this horn that came up from among the other ten horns was nothing other than the elements of Roman Catholicism, developing into popery. It was the "man of sin," the product of the substitution of man rule for the Holy Spirit rule, the date for which change historians have fixed at about the year 270 A. D. This horn was to "speak great words against the Most High," and to "wear out the saints of the Most High, and think to change times and laws: and they shall be given into his hand until a time and times and the dividing of time. But the judgment shall sit, and they shall take away his dominion, to consume and to destroy it unto the end. And the kingdom and dominion, and the greatness of the kingdom under the whole heaven, shall be given to the people of the saints of the Most High, whose kingdom is an everlasting kingdom, and all dominions shall serve and obey him" (vs. 25-27).

The "time and times and the dividing of time," marking the period during which the elements of the papacy should have full sway and should wear out the saints of the Most High, etc., are interpreted as three and one half years; a time in prophetic reckoning being one year, times two years, and the dividing of time one half year. Three and one half years would be forty-two months, or, if reduced to days according to the Jewish reckoning of thirty days to the month, twelve hundred and sixty days. Taking each day for a year, which is proper prophetic counting, we have twelve hundred and sixty years, and this added to the year 270 brings us to the year 1530, the date of the beginning of organized Protestantism, and the end of the universal sway of the papacy. Following this, "the judgment shall sit, and they shall take away his dominion, to consume and to destroy it unto the end" (v. 26). Since her universal spiritual supremacy ended, the judgment against Roman Catholicism has gradually proceeded and her political power has waned. "And the time came when the saints possessed the kingdom" (v. 22). The saints' possessing the kingdom is the culminating point in this line of prophecy, and means nothing other than the victory over human ecclesiasticism which the saints now possess.

In the 11th chapter of Revelation we have the wearing out of the saints expressed as treading under foot the holy city, and the time-period of "a time and times and the dividing of time" expressed as forty-two months (v. 2). In v. 3 the same time-period is expressed as twelve hundred and sixty days. During this time the two witnesses—the Word and the Spirit—prophesy in sackcloth, which represents the low estate to which they were relegated during the dark age of popery. It will be remembered that the twelve hundred and sixty days (years) end with the year 1530. Following this comes three days and a half (three centuries and a half) of Protestantism during which the two witnesses (Word and Spirit) are, in the governmental sense, operatively dead, the organized systems of man rule having usurped the place of divine government and authority which these witnesses originally held. At the end of the three days and a half, three hundred and fifty years (which, added to 1530, brings us to the year 1880) "the Spirit of life from God entered into them, and they stood upon their feet" (v. 11). They ascended to their place in the ecclesiastical heaven, to the true church, and were thus victorious. This brings us to the present reformation. This is soon followed by the sounding of the seventh angel, which represents the end of time when the 'kingdoms of this world shall become the kingdoms of our Lord and his Christ; and he shall reign forever and ever' (v. 15). The curtain drops.

Another scene is presented in the 13th chapter, where the rise of the papacy, or Roman Catholic power, is represented by a leopard beast having the same "mouth speaking great things" that appeared in the "little horn" of Daniel seven. "And power was given unto him to continue forty and two months" (v. 5), which is the same time-period, again, of twelve hundred and sixty years. Following this the period of Protestantism is represented by a beast "coming up out of the earth; and he had two horns like a lamb, and he spake as a dragon" (v. 11). The length of the time-period of this second beast is here omitted, but the sphere of its activity is succeeded (in chap. 14) by a victorious church, the fall of Babylon, and the present reformation work in which the everlasting gospel, the gospel that really saves, is once more preached "unto them that dwell on the earth." In connection with this also is the judgment which Daniel says is "given to the saints of the Most High;" that is, the judgment against the false religions of spiritual Babylon.

In the 18th chapter, in connection with Babylon's fall, we have God's people called out of her. "And I heard another voice from heaven, saying, Come out of her, my people, that ye be not partakers of her sins, and that ye receive not of her plagues. For her sins have reached unto heaven, and God hath remembered her iniquities. Reward her even as she rewarded you, and double unto her double according to her works: in the cup which she hath filled fill to her double" (vs. 4-6). Thus the time is come that 'judgment is given to the saints' and the 'saints possess the kingdom.'

Spiritual Babylon represents Rome first, and Protestantism second. In the Critical Commentary by Jamieson, Fausset, and Brown, in the comments on Rev. 18:4, we have the following quoted from Hahn in Auberlen: "The harlot is not Rome alone (though she is preeminently so), but every Church that has not Christ's mind and spirit. False Christendom, divided into very many sects, is truly Babylon, i. e., confusion." The literal Babylon was an ancient city situated on the Euphrates River. In it God's people Israel were held captive for seventy years, or until liberated by the Persian king Cyrus. This is used as a figure of the captivity of God's spiritual Israel in spiritual Babylon. The word Babylon means confusion, and it is fittingly applied to the confused religion as represented by the whole picture of Roman Catholicism and the Protestant sects.

In the 34th chapter of Ezekiel the gathering of God's people and their deliverance from false relations is represented by a shepherd seeking out his flock and delivering them. "As a shepherd seeketh out his flock in the day that he is among his sheep that are scattered; so will I seek out my sheep, and will deliver them out of all places where they have been scattered in the cloudy and dark day. And I will bring them out from the people, and gather them from the countries, and will bring them to their own land, and feed them upon the mountains of Israel by the rivers, and in all the inhabited places of the country. I will feed them in a good pasture, and upon the high mountains of Israel shall their fold be: there shall they lie in a good fold, and in a fat pasture shall they feed upon the mountains of Israel" (vs. 12-14).

The cloudy and dark day of Protestantism, when the light of truth shines, not in its entire brightness, nor yet as entirely obscured, is also referred to in the 14th chapter of Zechariah. "And it shall come to pass in that day, that the light shall not be clear, nor dark: but it shall be one day which shall be known to the Lord, not day, nor night: but it shall come to pass, that at evening time it shall be light" (vs. 6, 7). Thank God, the day of mingled light is past, and we are in the full light of the evening, when the whole truth is once more preached in its fullness, without hypocrisy and without reserve.

Thus we see that the present movement among God's people toward holiness and unity, out of denominationalism, is prophetically represented as a new epoch for the church.

Louder, Louder.

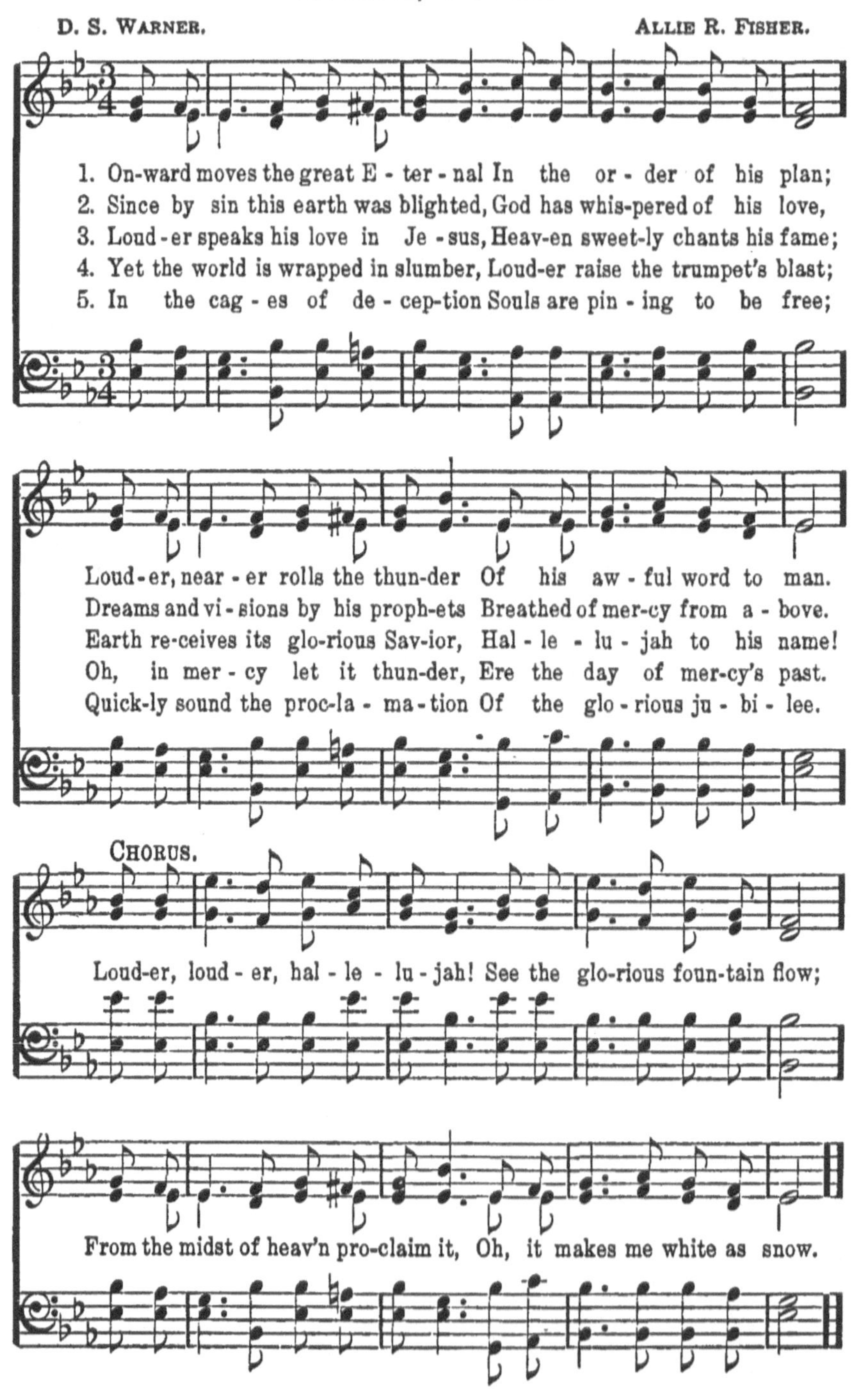

Louder, Louder.

D. S. Warner.   Allie R. Fisher.

1. On-ward moves the great E-ter-nal In the or-der of his plan;
2. Since by sin this earth was blighted, God has whis-pered of his love,
3. Loud-er speaks his love in Je-sus, Heav-en sweet-ly chants his fame;
4. Yet the world is wrapped in slumber, Loud-er raise the trumpet's blast;
5. In the cag-es of de-cep-tion Souls are pin-ing to be free;

Loud-er, near-er rolls the thun-der Of his aw-ful word to man.
Dreams and vi-sions by his proph-ets Breathed of mer-cy from a-bove.
Earth re-ceives its glo-rious Sav-ior, Hal-le-lu-jah to his name!
Oh, in mer-cy let it thun-der, Ere the day of mer-cy's past.
Quick-ly sound the proc-la-ma-tion Of the glo-rious ju-bi-lee.

Chorus.

Loud-er, loud-er, hal-le-lu-jah! See the glo-rious foun-tain flow;

From the midst of heav'n pro-claim it, Oh, it makes me white as snow.

CHAPTER XIV

THE GOSPEL TRUMPET

Consolidation of Herald of Gospel Freedom with the Pilgrim, forming
the Gospel Trumpet—Rome City its birthplace—Move to Indianapolis—Difficulties and privations—Paper issued irregularly—
Printed on hand-press—Move to Cardington, Ohio, and later to
Bucyrus—To Williamston, Mich., in 1884, and to Grand Junction
in 1886—Substantial progress.

After the Board of Publication of the Northern Indiana Eldership had passed
the resolution in November, 1880, that they were willing to consolidate the Herald
of Gospel Freedom with any other paper that advocated the same gospel principles, a consolidation was effected with a small paper called The Pilgrim, published
in Indianapolis, by G. Haines. The Pilgrim was a monthly and had been issued but
about eight times. The Herald equipment, it should be remarked, had been donated to Brothers Warner and Haines by the Churches of God in Indiana for the new
paper.[9] The decision to effect this consolidation was made in a joint meeting of
the Board of Publication and the Standing Committee held in Yellow Lake Bethel,
Kosciusko County, Ind., Dec. 23, 1880. In an old memorandum tablet of Brother
Warner's is recorded what is apparently a report of this meeting, in his own handwriting. One paragraph, which reads as follows, is of special interest:

"On motion it was agreed to consolidate the Herald of Gospel Freedom with
the Pilgrim, at Indianapolis, Ind., and call the new the Gospel Trumpet."

Though he modestly does not say so, it was Brother Warner himself who suggested the name Gospel Trumpet. He felt impressed that the new paper should be
called by that name, the idea being associated with such scriptures as the following:

[9] It seems the idea prevailed within the Eldership that "every member should be under the control of Christ alone in the performance of work appointed him." They said, "We
believe that the Lord wishes not his church burthened and perplexed with financial cares.
Therefore, Resolved That it is not good that she should own and control a printing-office."
They said further, "We are willing to assist and support these two brethren in the joint
publication of the Gospel Trumpet provided they are permitted to have full control of the
same and so long as they keep themselves and the paper wholly in the Lord's hands and
to his glory."

They, of course, did not understand that by means of a corporation, board of trustees,
or other legalized body, the church could control its printing business and yet not be "burthened and perplexed with financial cares."

"The great *trumpet* shall be blown, and they shall come ... and shall worship the Lord in the holy mount" (from Isa. 27:13). "The Lord God shall blow the *trumpet*, and shall go with whirlwinds" (from Zech. 9: 14).

A scripture containing the word "trumpet" always appeared in the heading of the paper. After a few years the heading contained the design of a flying angel blowing a trumpet from which was suspended a scroll containing this inscription, taken from Zech. 5:2-4: "He said unto me. What seest thou? And I answered, I see a flying roll.... Then said he unto me.... Every one that stealeth shall be cut off as on this side according to it; and everyone that sweareth shall be cut off as on that side according to it. I will bring it forth, saith the Lord of hosts."

At a later date the design was changed, the angel was reversed, and the following was substituted as an inscription on the scroll: "All ye inhabitants of the world, and dwellers on the earth, see ye, when he lifteth up an ensign on the mountains; and when he bloweth a trumpet, hear ye" (Isa. 18:3). For many years the heading design contained one or more angels blowing the trumpet.

Brother Warner was a man wonderfully anointed of God for a special work. Since he had received the experience of sanctification, in 1877, the Lord had been gradually revealing to him that the true and divinely intended state of the people of God was not that of being scattered in a multiplicity of sectarian divisions but of being perfectly one in Christ, not only in spirit, but in name and in visible aspect. He felt that the teaching of genuine holiness would, in connection with the light of the prophecies bearing on the subject, bring the church out into her pure, undivided state. For such a reformation he was indeed a chosen instrument of the Lord. It was God's truth he was preaching. It led, of course, to a crisis in which he received much persecution and was deserted by many. The Trumpet, he realized, was a very effectual instrument God had placed in his hands for accomplishing the great reformation-work in this evening time of the Christian era. The time was ripe. True saints of God in various places, in whom was the Spirit of the Lord, were desiring and anticipating a oneness for God's people, and when the Trumpet appeared it was just what they were wanting. The fact that it was considered insignificant and ignored in popular religious circles proved its mission none the less divine. God's work is frequently accomplished by insignificant instruments. The Trumpet shared Brother Warner's difficulties and deprivations. The description of these in the spiritual phase will be reserved for the next chapter. What we shall note here are some of the mere facts of its history.

The oldest copy of the Gospel Trumpet now in the files of the Publishing Office is of the issue of March 1, 1881. The paper began with January 1 of that year, at Rome City, Ind. Two issues were printed there, then the equipment was moved to Indianapolis. The removal occasioned some delay, so that there was no paper printed during the month of February. The new location was over N. 70 North Illinois St. The paper started as a semimonthly, at a subscription price of seventy-five cents a year. Agents were allowed a commission of fifteen cents on each subscription in clubs of five or upwards. Its object was stated as being, "The glory of God in the salvation of men from all sin, and the union of all saints upon the Bible." It was a four-page, five-column paper of about 13 by 19 inches in size. It at first contained considerable matter on prohibition; but the thing that brought it persecution and isolated it from the fellowship and sympathy of nominal professors was its teaching against sectarian divisions.

THE GOSPEL TRUMPET.

On motion it was agreed to consolidate the Herald of Gospel Freedom, with the Pilgrim — at Indianapolis Ind. and call this new, the Gospel-Trumpet

Fascimile of a copy of the Gospel Trumpet dated Mar. 1, 1881, the oldest in the Company's files. A paragraph from Brother Warner's notes.

Financial privation was one of the handicaps that had to be contended with from the start. On the moving of the equipment to Indianapolis, new type to the amount of $147 had to be purchased. At this time also a new Prouty power-press costing $590 was contemplated, the old press being a Washington hand-press. It was some years, however, until a power-press was installed. In the issue of May 15, 1881, appears the following editorial:

> We are experiencing that it takes a man wonderfully burned out for God to publish a paper that is simply true to Jesus and up to the Bible standard of salvation from all sin. A thousand points of expediency and policy must be disregarded, and the eye fixed on God alone. O reader, you that love God and the truth, do not forget to pray for us. We are here in the city with a family to support, and publishing expenses to meet, and many are withdrawing from us because we will not sanction their idols; but God is always present, and we fear no evil. Thus far, since the paper is all on God's altar, he has supplied our needs. Glory to his name!

Another difficulty that had to be contended with almost from the start was the unfaithfulness of some of those associated with him. He was scarcely settled in Indianapolis when the partnership with Haines had to be dissolved, and the latter then started an opposition paper. The following editorial from the June 1 number will explain:

THE OPPOSITION PAPER

> No person that has the real cause of God at heart can fail to deplore the fact that in this city two papers are now being published, both claiming to be holiness papers, having of course conflicting interests.

> That this state of affairs must weaken and wound this sacred cause, and hedge up its way by destroying the confidence of the people in the great truth of holiness, is very apparent to all thinking minds. This being true, fearful responsibilities rest somewhere, and the people have a right to know where.

> It is a painful task to refer to the reproach that is brought upon the pure cause of holiness; but it is largely known, and can be remedied only by a statement of the causes and terms of the dissolution of the Trumpet firm. Two papers in the same place with rival interests can not both be of God—there is no use trying to smuggle the fact.

> The blame must be located, and though its location exposes personal character, it must be done. Paul wrote even with tears of some whom he pronounced enemies of the cross of Christ. Alas, how often the blessed Son of God is sacrificed at the shrine of selfishness, and sold for a few pieces of money!

The office having been donated by the Church of God in northern Indiana, for the use of the Trumpet, we entered into a consolidation and partnership, agreeing that "each should do one half of the labor, pay one half of the expenses, and receive one half of the income."

We went to work in good earnest, published two papers at Rome City, and then shipped the office to this city.

But before it arrived we found ourself bound to a chilling iceberg, an austere, worldly, complaining, and mere money policy. Though rather incongenial to our feelings, we thought it probably all for the better and were willing to go ahead; but ere long the Spirit of God clearly indicated to us that we should not work with this man. We gave the matter all into the hands of God, and told the Lord that if he wished a dissolution, he should bring it about in his own time and his own way.

We had made no note of labors at Rome City, but thought when we set up here we should be under the necessity of doing so; but wishing to avoid every shadow of blame for the separation that we knew was coming, we continued to waive our right in the agreement, and went on working for the Lord, while partner gave his time to the Cincinnati Times-Star, with the exception of an occasional call of a few minutes at the office.

It pleased God to withhold a competent income from the paper. This soon wrought a divine purpose, and partner proposed to dissolve—offered to give or take one hundred dollars, and the party taking the office pay all the debts on the firm. Having the will of God clearly revealed to us, we could not, without disloyalty to God and infidelity to the brethren who donated the office, abandon it. We also had one hundred and seventy dollars in the office that partner did not, having released notes to that amount against those churches when they kindly donated the office.

We remarked, however, that as the office had been given for the use of the Trumpet, it was not right that, withdrawing from the paper, he should ask that amount of money. But the answer was that the Pilgrim field which had been merged into the Trumpet was worth that to him. We therefore consented to pay the one hundred dollars to satisfy him for the field. But when we remarked that he of course would feel himself under obligations not to start another paper here, both because of the amount received for the field, and for shame's sake, as it could only expose the cause to reproach, we were surprized that he would not make a fair promise. We insisted upon it as our right, and he remarked finally that he did not think he would start another. Just then the Spirit said, "Trust it in the hands of the Lord, God will himself manage the matter." From that time we said no more about it....

We feel that our skirts are clear from the harm that holiness must suffer from this bad example to the world. And if God can bless the little opposition sheet (for such is the spirit of its first issue) we shall be thankful.

Bless the Lord! We have nothing to fear, because we have nothing to lose. The Trumpet is indeed all burned up for God; but out of its ashes shall continue to rise honest, holy, God-fearing pilgrims, instead of "happy pilgrims" who rejoice in unrighteous gain. God is now on trial. He is our only resource. On the other hand, a crafty policy slyly gets up a little paper, changes the association meeting from **home** to Terre Haute, presents it to the congregation, gets **four votes** in its favor, then himself pronounces it adopted; is elated that he was "sharp" enough to get the one hundred dollars and the field also, and now boasts that he will take away the Trumpet subscribers. O Lord, pity and save such a one for Christ's sake!

Just now we feel a deeper concern for his salvation than for all we may suffer through his competition. Though doubtless we shall lose some readers through this assumed organ of the State association, a thing that lives only in name, and whose head, professing to be called to labor in the vineyard of the Lord as a gospel minister, prefers the vineyard of the worldly paper as more lucrative, we are thankful that the Gospel Trumpet rests only upon God and its own merits.

Our Father in heaven still owns the universe. Truth has not lost its power, neither have the **four votes** cast at Terre Haute dethroned the Almighty. Halleluiah! Jesus reigns.

After dissolution of partnership with Haines, Brother Warner was supplied with a colaborer in J. C. Fisher, who took a half interest, and was very effectual in starting the work in Michigan, where he resided.[10]

Illustrative of the poverty of the Trumpet in its infancy as well as the construction of the first publishing office, is another editorial from the June 1 number here given. The location of this new office was on Brother Warner's lot at 625 West Vermont St., adjoining his residence.

AN OFFICE FOR THE TRUMPET

As we have over a mile to walk to our office and have to pay $5 a month for rent, we felt led of the Lord to build an office on our lot. We had a small stable that would afford some material, and, trusting that God would send help, we began to tear it down in the name of the Lord. So the other day a dear old saint who is a carpenter came to inquire what we had to build with. We told

[10] See next chapter.

him, when he said he had some lumber to add, also door and plenty of windows, which he would give very cheap, and give work also.

We are now looking to God for some means, perhaps thirty dollars, to buy shingles and some other material. Now, dearly beloved reader, as both our family duties and the necessity of curtailing expenses, as well as saving time, require us to build this office, it may be that on account thereof we shall not be able to issue a paper for the 15th of June. Please remember this and do not be disappointed if no paper reaches you. There are two other reasons why it will be somewhat difficult to issue the next number. First, we have a tabernacle in operation and we desire to work all we can in these direct efforts to save souls. And, second, we think of taking charge of the office and doing most of the work on the paper ourself hereafter; and having but a slight experience in compository work, we shall need to have more time on the first paper. But withal we shall issue a paper if possible. If the Lord has given you a few dollars for the office, send it on. Amen.

In explanation of why he was not able to issue the paper regularly he writes as follows for August 15 of that same year:

The announcement that the paper would be on time would have been carried out so far as the work on the paper is concerned, but it did not please the Lord to send us the means to purchase the paper, hence the delay. Well, we are willing that God should stop the Trumpet altogether if he will. It belongs wholly to him, and so do we, and, bless God, we have nothing to say about it. Oh, how perfectly dead to all self in the matter! We will say to our readers that the Trumpet shall only be issued as the Lord furnishes the means; every two weeks if possible, if not, let all know that it was not in our power to do so, and that all our subscribers shall have the worth of the money paid. Owing to the past delays and the fact that we are led to attend some camp-meetings, we skip one number with the present issue.

In the November 1 number we notice more privation.

We did not move, neither were we able to plaster our office. How then do you think we managed to get out this paper? We will tell you. Dear Wife tendered her kitchen to the Lord for the use of publishing salvation. Praise the Lord! By thus crowding in a sufficient amount of the office to get along for the winter we shall save fuel, and the expense of finishing the office until next fall. Thank God, we are willing to get along any way for Christ's sake, so that we may fulfil our mission and publish truth and righteousness. We are not at all mortified at these humble facilities from which the Trumpet goes forth to its readers. Christ started his earthly mission from a manger. Oh no, we are not ashamed to let all men know that the Trumpet is published in the rear of a small cottage. God's presence makes the whole domicil sacred. Oh, how wonderfully he pours out his glory on our souls in this work!

On the other hand, there were others in whom God had planted a love for the truth. Among these was Brother Warner's faithful printer. God had preserved a few who should contribute sufficient to the paper to keep it going.

HOW IT LOOKS TO OTHERS

We know that many think it big to be an editor, hence before and ever since we entered upon this work we have feared and dreaded being actuated by such motives. When we go out to work in the field and we just tell God to let the Trumpet stop if it is his will and we will keep right on evangelizing, the Spirit's voice soon compels us to return to this sacred charge.

Once when we had the office up in the city, God tried us thoroughly. We had no money to pay the printer, and he was out of meal-tickets, which must be paid in advance. We were sent for to come to a meeting in Terre Haute. A brother wrote that he would pay our fare, so we borrowed the money and went down on Saturday morning. We told the Lord that if he did not want the paper to continue, to let the printer leave and get work somewhere else. As we walked from the depot to the office on our return, Monday eve, we said, If that young man is in the office it is the wonderful dealing of God. We entered and found him cheerfully working away. On Saturday he ran the press all day without a bite to eat. As he told us this our heart was melted. We entered our little sanctum and poured out our soul to God, and he sent the Spirit as the dews of heaven upon our heart.

When we started for the Camargo camp-meeting, we had a few dimes. Having been provided with a free pass, through the kindness of Brother — —, who wrote that for months he had not thought of the camp-meeting without seeing us on the program and that we must be there without fail, we left with Wife all our change but two nickels. Told our printer that as we had no money to give him he might quit if he saw fit and hunt a position where he could get his pay. We remarked that as the Trumpet was not ours we had no choice whether it lived or died. Well, it cost us five cents to reach the depot by street-car, and the other nickel to carry us and baggage from the train to camp-ground, so we just had enough. Praise God from whom all blessings flow! Though we were brought there by the direction of God's Spirit through Brother — —, the high priest in charge, probably out of self-interest, gave us no place in the pulpit. But God gave us a field to work in, and the hearts of the "people who do know their God," and, blessed be his name, in that meeting he gave us over sixty-one dollars. So the Trumpet still sends out the certain sound. Here is a sample of many letters received the last few months. It will show how others see the Trumpet in relation to God's will and Satan's dread:

> "Ah yes, Brother Warner, it is the Trumpet the devil wants stopped. You may evangelize all you please, so the Trumpet goes under, and the devil doesn't care. Do stand by the Trumpet at all hazards."

> Of course we know that all such expressions relate to the awful and offensive truth of God that we give place to in the Trumpet, and not to any ability we possess to write or conduct a paper. We are too sorely and constantly pinched by a sense of our own ignorance to think anything else.

In the November 15 number, under the heading, The Trumpet Will Go On, we have the following:

> God has blessed us with excellent health and strength. Praise his holy name! We can work without apparent fatigue from 5 A. M. to 11 P. M., and we propose doing so, by the continued help of God. We feel that the gates of hell can not stop the truth. And if we can not issue the paper regularly every two weeks, we will issue as often as we can, and give everybody his or her full number of papers. The Lord holds us to this work, and he can not forsake us in the work whereunto he has called us. Let all the readers of the Trumpet obey the voice of the Spirit of God, and there will be means both to enlarge and carry on the paper for the glory of God. Oh, if the God of salvation could but reach some who are blessed with means and draw out about two hundred dollars it would pay all the Trumpet debts, get the necessities to enlarge the paper, and provide a good little stock of paper to start with. We will work, and pray, and trust, and God and the dear people will provide the means.

At the beginning of the second year the price of the Trumpet was raised to one dollar.

> For some time before the Trumpet raised to one dollar, nearly everybody sent us one dollar instead of seventy-five cents. Thus the Lord has fixed the price, and he will provide for its enlargement.

The enlargement came with the first issue in February. It was made a six-column, four pages—15 by 22. In the first issue of the new size we find the following editorial:

> We printed two thousand papers this issue. It is quite a task

on our hand-press; but, praise God, he gives us blessed health and strength, and we are perfectly satisfied to work on with the means the Lord has furnished, until he sees proper to give us others.

Early in the autumn of 1882 the publishing office was moved to Cardington, Ohio. Here was a congregation of saints among whom the publishing work could be better supported. A very pleasant office, warm and well lighted, was rented for thirty dollars a year. Brother Warner acknowledges his enjoyment of the great kindness, love, and cooperation of the true saints there. It seems, however, that even there the work did not make much progress. The old press had by this time become very unsatisfactory. Brother Warner sought to hire his printing work done elsewhere, but his effort resulted in his having to print the first issue of 1883 on a job-press, with the paper reduced in size to a four-column 11 by 15. The price was dropped to seventy-five cents, then to fifty cents. The following editorial will give an insight to his situation:

THIS LITTLE TRUMPET

Having had our last issue printed on our neighbor's steam-press, we concluded it would pay us to trade our old press on a jobber and have them print the paper regularly.

Our chief reason for so doing was this: in the time that it would take us to print them on the slow old press, we could make more on job-work than would pay the printing. But, behold, when our neighbors learned that we were getting a job-press, they seemed to think we were intruding on their territory, and not having the utmost confidence in their typographical ability they thought to make us pay a sort of royalty for the privilege of doing job-work here, by raising the price of printing the trumpet from four dollars to eight dollars an issue; and while we conceded the perfect right to charge that price, we were happy for the privilege of saving that amount and printing on our job-press.

Of course, we can print but one page at a time, which makes four impressions for a folio; and if we print as large as the Trumpet has been, it will take eight times running through the press, which, after all, can be done in about the same time it took to print it in two impressions on the old press, and takes one to run instead of three.

When the paper comes to you only half the old size we will call it but a half number, so we will not defraud our subscribers in the least. But we desire to send you eight pages every two weeks if we possibly can. When we can not, please bear with us until the kind providence of God and the liberality of the saints help us to get a paper-press.

The eight-page proposition did not then materialize. About this time was adopted the motto, which was carried for many years: "First pure, then valiant for the truth." The home of the Gospel Trumpet was not long at Cardington. Brother Warner was desirous of having a permanent home for the Trumpet, where he would not have to pay rent. When he moved to Cardington, he did not feel that that would be the permanent place for the paper. Kind brethren in Michigan made very liberal offers and asked him to come there; but a place was opening at Bucyrus, twenty miles distant, in Crawford County. While he was in prayer pleading earnestly for God's direction, three teams drove up. It was the brethren from Bucyrus, who had come to move the office to that place and also help it out of financial difficulties. There was great joy in Brother Warner's heart as he realized that God had answered prayer and sent help. One of these brethren, D. D. Johnston, assisted in the matter of finances. He purchased a lot and furnished material with which to erect a building. His name appeared as publisher in August, 1883.

Brother Warner proceeded to build a small office on the lot at Bucyrus. In the last number printed at Cardington he writes as follows:

> While you read this paper, the editor will be personally at work erecting a house in which to carry on the work of the Lord. If we were building a house for ourself we should want to count the cost before commencing; but we are building this house unto the Lord, and the earth and the fulness thereof are his, hence, we need not stop to count since he says go forward. The undertaking is wholly by faith. While at work with our hands we shall pray without ceasing to our heavenly Father to send us the means.

*   *   *   *   *

> We have had experience enough in our business to know that we never can carry on the paper and pay rent. It is claimed that a paper is not self-supporting with most any number of subscribers without receiving advertisements. Just yesterday in the office of a temperance paper we were told by an editor and publisher that we ought to take in one thousand dollars every year for advertisements, and he could not see how the paper could be carried otherwise. But, beloved, it must be carried otherwise or not at all. Neither do we wish to do any secular job-work if we can help it. We shall dispose of our job-press and material as soon as possible. Now, beloved, when we shall have obtained a good paper-press (and it is already bought, thank God) and a place free of rent, with much self-denial and care we shall be able to send you a paper 22 by 32 every two weeks.

> Some of our dear brethren have in love censured us occasionally. We find generally these two points, sometimes in the same letter, namely, "Why do you not send your paper out more frequently and more regularly?" the other, "I think you have not been on your guard enough to keep out of debt." Well, there it is. We could have kept entirely out of debt if we had issued fewer papers, and we might have issued every two weeks had we gone

more in debt. But no one of our experience could possibly have issued more frequently, with our income and slow facilities. Our dear brethren are without a knowledge of what they are talking about. But now, beloved, as we are in this desperate effort to get entirely out of debt and to get situated so as to cut off much of our past expense, we hope that all will send us the help they can.

The move to Bucyrus was made in May, 1883. About that time the first good press was purchased. It was a rebuilt Country Campbell, allowing either belt- or hand-power to be used, and costing perhaps six hundred dollars.

The trying times through which the Trumpet had to pass in its early years are known only to God. It was perhaps his design that it should be tried as gold is tried. There were always a few consecrated hearts who contributed of their means. Some put everything they had into the work. Thus the work was kept alive. Little did Brother Warner realize, when he was located at Bucyrus and the prospects looked good, that there he should go through the bitterest trial of his life. The light of the Trumpet came very near being snuffed out entirely. Bucyrus was the narrows in the Trumpet's voyage, through which it barely passed. This will be described in our next chapter.

The office of the Trumpet remained at Bucyrus nearly a year. Some brethren in Michigan were desirous of having it moved to their locality. Progress had been made at Bucyrus, but it was through the furnace of trial rather than any extension of influence. But doubtless all this experience was necessary as an equipment for greater usefulness.

The move to Williamston, Ingham County, Mich., was made in April, 1884. A Mr. Horton, a business man of Williamston, in whom the Lord had planted a love for the truth, went to Bucyrus and had the office equipment shipped. The saints in Michigan had in the meantime obtained possession of a two-story building 28 x 84, and they had it partitioned, or remodeled, to suit the need, the upper story to be used for a hall or assembly-room, the rear of the lower floor to be used for living rooms and the front for an office. Brother Warner rejoiced with tears when the work got started in its new and enlarged quarters in Williamston. The first number of the paper published there was dated April 15. From its columns we quote the following greetings:

> We are happy to greet your ears once more, beloved, with the sound of the trump of God. The devil has spent all his infernal powers in vain to crush this work of God. We have thoroughly learned his attitude toward us. In his hellish clamor about us for many days, saying, 'You must give up the Trumpet,' he has clearly committed himself against this cause, and all who are against this dissemination of the light of God we know are on the devil's side, either wilfully or ignorantly. Oh, how hell has poured forth upon us! Night after night we had to leave our bed at two, three, and four o'clock, and go to the office and cry unto God to drive away the hosts of hell that had encamped against us. And every

time the power of God dispersed these infernal spirits of darkness, the Lord recommissioned us to blow the Trumpet in Zion, and sound an alarm on his holy mountain, and we were made joyfully conscious of his approving smile for not having backed down before the legions of hell. But the devil having drawn to his side the best agents he could ever expect to use against us, was fierce and determined to hush the trumpet-sound of freedom from all sin and Babylon yokes. Oh, halleluiah!

During this terrible combat with the powers of darkness, we had to do more fighting than working, hence the work went on slowly. We were ready to print about the first of February, then the Lord called us by telegram to Kalamazoo, Mich. The next day our printer accidentally spoiled the rollers, so that he could not print. So the work lay until our return. After looking to the Lord until he assured us that the office would be cleared from the mortgage, we ordered new rollers, and went to work again in the name of the Lord. About the time we were ready to print, God sent Bro. Thomas Horton, from Williamston, Mich., who paid off the five hundred-dollar mortgage, some other debts, chartered a car, loaded us up, and moved office, household goods, Master Willie, and ourself to this place. Wife and child having remained behind to visit with friends. Moving just at the time caused a few days delay in this issue, but now we expect to greet you regularly. Praise the Lord! "The Lord giveth, and the Lord taketh away, blessed be the name of the Lord!" So said Job. If it was the devil that took it away, he had to get a permit from God before he could do it, therefore it was of the Lord, and "blessed be the name of the Lord"; for when he permits the devil to take anything away he has given to his children, he always returns fourfold. We have understood this principle long ago, and have thrown it in the face of the devil every time he has shown his teeth at us. Blessed be God forever and ever! And thus hath God done unto us again. We left an office where we were hampered up in 14 × 26 feet, and here has God furnished a building two stories high, 28 × 84 feet, all of which is dedicated to the Lord. It contains a large meeting-hall, and plenty of room for office and all families connected with it. It is, however, under repairs, and we have taken temporary quarters for a few weeks.

Every change that was made gave occasion for new hopes for the advancement of the publishing work. Accordingly we read in the first issue at Williamston: "After one more issue we expect steam-power, and there is no telling what God will yet do for the Trumpet if the devil doesn't quit his hellish opposition." An engine was purchased during the first year at Williamston. It was of three horse-power and cost two hundred dollars. Thus, after the trying times of the first four years of its life, the Trumpet work began to make substantial progress and the reformation cause to expand and become permanent.

The next move for the Gospel Trumpet was in the summer of 1886. Near Bangor, in Van Buren County, was a yearly camp-meeting. There were many saints in the vicinity and near Grand Junction, seven miles north. At the Bangor camp-meeting in June, 1886, the subject of moving the Trumpet Office to that part of the State was considered. It seemed to be the mind of the Spirit and of all the saints that the removal should be made. A commodious and substantial building in the town of Grand Junction was offered for eight hundred dollars, or about half its worth. The saints agreed to purchase the property, and money was raised to pay moving-expenses. An encumbrance of five hundred dollars on the machinery was also paid off. Accordingly it was decided to move. One freight-car held the entire outfit of office material, machinery, and household goods.

Grand Junction, "where two lightning tracks lay crossing," was a small town of a few hundred inhabitants, the junction of the Chicago and West Michigan (now the Pere Marquette) and a branch of the Michigan Central Railways, ten miles from South Haven on the lake and thirty miles west of Kalamazoo. This became the permanent home of the Gospel Trumpet during twelve years of its history.

Before the move to Grand Junction, Bro. S. Michels, of South Haven, assumed with his means a portion of the financial responsibility. Being thus directly connected with the publishing work, his name appeared as publisher, which position he held till relieved by N. H. Byrum, in 1895.

About a year after the publishing office was located at Grand Junction, the publishing work, and the church as well, suffered the defection of J. C. Fisher, who had been on the editorial staff and had been useful in the ministry.[11] He was succeeded as assistant editor by E. E. Byrum, who remained on the staff for many years, and after Brother Warner's death became editor.

The Gospel Trumpet was a mighty factor in the reformation work, a very effectual means of spreading the truth. At Grand Junction the Office grew to a substantial printing-plant, sending out tons of literature. Books were printed, a children's paper was started, and the Trumpet became a weekly. It was here that Brother Warner's death occurred, in 1895. We close this chapter with the publishing work located at Grand Junction. Brief reference to its present status will be made in another chapter.

---

[11] See Chapter XV for further mention of this.

Office and Home of the Gospel Trumpet. Grand Junction, Mich., 1889.

CHAPTER XV

THE CRISIS[12]

Unity effected only out of and away from sects—No other alternative
for God's people—Brother Warner a reformer—His stand meets
Satan's opposition, but vindicated by Spirit of God-Extracts from
Gospel Trumpet—Declares himself free from Northern Indiana
Eldership—Same stand taken by Michigan saints—Counterfeit
doctrines—Trying time at Bucyrus, Ohio—His wife's estrange-
ment—Comments by contemporary editors—Trouble over donation by a Mrs. Booth—Letters of sympathy and encouragement—
Work spreads into various States—Emma Miller's healing of
blindness—Other marvelous healings—Defection of J. C. Fisher—
How the reformation is distinguished from all other movements.

True to prophetic fulfilment, the time was at hand for the restoration of the
church to her normal state of unity and holiness. The scattered condition of God's
people in the various sectarian denominations was not always to continue, for
such could not be the ideal state of the church; it could not be her final state in
which Christ could expect to receive her as his bride. For her there was a better day
at hand. From Romish night to the light of justification by faith, possessed among
Protestant sects generally since the sixteenth century reformation, had been a
great step upward. Also the Wesleyan reformation, bringing in the light of perfect
holiness as a Christian attainment subsequent to regeneration, marked an advance
for the truth in its progress by stages unto the end of time. There needed to be yet
another step, another reformation, which should bring the church to her fulness of
glory, and visualize her unity and solidarity.

It would seem that the holiness movement that arose in the sixties and seventies should have accomplished this, but it served only as an approach to it. True
holiness indeed destroys the elements of sectarianism, and forbids a continued
state of division among Christians. But the holiness movement, as such, came to
have holiness only nominally for its object. It undertook no antagonism to sectarian divisions, though it deplored them. It stood for nothing more than holiness
as a subject to be taught and experienced, and satisfied itself as best it could to
remain within the denominations. It drew back when the real issue came, and in
consequence it has long been dissipated in the sects, having for forty years accomplished little or nothing toward bringing God's people into unity.

[12] Desiring to trace the earlier history of the Gospel Trumpet, I have permitted the
preceding chapter to overlap this one a few years.

Christian unity can never be brought about within the sects nor in connection with any recognition of allegiance to them. It absolutely can be effected only out of and away from the sects, by obedience to God and a severance of sectarian ties. Since true Christian unity is incompatible with sects, and since coming out of sects is opposed by the sect spirit and invites persecution by the sects, the only course for the people of God to take who have received the light on the true church is to cut loose from human institutions and abide in Christ alone, even though it places them in a relation hostile to the so-called churches. For those first leaving the sects there was no body of saints already called out to which they could be added. What could it mean to them but a crisis? And what would it constitute in the progress of events but a reformation? But the Spirit of the Lord was thus leading. Since sects are hostile to the movement out of sects, the Spirit of the Lord becomes necessarily hostile to them; for he indeed leads his people out of sects. But the time had come. God's spiritual ones were looking and longing for some development or other by which they would cease to be divided in sectarian bodies. No one had put it into their minds; their anticipation of it was prompted by the Spirit of God, which was in them. There needed some one to sound the trumpet of the Lord, some one to take the lead and make a positive declaration against the sin of division, some one through whom God could voice the call, "Come out of her, my people, that ye be not partakers of her sins, and that ye receive not of her plagues" (Rev. 18:4).

God had in Brother Warner prepared just such an instrument. His was the spirit of a reformer. He shunned not to declare God's judgments. His ministry had a definite message, and represented the burden of God for the purity and unity of his church. Looking back upon Brother Warner's career it would seem, as the writer has already intimated, that his connection with the Church of God (Winebrennerian), which assumed to have no creed but the Bible and to be indeed the true church of God, had doubtless served to emphasize to him the true church ideal and to shape his course along right lines. And his rejection by the Ohio Eldership for the preaching of holiness awakened him to see that that body was not what it claimed to be, but was, after all, only a humanly ruled institution, only one sect among the many. The light he already had on the church was sufficient to forbid his reuniting with them. Thus the so-called Church of God had contributed to him the right idea of the church, and the holiness movement had brought to his understanding the line on which God would bring out a pure church, namely, the line of holiness; and thus was the divine Hand leading him and fitting him for the work to which he was called.

We can only imagine what it meant to step out on God alone and preach the divine judgments against the apostate religions of the day, to decry the evils of denominationalism, and to undertake on that same line the publication of a paper. That his work was despised and that Satan undertook to crush it in its very beginning can not be wondered at. Its humbleness and apparent insignificance looked uninviting to the worldly-minded; but the deep spirituality and divine manifestations that characterized it were a sufficient vindication to those who were capable of spiritually discerning the truth. There was something that said, "This work is of God." There was a sense of spiritual freedom and of love and Christian fellowship that bore convincing testimony to those who would but listen to the dictation of the Spirit that this is indeed the truth.

But Brother Warner was not alone. God had reserved his thousands who no longer were bowing the knee to Baal. From them he received encouragement and support, though for a few years it seemed his work had to go through the crucible of trial. Accordingly we trace his difficulties and sorrows, as well as his victories, until the cause becomes fully established in the earth.

From what we learn of Brother Warner's earlier views and attitude, he never had a party spirit; he never was a sectarian. Even from his early ministry the love and fellowship that exists among the people of God he recognized as the paramount bond of Christian union. After his conversion, when dealing with the question of what church he should join, he is found casting about to determine which one represented the real church of God. As the followers of Winebrenner had the right name, and seemed to him to be correct in doctrine, he was led into that denomination. With the insufficient light he then possessed he probably failed to see the man rule that prevailed, instead of the Holy Spirit rule that characterizes the divine, theocratic government in the true church of God. He discovered, of course, the clash of this man rule with the free, independent inclination of the Holy Spirit, by which he preferred to be led. But he bore with it patiently, believing that he was in the true church; and it took years to discover to him that the body to which he belonged was but a sect.

It was through the attainment of the Bible standard of holiness that he was gradually led into the truth respecting the church and sects. Early in 1878 he wrote: "The Lord showed me that holiness could never prosper upon sectarian soil encumbered by human creeds and party names, and he gave me a new commission to join holiness and all truth together and build up the apostolic church of the living God." He soon began to receive light on the Scriptures, which revealed to him that the church was to be restored to her primitive glory in the evening of the dispensation. The chapter on a Spiritual Shaking, taken from his book, clearly shows that when the chapter was written (1879) he understood that God was going to bring out a pure church. He published this in 1880, which became the date from which the present epoch of the church may be reckoned.

It should be remembered that during this time he was connected with the Northern Indiana Eldership; but as this was a body already separated from the old Eldership because of their purpose to keep on the Scriptural basis, he really believed that this body was the true church, for that was its claim. Thus he was really out of sectism in heart and was associated with a body claiming to be the church of God. During the last year (1880) of the Herald of Gospel Freedom, when it was fully under his editorial charge, its columns, while teaching holiness, breathed the principles of the one true church. One of its stated objects was "the union of all true believers in the Spirit of God and upon the inspired Word." Because of insufficient light on the governmental aspect of the true church, he was slow to discover that even the new Eldership was only a body ruled by men. As light came on the Holy Spirit government, he looked upon the man rule elements in the Eldership as inconsistencies that needed removal. It was human machinery that he thought needed to be dispensed with. We must concede, therefore, that in the meantime he was, to all intents and purposes, out of sects.

We speak of this period as the crisis because he took such a bold, uncompromising stand against sects and taught holiness and the principles of the church with such thoroughness that it seemed to awaken every satanic element that had been slumbering under the guise of false profession. People had either to accept the truth or go into darkness. To him it meant the break-up of old relations, the drawing of new lines of fellowship, exposure to persecution, and everything that might befall the career of a reformer. As the teaching of the resurrection and the repudiation of circumcision constituted the offence of the cross in Paul's day, so the preaching of the Bible standard of holiness and the renouncement of all sects became the offence of the cross at this time. We shall give several selections from the earlier issues of the Trumpet that are representative of its teaching. In the issue of Mar. 1, 1881, we have the following:

BRANCHES

Where in the Bible do we find the idea of sects being branches, as people talk about? "What branch of the church do you belong to?" is a common expression in these times of antiscriptural language and practise. Why do not people read their Bibles better and learn that every individual believer is a branch in Christ— John 15?

If a whole sect is a branch, then the individual must be a sub-branch; but this would make each one dependent upon the sect for his union with, and life from, Christ. This would be second-hand salvation. We should not like to risk the coupling—I prefer a direct union with Christ.

Taking Christ's parable of the Vine and Branches, there is but one way to represent branch sects; that is, imagine the branches adhering directly to the vine but pressed together and tightly bound into several bunches. Thus drawn together each bundle would have the appearance of a branch; but upon closer examination it would be found to consist of many branches each adhering to the vine, except a good many dead sticks, that had been killed by the unnatural confinement, and had rotted loose from the trunk.

We think it is the great business of the pure gospel sword of holiness to cut those soul-killing chords, that the Father may purge the several branches, and that they may all straighten out in natural position—live, grow, and bear fruit unto holiness.

His account of how he was led to sever his connection with the holiness association, which he began to see was but a milder form of sectism, is given in an editorial for June 1, 1881.

THAT YE BREAK EVERY YOKE

Saturday, April 22, the hand of the Lord was heavily upon our soul, had no relish to converse with any one but God. Finally in company with two brethren we went into the house of God at Hardinsburg, Ind., and placed ourselves under the searching eye of God, when the Spirit of the Lord showed me the inconsistency of repudiating sects and yet belonging to an association that is based upon sect recognition. We promised God to withdraw from all such compacts. But being dearly attached to the holiness work, we attended the Association at Terre Haute, and tried to have the sect-endorsing clause removed from the constitution. Its substance is as follows, speaking of local associations:

"It shall consist of members of various Christian organizations and seek to work in harmony with all these societies."

We offered the following substitute: "It shall consist of, and seek to cooperate with, all true Christians everywhere."

We had supposed that fellowship and cooperation should not exclude any person or truth that is in Christ Jesus, and that we should not be compelled to bow down to anything not in, nor of, Christ Jesus.

We were positively denied membership on the ground of not adhering to any sect. And now we wish to announce to all that we wish to cooperate with all Christians, as such, in saving souls—but **forever withdraw** from all organisms that uphold and endorse sects and denominations in the body of Christ.

In the same issue (June 1) he reviews a position taken by T. K. Doty, the editor of the Christian Harvester. We present this article, and also two others, in order to show his argument on the question of the church and sects.

SQUARE COME-OUTISM

"Probably this means the doctrine of coming out of all the sects, and giving the church of Christ no visible organization."—Christian Harvester.

I wish to ask the editor of the Harvester if human sects are essential to the visible organization of Christ? The above language so implies.

Then, according to this statement, the church of Christ was without a visible organization hundreds of years, until the present-day sects arose. And if the visible organization thus provided is a necessary adjunct to the church, then the apostle Peter made a mistake when he said that God had already "given unto us all things that pertain unto life and godliness."

Again, if the formation of sects gives the church of Christ a visible organization, will the Harvester please point out the time, in the history of the church, when that important event occurred?

Was it when the first sect was formed, namely, the Roman Catholic sect, in the beginning of the apostasy? Did she give the church of Christ a visible organization? If so, what need of subsequent efforts at organization?

We presume that the Harvester does not admit that this corrupt hierarchy is the church of Christ. So there was one sect formed, and Christ's church still not visibly organized.

Out of her came the Church of England. She claims to be the identical church of Christ. Does the Harvester admit the assumption? If not, then he must admit that a second sect failed to organize and represent the Church of Christ.

Again, from the old mother of sects came forth the Lutheran sect and her daughters—granddaughters of Rome. Did any of them organize the visible church of Christ? If so, which one?

Or was it left for John Wesley to organize the church of Christ in the formation of the Methodist Episcopal sect? If that sect is really the identical church of Christ, then the editor of the Harvester is in a hopeless condition, since severed from that body; but we presume that he still felt that he was in the church of Christ after dismembered from that great sect, therefore it is not identical with the church of Christ, and her organization was not the organization of Christ's church at all.

Having now followed two branches of Rome to the second generation without finding in any of these sister denominations the identical church of Christ, we must pass on to the third generation.

Is any of the sects that have branched out from the Methodist Episcopal sect the church of Christ? If so, will the Harvester point out the one? Will he assume that the one he represents is the church of Christ? If so, then he has been without Christ's church until recently. If not, then the founding of the Wesleyan Methodist sect was not the organization of the body of Christ. It is a fact which no man of intelligence will deny, that no one sect on earth is the identical church of God.

But it may be claimed by some that all the sects taken together constitute the true church in her visible organization. This is also a great mistake. How can all these bodies sum up the one organic visible church of God, when they have no organic relation to each other? In what a disgraceful light sectism presents the church! Does that look like a divine and heaven-born family, that is composed of numerous, rival, jealous, independent, and conflicting organisms? Oh, I beseech you for Christ's sake, do not dishonor God by confounding his church with Babylon confusion!

Instead of sects giving the church of Christ a visible organization they mar and destroy the visible organization and unity of the church of Christ. A striking want of identity in the membership of God's church and human sects also proves conclusively that no sect, nor yet all sects together, constitutes the divine fold. Their walls are not the walls of God's house at all, neither are "their thresholds" his threshold. Many are in them who never entered God's church, and, thank God, many have entered by Christ the door who have never attached themselves to any of the factions that are not of God, but the result of sin. If, then, the constituent elements of sects are not identical with the elements of God's church, sects themselves are not identical with her, and consequently their organization is not her organization.

QUESTIONS ANSWERED
(AUG. 15, 1881.)

First: "Does the come-out element constitute the true church of God?"

Answer: All true Christians in heaven and earth constitute the true church of God. Eph. 3:15.

Second: "In what particular is the separationist, or come-out church, better than the Wesleyan Methodist Church?"

Answer: This language places antisect Christians in a false light. They never teach such a thing as a new sect, whose distinguishing characteristic is simply the coming out of all other sects; such is the impression made by the question, and it is a false one. The Christians branded "come-outers" have founded no church or sect, nor do they intend to; but, on the contrary, they have abandoned all sects to live in the one church that Christ founded, and into which we were inducted by regeneration. This fact is known by hundreds who nevertheless misrepresent them continually: this goes with them. God's church is composed altogether of "come-outers." The word "church" (**ecclesia**) means the "called out," they are called out of the world, out of heathen religions, and all corrupt and bogus Christianity. But while the come-out element is embodied in the very word "church," she is not to be called "Come-out" church. She embodies water baptism, but is not a Baptist church. She teaches the Sabbath, and the second advent, but is not a Sabbatarian nor Adventist church. Her members are all brethren, and united, but she is not the United Brethren church. The sin of all this is in making one of the subordinate elements of the system the center, and not God in Christ Jesus. But to the question. The Wesleyan Methodist sect is an organized party in Christendom, a schismatic, or cut-off party, all of which is condemned in the Bible. "There should be no schisms in the body." The origin of all such disintegrating factions, whether for Paul, Peter, or Wesley, is carnality, as the Word of God teaches, "the result of sin," says the Harvester. The Wesleyan Methodist sect is human, fragmentary, and earthly, and will be utterly annihilated at the coming of Christ, with every other schismatic party. The church of the living God, in which "come-outers" inhere, to the exclusion of all human organisms, was purchased, built, and sanctified by Christ Jesus, who is its head, door, and foundation. It is the "pillar and ground of the truth," and will stand through all eternity, that's the difference.

*   *   *   *   *

Fourth: "Wherein does the come-out church excel the Wesleyan, and manifest its divine origin?"

Answer: This is virtually a repetition of the question above answered. We have often said, Why do not opposers of holiness go to the standards of the doctrine and controvert what they say? They never do. Again, we ask, Why do not sect apologists attack what "come-outers" teach? They teach the one true and catholic church of the Bible—this can not be overthrown, therefore sect worshipers seek to hide their sin in misrepresenting all who abandon sects. Come out of Babylon, brother, then you can see much clearer.

THE SHAFTING GIVING WAY
(NOV. 1, 1881.)

If it were not such a solemn thing, it were really amusing to see how many are floundering about on the question of organized divisions in Christendom. They admit them evil, predict their downfall, and then, shrinking from the result of their own admissions, they fly to their protection and raise the hue and cry against those who bring the gospel of God to bear upon these ramparts of sin.

L. Hawkins, of the Banner of Holiness, admits the design of Christ is the spiritual and organic unity of all believers, and that an advanced degree of holiness would demolish these walls of separation, and then, as if alarmed at their fall, he pleads for their toleration at present.

The Harvester adds, "Then let us hail every sign of real unity as from the Lord, and, as holiness laborers, not be afraid when the temporary shafting of denominationalism begins to give way."

So it is admitted that denominationalism is bolstered up with temporary shafting. This reminds us of a pamphlet we read some years ago, in defense of sect organizations. The writer confessed that the denominations were not the real "house of God which is the church of the living God," but that they were necessary scaffolds for the erection of the house, and that when the house shall have been completed, the scaffolds will all be taken down. Well, in view of the prospects of Christ's speedy coming we prefer to keep off of these old rickety, rotten-timbered scaffolds that are destined so soon to tumble down and be consumed with all the rubbish of Satan's invention. For our part we are ready for the sect shafting to give way any day; for we are builded into the house of God itself, and have nothing to lose or to fear. But many are not ready for the catastrophe. While fearing and even predicting the fall of those Dark-Age structures, they are unwilling to abandon them. They sit trembling upon their lofty but narrow Methodist, Baptist, United Brethren, or Presbyterian plank, while with one hand they try to hold onto the walls of God's church. We can always tell whether a man is resting upon one of these scaffolds or whether he is building only on Christ, the sure foundation. If on the latter, he has nothing to fear; if on the former, he is sure to command a halt when he sees the true priests of God blowing the trumpets about these walls. Such always think the time has not yet come to abolish sects and denominations. "Oh! no! do not push against our scaffold poles yet; be careful down there! Please don't lean against that shafting, there is danger of its falling!"

One dear minister took us aside at the Alvan (Ill.) camp-meeting last summer and inquired of our views. We told him, of course, that we believed in no church but the body of Christ, etc. He conceded about all we contended for, but, unwilling to abandon his elevated plank, he humbly besought us not to be so hard on them. Poor fellow! We think all had better climb down from these shaky concerns; for God has announced her fall. "Babylon the great is fallen, is fallen, and is become the habitation of devils, and the hold of every foul spirit, and a cage of every unclean and hateful bird. And I heard another voice from heaven, saying, Come out of her, my people, that ye be not partakers of her sins, and that ye receive not of her plagues" (Rev. 18:2,4). "Then let us hail every sign of real unity as from the Lord, and not be afraid when the temporary shafting of denominationalism begins to give way." This is good advice, but does Brother Doty walk in it? Does he hail as from the Lord those whom the Spirit of God has led out of those cut-off parties, which divide the people of God, and who stand in the "one fold" and body of Christ? or has he not done his best to represent them as teaching "no church," "no organization," and as building another sect, etc.? Is it consistent to admit that sects are without a warrant in God's Word, and that they are the "result of sin in the body of believers," and express a hope for the unity of God's people, and then join with all the popular holiness journals in opposing those who have abandoned all those unscriptural schisms? Is it consistent to say, "We don't want an ism gospel," and yet adhere to and stuff the Harvester full of the gospel of Wesleyan Methodist ism?

Church building in which D. S. Warner and five others severed their relation with the Northern Indiana Eldership in 1881. It is located at Beaver Dam, three miles north of Akron, Ind.

Group of Individuals, former members of the Northern Indiana Eldership, who with Brother Warner severed their connection with the Northern Indiana Eldership in 1881. At top, Mr. and Mrs. F. Krause; center, D. Leininger; bottom, Mr. and Mrs. W. W. Ballenger.

An event that had to occur sooner or later was Brother Warner's separation from the Northern Indiana Eldership. At the Eldership meeting which convened at Beaver Dam, Kosciusko County, Ind., in October, 1881, he proposed some measures by which that body might be made to conform more perfectly to the Bible standard with reference to government. In this he would not be heard, and on their rejection of his reform measures he realized, probably for the first time, that the new Eldership, bent on continuing their human organization, was a sect with which he must sever his connection, and he then and there did so. This event does not properly mark his coming out of spiritual Babylon, as some have supposed. In heart he had already been out, and had preached against sects. But he ignorantly supposed that the Northern Indiana Eldership of the Church of God was not a sect and therefore that he was keeping clear of sects. Thus his act at Beaver Dam was a *keeping* out of Babylon as much as a coming out. It was the latter only in the outward sense, but of course it emphasized and gave more definite character to the anti-sectarian stand he had previously taken.

There were others in attendance at the Eldership meeting who had heard his preaching against spiritual Babylon and who also took the same step with him. They were David Leininger, William Ballenger and wife, and F. Krause and wife. We give their names and also their pictures as being of those originals who declared themselves free from all outward forms of Babylon.

A similar thing occurred in Michigan. About the same time the Northern Indiana Eldership was formed, there originated near Pompeii, Gratiot County, Mich., the Northern Michigan Eldership of the Church of God. This body was formed because its members had been isolated from and generally dissatisfied with the old Eldership, which sanctioned secrecy and was steeped in tobacco. About the fall of 1878 there joined this new Eldership J. C. Fisher and his wife, Allie R. They had never heard of Brother Warner at that time. In the spring of 1880, J. C. Fisher had occasion to visit Indiana on business, and it happened that while there he heard Brother Warner preach, and he accepted the doctrine of holiness and received the experience. The following autumn the Fishers sent for Brother Warner to come up to that part of Michigan and preach holiness. It was then that Allie R. consecrated for and also received the experience of sanctification.[13]

A year later, just before the annual meeting of the Eldership (October, 1881), the Fishers and others, thinking to get the Eldership to accept holiness and thus make good the claim of being the true church, started a holiness meeting at Carson City, where the Fishers lived, and again had Brother Warner present. This was right after the meeting in Indiana where Brother Warner had declared his separation from the Northern Indiana Eldership. The situation was similar to what it had been in Indiana. Brother Warner had been preaching on the true church and setting forth its divine government, and the hope of these Michigan saints was that if they could get the Eldership to accept holiness they might get them to do away with the human machinery and fill the true church requirement. In this they

[13] She relates that her consecration occurred in the house of an Elder Walker, and that so great was the power and manifestation of God in Brother Warner while he was praying for her that Walker and his wife through fright fled into another room, where he was found squatted in a corner. In Brother Warner's report of this trip he speaks of a meeting near Lacey's Lake (in Eaton or Barry County) as follows: "Was happy at this place to meet a people who have come out of various denominations, ignoring human creeds and sects and endeavoring to walk in the oneness of the Spirit."

were disappointed. Before the holiness meeting was over the Eldership showed its opposition. Upon this the Fishers and a good number of others, nearly twenty in all, withdrew from the Eldership.

Joseph C. and Allie R. Fisher.

Thus there were two centers where a stand of independence with regard to the Eldership and human ecclesiasticism had been taken. These two congregations of saints—at Beaver Dam, (Ind.), and Carson City, (Mich.),—were the earliest in the United States (so far as the author knows) who had stepped completely out of Babylon and had taken for their basis that of the New Testament church alone. An annual camp-meeting was established at each place.

Group of Michigan saints, some of the first to declare their freedom from sectarian relations. Above, Mr. and Mrs. Frank B. Reeves; center, Mrs. C. E. Reeves; below, Mr. and Mrs. John T. Lyon.

The Michigan saints in order to express in definite form their position and intentions drew up the following resolutions:

Whereas we recognize ourselves in the perilous times of the last days, the time in which Michael is standing up for the deliverance of God's true saints (Dan. 12:1), the troublesome times in which the true house of God is being built again, therefore,

Resolved, That we will endeavor by all the grace of God to live holy, righteous, and godly in Christ Jesus, "looking for, and hastening unto the coming of the Lord Jesus Christ," who we believe is nigh, even at the door.

Resolved, That we adhere to no body or organization but the church of God, bought by the blood of Christ, organized by the Holy Spirit, and governed by the Bible. And if the Lord will, we will hold an annual assembly of all saints who in the providence of God shall be permitted to come together for the worship of God, the instruction and edification of one another, and the transaction of such business as the Holy Spirit may lead us to see and direct in its performance.

Resolved, That we ignore and abandon the practise of preacher's license as without precept or example in the Word of God, and that we wish to be "known by our fruits" instead of by papers.

Resolved, That we do not recognize or fellowship any who come unto us assuming the character of a minister whose life is not godly in Christ Jesus and whose doctrine is not the Word of God.

Resolved also, That we recognize and fellowship, as members with us in the one body of Christ, all truly regenerated and sincere saints who worship God in all the light they possess, and that we urge all the dear children of God to forsake the snares and yokes of human parties and stand alone in the "one fold" of Christ upon the Bible, and in the unity of the Spirit.

It should be noted that even at this time, while they could see the evils of human machinery in the church, they had not as yet a perfect knowledge of how the divine government would be. They wondered whether they should form a new Eldership or whether they had anything at all to do in the new procedure, cut loose as they were from all human organizations. At this time Sister Fisher was given a vision. It was of a tower which she and others were constructing with stones that were piled about them in heaps. The foundation was already laid and they were engaged on the superstructure, their work being to polish the stones and fit them for the tower. When polished, the stones were clear as crystal. They were asked where they got such beautiful stones. She replied that they were simply such stones as could be found anywhere. Their beauty was brought out through the work that was put upon them. The capstone, or headstone, was also perfectly clear, but it had a blood-red spot in the center which shone and which shed rays of light like streaks of blood down through all the tower.

The vision seemed to her so wonderful. She awoke to a full consciousness and said, "Lord, what is it?" He answered, "This is my church." Immediately the Scriptures in 1 Cor. 3:11-18; Eph. 2:20-22; and 1 Cor. 3:9 came to her mind. She then understood that the church was organized by God, and that it was man's part to work with him, and let him be Leader and Foreman, and that Jesus was the head of the body.[14]

They soon learned to be led of the Spirit and that they were complete in Christ in matters of government as well as everything else. Conscious of their freedom from the bondage in which they had been held and that they had taken their stand on God alone, they were blessed with the Spirit of God upon them and their assemblies in a remarkable manner. The joy of the Lord was their portion and they were satisfied. Thus the reformation had taken complete form. The light began to spread and the work became established in various places. A sister Harris, living near Bangor, in the southwestern part of Michigan, was called up to Gratiot County in July, 1882, to attend the funeral of a niece. While there she heard J. C. Fisher preach and she invited him down to her part of the State. He went the following October and held meetings there, which were very successful, resulting in a number getting saved. An annual camp-meeting was started there the next year. This camp-meeting has been continued ever since, though it was taken to Grand Junction, seven miles north, in 1892. Thus this part of the State was one of the first sections where the work of the reformation was established, and Grand Junction became, at a later date, the home of the publishing plant for a number of years.

That God was working on a similar line in other parts of the world may be seen from a letter written from England and quoted in the Gospel Trumpet from the Christian Harvester.

SOUL PROSPERITY WITHOUT THE PENS

We extract the following from a letter in the Christian Harvester from E. Morgan, Maidstone, England:

"We have a number of people who enjoy holiness, men and women, old and young, who do not belong to any sect. They have the presence of the Holy Spirit with them in a much richer and more powerful way than the friends in the churches. This seems to indicate that the Lord will raise up an army to do his work, and perfect love will be the uniting power that will keep them one."

It is not at all to be wondered at that those who have obeyed God and come out of all human sects should have a superior degree of God's grace and Spirit with them, who are free from the oppression and interdiction that we hear so much of in all our holiness papers. Yes, God is now raising up that holy army who stand free in Christ, bound only by the truth and the love of God.

---

[14] This vision is very similar to the one recorded in the Shepherd of Hermas, in the second century. It was a remarkable coincidence that while Sister Fisher had never heard of the vision of the Shepherd of Hermas, she and her husband had ordered the set of books known as the Apostolic Fathers (in which the Shepherd of Hermas is included), and on the same day of her vision the books were received and unpacked, and on looking into them her husband opened right at the vision in the Shepherd of Hermas. They were astonished to find that her vision was there recorded and explained as the church.

From the above, we see, as well as from the testimony of hundreds in this country, that the assertion that coming out of sectism results in spiritual death is a groundless falsehood. The result is always the opposite, unless it be in some instances where souls have been overwhelmed with the hellish rage and deceitful, persecuting spirit of the sects, which has induced a superindignation.

Brother Warner's separation from the Northern Indiana Eldership was the subject of comment by his contemporary editors and others. His reply to a letter on the subject of his leaving the church is here given.

A dear brother writes to us as follows: "I think you have erred in leaving the Church of God, and yet God is blessing you and the Trumpet."...

To talk about "leaving the church of God and yet receiving the blessing of God," is Babylon confusion. There is absolutely no way given under heaven and among men whereby we can leave the church of God but by ceasing to live by faith in and obedience to Jesus Christ, or falling into and continuing in sin; in which case God does not and can not continue his blessings upon that soul as before. Therefore, when certain preachers in Ohio published that I had left the church (which was false, for they themselves cast me out of their synagog for the crime of preaching real experimental holiness), they declared the fact that what they worship in the name of the "Church of God" is only a "creature" of men, to which they invite members and report "accessions" through a different process than that of regeneration, which is the only means of accession to God's church. And when people talk of our having left the church, because we withdrew last fall from a human corporation called the "Northern Indiana Eldership of the Church of God," they simply show that the devil's counterfeits still pass current with them; they call that the church which does not answer the Bible description of the church. Oh, how hard it is to get rid of the marks of the beast, and the number of his name!

The Bible speaks of churches of God in Galatia, in Achaia, in Asia, etc., but we do not read of any northern, southern, eastern or western Galatian, Achaian, or Asiatic Elderships of the church of God. You see this thing—Northern Indiana Eldership of the Church of God—is too long for any use, so we just take the broadax of God's Word and chop it in two between "of" and "the" and throw the first part to the moles and bats, according to the sayings of the prophet. Then we have the church of God left, which is the body of Christ, "the fulness of him that filleth all in all." Glory to God and the Lamb, "we are complete in him"!

If some more would suffer the excision of this useless appendage, there would be quite a vacuum made for the reception of this "fulness." The term "Eldership" as used in this case, is both contradictory in itself and a perversion of God's Word. Where the apostle Paul speaks of "laying on of the hands of the presbytery," the Bible Union and some other versions render "hands of the eldership," and I think correctly, too. So I accept the word "eldership" as a Biblical term. But what is its obvious meaning? Simply the elders of the church in one locality, or in a district, or country, as the case may be. To apply it therefore to an organized corporation is a misapplication, a perversion of one of the words of God's Holy Book. It is contradictory, and asserts a falsehood, because the corporate "body" to which it is applied is not composed of elders, but of brothers and sisters, a few elders, and without doubt some sinners and backsliders; so this use of the word changes the truth of God into a lie. Like every other body that is not identical with the body of Christ, this "new Eldership," as it is often called, is a rival of the body of Christ, and is used by the devil to generate party spirit and sectish bigotry. Nothing is more natural than the disposition of carnality to want to get up something besides the glorious church of the Firstborn.

The reason is obvious. Christ built his own church, adds the members, and spews out the unworthy; 'He is head over all to his body, the church,' the only real ruling power, except as he chooses to execute his will through some of the members. Hence this gives no place to aspirants who wish to work up something that men can build, so as to receive the glory, and become lords over the work of their hands. As Sister M'Creery says in her history of the origin of the Free Methodists—during the six years that they were contented to work with a single eye, and let God build up his own church, and receive all the glory, the Spirit was with them in mighty power to save souls, because they had no craft to look after; but after they set up the Free Methodist idol, it was all, "He 'o he, go up Free Methodism!" And ceasing to work exclusively for God's kingdom of righteousness, peace, and joy in the Holy Spirit, and founding another sect, that they call "Our Church," they necessarily became double-eyed, and lost the real power of God. So after our meeting last fall we heard the call to rally up the party spirit; and to apologize for the addition of this sect corporation to the several hundred already in the mazes of Babylon, it was called the "Northern Indiana Eldership of the Church of God, opposed to Secret Societies." Just as though the church that Christ himself founded did not oppose secret societies, therefore it is necessary to form another "body" for that purpose. Thus every sect on earth is an insult to God; even their formation implies that we are not complete in Christ, hence the "necessity," as B. T. Roberts said, of our organizing another sect.

The Trumpet's New Year's greeting, at the dawn of its second year, has an interesting tone.

NEW YEAR'S GREETING

To all who may read this Trumpet, and especially to all who love the truth, we send you our brotherly greeting, a "Happy New Year," and a heartfelt "God bless you." Our heart overflows with love and gratitude to God, and all his loving saints, for all the benefits and mercies that filled the expiring year. Dearly beloved friends and patrons of the Trumpet, and lovers of its hated truth, we are happy to report from this watch-tower of Zion that we see nothing but success, victory, and glory. A beloved father in Israel in New York on first seeing the Trumpet recently wrote us of his inexpressible gratitude, and he remarked that he had tried to have one established in Chicago, but says he, "There was no one interested in the truth, that seemed to have sufficient means to undertake the project." Well, glory to God. He has chosen the weak things, and the moneyless, to carry on a work which to all human appearances, in this sect-loving and idolatrous age, could not be accomplished without considerable capital, and on a free basis—the wonderful work of God. How has he "surprized the hypocrites," and confounded the prophets of Babylon! G. D. Watson but uttered the predictions and carnal prayers of thousands when he said through an antichrist sheet in this place, "Brother Warner can not succeed in that line." What is this but a thrust at Jesus Christ! It virtually says to the Son of God: "In the prosperity of our churches, there can be nothing but failure in the attempt to build up 'God's Church.'" Oh, these devotees of Babylon would blot out of existence, if they could, the church that Christ founded over eighteen hundred years ago, to augment the glory of our "great Methodist Church" founded less than a hundred and fifty years ago!

Well, Brother Warner may have failed in many respects; but no man that reads the Trumpet can deny the fact that God and truth have most gloriously triumphed. And the Trumpet, too, through the God-approved truth it holds forth, has proved a glorious success, notwithstanding the different measures Satan has devised to hedge up its way. One poor whited sepulcher had the impudence to say with a satanic chuckle, "We will crush the Trumpet" and "take all Brother Warner's subscribers." A gentleman in this city when asked to take the chaff, and baby-soap, sheet, remarked, "If you succeed with this paper will it not break down the Trumpet?" and received the following reply: "That's just what we want to do." He told a brother this, and said he did not think there was much holiness in that, and did not want the paper. Yet one, M.

L. Haney, who was canonized at the Jacksonville convention as "the Patriarch of Holiness in the West" and everywhere else, is so blind that he has twice presumed to intimate that that enterprise might be of God, saying "If your paper is of God." Nearly all the professed holiness periodicals have been hauling barrels of water and pouring on the altar of God's truth and filling up the trench round about; but God is all the more glorified in this test between the Trumpet and the prophets of sects. Praise his name!

The Gospel Trumpet has proved Satan false in more than one way. In all love, we suggest to all those papers and preachers that have been in the habit of telling the people that "separation from the sects invariably results in spiritual death" to read the Trumpet, then shut their mouths, and cease their lying against the truth. There is not a sect-endorsing paper in the land that presents as strong array of testimony to clear definite holiness, Holy Ghost power, wonder-working faith, and fruitful lives. And we have abundance of live, glowing reports and experiences that we have not had space to use, and nearly all have spared us the necessity of telling you that the writers are without the camp of creed factions. We have published numerous expressions of appreciation, because, by their strong relish for the truths of the Trumpet coupled with their vigorous spiritual health and usefulness in Christ, they condemn all who reject the food we issue, as perverted and spiritually diseased. To the former class the Trumpet is heavenly music; but to the latter, it is an annoying sound, because their hearts and ears are not sufficiently circumcised to endure sound doctrine. The Trumpet has demonstrated the fact that God is able to carry a war against the devil in his strongest, last, and most desperate fortress.

God has in a remarkable manner heard and answered our prayers; not always however in the way we expected, but far better than we imagined. Last spring we prayed the Lord for a more speedy press, but the furnace of trial through which he brought us was better for our soul than a hundred presses and ten thousand subscribers. Glory to the God of Daniel, and the Hebrews! Oh, what lessons we have learned in the salt and fire school of Christ! We would gladly pull the lever of the Lord's good old hand-press for forty years to come, rather than have missed those furnace-wrought visions of God, of his church, and of the great sect abomination. To all the patrons of the Trumpet, we would return many thanks for the means you have furnished the Lord's cause, and the many appreciated contributions you have sent us by the inspiration of the Holy Spirit. You have largely made the paper what it is, and by your continued labor of love and sacrifice for Christ's sake you will continue to improve and enlarge the paper and extend its sphere of usefulness. We regard the real test-ing-point in the Trumpet as past; God has established the work of our hands. Our circulation is steadily increasing; we have been printing sixteen hundred papers each issue, sixteen fifty this time, and we do not have fifty papers left when we get through mail-ing. The demand for canvassing and sample copies continually increases.

To Babylon and all her concomitants, we promise nothing but fire, sword and hammer, and confounding blasts from the armory of God's Word. We have scarcely begun the bombardment of the wicked harlot city. By the grace of God, we expect to deal with sin and sinners as we never yet have done. Some have intimated to us that we have been too personal in rebuking Church sinners: but, before God, we are ashamed of and repent for our mildness and want of personality in the past. And now we give fair warning to hypocrites, and all whose walk has not been upright before God, that if you don't repent and publish your confession of sin, the Lord has made it our duty, so far as we know, to expose and re-buke you before all. We know no man after the flesh, and we seek to please no man. If God can not carry on the paper by us seeking only to please Him, the Trumpet will surely be discontinued. But God is our sufficiency. "I shall not want." "For the Lord God will help me; therefore shall I not be confounded; therefore have I set my face like a flint, and I know that I shall not be ashamed" (Isa. 50:7).

While it is our duty to reprove all outward sin, we must keep the fact prominent that all reform must begin at the heart, which God only can change; inward transformation is only upon the condition of faith, and, therefore, must be definitely presented in the Scriptural order of pardon and adoption to the sinner, and entire sanctification to the believer. We regret that some attempt to beat down the ice-mountain of sect by the hammer of the Word, without the melting fire of the Holy Spirit. Getting people out of the sects any other way than by leading them to Christ for heart purity and the reception of the Comforter, which leads the soul from all sects and into all truth, is but enlisting men into carnal crusade against Babylon, and can result in little good, and has, in some instances, hedged up the way and turned back the tide of God's truth more than it will be able to advance it. Because the Bible experience of entire sanctification is the true objective of Christ's atonement and shed blood, and because thorough holi-ness destroys sects and denominations, as frost would disappear under the beams of the June sun, and as the promotion of true ho-liness is the only remedy for schisms and every other form of sin in the body of professed Christians, therefore the Gospel Trumpet shall continue to "praise the beauty of holiness" and proclaim the power of the blood of Christ on the gospel line of definite holiness and perfect heart-purity. We ask the cooperation and prayers of all true saints of God, who love the freedom of Christ Jesus our Savior.

The truths of the reformation were disseminated largely by the Gospel Trumpet, and in many parts of the country there were those with whom its teachings found a hearty welcome. A few bits of correspondence addressed to Brother Warner and taken from the Trumpet of early in 1882 are here presented.

I like the Trumpet very well; hope it may sound out long, loud, and clear to call the people back to the old paths, the good way. Yes, truly it is the good way, the strait and narrow way, the new and living way, and the high and holy way. You may count me a subscriber as long as the Trumpet sticks to the Bible. Your brother purified and being tried,E. B. B.

He keeps them that put their trust in him. I pray God the time may soon come when Christians shall be united as one in Christ Jesus, the living Head, and throw away all divisions, taking Christ for their head and having their names enrolled on God's book in heaven. May the Lord bless all the saints. May God bless you, Sister Warner, in giving up part of your house in order that the Gospel Trumpet may still be printed. Oh, we can't give up the Trumpet! Oh, that I could do something! I will do what I can to help you. The Trumpet must go on. Enclosed find the widow's mite.L. B.

We are strangers, never have seen each other, yet we know each other by the Spirit that is given us. I am glad you have grace enough to run the Gospel Trumpet without any visible means. They that overcome inherit all things. The Lord will not forsake you in the work. He will help you to carry it through. I gladly send you one dollar and would gladly send you more if I could at present. I have no love for sects in my soul.L. M.

Success crown your labor of love in the kingdom and patience of Jesus.

May sectarianism totter and fall to its very base, and glory and unity fill God's kingdom of peace and righteousness.

God grant that the trumpet of salvation may continue to sound its certain blasts, until Babylon be overthrown by the power of God and truth.Mrs. L. L. and Eld. J. M.

God bless you abundantly. Amen. My heart is with you to do the whole will of God, regardless of great or small men, bigots, or devils.T. F. D.

I have received two numbers of the Trumpet; the sentiments

therein taught are mine and have been for fifteen years. My wife stands with me. Let the Trumpet continue to sound louder and louder, until the walls of sectarian Jericho fall.J. C. A.

The more I deepen in Christ, the better I understand the doctrine Brother Warner advocates; and the more I understand the doctrine advocated and acquaint myself with the early history of the Friends, the greater similarity I find between the two. He does not insist upon entire separation from the world in every form stronger than they did.F. W.

God bless you and yours and the great and glorious work in which you are engaged. Would like to help you scatter pure gospel truth without isms or man-made walls. The Lord hasten on the day when they shall all fall to rise no more. Glory to God! Yours saved,J. L. K.

In the issue of Jan. 16, 1882, Brother Warner answers a number of criticisms by contemporary editors.

TO OUR CONTEMPORARIES

"Modern come-outism, or, better said, no-churchism." We hold that uniting with the people of God in church fellowship, even of our own choice, does not necessarily constitute us sectarians.—Gospel Banner.

In all love we would ask our kind Brother Brenneman to inform us of those modern "no-church" men of whom he speaks; give us the address of any man professing godliness who believes in and claims membership in no church.

Second. Is the body of Christ no church?

Third. If there is any way to get into the church besides Christ and through the Holy Spirit—if the church is something that men open the door of and admit members into—please give us "thus saith the Lord" for it.

Fourth. If uniting with one party or sect of the professed people of God does not constitute one a sectarian, then why should union with a Masonic lodge constitute a man a Freemason?

Fifth. If a person is in Christ Jesus, is he not in the church, and is he not already joined to all others that are joined to the Lord?

Pure Religion very smartly, as she supposes, ranks "come-outers" with "all other sects," by which she virtually admits that they are as good as the others, and then says that it takes the following elements to make a good "come-outer": 1. It is necessary that the person be "turned out of some church," meaning of course one of those "other sects," for a little sober, candid reflection upon the

Bible will show any person that such remarks can not apply to the true church at all; for "the Lord added to the church daily such as should be [or, were being] saved," and 'no man [or ecclesiastical court] can pluck them out of his hand.'

If the editress of Pure Religion were half as zealous to know what the Bible teaches as she is to exhibit her wit, she would doubtless have learned that the church is not something that men organize and admit members into, but that it is "a holy temple in the Lord," "God's building, God's husbandry."

2. The editress thinks that to be a good "come-outer" the person should have a small stock of religion and "quite a good stock of ignorance." We presume that she did not consider that in those words she condemned as nearly graceless and very ignorant such men as Luther, Melancthon, Fox, and Wesley, who at the very time when they stood out of and condemned all sects and did not contemplate joining or forming any, wielded their greatest power for God.

The Good Way recently informed us that Wesley never contemplated the forming of a sect. What was he then but a "come-outer"? It is an undeniable fact upon record that he deplored the unhappy divisions and parties of Christendom.

It is the uniform testimony of the history of the Reformation that every reform effort was attended by a much greater power and demonstration of the Spirit of God before it culminated in a new sect than ever was manifest in that sect afterward. I think I can safely challenge a single exception to this fact. During ten years labor in the denomination that grew out of the labors of J. Winebrenner and his coworkers, it was the constant admission of the old fathers and mothers that no such power of God had been witnessed in that body as was before they assumed and received the name of another religious denomination. The same is true of early Methodism, and in a remarkable manner is it true of the Free Methodists. Let me give you a few extracts from the "History of the Origin of Free Methodism," by Sister Sidney M'Creery, who with her husband, Joseph M'Creery, was associated with B. T. Roberts and William Kendall from the beginning of the great holiness revival that resulted in their separation from the Methodist Episcopal sect. Hence she testifies what she knows and declares what she has seen.

The record is that for six years they worked and prospered wonderfully under the power of God and freedom from all sect yokes, and that from the formation of a new sect by B. T. Roberts the glory departed from the Nazarites, as they had been called. She says:

"B. T. Roberts in his discipline says the Free Methodist organization was a necessity. Was it? Let the hundreds testify who were so wonderfully and lovingly united together in the Holy Ghost. The truth is this: God's heritage and work were spoiled by the laying on of man's hands.

"While enjoying this spiritual fellowship all was peace and harmony and the work of conversion went on, the saints rejoiced, and the sectarian devil was mad, sinners in Zion were afraid and trembled as they saw the weakest saint upon his knees.

"B. T. Roberts started out with a trap in hand, making a new test of fellowship. He visited far and wide among the live pilgrims, preaching sect fellowship as the one thing needful, and that they could go no further without it.

"In most cases it took them by surprize. They examined themselves and reasoned thus: We are already in fellowship with the Father, Son, and Holy Ghost, and in holy spiritual fellowship with the saints, and God has given us the victory again and again while fighting against the unholy sects. What can the sect yoke do for us? We are now free to go everywhere preaching and teaching in the name of Jesus. Thus many stood out for a while. Oh, what robbery, what treachery, to pervert and use this work of God, which began so gloriously, to the building up of a carnal and selfish organism! At every gathering, large or small, the sect yoke was presented and held forth as 'the cross'.

"My husband was satisfied with God's way of ordering the battle; yea, more than satisfied; he rejoiced and was exceeding glad to see the prosperity of Zion in our midst. While B. T. R. said in action by the formation of his sect, 'I have suffered enough reproach and shame; I will number Israel and become as other nations,' then the work of building up 'our church' commenced. How the enemy triumphed! At all the gatherings the spirit of sectarian zeal was worked up to the highest pitch, and so fulfiling the scripture which saith, 'Who changed the truth of God into a lie, and worshiped and served the creature more than the Creator, who is blessed for ever.'... "And today he (B. T. R.) has no more influence than any other sect bishop, whereas he was once a terror to evil-doers and a praise to them who did well. From this time the battle of the Lord ceased and the enemies rejoiced. Some who remember the former days of liberty and power ask B. T. R. why the same power is not manifested now as formerly. He answers on this wise: God then gave the people a special blessing for a special work. Very good; but why not continue under these special blessings and in this special work? What an absurdity, what inconsistency to build another sect in order to go through the same variations and evolutions of its predecessors! Was it pleasing in the sight of God to manufacture another class of backsliders? Was it a necessity? Wherever I go I find the burden of Free Methodist preaching is to backslidden membership, whereas before its formation—while they remained in God's order, where he placed them—every man, woman, and child was able to do a full day's work. In visiting many places I find them (the F. M.'s) nearly, if not quite, extinct. In missionary fields the work takes well for a season, but when they begin proselyting and making it a 'necessity' to gather them into their peck measure, then the Lord leaves them to themselves. As I am passing through the land I often meet with those with whom I was acquainted during the war of the Lord, and immediately they refer to the former days of power and salvation and say, 'We don't have such meetings nowadays; I would go a long distance to enjoy such privilege.'"

We might multiply quotations, but these will suffice to show the fact that the formation of sects is the destruction of Christianity. Thus it is an undeniable fact, that when men enjoyed the stigmatized "come-out" "stock of ignorance," they have been used of God far more than after they suddenly became wise (?) in building up a wall about themselves or entering a sect pen built by some one else.

The Vanguard calls coming out of Babylon "a kind of spiritual rash"; and Pure Religion and Gath Rimmon both think that very smart, and serve it up to their readers. May the Lord forgive this lightness. Had we not better look into the Word of God and see what the Lord saith, than to indulge in mere witticisms? Does the Word of God teach that it is a "spiritual rash" to belong to Christ alone and hold only to him, "the head over all things to the church, which is his body, the fulness of him that filleth all in all"? Was Christ afflicted with a spiritual rash when he said, "There shall be one fold and one shepherd"? Was that the infirmity that Paul had when he said 'there should be no schisms in the body'—no Methodist schism, no Wesleyan schism, no Free Methodist bond schism, nor United Brethren; yea, **no** schism?

Now, brethren, if you dare drop the scales from your eyes and look squarely at the Holy Bible, you must admit that every one of those sect organizations which you call churches are schisms, just what God condemns and forbids. Unless you are shamefully blind, you know it to be the truth and nothing but the truth, and your slurs and sarcasms can not revoke that truth nor enable you to stand when you are judged by it.

*   *   *   *   *

There are other exchanges that have uttered hard things against the Rock on which I stand. Now, I simply want you to know what you are doing, then if you wish to continue kicking against the goads, you may do so. Do you believe that Christ purchased and founded one church of the living God? Do you believe that the "body of Christ" is the church? Do you believe that Christ is the only door to the church, and that "by him if any man enter he shall be saved"? Do you believe that the Holy Spirit sets the members in the body, the church? Do you believe there should be "no schisms in the body"? Do you believe that believers are "made perfect in one" and that "thorough holiness destroys sects and denominations"? Do you believe that 'divisions and offences are contrary to the doctrine we have received' of Christ? Do you believe that Christians should not be "unequally yoked together with unbelievers"?

In the name of our Lord Jesus Christ I ask any paper to speak out and tell me which of these points you dispute. And if you say you believe them all, as some of you have, then I ask, Why do you object to my believing the same? for that is just what I believe. The only difference is, I act consistently with my faith, while you say and do not.

You admit there is but one church of God, still you think hard of me for not allowing that all your "churches" are of God. This is God's truth and you can not deny it. You say that sects are wrong, but advise God's children to continue in the wrong. I claim that sects are wrong, and therefore say, Come out from among them, as saith the Lord. Men professing godliness should act consistently with their belief.

If you believe that Christ is divided and there are many folds, many bodies, many Lords, many faiths, instead of "one fold," "one body," "one Lord," and "one faith," then you may consistently with your faith antagonize the Gospel Trumpet; but you must abide the consequences of fighting against God's Word. And remember this, that in the day of judgment it will do you no good to have put false colors on the truth you are opposing. You will not plead before the bar of God that I taught "no-churchism," "no organization," etc.

If you are ignorant of the Trumpet's teaching, you will be condemned before God for opposing and speaking evil of the things you do not understand. You should hold your peace until you know what you are talking about.

If you do know what we—myself and contributors—teach, you know that every paper insists on organization, the very organization set forth in the New Testament, and you do know that we all advocate the church, and never have encouraged anybody to leave her; but we chose to learn from the simple Word of God what the church is, and not from your Dark Age creeds and confused tongues. Now, all you who have lifted up your heel against Christ and his body, the only true church in heaven and earth, have done so because you have some sect idol in your heart and can not receive the truth or endure sound doctrine, or else you have not the moral courage to assault the devil in his stronghold of divisions. What does Satan care for your clamor against the "sin in the sects" so long as you give him the best means of bringing God's house or kingdom to naught—the sin of sects? I pity your sad confusion. May God give you all repentance to the acknowledging of the truth.

An editorial in the July 25 number answers an objection by the editor of the Sword.

THAT'S RIGHT

Brother Dolan makes a sweeping cut with his Sword like this: "Sectism is of the devil, and no-sectism is of the devil."

Amen. That's true. An ism spirit may attach itself to any principle, false or true.

As many sects have been developed by making a center of some subordinate point of the Christian system as by rallying upon some mere human tradition.

Whether men worship the moon or an idol of their own make, it is an equal insult to God; and whether men worship a gospel principle, or a doctrine of devils, is of little if any difference in the sight of God. Either case is idolatry; because Christ is supplanted as the center by something else either subordinate or foreign. When men get a chronic lopsidedness, so that they will scan greedily over a paper and drop it as soon as they see nothing on their hobby, whether it be sect or antisect, Sabbath or antisabbath, or anything else, notwithstanding it may contain much good, pure food, many blessed thoughts about Jesus, they have put something else in the place of Christ, and their religion runs about like a grindstone with its axis near the outer circumference and passing diagonally through the stone.

We once heard a Disciple preacher say that every sect that holds some truth that no other sect holds, has a right to its existence. This provides for as many sects as there are truths in the religion of Christ; but God allows no "schism in the body." Nothing but the exclusive 'holding the Head,' 'seeing Jesus only,' and the full enjoyment and constant "praising of the beauty of holiness," can keep us from all isms.

A selection from the Vanguard, copied in the Trumpet shows the spiritual state into which a number of leading holiness editors had by this time drifted because of a failure to follow as God was leading.

BACKSLIDDEN

Brother Brooks in the last number of the Banner (and his authority as the oldest holiness editor in the country can not be doubted) says that the aggressiveness has gone out of the holiness movement, and ceasing to be aggressive it is a dying thing. In most places its numbers are decreasing, only a few accessions.

Well, he tells the truth. The holiness people as a general thing through the country are backslidden from God. A large per cent of them never had anything but a reclaimed backslidden experience to leave. They got back to God and called it by the new name of holiness, taught to do so by superficial teachers that wanted to swell the Banner reports.

      *   *   *   *   *

The chief cause of this awful declension that has rolled back the tide of the salvation of the world a decade is that the editors and evangelists, failing to become more and more aggressive at every point against sin in the church and out, especially among holiness people, have backslidden as a class....

Brother Brooks told me he could not put radical truth into the Banner without Brother Haney and Brother Kent and other such temporizers writing and denouncing him; so Brother Brooks would yield and backslide from Holy Ghost power.

Bro. Isaiah Reid told Brother Sherman he did not want anything in his paper that would indicate that the holiness people were not all right; he was planning to have the Highway as a support for his old age. A year ago he called for a thousand "firemen" in the holiness work as the only thing needed. He has spent his energies this year in regulating the fiery come-outers from wrecking the train, and evidently wants the oaks of Bashan slashed down with a little hatchet, and not with a broadax. Rams' horns, goad sticks, and the unsectarian "jaw-bone of an ass" Philistine-killer, he evidently does not take much stock in. Brothers Inskip and Macdonald are not square on the Freemason question and are churchy. While the shell remains in part of radical holiness, that only is the real thing, much of the spirit is gone. You may call it fault-finding, sour godliness, or whatever you please, these are God's facts about your case. You know the whole batch of you are afraid to throw red-hot truth uncompromisingly everywhere. We except from this catalog Baker and Arnold of the Free Methodist, Warner of the Trumpet, Johnson of the Stumbling Stone (if he had the Holy Ghost), and the Sword, and some others.

Now Brother editors and evangelists, suffer the word of exhortation from a "jaw-bone," break up your fallow ground, do your first works, burn up Haney's chapter on dress, not resolve against it; pay your debts, or go and acknowledge them at least; cease to print such dawdle as Brother Bryant's church holiness writings; seek for and get the Holy Ghost again; and lead the people up into the land.—Vanguard.

Satanic forces were arrayed against the reformation work in every conceivable way, not only by mobs and undisguised, professional evil (though this form of attack was usually instigated by the sectarian element), but also by deception—by teachers and editors who were apparently right on some main question in order to deceive, but wrong on some other vital points. A writer in the Trumpet points out one of these destructive agencies.

A DESTRUCTIVE HERESY
BY D. W. M'LAUGHLIN

There is an eternal antagonism between true holiness and fanaticism in all its phases, and the individual possessed of the fulness of the Holy Ghost will be able to detect fanaticism in others whether it be in outward act or deportment or in the more subtle form of heretical teaching. The Spirit and the Word agree, and the Holy Spirit moves and works in harmony with the written Word and never contrary thereto.

*   *   *   *   *

The writer has been receiving from time to time during the last four years copies of the Stumbling Stone, and while much truth is found in its columns as to the evils of sect divisions, the destructive heresy of Count Zinzendorf (that sanctification is not subsequent to regeneration) is held with inveterate opposition to the gospel order. Consequently, from this standpoint, the holiness movement is of the devil, and the second-grace Christians are in need of the first grace. The Stumbling Stone seems to attack every movement extant, even to the Salvation Army, as well as all holiness associations and bands for the promotion of entire sanctification. Even the position of the Gospel Trumpet he calls a holiness schism, because the editor makes a distinction between justified and sanctified believers. And he proposes to "kick Brother Warner's justification cobhouse into pi," by which he exhibits his ignorance of the real plan of salvation. He might as well talk of kicking God's Word into pi as to overthrow the two distinct works of grace, justification and sanctification....

By the above and similar remarks the Stumbling Stone editor reveals the antagonism in his heart to the "second grace" in the Bible economy of salvation. Now, my honest conviction is that a come-outism that sets itself squarely against holiness as a definite experience subsequent to pardon, is surely of the devil. It is a fact that wholly saved souls who are spiritual and discerning men detect at once the carnality in such persons, and, quite naturally, are led to conclude that "if such spirits are the fruits of come-outism I will have nothing to do with it." Thus, this spurious antiholiness come-outism is a snare of Satan to deter honest souls from separating from sectism, leaving them under the pressure of unholy corporations, which often results in compromise and the loss of the Spirit of God. A come-outism that sets itself to fighting the sects in a vindictive spirit, condemning and unchristianizing all who do not at once come out, can not be of God. Let us lead the children of God to the true apostolic unity, but never attempt to drive them out of Babylon; and, above all things, let us keep sweet and deal kindly with persons who, under the blinding influence of sectarian education, can not yet see the sin of sects, and the true church of God.

Sound teaching, in connection with the come-out movement, is of the utmost importance. False doctrinal theories and extravagant notions cause untold disaster to the cause we represent....

In the issue of May 1, 1883, when the Trumpet was yet printed at Cardington, Ohio, Brother Warner speaks of how the cause was sifted at that place.

SALT IN CARDINGTON

God's cause has passed through a terrible sifting in this place. All the powers of darkness and of Satan's hellish rage have been let loose upon the few loyal, holy little ones here. Wicked sect members have boasted that this cause was crushed out. One Methodist son of Belial, steeped in tobacco and the poison smoke of his torment, has even boasted through the secular press that he had succeeded in putting down holiness. A Quaker preacher and family have let their tongues run with the base, vulgar, and profane of the place in speaking against this way. But bless God, the devil is sadly mistaken. Several souls have recently become established, unblameable in holiness. The Lord is with us in power, the hidden ones have four meetings every week, and God is wonderfully blessing us.

In the chapter on the Gospel Trumpet we have already referred to the trying ordeal through which Brother Warner had to pass while the Publishing Office was in Bucyrus, Ohio, in 1883. A general assembly of the saints in Ohio was announced to be held on Friday, November 9. The place was Annapolis (now called Sulphur Springs), seven miles northeast of Bucyrus. In Brother Warner's call to this first general assembly in Ohio he wrote as follows:

We expect to see a large turnout of the saints of the living God from Van Wert, Paulding, and Wood Counties, and some from eastern Ohio; and come ye, dear ones, from Pennsylvania. Come, O ye sanctified hosts of the Lord! Let us eat together in the name of our Chief Shepherd and only Head and Leader. Come in the power of the Spirit; come to have the spiritual gifts stirred up and strengthened; come to sharpen each other as iron sharpeneth iron and to have the faith once delivered to the saints developed in us up to the Bible standard; come to make a more perfect consecration. Come, O ye lame and halt and blind and deaf, for the power of the Lord will be present to heal all who believe on him. Come, O ye sufferers, and give yourselves up to the mighty God and be made whole. Come, poor sinners, and be saved in the day of his power. Come, O ye poor and wayward Christians, and have your hearts established unblameable in holiness. Come, ye who are in bondage of sect captivity, and learn your way out of the wilderness unto the city that is set upon a hill, which hath foundations, and whose builder and maker is God. Come from far and near, whoever seeks the old paths and the peace of Jerusalem. Come, for the little ones will make you welcome; yea, the Spirit and the bride say, Come, and whosoever will, let him take of the water of life freely.

Little did he realize, when giving this invitation and bold promise of such benefit to all who should have any need of the divine favor, that Satan would come also with various forms of deception and attempt to divert the reformation movement into false channels and to so confuse the truth with clouds of error and fanaticism that men may not see it.

The meeting began on Friday evening at Conlay Bethel, some distance in·the country from Bucyrus. Saturday, the second day, was appointed a fast day. The first conflict came with some elements of fanaticism manifested by three men from Van Wert and Paulding Counties, who believed it wrong to wear collars, collar buttons, lace, eye-glasses, etc., and confessed that they came to the meeting purposely to make Brother Warner and the other saints take off these things. They were a great interruption of the meeting until Brother Warner finally rebuked them. After this they feigned great humility. They prostrated themselves on three sides of the table behind which Brother Warner was preaching, and would moan and groan during his discourse.

On Saturday evening the meeting was moved to the hall at Annapolis. Here another element was met. L. H. Johnson, who published in Toledo a paper called the Stumbling Stone, had arrived and even before the evening service began had mounted a wagon and begun to teach his false doctrine. He rejected the New Testament ordinances and also opposed sanctification as a second work of grace, though he was also on the anti-sectarian line. He was very bold to break in on the meeting with his harangue against the true way, which he did particularly on Sunday. On Sunday evening the saints, wishing to get away from the confusing and delusive elements, withdrew to a private house where they felt they had escaped from the atmosphere impregnated with devils, and where the meeting continued victoriously all night—until 5 A.M. On the next day, Monday, at 1 P.M. the meeting was held at another private house. This time the deceiving elements appeared and undertook to get the upper hand. The saints, being forbidden in the Scriptures to have any fellowship with devils, withdrew to another room, where the meeting progressed peacefully. One sister ventured to stay in the room occupied by the false teachers. She was suddenly seized by the awful powers of darkness and she felt she was lost. To a sister who came to her she said, "Oh, I feel so bad; take me to the altar!" She was led to the saints' apartment, where she bowed at the altar and soon began to manifest a frightful appearance. She jerked and cried, "I have a devil; stay away from me!" Her face blackened and twitched with frightful contortions, her eyes glared, her tongue darted out like a serpent's, and when any one approached her, she would spit and claw furiously. Hands were laid on her and she was instantly delivered and clothed in her right mind.

This was but one of the many remarkable manifestations. The meeting ended on Tuesday evening, and on the whole with victory on God's side, but it had been a trying time indeed. Brother Warner devoted a whole page of the Trumpet to the report of this Assembly. We quote the beginning of the report:

> We have never been called upon to portray any meeting that so transcends our powers of description. We can now better understand the language of John when he said that "if all the works of Christ had been written, I suppose the world could not contain the books." A full account of the meeting would make quite a volume. For some time we felt that the meeting would be one of unusual interest. As we received intelligence of the saints' coming from time to time, the Spirit of God was poured upon our soul, insomuch that we could not restrain the praises of God as we walked the streets. And their coming was as the heavens bowed to earth. Our little habitation was thronged most of the day on Friday, and in the evening we all went to the Conlay Bethel, where the meeting began. Since the first assembly in Michigan, where Satan was also loosed and a terrible conflict ensued, resulting in his being cast out, all the meetings of the sanctified and free saints of God that we have attended have been blessed with great unity and peace; and as there were such a host coming to this assembly, all of which we knew were of one mind and one heart in the truth and Spirit of Christ, and most of whom had never met before, we looked for a meeting that would be a sample of the reign of heaven. How apt we are to forget that we are still in the field of battle, and that Satan is now loosed for a little season, having great wrath because he knows his time is short! In the very first meeting we felt that Satan had also gathered his angels together where the sons of God came to worship the God of the Bible (Job. 1:6).

Certain of the brethren and sisters had been previously shown by visions some of the things that occurred at this meeting. The Lord was on the side of his saints and vindicated the righteousness of his cause by manifesting himself in their meetings as well as to their spiritual consciousness. Outwardly, of course, the meeting bore an aspect of confusion; but Brother Warner learned to see the good in everything. Referring, at a later date, to this assembly, he said:

> This providential bringing together of the children of light and the powers of darkness has proved a great blessing to the saints in that it has clearly brought to light which side men occupy.

The Bucyrus assembly was but one engagement with the forces that at this time had gathered to oppose and overthrow the reformation work which Brother Warner and the Trumpet had begun. Other instruments were to figure in the struggle, and another terrific battle was soon to follow. There were two prominent holiness teachers who were not in sympathy with Brother Warner's position regarding sects. They opposed the coming out from denominationalism. R. S. Stockwell was a young minister who had helped in the meetings and who had been loved and respected by both Brother Warner and Sister Warner, but had become exalted in himself and deceived, and had sprung a very pernicious doctrine, the doctrine of marital celibacy. He held that the sex relation was carnal; that when a person was fully cleansed, the love for a husband or wife was no more than the love for any one else; especially, that if a husband and wife were not in harmony it would be wrong for them to maintain the conjugal relation or be to each other anything more than to any one else; and that they would have more love for others with whom they were in harmony than for their own companion, etc. The attainment along this line was an advanced experience, a sort of third work of grace.

Sister Warner was a splendid woman and had been a faithful companion to her husband. She had borne her part well in the arduous duties of their evangelical career. But there had come in some disorder that had begun to affect their fellowship. Brother Warner mentions it thus in his "Meditations."

> First there appeared mysteriously withal,
> Some leprous spots on our domestic wall.
> The plague soon marred our holy fellowship,
> Then ate like moth the threads of love that knit
> Our hearts and souls in sweet connubial bliss,
> And made us one in sympathetic flesh.

It is probable that this would have been but temporary had not deceiving forces combined to turn her mind and estrange her from her husband. She came from a well-to-do family, and it is possible that the contrast of a life more or less destitute of physical comfort had some weight with her at this time and made her susceptible to the suggestion that perhaps the Trumpet could be more successfully managed in the hands of some one else. There were those who were desirous of taking it over and had the means to invest in it. Under Stockwell's instruction she endeavored to consecrate for the "third work," and under his enamoring influence the enemy took advantage of her state of mind, and she came into affinity with spirits that antagonized the work that the Lord had been accomplishing through her and her husband. Once in the hands of these enemies, the "flying roll," which had begun to carry messages of salvation to thousands, would of course have to cease its mission. A league of babel spirits, though dissimilar in character, comprising free-love, antiordinance, anti-second-work, and anti-come-out elements, had united against Brother Warner.

In a meeting at a private house in Bucyrus, Stockwell, who had begun to assume a papal-like authority, gave those assembled about an hour's harangue, which was like a gathering storm about to break on Brother Warner. There were peculiar manifestations at this meeting. On a lounge lay a woman of frightful appearance, her face drawn, her eyes sunken, and she was uttering moans. Another, a man with distorted limbs and scowling countenance, also gave evidence of an attack upon his body by some supernatural power. It was claimed by Stockwell that these were divine evidences that some one needed to be set right; just who, the Lord would make known. Each began to say, "Lord, is it I?" Brother Warner had been asking the Lord for wisdom and had been shown that after some trial of suffering he would be able to take God himself for his wisdom. Now, since his wife had taken sides with others who held that he was not right, and since he was ready to suspect himself as being in error rather than his wife, he felt that possibly they were right in their contention that the error lay with him. In his intense eagerness to be right with God and have the blessing of fellowship restored in his family, he became a victim. He bowed before them

> A suppliant, in that infernal maze,
> To evil spirits' much elated gaze.

His critics gathered around him and waited with agonizing groans while Stockwell pried into his consecration and asked whether he was willing to sell the Gospel Trumpet. They said they felt that such was God's will and that if he was not able to see it he should be wise and act upon their judgment, and that his soul would be blessed in so doing. Brother Warner consented, but reserved one condition — that should God, ere the transfer be made, interdict the order and show him differently, he of course would obey God. They said, "No, but that 'if' you must leave out." Finally he was persuaded to drop the if. Then the agonies of those who, it was claimed, were groaning for him, ceased and gave place to fiendish laughter, as they supposed God's "flying roll" was taken. This was the crisis that had come upon his soul; this the price he had to pay for a decision to preach uncompromisingly the truth that should create a shudder in the ranks of hell and work a reformation in the world. Opposing forces had succeeded in getting him to consent to give up the Trumpet and yield to the suggestion that he was not right.

But the promised blessings did not come to his soul; on the contrary he was plunged into spiritual darkness. He had weakened and given over his sacred trust. What a night of suffering followed! Only with the morning that swept away the horrors of night came a spiritual illumination and consequent victory. His very disappointment had brought reason to its throne and changed the aspect of the situation. And the Lord broke the satanic spell, filled his soul with peace, and enlightened his understanding as to the devilish powers that had been seeking to crush his soul. He went to the little publishing office, bowed in thankfulness, renewed his covenant, and was swallowed up completely in God once more. He then felt that he could henceforth take the Lord for his wisdom against all the suggestions of men or devils transformed as angels of light.

John N. Slagle, befriender of D. S. Warner.

But now he began to realize that his trueness to God would mean the sacrifice of his own bosom companion. This, then, should be the lingering phase of his sorrow. For about one week the battle alternated between victory and the attacks of hell. Morning would bring apparent release, and Satan's hosts would flee, only to renew the conflict when the shadows of evening gathered around him. His strength wore away. He prayed that he might be comforted by some friend, if one were left. There was a brother, a John N. Slagle, whom God had reserved and who had expressed to Brother Warner a forewarning of some trouble. This brother came to him and took him to his home, seven miles in the country, where was enjoyed a sweet sleep and a respite from the storm's rage. The poem Meditations on the Prairie, is very touching in its description of these experiences. What this humble servant of God had to pass through in this trying ordeal only One can know. In one long sleepless night of parching fever and inward pain a portion of his hair suddenly turned grey. What wonder that the Trumpet during this period was sometimes late in reaching its readers or that for four months it failed to appear at all!

Sidney, only living child of D. S. Warner.

With repeated endeavor Brother Warner tried to win back his alien wife. They had one child, a boy of three years. He had fears that he should have to be separated from the child also; but it seemed the mother's affection for both husband and child had forever flown. She wrote her husband that he could come and get the child for aught she cared.

> The train that bore us onward to that son
> Seemed slow that day, so very slow to run.
> We met, and lo, upon his little face
> A famine of parental love we trace.
> Three days we tarried there in strong appeal
> That God would make that woman's heart to feel
> One touch of love, yea, but one precious beam
> Of fond affection where a living stream
> Once issued forth to bless our happy home,
> But now, alas, congealed in icy zone.
> In vain was wished one moment's private talk;
> At last 'twas begged that we together walk
> Outside the city, where repose the dead,
> In silence slumb'ring in their narrow bed,
> And where, between two virgal evergreens,
> A little mound more dear than any seems:
> The grave of our Levilla Modest child,
> On whose sweet brow but three bright summers smiled.
> She was her mother's idol and firstborn,
> Her childish virtues memory still adorn.
> But this request she coolly yet declined,
> As if no love to living or dead remained.
> Then, taking that one warm and little hand,
> We slowly walked to where cold marbles stand.
> Dear Sidney chatted merrily on the way
> Not knowing what within our bosom lay:
> 'Twas hard to answer to his prattling words
> With but the tearful tribute grief affords.
> Poor child! God bless him! We devoutly pray
> He ne'er may feel what father felt that day.
> We came to where there had been laid to rest
> The form, now cold, that we had known was blessed
> To hold a pure and lovely spirit-bud
> That went to blossom in the home of God.
> And there beside the foot of that small mound
> We knelt in prayer upon the turfy ground.
> Dear Sidney—bless the child—rememb'ring how
> In family worship he was wont to bow
> Close to our side in sweet becoming grace,
> He gently came and now resumed his place.
> His tender heart beat with devotion there

As soft his name was breathed in fervent prayer.
But oh, that hour! what deep emotions rose!
No earthly language could our heart disclose.
For our child's dear sake some feeble words were used,
But they failed to carry what was inward mused.
Oh! how our heart longed for the poet's flight
To sing relief to deep affection's blight.
When touched emotions ripe like a swelling flood
And merge the soul, oh! it is then we would
That some kind angel could but lend his harp
To start the flowing of a surcharged heart.
But mundane language gave no wings to thought;
Our feelings could in tears alone flow out.

Brother Warner endeavored to regard this alienation of his wife as Providential. He took it all for good and felt that by it he would experience all the more of Heaven's riches in his soul.

Through the kindness of a brother who happened to have a copy of the Christian Harvester of May 1, 1884, we are able to give to the readers the article by Mrs. Warner in which she renounced the movement which she brands Come-outism.

COME-OUTISM RENOUNCED

The following communication pretty fully explains itself. It was written by Sister Warner, the wife of D. S. Warner, the Come-out leader, and editor of the Gospel Trumpet. Those who know Sister W. generally, among the straight holiness people, have confidence in her integrity. God bless her, and may she save her husband from his strong delusions. She desires the holiness papers to copy her article:

Dear Brother Doty: My soul praises God today for a perfect salvation in Jesus. He sweetly abides in my heart, and I do know that his Word is true. His promises to save from all sin and keep in perfect peace are most wonderfully verified in my case; praise his name! Salvation is sweeter to my soul every day I live.

"And how sweetly Jesus whispers,
Take the cross, thou needst not fear;
For I've trod this way before thee,
And the glory lingers near."

Yea, praise God for the cross, and the glory that always follows.

I feel it my duty to say to all God's children, that he has opened my eyes to see the evils of come-outism. I am free from it, and forever renounce it and praise God that he has so completely delivered me from the spirit of it. I am thoroughly convinced that this effort to unite God's people by calling them out of the church- es is not God's plan of unity. It simply cuts off a few members by themselves, who get an idea that none are clearly sanctified unless they see as "we" do; and, then, they have a harsh grating that is the very opposite of love. I have found that the predominant spirit of the come-out movement is the same self-righteous, pharisaical spirit that Christ rebuked when he was here on earth. They hold and teach that no one can be entirely sanctified and belong to a "sect."

It is not necessary for me to speak of the fanaticism and absur- dities connected with this movement; but I am not at all surprized to hear of men losing their minds after passing through such a meeting as the assembly at Sulphur Springs last November. I have seen more Babylon confusion outside the churches than in. I know whereof I speak, for I have been connected with the move- ment from its beginning, and, as you all know, at the very head of it. And while I believe it my duty before God to renounce it, and stand aloof from it, I have all charity for those connected with it. I am confident that I have nothing in my heart but love toward them all, and love to my husband; nor do I reject him, but I can not endorse either the movement or its organ, the Gospel Trumpet. I must obey God, and walk in the light he has given me, or forfeit salvation, which I can not afford to do. I have suffered the loss of all things, but rejoice to know that I am counted worthy to suffer for Jesus' sake.

In taking this step for God I have not been hasty. I have been convicted of this duty for some time. Circumstances and the man- ifestations of the spirit of this movement have been such for sev- eral months past that I fear further delay on my part would be disastrous to the cause of Christ and my own soul. I humbly ask the prayers of all God's children that he will keep me firm and sweet while passing through the furnace.

Mrs. S. A. Warner.

Upper Sandusky, Ohio, Apr. 22, 1884.

Brother Warner deplored his wife's going into print with their trouble. A num- ber of the so-called holiness papers made remarks that were reflective on Brother Warner and the cause of truth. On account of this, he felt it necessary to make some reply in the Trumpet and set forth the facts concerning his wife. In the issue of July 15, 1884, he made a very clear delineation of the whole affair. He showed the sad deception into which his wife had fallen, how it had affected her conduct, and hardened her conscience to do things she was never known to do before, even to being untruthful, and yet publish her testimony abroad that she was more sweetly saved than ever. Near the close he says:

And this is the kind of holiness the sectarian sheets have

such a jubilee over. This work of the devil which has at present broken up a family, brought a reproach upon the cause of holiness, robbed us of our sweet child for over three months past, and which has filled all hell with a jubilee, the Highway of Holiness says "should be received with thankfulness." Yes, it is received in hell with thankfulness, and just to the extent that Babylon glories in the same she proves that she is in league with hell.

While our heart is sad for the sake of our dear companion, we have great reason to give everlasting thanks to God for the glorious fruits of these furnace flames. Oh, how our weaknesses have been searched out and our patience perfected!

> We would not cast away the gold
> We've gathered in the furnace flame.
> Nor would we wish again the dross
> Here purged in our Redeemer's name.

In the Trumpet of July 1, 1884, a quotation is made from the writings of John Bunyan in which are recalled the persecutions that culminated in his imprisonment. He tells of how Satan, failing in one plan to overthrow his work and make it ineffectual, tries another, which was to stir up the minds of the ignorant and malicious to load him with slanders and reproaches, and finally to have him arraigned and put in jail. With this quotation Brother Warner makes the following comparison:

In all these sufferings Bunyan had, besides the grace of God, the consolations of a true wife to sustain and comfort him. With his great heart glowing with love for the truth, and deep affection for her that had been such a true friend in the past, just suppose for a moment the devil had in the time of his greatest persecution from sectarian idolaters, overthrown his faithful Elizabeth, and so blinded and deceived her as to make it appear her duty to renounce him and the truth he was devoted to, in all the papers of that day. Suppose he had found her all at once fellowshiping his persecutors and slanderers, and receiving the friendship and applause of the popular sects of that time, rather than suffering persecution with her husband for Christ's sake; do you not believe that such a trial would have more cruelly "pulled the flesh from his bones" than twelve years' imprisonment with a good and faithful wife at home sharing his reproach and offering her daily prayers to God on his behalf?

Of course the woman could not have published any sin of the man of God, nor would it have been necessary. All that she would have needed to do would have been to renounce him and the "come-out movement" that he was engaged in under God, and remind them that she "had been connected with the movement from its beginning, as you all know, and at the very head of it," and then throw out a few hints that she had "suffered" a great many things, and that "circumstances and the manifestation of the spirit of this movement have been such for several months past that I fear further delay on my part would be disastrous to the cause of Christ and my own soul." This were sufficient to confirm all the vile slanders that Satan had sent out against her husband, with all who hated the truth he taught. Oh, yes, that would settle the matter. Yes, yes, you know all the terrible things that are reported of this awfully deluded man, and now his wife comes out against him, which proves that these things are true. And if the devil were as smart then as he is now, he would have led the poor apostate guilty woman to put on a very lovely aspect in her public comforters, to the idolaters of those times, in order to have the more influence. Yea, doubtless, while selling her husband to the devil for the friendship of his enemies, and selling Christ, whose truth he dared to speak, she would have hypocritically said, "I love my husband," and "Jesus sweetly abides in my heart." Oh, what a record the day of judgment will unfold! But God be praised that Bunyan was blessed with a true companion; but let him whose lot is otherwise "bind this to him as an ornament," as Bunyan did the vile slanders heaped upon him.

After a few years there appeared in the Trumpet, in the issue of Jan. 7, 1892, the following statement, from a person who knew Mrs. Warner from her youth and who here speaks of her divorce and remarriage:

> Nothing has ever been more surprizing to me than the steps she has taken. It may not be generally known that she got a bill through the court at Upper Sandusky, Ohio. The grounds upon which she filed her complaint betray a dreadful absence of conscience and the fear of God, stating that she had "been a faithful wife to him ever since married," and that "he had been wilfuly absent from her for over three years"; when the facts are, she had wilfully abandoned him over six years before, during which time he twice visited her and wrote many letters kindly urging her to return and that without any conditions. And she was so far from being a faithful wife that she did not even answer his letters.
>
> Brother Warner did not feel led to appear against her, but faithfully admonished her for her soul's sake not to put on record in the county court and the high court of heaven statements that she knew to be so directly opposite to the truth. And, worse yet, the woman has recently shown her disregard for the counsel of the Bible by marrying another man.[15] We insisted that these few

[15] Once after her second marriage, while living in Cincinnati, she wrote a letter to her boy, Sidney, who was in the care of his father. Brother Warner had been to visit her twice since their separation, and he was constrained to go again. So he took the boy and went to the city address as given in her letter. She happened not to be at the house just then. So the two walked about leisurely until she should return. While on the opposite side of the street

> words of explanation be published to cut off all occasion for unreasonable men to speak against the cause of Christ and against his servant. —E. J. Hill.

In the Trumpet of June 1, 1893, an editorial speaks of her death, as follows:

> While holding meetings in Portland, Ind. on Wednesday, May 24, we were informed that there was a telegram at the office for us. On going there we were startled with this brief dispatch: "Sarah died this morning in Cincinnati. Signed, L. F. Keller."

> He is a brother of the one we ought to be able to call our wife, and this fact rendered the familiar name "Sarah" all sufficient in the dispatch. O my Lord, is it possible that she is cut off in the midst of her days! She who seemed so fresh and well is suddenly called to be the first to break the circle of six children, all of whom were early instructed in the fear of the Lord. Ah, we can not help the conviction that had the dear woman never been alienated by the adversary to break her solemn vows, and held by a blind and erring influence from returning to the obligations of a mother and wife, yea, and had she not been by that influence led to obtain a bill, and that on absolutely false grounds, she would be alive, well, and happy today. But alas, all is past now....

> We wrote immediately to our friend who had kindly informed us of the departure of the one who once so filled the vision of our heart, for the particulars of her death, and received a prompt reply that she died with acute typhoid fever, to which was added peritonitis, and that she did not express herself about the future. Out of a full heart we would love to say much, but we have space only for these thoughts. May God comfort the sorrowing mother, brothers, and sisters.

> The unhappy woman, having forsaken her God, her husband, and child, became married over a year ago to another man. But alas, how often the path that leads from God is cut short!

As to what became of Stockwell, the author has found no trace. When Brother Warner recovered his spiritual poise, after the terrible conflict at Bucyrus, he renounced Stockwell, and the latter at once dropped all profession.

An incident that occurred at Medina, Ohio, before Stockwell's defection, gave Brother Warner some trouble. A Mrs. Booth had had a vision in which she saw herself caught up with a thousand-dollar note. Stockwell, who was at that time apparently in sympathy with the Trumpet, interpreted her vision to her as meaning that she should give the one thousand dollars to the Trumpet. She then decided

---

from her house they saw her returning. She reached the house first and entered the hall and stood waiting for them. When they reached the door she railed out in terrible abuse on her former husband. That was his only reception. He had on his former visits to her felt the Spirit dictating that there was no hope of a reconciliation; and likewise on this occasion, as his child clung the closer to him, the Spirit said, "It is enough; leave off thy fond pursuit."

to do so and threw the money into the lap of Sister Warner, who refused to accept it. Stockwell then said *he* would take it, which he did, and with it paid off the debt against the Trumpet office. After this was done, Mrs. Booth came to Brother Warner one day in company with an attorney for the purpose of recovering the money, whereupon Brother Warner adjusted the matter by mortgaging the Trumpet equipment for one half the amount and giving a note for the balance. The report got out in some manner that he had fraudulently taken the money from Mrs. Booth. In explanation he speaks of the matter as follows:

> We feel rather like treating with silent contempt the wicked aspersions that have gone through many papers, secular and religious, against our character; but as friends demand it of us we will just say that the report that we fraudulently took from a Mrs. Booth a thousand dollars by mesmeric influences is wholly and basely false. If we have been correctly informed, it was fabricated by a lying infidel in Bucyrus and furnished to a Cincinnati Enquirer reporter by him. That paper, after consulting more reliable parties in Bucyrus, on the 15th of last February published an article refuting all the reflections that had been cast upon us. The Church Advocate, having published the Enquirer's slanders, also took back the charges against us. The fact is, we never had any hand in obtaining that money. We were at our home and knew not that the woman had a thousand dollars or any money at all, until a letter was sent me stating she had given the same. We also have letters from her stating that she had cheerfully and deliberately given the money; that God had called her to do so and that she did not regret the step she had taken. But subsequently she fell through the opposition of her husband and Satan, and we gave security for the money because it was demanded, though we were under no legal or moral obligation to do so.

One can imagine that during his severe trial at Bucyrus Brother Warner felt very much forsaken. But God had many others who were ready to stand with him. There were those who were solicitous with reference to his welfare. In one of the issues of the Trumpet we find this little note:

> A brother writes thus, inquiring of us, "O Daniel! is thy God continually able to deliver thee?" Through the amazing grace of God we are able to answer from the lion's den and from the seven-times-heated furnace, Yes. Glory to the God of our salvation, he keeps our soul above the world, the flesh, and the devil, and from all sin. He keeps us from these two opposite regions of death, namely, the cold, hard-hearted, grating, fruitless spirit of carnal sect-hatred on one side; and from the soft, spurious, self-soothing, carnality-pleasing, and sect-compromising, all-bogus love delusion on the other. God helping us we shall never move out of Mic. 3:8 and Psa. 149:6-9.

He received many letters from those who were sympathetic and who were thankful for the Trumpet. The following are a few:

I am so glad to get the Gospel Trumpet. I think it is the best paper I ever read. It speaks the Bible truth.

May the Lord bless you in the good work, and give you grace and strength to withstand all the fiery darts that Satan and his hosts can hurl at you. God and Christ shall be for walls of salvation about you. Whom shall we fear when God is our friend? I am trusting in Jesus for a full and free salvation. 'Without holiness no man shall see God.' It does my soul good to read the testimonies of how God is healing both soul and body, I believe he is willing to manifest as much power on earth today as he did when Christ was here in the flesh. Your sister, saved through the blood,

L. B.

We are continually praising God for the way he is keeping you through every severe trial. When we understood the reality of your trials we all wept as if we had been at a funeral. How our hearts go out in sympathy for you! O dear brother, hold on to God; he will not forsake those that trust in him. You must come to our camp-meeting without fail, for we know God wants you here; but the sect people are hoping you will not come. Your sister,

M. J. F.

May God reward you in your great work. Some good friend is sending me the Trumpet, and I do love to read it, because it has the right ring. It sounds as if it had been baptized in the Holy Ghost and with fire. I never saw until I was baptized with the Holy Ghost the corruption of sectism. I am so glad that there are a few that do stand for Christ and him alone. Your brother,

H. B. C.

My prayer is that you may continue blowing the Trumpet, and that it may always give a clear and certain sound. I had a pretty sharp discussion with a minister today on the subject of sanctification. By the grace of God I was under the necessity of telling him that he was not a competent witness on the subject, having never received the experience. Oh, why will men attempt to explain and preach that of which they know nothing! May the God of all grace be continually your refuge and your exceeding great reward.

M. M.

That the Trumpet had the right ring was a fact recognized wherever there were spiritual Christians who had felt the oppression and seen the evils of human control in the so-called churches, and of course that meant in all parts of the country. There were many ready to fall in line with its teachings. Besides Beaver Dam, in Kosciusko County, Ind., and Carson City, in Michigan, as original centers, there had come to be congregations in other parts of the States named, and in Ohio, Pennsylvania, Missouri, Iowa, Kansas, and others. The reformation was in all places marked with spiritual vigor, enthusiasm, joy, love, fellowship, confidence, and activity. People who came in contact with it and who were not already prejudiced by sectarianism, were made to feel, by a spiritual discernment, that "this is the way" and "these people have the truth." A spirit of victory pervaded the work everywhere. God manifested himself by the outpouring of his Spirit and by miraculous healings and answers to prayer.

A remarkable instance of healing occurred at the first camp-meeting held near Bangor, in southwestern Michigan, in June, 1883. Emma Miller, who lived in Battle Creek, had been an invalid for nearly three years. Her eyes had become affected and she had to be led about. For nearly the whole period of three years (or, lacking one month) she had not read a line of print. After her conversion, which occurred nine months previously to her healing, she was plainly shown by the Lord that she would be healed. On being invited to the camp-meeting she was again shown, in answer to her prayer, that she would be healed. She requested her friends to provide her with paper and envelopes, promising to write to them. In this confidence she went to the meeting.

On the fourth morning of the meeting, after continued prayer had been offered, she was impressed she would be healed that day. Brother Warner had been called away from the meeting, but J. C. Fisher and others were present. Here was a case of blindness. Her eyes were covered with a film and the lids were closed through paralysis and she could not open them. But nothing daunted the little body of spiritual workers here assembled. Fasting and importunity characterized the earnest prayer. About 5 P. M. of the day mentioned, while Sister Miller was seated on the rostrum, where she had been requested to sit that all might see, suddenly her eyes were opened and she gazed upon the audience and praised the Lord. The people were amazed. Some fell to shouting, which was heard two miles away. Others trembled and cried. After praising God for an hour or more Sister Miller went out into the bright sunlight without any unpleasant sensation, the first time for nearly three years, and wrote two postal cards. Her eyes became bright and strong. Sister Miller (now Mrs. A. B. Palmer) is still living and has had her sight ever since.

Marvelous healings were common, but as this one was a healing of complete blindness and was one of the earliest cases, it is here mentioned. Another divine manifestation was the power given to the ministry over devils. Since the early centuries it has not been characteristic of any spiritual movement prior to this one, so far as the author has learned, that devils were in such subjection and had to come out of those possessed.

By this time quite a force of ministers had been raised up in various portions of the country. Over in Missouri was a man named Jeremiah Cole, who had been led into the light independent of any human instrumentality. He had suffered from dyspepsia for twelve years; he had been so bad he could eat only specially prepared articles of food. He was instantaneously and wonderfully healed in answer to his own importuning prayer, so that he could eat all ordinary foods without discomfort. His own healing led to the healing of his sister, Mary, who had been an invalid all her life. She began to have spasms at two years of age, and later dyspepsia and other ailments, until her life was one of continual suffering. Through her own prayer and that of her brother, she also was led to claim her healing, and the work was done. Both of these persons became effective ministers in the reformation.

In northwestern Ohio God had raised up several persons (among whom were A. J. Kilpatrick, William N. Smith, J. N. Howard, and Sarah Smith) who also became prominent workers. In western Pennsylvania was G. T. Clayton, and in yet other parts of the country, far and near, were those who had received light on the church, in some cases without any teaching from any one, and who were by the Spirit of God added to the ministry.

APOSTASY OF FISHER

A sad defection from the ranks of those who had been active in the reformation work was that of J. C. Fisher, which has been already referred to. He was a very effectual preacher. It was through his efforts that the original company was raised up at Carson City, Mich., where he lived at the time. Also it was through his instrumentality that the work was started in southwestern Michigan and in some other parts of the country. Through a lack of his consecration, sad to say, he became unfaithful in his marriage relation and found affinity with another. After being patiently and faithfully counseled by Brother Warner and others, and after it became evident that he was rejecting all admonitions, and in fact had married another woman, he had to be renounced and cut off from the fellowship of the saints.

This was a distinct loss to the cause, for Fisher had been a very successful evangelist, and had a great influence. His error, however, was plain, and there were scarcely any who were sufficiently in sympathy with his actions to be to any extent drawn away with him.

As a part of this chapter, we wish to include an article from one of the earlier Trumpets, written by a contributor, which touches the central principle of the reformation, the principle which distinguishes it from all other movements. It is on this line, the ruling authority of the Holy Ghost, that the reformation proceeds.

RULING AUTHORITY OF THE HOLY GHOST
BY D. W. M'LAUGHLIN

Notwithstanding the apostasy of the Romish Church, her utter departure from the faith because of the substitution of a man-made system of ecclesiasticism for the personal presence and authority of the Holy Ghost, Protestants have not profited (but in part) by her fall; they have very generally fallen into a like snare.

The apostolic church fully recognized the personal presence and authority of the Holy Ghost. He was fully accepted as their teacher and guide. They fully embraced the words of Jesus: "When he, the Spirit of truth, is come, he will guide you into all truth"—yea, "teach you all things," even the "deep things" of God. Hence, we hear Peter saying unto Ananias, "Why hath Satan filled thine heart to lie to the Holy Ghost?" The presence of the divine Spirit was to them a certainty.

In Acts 13:2 we read, "As they ministered to the Lord, and fasted, the Holy Ghost said, Separate me Barnabas and Saul for the work whereunto I have called them." Here the authority of the Holy Ghost is recognized. Thus we see that the early church needed no man-made system; being filled with the Holy Ghost they fully accepted him as their teacher and guide. But in process of time the church lost her primitive power; the presence of the Holy Ghost seemed less real. The necessity of a teacher and guide was felt; hence the absence of the Holy Ghost necessitated the substitution of another teacher and guide, a "dead ecclesiasticism," called the Holy Catholic Church (?), with the prerogative of the divine Spirit—thus priesthood was exalted and invested with power to forgive sins; and the pope made the "visible head of the church," or the vicar of Jesus Christ upon earth. But the church felt the need of an "infallible teacher"; the loss of the divine Paraclete necessitated a substitution, if the resemblance of the apostolic church be maintained; hence the system must supply the lack. Thus the dogma of infallibility was conceived, ending in the exaltation of the pope of Rome above all that is called God, or that is worshiped—the "man of sin" "sitting in the temple of God, shewing himself that he is God."

Any man-made system of ecclesiasticism must necessarily be lifeless and powerless, just in proportion as it fails to recognize the personal presence and authority of the Holy Ghost, and sets up its own order and authority.

Indeed the modern church has so far lost sight of the veritable presence and authority of the personal Holy Ghost, that everything seems reduced to man-ordered system—yea, an endless treadmill of works. The form of religion takes the place of vital godliness, and the people seem to have forgotten that there is any Holy Ghost.

It is said history repeats itself; let us consider what meaneth the cry of "fanatic" now so prevalent in the sects as used against the holiness movement. Perhaps we may learn a lesson from Rome—why did the Romish hierarchy persecute the Reformers? Simply because there had been substituted a wire-bound ecclesiasticism (a man-made system) for the presence and authority of the personal Holy Ghost; a lifeless system—yea, a dead ecclesiasticism was thought to be the one holy catholic church. It was not allowed that any could be loyal to God unless loyal to the system, hence the cry of "heretic," which today finds its counterpart in the term "holiness fanatic" as used by the dominant sects against holiness men. In their devotion to churchism they lose sight of the personal Holy Ghost, and exalt the system. We must go back to apostolic ground; the presence and power of the Holy Ghost must mark (or make manifest) the church. The blinding power of churchism will deceive nominal professors in the Protestant sects just as effectually as it did in the Roman Church. It is eternally true that the natural man perceiveth not the things of the Spirit of God. The great Sanhedrin judged it right that Jesus Christ, the Lord of glory, judged to be a vile deceiver, should be crucified between two thieves; the Romish Church considered it right to burn "heretics"; and in all ages the mystic Babylon of Revelation has persecuted the true saints of God.

Thus it will be till the time of the end.

THE ONE CHURCH

Through the night of doubt and sorrow
Onward goes the pilgrim band,
Singing songs of expectation,
Marching to the Promised Land.

One the object of our journey,
One the faith that never tires,
One the earnest looking forward,
One the hope our God inspires.

One the strain that lips of thousands
Lift as from the heart of one;
One the conflict, one the peril,
One the march in God begun.

One the gladness of rejoicing
On the far eternal shore,
Where the one Almighty Father
Reigns in love forevermore.

Onward therefore, pilgrim brothers,
Onward with the Cross our aid!
Bear its shame, and fight its battle,
Till we rest beneath its shade.

—Sabine Baring-Gould.

Perishing Souls.

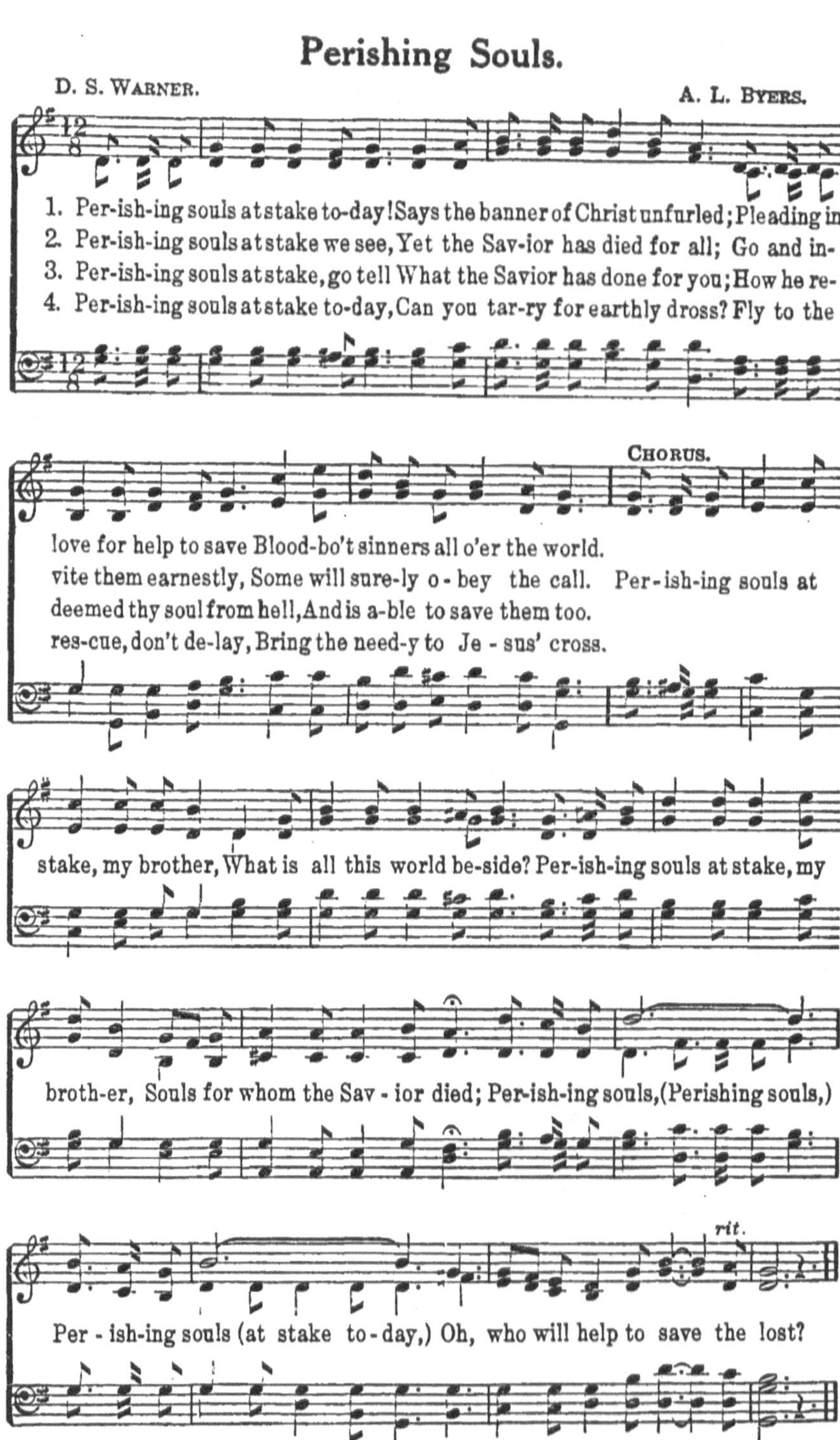

Perishing Souls.

D. S. Warner.   A. L. Byers.

1. Per-ish-ing souls at stake to-day! Says the banner of Christ unfurled; Pleading in
2. Per-ish-ing souls at stake we see, Yet the Sav-ior has died for all; Go and in-
3. Per-ish-ing souls at stake, go tell What the Savior has done for you; How
he re-
4. Per-ish-ing souls at stake to-day, Can you tar-ry for earthly dross? Fly to
the

love for help to save Blood-bo't sinners all o'er the world.
vite them earnestly, Some will sure-ly o-bey the call.
deemed thy soul from hell, And is a-ble to save them too.
res-cue, don't de-lay, Bring the need-y to Je-sus' cross.

Chorus.

Per-ish-ing souls at

stake, my brother, What is all this world be-side? Per-ish-ing souls at stake,
my

brother, Souls for whom the Sav-ior died; Per-ish-ing souls, (Perishing souls,)

Per-ish-ing souls (at stake to-day,) Oh, who will help to save the lost?

CHAPTER XVI

EVANGELISTIC TOURS

Trip into Pennsylvania—Various healings—Attacked by intoxicated man—Woman delivered from devils—Visits Winebrennerian camp—An incident of Beaver Dam assembly—Company of singers formed—Wonderful meeting in Indiana—Storm stayed in answer to prayer—Mob near Rising Sun, Ohio—A Western tour—Strange manifestations at St. James, Mo.—To Denver—Meetings in Canada—In the Southern field—Mob element in Mississippi—Visits Mammoth Cave—Visits the church in California—Scenery of the Rockies.

The responsibility of publishing the Trumpet required, of course, that the editor spend a good portion of his time at the Publishing Office. But Brother Warner's zeal for the evangelistic work, as well as the demand for his services here and there in the field, took him forth a good deal on various tours. An account of the principal tours he made, and the events in connection therewith, is sufficient for a chapter by itself.

For the first few years after the Trumpet started, he made frequent trips. Of these we shall give no account, but shall begin the chapter with a trip into western Pennsylvania in the summer of 1884. A camp-meeting was to be held two miles south of Sandy Lake, in Mercer County, beginning August 23. This was the second meeting for that place, as one had been held there the previous year. He planned to attend this meeting after holding a grove-meeting in Medina County, Ohio, and he accordingly announced there would be no Trumpet issued for August 15, since he expected to make this tour. Portions of his report of the Sandy Lake meeting are here given. Quotations direct from Brother Warner will enable the reader the better to comprehend the man and to feel the touch of his saintliness; for there breathes out from his words such a spirituality and devotion as is possessed only by those who are thoroughly abandoned to God.

Glory be to the God of salvation-power! These words seem best fitted to begin our report of this heavenly convocation. We were met by conveyance at Stonesboro, and the very instant we entered the precious grove of the saints' encampment we felt the presence of God. Indeed it was wonderful. We were engaged in conversation as we drove in and were not thinking of or expecting such a glorious manifestation of God, when we were suddenly filled with the consciousness of his holy presence, impressing heart and lips in praises to his holy name....

We had been unwell some days in the city, and felt half sick on the train; but as soon as we breathed the God-pervaded atmosphere of that beautiful pine-grove, all our infirmities fled away and we could shout the praises of God in a sound body. How hallowed and sweet the recollections of God's blessings upon that ground one year ago! How dear to our heart the precious chambers in Brother and Sister Carmichael's tent, where we often spent much of the brief interval between the three daily services, in nearly all of which the Lord used us to read and teach his Holy Word to the dear saints. In that precious retreat he daily filled our soul and recuperated the wasted energies of our body and mind so that we could stand and feed the Lord's sheep. Praise God, we found the same little sanctum prepared for us again. Thank God, there were plenty to share the work of the gospel ministry this year.

The blessed Holy Spirit wrought in the hearts of the people from the first service to the close of the meeting. On Tuesday we went to the stream a mile from the camp and immersed fourteen of the dear, happy saints of God. It was a glorious and wonderful time. The Spirit of the living God was poured out in mighty power. Some went down into the water shouting the high praises of God, and nearly all leaped and shouted as they came forth from the symbolic grave. What glory shone in the faces of those blood-washed ones! The place was one of beautiful scenery. On either side the stream stood the dense and lofty pines. As this blood-washed company faced the stream, with their eyes lifted toward God and their faces all lit up with heaven's glow, and sang the sweet songs of redemption, we were reminded of Bunyan's company of pilgrims that stood in white robes awaiting their invitation to cross to the celestial paradise....

Do we astonish you when we say that while sinners were melted to tears by the power of God during the baptism, and said, "This is the right way. This is the right way," an apostate and hypocrite preacher by the name of — — stood back and spake against "this way" of the Lord? Woe unto such empty clouds, wandering stars, wells without water!...

Brother Fisher was quite sick when we reached the grove, and after having been strengthened several times to preach the word he was finally and instantaneously healed by faith and the laying on of hands. The next evening the healing power was mightily upon him, and four of the dear saints were healed of various diseases and old complaints. In the early part of the meeting Brother and Sister Frost's little girl was healed of a very bad case of catarrh. The morning Brother and Sister Fisher left, the Lord woke us between three and four o'clock in the morning and led us forth into the woods to commune with him. Our mind was led to ask for a more perfect faith. Praise God, he gave it. Early we walked to Brother Farrah's house, where we found Sister Clayton very sick with sick-headache. In the name of the Lord we laid hands on her head, and she was immediately healed by faith in Jesus. Several others of the saints were healed that day....

One evening in company with Brother and Sister Fisher we went home with Brother and Sister Frost. Sister Owen lives a close neighbor to them. Her daughter had two days before been taken sick. That night she was taken very bad, and she suffered extremely. Mr. Owen wished to go for the doctor, but Lula begged her pa to send for us. Though he had been extremely prejudiced against us by some ungodly sectarian neighbors, he could not refuse the wish of his suffering child. He gave his consent, and at two o'clock we were called up, and went to the house in the name of the Lord. Lula had been praying the Lord to forgive her sins, and seemed to have found pardon, but she was in great suffering. Brother Fisher and I laid hands upon her, and in less than a minute her intense suffering ceased, and she rested until morning. Her body gradually recovered strength, and two days later she was out to the meeting. Praise the Lord, O my soul! The power of God since then so softened the heart of Brother Owen that he has turned to serve the Lord. His heart is so changed that he not only loves God but us also. May God bless the dear brother.

Praise the Lord for the wonderful bond of love that binds our hearts together in the Son of God! Blind sectarians ask us, "What have you got to bind you together?" We reply by asking them, "What have you got to part us asunder?" Oh, bless God for the balm in this union! We never know the strength of the divine bonds of love until all the sect bonds of the devil are cast away and we are led to suffer together for the gospel of God and the name of Jesus. Oh, happy bond of perfect love, which binds all the pure in heart to God and to each other!

After the close of the Sandy Lake meeting he went by invitation to Greenville, in the same county. He first held an evening service on the streets, in which he spoke to a large audience. This was on Friday evening, September 5. The rest of the services at Greenville were in a grove in the country. In his report he tells of his being mercilessly beaten by a drunken man and of his wonderful escape from injury because of divine protection.

We praise God for having sent us here. We are confident that much good was done. One brother, who had been wonderfully converted and blessed, had actually made an appointment at a schoolhouse and talked to the people by the Holy Spirit. People were moved, and asked the man to speak again. But he consulted his Methodist priest, who told him it would never do in the world for him to attempt to speak and exhort without license, and that if he did so he would be brought up and tried. The poor man was scared down and was on back ground; but he promised us to rededicate himself to God and go straight forward in God's will. May God bless and help him. Such is the pernicious work of the devil under the mask of what he calls "our church." We hope in the providence of God to return to Greenville again. A sister told us that we would receive persecution for pay. Well, praise God, we were well remunerated in that kind of currency for Christ's sake. It has brought the "leap and rejoice" with "the spirit of glory and of God" in our soul. After the grove-meeting we spoke again on the streets of Greenville to a very large crowd of attentive hearers....

After preaching in the grove Saturday night, we walked a mile and a half to find rest for the night. The mother and two of the family are fully saved. But the husband is intemperate and desperately wicked. He does not often stop with the family, as the little home belongs to one of the sons, who, with his brothers, affords protection to their mother against the father's abuse. The wretched man had been drinking liquor through the day, and was also well filled with the wine of Babylon's wrath received from his sectarian neighbors, who hate any child of God that lives godly in Christ Jesus outside of her pales. He seems to have come liquored up on purpose for a row. After entering the house, the frenzied man assaulted us with shocking oaths and threats. He was desperate, just in that state of intoxication in which he had more than his usual strength, and maddened beyond all reason. He soon struck me with all force in the forehead, but through God his blow was not more than a ball of cotton. We praised the Lord. Feeling a deep concern for the wicked man's soul, we dropped upon our knees in the middle of the room, raised our bands, and began to pray for him. But this enraged Satan more than ever. He seized a large rocking-chair and slammed it down on us with all vengeance, but through the Lord Jesus Christ our uplifted hands turned it off with ease. The storms of oaths and slamming of furniture was terrific. It looked as though there would not be a whole piece left in the room. The infuriated man grabbed a common wood-bottom chair by the back and struck down twice or three times at our head, which was safely shielded by the hand of the Lord. Glory to God in the highest! Our soul was filled with great peace in the midst of the storm; we had not the slightest fear of suffering harm.

The kind wife and a daughter, who were gloriously sanctified at the Sandy Lake meeting, tried to protect us, when the latter received a heavy blow on the shoulder from the chair, the legs having been threshed off by previous blows, making it all the better to maul with. Seeing that they were in danger of being hurt in our protection, we arose and began to retreat. The savage monster followed us out of the yard and some rods on the road with awful curses and open threats that he would kill us. Glory to the God of our salvation! There was not a hair of our head hurt, not a scratch or mark upon our body. The next morning we felt our right wrist was slightly sprained by stopping the terrible blows, but it soon disappeared. The man soon left, shortly after which his large son came, whose delay furnished the intoxicated man his opportunity for an onslaught.

Praise God, the Lord led me to do just as I had preached what a holy man should do when thus assaulted—commit our life to God, fear no evil, and let him be glorified in our death or deliverance, as he shall choose. Fearing the man might return that night and our presence excite to deeds of violence upon the family, one of the boys and I went to the barn to sleep, but I spent the night in thanksgiving to God for his sweet deliverance. Surely it is safe to trust God always.

It was while he was in western Pennsylvania that he received word from his wife that he could come and get their boy, Sidney, then a little more than three years of age. Accordingly he returned home by way of Upper Sandusky, Ohio, and got the boy. He then made a visit to the saints at Jerry City, Wood County, of which he thus speaks:

Then, following the apostolic example, we "declared what miracles and wonders God had wrought" where we have gone about preaching the kingdom of God's grace, and assured the dear saints as he did "that we must through much tribulation enter the kingdom of heaven." And the hearing of all the gracious dealing of God with our soul and in many hearts "caused great joy unto all the brethren." Many tears of sympathy and holy love flowed from the eyes of the beloved.

He arrived home at Williamston in time for the annual assembly; for which the large hall, 28×84, on the second floor of the Office building afforded a splendid place. It was a wonderful gathering of the saints. A number were ordained to the ministry, and among these he included himself, as where so many were assembled he probably decided that his call to the work should be solemnly recognized and confirmed by the laying on of hands of the elders present. As was evidenced by the success of this assembly, the work of the reformation seemed by this time to be taking a forward move. Since the Ohio assembly at Bucyrus, one year before, Brother Warner had learned to take a more fearless, unyielding attitude against deceiving elements such as had encompassed him there.

We shall ever have reasons to thank God for the benefit derived from the Ohio assembly last fall. Though much of the good anticipated was not realized because of the evil powers that were permitted to "encompass the beloved saints," yet the lessons learned as a result have furnished a protection against the devil in all subsequent meetings. The fact is, we were delivered from priestcraft and had a solemn abhorrence of everything that savored of lordism. Hence we declared the meetings free; yes, free for heretics, false prophets, and virtually for the devil himself. In our zeal to avoid all dragon authority we had also lost sight of the divine authority, and God had to permit that victorious conflict with the powers of hell to teach us the necessity of using, not lordism, but, the double-edged sword of the Almighty upon everything that is not clean and straight before God.

Since "we know that we are of the truth, and shall assure our hearts before God," "we know that we are of God, and he that heareth us not is not of God." And the only sense in which we give place to such as are deformed and darkened by antichrist traditions and "doctrines of devils," is in this wise: "We give place for them at the altar, where, by entire consecration, and faith in the blood of Christ they may be cleansed from sin and all foolish conversation received by tradition from the fathers." Glory be to God, there is now a flaming sword in the assembly of his saints, that can be endured only by those who know and do the truth, and such as honestly wish to know and obey the truth as it is in Christ Jesus. We believe that all future time and eternity will not erase the glory of this [Williamston] assembly from the memory of the redeemed.

After the assembly he held a meeting in Battle Creek, Mich. The following is a portion of his account of a woman's deliverance from devil-possession, which occurred while he was there. Such instances were found from time to time. For an example we give but this one:

For some months past Mrs. Samuel Worden, of Battle Creek, Mich., has created quite an excitement in the papers throughout the country by the exercise of a supernatural power of healing. People have come from a considerable distance to be treated, and letters have poured in from every direction. Some cases of healing were actually performed.

The woman and her husband, hearing of our meetings, came to hear the gospel and seemed willing to receive the truth. She confessed that they were not fully saved and filled with the Spirit as they should be, although she claimed to heal in the name of Christ and by the power of God. She soon came to the altar. God enabled us to see her condition pretty correctly. We told her she was in the "gall of bitterness and the bonds of iniquity." She acknowledged the fact and desired deliverance. In the course of a few days she professed to have found salvation. There seemed to be a change; but still there was something in her from which the Spirit of God in our heart recoiled. She tried to consecrate for sanctification, but could not claim that grace.

On Sabbath afternoon, October 26, the power of God was upon our little meeting. There were four cases of healing by the laying on of hands. Sister Worden said that she had suffered for many years in an awful manner with what she called a confused headache. She had hands laid on her for the healing. The Spirit came on us and her in mighty power. She claimed what had been prayed for, a complete healing of her body. Presently there were strange manifestations, which the most of us at once recognized as the writhing of evil spirits in her. We asked God to show her just what it was. Presently she said, "Brother Warner, pray for me." We asked her what she wanted. She replied, "That the devil might be cast out." This was the confession we desired to draw out of her. Hands were laid on her head, and the demons were commanded to come out of her in the name of Jesus Christ. The poor victim was soon convulsed and choked by the hellish spirits, which had to come out by the power of God. She obtained relief, sat up, but did not look clear. We all kept looking to God to complete the work. Hands were laid on again in the name of Jesus. Another struggle ensued. Then we perceived that to get complete deliverance there had to be a more perfect consecration, confession, and mortification. We proceeded to use the sword of the Spirit in every possible manner. But a miserable don't-care devil answered to every point of consecration.

Oh, what an awful condition the poor woman was in! How discouraging! The devils had so long held possession of her that they had almost taken possession of her own will and thoughts. And this awful enemy had so tortured her head that she had had a hard struggle to keep out of the asylum; so when he was pressed by the power of God he caused such distress and confusion in her head that he could use her mind and organs of speech. But by the grace and mercy of God conviction reached her conscience. The poor woman made some humiliating confessions, was humbled down, and wept. She confessed her association with Spiritualists, which Satan had tried to conceal before. Glory to God, his chief nest was now revealed. The Spiritualism devil was commanded to come out of her in the name of Christ. Oh, how he tortured the poor woman! Her throat became greatly swollen. How the legions of hell struggled against the power of God! She was pretty thoroughly decided for God; declared she would have every last evil spirit cast out if it killed her. Glory to God for the mighty Deliverer! Relief came by the hand of Jesus. A great measure of peace filled her soul. She sat up in the rocking-chair and her hands were raised while we sang songs of victory for the space of an hour.

Two days later she discovered that there was still in her heart something that was not right, and a close examination discovered that she had some lingering love for Spiritualists. She confessed it, when she soon found that more evil spirits were revealed. By the laying on of hands and the power of God she was fully delivered, after which she consecrated wholly and entered the sacred rest of entire sanctification.[16] On Saturday hands were laid upon her for healing. The mighty power of God came upon her and filled her soul and body, and she was perfectly healed from the awful tortures Satan had inflicted upon her for many years. Praise God for his wonderful mercy to the oppressed children of men! For years this poor woman had struggled hard to keep out of the insane asylum; now she says, "I am 'clothed and in my right mind.'" Her neighbors see the great change in her countenance. One woman looked upon her with astonishment, and said, "Why, how your face and voice are changed! surely these meetings are the true work of God."

The months of February and March, 1885, he spent in a tour to southeastern Iowa, and northeastern Missouri. He refers to his leaving home as follows:

In the kind providence of God we were permitted to start forth on this long-expected tour January 28. God bless the beloved ones we left behind in the Trumpet Office. Oh, how our hearts are knit together in the pure love of Jesus! Bless God for those he has given to be with us in the glorious work of the Lord! But the hardest of all was to leave my precious little Sidney, not expecting to see the dear child again for some three months. But praise God for the very kind provision he has made for the poor boy in the devout family of Brother and Sister William Crandall, residing at the edge of our town. Here he is taught to pray daily, and his little heart is developed only in the pure spirit of love and obedience. He is my only living child, three years old the 24th of last June. Though he has a happy home and two little playmates, still, as may be imagined under the circumstances, his dear little heart clings to his father with the most fervent love that a child is capable of possessing, as ours also does to him. But since God so lovingly cares for him, we must leave the blessed little angel in his charge and go forth to win to Christ souls that are lost in sin.

[16] In reference to this apparent instance of a person's being in a justified state while at the same time in possession of evil spirits it can be said, without attempting an explanation of whether such might be possible, that Brother Warner was always very particular to insist on justification as an essential condition to sanctification, and that if we knew all the circumstances in this case (allowing that the account may not be full) there probably would be no question in our minds.

He was gone nearly three months. The meetings in Iowa and Missouri resulted in good, yet nothing of unusual interest attended them. Early in June he made a trip to Daviess County, Ind. He had found in his evangelistic work that preaching on the street was a very effectual way of reaching the people. When he lived in Indianapolis, a few years previously, he and the saints in that place engaged frequently in preaching on the streets and in the parks. One Sunday afternoon, while preaching in Central Park, a man came to him and gave the names of persons in southern Indiana to whom he requested the Trumpet sent. Thus the Trumpet became the forerunner of his visit to Daviess County.

As we passed through the village of Odon, we notified the people that we would preach the gospel on their streets the next afternoon. Not being accustomed to such services, there was quite an interest. The people began to collect some time before the hour arrived. Store-boxes, sidewalks, etc., were converted into pews, and we had one of the best hearings we ever had on the streets. God mightily helped us by his Spirit to testify the gospel of his perfect salvation for an hour and thirty-eight minutes. Bless God, the truth swept all the sinnership religion into the pit, from whence it came. Though real Bible holiness had scarcely ever been preached in that place, and no holiness meetings ever held there, so far as we learned, yet every hearer, even lawyers, doctors, and preachers, acknowledged the practicability of perfect salvation and preservation from all sin through Christ Jesus. A Baptist preacher by the name of W—, who had been preaching to the people that no one can or does live without sinning in this world, and that all men sin day and night, sat close by us, and was convinced of the truth of the gospel and convicted of his sins. He sanctioned the word and acknowledged to others that it was all truth. We saw the tears in his eyes, and hoped he would become saved and qualified to preach for Jesus, instead of for sin and the sect.

Sabbath, the seventh, we held services in a grove near old Shiloh Bethel, south of Odon. As the appointment was circulated only after our arrival, there was not a large turnout. The Baptist preacher sat near us while preaching in the forenoon, and looking into his face during the discourse, our soul was pained to see that he had shut his heart against the truth and salvation of God. Instead of coming down to an equality with Christ, he chose to have a reputation among men, to indulge the lusts of the flesh and enjoy the friendship of the world. From that moment his "face gathered blackness." During the afternoon preaching he showed every disposition to avoid listening to the gospel of God. He came to some of the meetings afterward, just as the ungodly Pharisees followed Christ, to "catch something out of his mouth." On Wednesday evening Bro. O. Allen met and spoke to this priest of Baal, standing in a public place of the village, burning incense to the devil in gratification of the filthy lust for tobacco.

He later made another trip into Pennsylvania and attended the third annual camp-meeting at Sandy Lake. At the close of this meeting he, in company with others, drove about twelve miles to attend a Church of God (Winebrennerian) camp-meeting, held near Barkerville. His description under the title A Night in Babylon, is here given in part.

> On the way we met a good many people returning from the camp, and we were no little astonished to see so many of them smoking cigars. Finally the thought forced itself on our mind, "Can it be possible that they are selling such things on the camp-ground?" But considering that it was the Sabbath-day and the people holding the camp-meeting professed to be the "Church of God," such a thing surely could not be. The very thought was shocking and preposterous. When a half mile away we saw a smoke ascending at the camp. As we entered the ground we observed a crowd of sinners standing about a building with a sign, Boarding-Tent, and the smoke from their many cigars blended into a cloud, that we had seen from a distance. Soon after landing, we said to a brother, "Let us walk up and see what they have to sell there." We did so, and adventuring into the poison-fog we walked the whole length of the long building, all opened in front, displaying a large stock of every variety of ware that would be necessary to satisfy the pride, vanity, and lust of the horse-race or any vanity-fair throng of this ungodly world.

> We were shocked and amazed at this horrible traffic. The chief sale was tobacco. There the nasty, filthy stuff was piled up from one end of the building to the other. The vile curse of the earth, in every form and shape the devil ever invented, freely sold on a—oh, the blasphemy!—"Church of God" camp-ground!...

> It was all licensed by the preachers in control of the meetings. And such men have the wicked presumption to call themselves ministers of Christ! One of the "merchants of these things which were made rich" by the "abundance of the delicacies," though we understand he makes no profession of Christ, was ashamed of the unhallowed traffic, and though his contract included another year, he said he would never come back again. He confessed that if he were to open up such traffic on Sabbath at his place of business in town he would be prosecuted; but the superabundance of righteousness (?) of these tobacco-soaked preachers, it would appear, was to atone for the same sins on their camp-ground. Surely it has come to pass what is written in the prophets, "They overpass the deeds of the wicked" (Jer. 5:28).

> After taking some refreshment and having obtained permission to praise God, we engaged in our evening devotion, with

singing and prayer, to the God of our salvation. Our doors were soon crowded with young folks to hear the singing.

The tobacco-smoke was so dense that we could scarcely endure it without getting sick. But after a few songs and prayers were offered, every one cast his cigar away and listened with seriousness. This they did without a word said by any of us....

The meeting had been in progress four days, and no soul had been saved. Not a seeker. Not even a place for a penitent to kneel, no straw on the ground. The pulpit was the only place to kneel in the congregation; as though they did not expect a poor penitent to seek God, and that the preacher should do all the praying.

On Monday morning, the services were made later than the usual hour. The preachers were doubtless perplexed how to perform in the deadness of their souls. "The sinners in Zion are afraid; fearfulness hath surprized the hypocrites" (Isa. 33:14). Not one of them would venture to preach. The services were confined to one hour. After reading a psalm, the preacher announced that all should be free to serve God by prayer, and testimony, and song, requesting brevity of each. So, as our heart was "springing up" full of the love of God, we opened our mouth to praise the Lord in singing a verse occasionally. After several had spoken we arose and testified to the great "salvation we have in Christ Jesus with eternal glory." We aimed to be very brief, but occupied seven minutes by the watch, when they began to sing. But they being but a few and "feeble folk," their song would not have interfered materially with our remarks. However, we struck in to sing until they stopped, and then sat down....

After the services were dismissed we were ordered to leave the ground as soon as we could pack up and depart; and forbidden to sing, pray, or preach, within one mile of their tobacco-soaked camp.

When asked why they would not allow us to worship God there, the president said it was because we held a second work of grace, which they did not believe. Why should they fear to hear the testimony? If they really believed that there is no "second grace," they need not fear that any of their flock would obtain it. According to their position, they were afraid of the thing that does not exist. What brave soldiers!

One of the preachers arose in the speaking-meeting and said, "According to the little bit of information I have received concerning Christ's salvation, it is all received at once." Certainly a man that has only "a little bit of information respecting Christ's salvation" has only a little bit of salvation, and that little bit of salvation was doubtless all obtained at once, for it was so little it could not have been divided. And when that very "little bit" is analyzed it is seen to consist in a mere "name to live," a "form of godliness," anointed by love of self and love of sect....

The preacher who led the meeting is saturated with tobacco and addicted to horse-trading and worldly foolish jesting. In his remarks he said we should "exemplify Christ," that is, our lives should be like his. The Lord led us to ask him if he regarded himself an example of Christ's character; whether he could consistently say to boys and men generally, "Follow the example I set before you." Not having 'sanctified the Lord Jesus in his heart,' he was not ready to give an answer. He paced the pulpit, being speechless. We repeated the question, including both him and the president. Neither answered. We then told the latter something about their being of the same spirit the old Jews and pagans were of, who forbade the apostles preaching any more in their towns. We also called their attention to the abominable and wicked traffic we saw on their ground on the Lord's day, which was licensed by them and sanctioned by their filthy habit. They could allow that corrupting bane of society; but of a few little children of God who have obtained pure hearts and desired to "worship God in the beauty of holiness," they said, "Away with them"!...

Well, we are compelled to give the manifestations at that camp the credit of being the filthiest and vilest form of Babylon we have ever met. An unconverted man who was there and witnessed the scene said to them, "God deliver me from such a sect." They are destitute of God's grace. 'For the grace of God that bringeth salvation ... teacheth us, that denying ungodliness and worldly lusts, we should live soberly, righteously, and godly in this present world' (Tit. 2:11,12). But these live in the filth of the world, "walking after their ungodly lusts."

In a report written from this part of Pennsylvania three years later, he refers to his visit to the Winebrennerian camp, as just described, and says, "Well, that was the last camp-meeting held on that ground. Their doleful tents are rotting to the ground, and are the habitation of owls and bats."

Brother Warner felt that he needed, and that the Lord was going to provide, a company of singers to go with him in the evangelistic field. It was about this time that the company who should travel with him for more than five years began to be formed. It was at the Williamston assembly that summer that Brother Warner said to Nannie Kigar, of Payne, Ohio, and to Frances Miller, of Battle Creek, who attended the meeting, that he felt impressed they would form a part of his company to help in singing and other gospel work. Their voices were soprano and alto respectively. They, with a number of other saints, accompanied Brother Warner to the Beaver Dam assembly. On their way, as they changed cars at Ft. Wayne, they met and were joined by Sarah Smith, of Jerry City, Ohio. While they were at Beaver Dam the Lord added Sister Smith to the company. Her voice furnished a high tenor. She was an elderly lady and she was called the "mother" of the company. Bro. John U. Bryant and Bro. D. Leininger, from the Beaver Dam neighborhood, also traveled in the company for a time.

The Floating Bethel, used for several years on the Ohio River for Evangelistic Work by G. T. Clayton and Company. Burned Dec. 16, 1898.

After the Beaver Dam meeting, Brother Warner made a short visit to Illinois and Iowa, while the rest of the company remained at Beaver Dam and were soon engaged in a protracted meeting at the Hans Schoolhouse, where about fifty souls were saved and a great interest was created.[17] While on this trip he was healed of an affliction of the eyes. He thus speaks of it:

> During the Williamston assembly in September, Satan began to afflict our eyes. At the beginning we were impressed that it was an attack of the enemy. They grew worse until we were scarcely able to read or write. The next morning after our arriving in Iowa, the Spirit impressed a sister that it was Satan who had afflicted our eyes to prevent our labors in writing, etc. Instantly recollecting the same impression in our mind at the beginning of the attack, we knew it was of God.

> Our vehement faith in God and indignation against the devil were instantly aroused. We fell upon our knees and asked God to deliver us, rebuking Satan in the name of Jesus Christ. Praise

[17] Brother Leininger relates that at this meeting a Dunkard minister drew his fist to strike him. A daughter of this preacher was a hired helper in Brother Leininger's family. She had obtained the experience of sanctification, which angered her father. As Brother Leininger was going out of the meeting-house, this man stood at the door ready to do violence to him. He drew back his fist to strike, but it seems his blow was rather misdirected, as his thumb nail grazed his own nose and tore loose a bit of skin, so that he went home bleeding and discomfited.

God, the pain all ceased, and we were able to do a pretty good day's work. And our eyes have been well ever since. God suffered the attack doubtless to teach us a lesson concerning the origin of much of the suffering of the afflicted.

In the latter part of January he with his company of singers and coworkers went to Deerfield, Randolph County, Ind., arriving on a Saturday evening. The next morning they attended a meeting where a nominal Christian preacher had the service. They sang some of the sweet songs of victory; but this so confounded the preacher that he could not find anything in his Bible to preach, and after he had taken the pulpit he invited Brother Warner to preach. The latter preached a burning message. He had hoped for the use of the house, but it could be seen that the preacher intended to control the house that week, for he proposed that he and these people use it alternately. He was soon told that they were out on the blood and fire line, that they could not yoke up with the dead priests of Babel and would go elsewhere.

They went over into the edge of Jay County and began meetings in a United Brethren house called Prospect. Here the preaching created a furor among those who were joined to their sectarian institution and felt that it was in danger. It was like a thunderbolt in the community. The singing drew the crowds. The trustees became fearful. One of them went into the woods to pray to know what to do to get rid of these people who seemed to be taking things. The heavenly songs seemed to follow him. He felt he should attend all the meetings to see what occurred. He soon found that these people had something more than the United Brethren had. He was one of two trustees who embraced the truth, and of course desired that the meetings continue. Threats were made. A woman was heard to say, "They ought to be driven out of the country with shotguns." A Baptist preacher who came into the neighborhood said that they ought to be put in jail, and offered his service as one to help in the matter.

The United Brethren minister had been holding meetings, with but little success. A Mrs. R——, one of their number, had been praying the Lord to send somebody who would preach the truth in such a way that God would get unto himself a people who would serve him. She and a Mrs. W—— went to the altar together, with others. Brother Warner asked them whether they would be willing to separate themselves from denominationalism if the Lord should show them that duty. Sister W—— said in her heart, yes. Sister R—— turned over to her and said, "Now, they are trying to tear down the church, so let us just stick." There she turned bitter, and the very thing she had prayed for she was rejecting. She walked up and down the aisle wringing her hands and crying, "My church! my church!" Another woman said, "These people are either awfully good people or else they are desperately wicked." Once during the meeting flying missiles crashed through the windows. Glass flew across the room, striking a woman on the head and drawing blood.[18] Said Brother Warner:

---

[18] A man who lived in the neighborhood said in one of the meetings that he was going to kick Brother Warner. As the latter was among the last to pass out of the building, this man lingered at the door, while the crowd was waiting to see him do the deed. As Brother

People have dealt in cheap, shoddy religions so long that they feel like stoning us when we state the cost of that we are commissioned of Christ to offer the people; nevertheless, when men consent to pay the price they are always highly pleased with the results.

Such a display of sectarian idolatry was a good exhibition for some who had come out of Babylon, for they saw what they had been yoked up with. About eight persons made their escape in this meeting.

There were in attendance, as was usual in the meetings everywhere, people who gloried in hearing the sects spoken against. Such people, of course, while adding force in the start, were no substantial credit to the movement, as they were not genuine representatives.

During the winter the evangelists went to Marshall County, into a neighborhood that seemed very dark spiritually. After one of the evening meetings there, in which he had preached with marvelous power, Brother Warner was passing out the door when a young rough gave him a kick. He turned and thanked the fellow and said he always praised God when he received such treatment. As he started on he received another kick, for which he also praised God aloud. At the house where he was stopping the sister had two very wicked sons. On the night the kicking occurred one of these young men, instead of retiring to bed, sat in his chair at the fireplace, his face in his hands, groaning. When asked what was the matter, he referred to what had happened that evening and said he felt sorry for Brother Warner, for surely he was a godly man, etc. When he saw how Brother Warner received such abuse, his heart was touched, and he was much pained. He and his brother had both mistreated Brother Warner and those with him and had in their presence cursed his mother for feeding them. When they saw the love manifested their hearts melted, and they became warm friends to the saints of God.

From Marshall County the company went up into Michigan, into Van Buren County. Here, at Geneva Center lived a young man whom the Lord had saved and was calling into the gospel work, Bro. Barney E. Warren. The fact that he was under twenty-one years of age and that his father was unsaved and was opposed to his going into the ministry, was an obstacle. But his father, who was a very wicked man, became very much convicted during the meetings held in a schoolhouse in the vicinity. He was seized with such trembling that in his attempt to steady himself by holding to the seats he shook the very floor of the building. Finally, in a consecration-meeting in Bro. Joseph Smith's house, near Lacota, he rebelled against the Lord and started to leave the room. Before he reached the door the strength of his legs gave way and he sank instantly to the floor, and was unable to go farther. He then yielded. Brother Warner asked him if he was willing to let Barney go into the gospel work. His reply was, "Barney is the Lord's." The way was then opened for the young Brother Warren, and in the following April he became a part of the little singing company that should travel with Brother Warner for the next five

---

Warner passed out he raised his foot to kick, but he did not kick. He was asked why he did not. His reply was, "I was afraid the Lord would kick me". This man accepted the truth and became one of the permanent fixtures in the church in that place.

years, and should consist of, besides Brother Warren, who was a base singer, Sisters Nannie Kigar, Frances Miller, and Mother Smith. This constituted a complete quartet, with Brother Warner often reenforcing the tenor.

Evangelistic Company, 1886–1891.

B. E. Warren 　　　　　*Nannie Kigar* 　　　　　*Frankie Miller*

D. S. Warner 　　　　　*Sarah Smith*

B. E. Warren, Springfield, O.

There had come to be many saints gathered in the one fold in this part of Michigan. Bros. A. B. Palmer, S. Michels, W. B. Grover, and S. L. Speck were ministerial workers whom God was using in this vicinity. At this time Brother Warner was called to Williamston to help get out the second edition of the Songs of Victory, the first song-book published at the Gospel Trumpet Office. Of the first edition there were over fifteen hundred copies sold in less than three weeks. Holy song exerted a wonderful influence in the reformation. With reference to his return to Williamston we include a paragraph from his report.

The day we arrived at home a good steam-engine was brought into the Trumpet Office, by the kind blessing of God, Brother Fisher having previously engaged it. Thank God that we live to see this day. The glorious work is spreading like fire in the earth. Glory to God and the Lamb! Oh, what hosts of fire-baptized saints we have met! With the increase of numbers there is a continual advancement in clearness and power.

Thus there was a long day of waiting before a steam-engine was used in the Trumpet Office. Every improvement of this kind was always an occasion of much rejoicing for Brother Warner.

By this time the truths of the reformation were being extensively scattered. Besides the workers named in southwestern Michigan, there were G. T. Clayton in western Pennsylvania, C. Z. Lindley in Iowa, J. P. Haner in Kansas, and W. N. Smith and others in Ohio. The Lord was raising up ministers in various places, and many people were accepting the truth.

The first engagement for Brother Warner and his company, after the latter had been definitely formed, was at Walkerton, Ind., in April, 1886. They remained two weeks, and a few souls came out on the clear Bible line. There was a little persecution here, as was usual. They found the place dark with prejudice. Over forty of the professors in the place were joined in a holiness band. They professed sanctification, but most of them were connected with sects.

We went to their meeting on Tuesday night before we began operations in the hall. Being held in the United Brethren house, the meeting was led by Pastor S—, of that sect. God powerfully baptized our soul, and we praised him in prayer and testimony, which made the sect priest grow black in the face. He afterward tried to make out that we had come there and interrupted their meeting, and actually caused a report of that kind to go out. He spared no pains to fill the place with all manner of evil against us. Like Demetrius, the silversmith, his craft was in danger....

The Methodist priest delivered a lecture on Monday night in favor of secret societies; he labored especially to make a good character for the Odd Fellows. The Holy Spirit put it upon us to rebuke such agents of the devil. This the class-leader of that sect said made his blood boil. So he went about the town breathing out his venom against us and enlisting as many as possible in an effort to induce the proprietor of the hall to break his contract and close the hall. They succeeded in so influencing him; but the power of God turned his mind right around, and he not only gave the hall cheerfully to the extent of the time, but offered it as much longer as we wanted it or at any time we might return.

Threats were made, eggs were thrown, and there was considerable disturbance. But the effect of such abuse was the raising up of many friends for the truth and the salvation of a few souls. Brother Warner was again called home, and the company returned to Beaver Dam.

The next trip for the company was to the Prospect neighborhood, in Jay County, where the truth had been planted the previous winter. This was in May. Brother Warner and Brother and Sister Fisher went directly to Portland by train, while the company, including S. L. Speck and Clara Morrison, were conveyed from Beaver Dam in a wagon. Of this trip across the country in a wagon, Sister Frances Miller wrote an account in her diary. It is interesting reading in these days of automobiles, when such a trip can be made in a few hours, and we here include it as she wrote it.

> The brethren from Beaver Dam carried our little company from that place to Sweetser, Grant County, by lumber-wagon. We started at 5 A. M., and reached our destination about 9 P. M. We had a glorious time by the way, praising God and singing those beautiful songs. About two miles beyond Roann we drove in at the edge of a beautiful piece of woods and stopped for dinner. We placed the seats in a circle and spread our dinner upon Father's green carpet, then thought we would praise him with a song, supposing we were alone in the woods.

> In a few moments we were surrounded with cattle. There must have been at least twenty-five or thirty, with their eyes wide open, gazing at us. We felt that God had put the love of music in these dumb animals, and we sang two or three songs for their benefit.

> Mother Smith then asked God to bless the food, and we all thanked him for it, in our hearts. After the horses had finished their dinner we pursued our way, rejoicing because we had Jesus in our souls, and he made melody through us to the Father.

> The next morning the Beaver Dam brethren returned home, and brethren at Sweetser brought us to Prospect, Jay County. We started at 7 A. M. It was a beautiful morning. The recent rains had laid the dust, and we had pike roads most of the way, making traveling delightful. In the afternoon the clouds began to gather blackness, and in a short time a terrible storm was upon us. The rain came down in torrents, drenching us through and through. The wind was furious. It seemed almost every moment as though it would take us up. Then the hailstones came down so thickly the horses refused to go. We were seemingly in the midst of an ocean of water. The recent heavy rains had flooded the country, washing away several bridges.

> We had quite an adventurous trip; forded one river, and the horses, while pulling us through a deep creek, pulled loose from the wagon, leaving us in the water. We were able to get to land, however. This was about two hours after the storm, and while the brethren were repairing the wagon we gathered hailstones by the

handful in the fence corners.

Well, I am satisfied that none but the pure in heart could relish such a storm. We did enjoy it; and God so filled our hearts that we praised him through it all. And when the wind was blowing the thickest, the calmness in our souls was indescribable. We knew God had power to prevent the storm; but in his wisdom he saw it was just what we needed, and his will being ours, we thanked him for it and left the consequences of our becoming wet in his hands, knowing all would work out for our good.

After the storm, it turned quite cold. We had thirty miles yet to drive; but we had the holy fire burning within us. We reached Brother Key's about twelve o'clock that night, waking Brother and Sister Key with the song, "Oh, 'twas love, 'twas love, that found out me!" The next morning, Saturday, May 15, we arose feeling refreshed after a few hours' rest, not one of us feeling any the worse after our exposure of the previous day.

Oh, what a wonderful God! Let us praise him for his goodness and for his wonderful works to the children of men. We drove out to Prospect that morning, six miles, and to our surprize and joy met Brother and Sister Fisher, who had come with Brother Warner. Our hearts were made to rejoice to meet the dear saints at Prospect, with whom we had labored in the Lord last January. We had a glorious time and witnessed the salvation of many precious souls.

This second meeting at Prospect was to be held in a grove; but on account of the weather being cold and damp, and the meeting-house being refused, the meetings were held most of the time in a granary building owned by a brother, Jesse Wickersham. This brother had given the land on which the Prospect meeting-house stood, and had contributed largely to its erection, with the understanding that the house should be open to all true worshipers of God. But here the sect refused the house, the preaching of the truth on the former occasion having been too much for them.[19]

In August of this year (1886) was held the first of the annual grove- or camp-meetings in the Beaver Dam vicinity. It was in W. W. Ballenger's grove. For the next five years the annual camp-meeting was held in J. Kuhn's woods; and then, beginning in 1892, it was held for five years in D. Leininger's woods. Beginning with 1897 this meeting has since been held on the beautiful ground overlooking Yellow Lake.

---

[19] On the second Sunday the meeting was held in the grove. After the people had assembled a very frightful storm threatened, and people began to leave. Brother Warner stopped in the midst of his preaching, and with his hand lifted to heaven prayed God to scatter the storm and not let it hinder the meeting. He assured the people that they need not leave, that it would not rain. Some had begun to depart but stopped to see whether his prayer would be answered. It did not rain. There were other instances of this kind in Brother Warner's career.

Before attending the Indiana grove-meeting in August, Brother Warner felt impressed that from that meeting he should labor on a line eastward from that place. In conjunction with this came urgent calls from that direction, and brethren even made preparation for his coming before asking him. The first place was Arcola, Ind. We quote from his report in which he speaks of this part of his trip:

On Friday morning, August 13, with our heart melting with pure parental love for our child, we kissed his innocent cheek and left him in silent slumber, not daring to wake him lest his little heart should break with grief at our departure, and our soul also be filled with sorrow at his pitiful tears. O God, thou knowest the abundance of thy grace that enables us to tear away from this affectionate child! The poor boy has recently been sick insomuch that many of the saints despaired of his life. O Lord, only thou knowest the great trial of our soul when we felt the awful sickness of our boy, by the Spirit of God, while we were making up the last Trumpet at Williamston, and packing the Office, which none of our company had any experience in! Our presence was much needed, so that we did not feel permitted to go, though we keenly felt his sickness and told some of the saints that we felt he was sick. After suffering those feelings a week, we received a letter stating that he had been very low but was better. This took a great load off our heart, and a few days later a second letter stated that through the laying on of hands in prayer the Lord had gloriously healed the poor little fellow.

Oh, praise our God for his great mercy toward us, that he has spared our soul the great sorrow of such a bereavement as would have been the departure of this last and dear-beloved friend in the flesh! And yet we know that had the blessed Lord seen fit to take him, as in all the trials of the past we would have been "exceeding joyful in all our tribulations." This trial of our faith was a great blessing to us. It gave us a sure evidence that notwithstanding our intense love for the child we could leave him in the hands of God, and feel sweetly resigned to his will who had worked for us elsewhere. We found the precious boy feeling well, but still so slim and poor that it touched our heart to look upon his lean face. The Lord bless Brother Leininger's family, with whom the child was staying during his sickness, and all the beloved saints who did all they could for the comfort and help of the dear boy.

We started at three o'clock in the morning, the Lord having sent a glorious shower before us to cool the air and put away the dust. As the day began to break, we were blessed in looking at the sublime and beautiful clouds which Father piled up in the heavens, of every shape, tint, and hue. Looking to the north we saw the perfect form of a great hand pointing to the East, and the Spirit of God filled our heart as we acknowledged it the hand of our Father, and that we were going in the direction Father was pointing. We felt something like Nehemiah must have felt when he said, "The hand of the Lord is good upon me."

Residences of Joseph F. Smith and D. Leininger – Two of the "homes" where Brother Warner and the earlier evangelists and workers always found a welcome. The upper residence is that of Joseph F. Smith, near Grand Junction, Mich.; the lower one that of David Leininger, near Beaver Dam, Ind.

Early places of worship in Michigan – These two old buildings, now crumbling to decay, were used thirty-five years ago as houses of worship by the saints at and around Grand Junction, Mich. The one in the upper picture, known as "Smith's," is about three and one half miles northwest of Grand Junction; and the other, known as the "log house," is about the same distance northeast.

We sang the praises of God much of the way, and the gentle breezes carried the sweet sound over the surrounding country. Once we finished a hymn just as we were ascending a hill. At the top of the hill, to our right, stood a house. The song had sounded on ahead of us and found an echo in the heart of a blessed old mother in Israel, who was clapping her hands and shouting the praises of God, and who waved her hand and nodded her head toward us as we came opposite the house, as good as to say, "I felt the Spirit of God in the song and it has set my soul on fire." Oh, how it stirred our soul, as we saw the joyful demonstrations of the dear old sister! We reached our destination in good time and had a blessed meeting that night.

That his frail body should endure the strenuous evangelistic work—the much travel, loss of sleep, and the strain of preaching and laboring for souls—as well as editing and writing for the Trumpet, is in itself a miracle. On more than one occasion, when he was exhausted, he was miraculously strengthened by the power of the Spirit. The following is a portion of his account of the meeting at Antwerp, Ohio, held while on this tour:

Having labored hard all day in the Lord, our body was so worn that we felt scarcely able to stand on our feet, so closed the meeting about dark. But finding some unsaved souls had just come who seemed concerned about salvation, we asked God to touch our body with renewed strength. Praise God, he did as we asked. We called the people to order and renewed the battle of the Lord for the rescue of perishing souls at stake. Praise God, a rich harvest of souls followed. We labored on until after ten o'clock. Two or three times we announced the meeting closed, when other souls were found under conviction and were constrained by the Spirit of God to yield. About eight were converted and a few sanctified through the blood. The work was wrought in mighty power. Strong men shouted in their new-born joys sent down from heaven by the sweet Spirit of adoption. Oh, what a heavenly sight! Even little boys, who had just found the Lord, were so powerfully blessed of God that they clapped their hands and leaped with the glory. In twenty years of labor for God we never saw anything like it. It verily seemed their little bodies must burst asunder by the power of the Spirit....

Every meeting is getting richer and more wonderful. O my Lord, whereunto will this great kingdom yet grow? Truly the saints of the Most High have taken the kingdom and the dominion and the greatness of the kingdom under the whole heaven.

Leaving his company at Jerry City, Ohio, he returned to Van Buren County, Mich., long enough to attend the assembly at Geneva Center where saints from over an extensive territory were gathered. He makes the following reference to this meeting:

Tuesday afternoon, the great day of the feast, near the beginning of the service, we sang, Perishing Souls at Stake, when the Holy Spirit overwhelmed all our souls with the awful condition of this dark world and the worth of millions of souls who would receive the pure gospel and be saved if it were brought to them. Oh, how all our hearts were melted in sympathy for "perishing souls at stake today!"

Up to that time we had been looking for one of the dear ministerial brethren to work with us; but then we said, O Lord, send them everywhere, and we will trust thee to 'make all grace abound unto us, so that we always, having all sufficiency in all things, may abound unto every good work.' Through the Lord Jesus Christ we feel abundantly able to do as much preaching and laboring with souls as one man would be supposed to perform, and also one man's work with the pen....

How beautiful the sight of God's host, all mustered to the battle by the Lord himself! No jealousy, strife, and selfish manipulation for the best places and fattest fields. Every soul feels that he has the very best place while he abides in Christ and Christ abides in us. Oh, what fools the devil has made of poor blind Babylonians whose backs are galded by the sect harness and whose hearts are often crushed beneath the sect machinery! We speak from experience. For ten years we felt this cold, heartless heel of selfish oppression. More than once we wet our pillow with the tears that the accursed Baal-idol pressed from our wounded heart. By the grace of God we shall "render unto her double," as God hath commanded us.

Instead of wire-pulling and ungodly plotting against one another, and each one greedily looking for his meat from his quarter, each worker in the Lord's vineyard is looking to the Lord to guide his feet in the paths of His own will. And all go out in perfect freedom whither the Lord will and yet all work in perfect harmony, under the sweet and heavenly management of the Holy Spirit.

Of his return to Ohio and of an attempt by a mob to capture and mistreat him we have his account in the Trumpet of Nov. 1.

After the assembly of the saints in Michigan, we returned to our little company of fellow workers in Ohio; found them all together at dear Brother and Sister Miller's, at Jerry City. Praise God, it was joyful to our souls to meet all well again. How all hearts praised God for the tidings of his wonderful works in the assembly! Of course dear Brother Barney began to bound like a rubber ball, almost to the ceiling, when he learned of the salvation of his brother William. Doubtless angels in heaven took a part in the celebration of God's holy praises....

October 1 we came to Bro. S. Phillips', near Rising Sun. We held some meetings in a house on his place. We enjoyed preaching the glorious gospel of Christ to the people that came together there....

October 7, we moved a few miles farther east and one mile north, to the house of dear Bro. Daniel Roush, where we invited the neighbors together to hear the word of the Lord. The room soon proved too small, and the weather being pleasant, we obtained a tent from Brother Phillips, that covered about 18×20 feet, which we attached to one end of a large porch; these together made quite a good meeting-room. The Lord helped us to preach the glorious gospel of Christ, and we poured out the vials of God's wrath upon every evil way. The Lord worked, and souls were saved almost every day.

Thursday, October 14, the Lord sent a very strong wind and we had to take the tent down. That night we held the meeting in the house. The night being dark and rainy, the congregation was not very large. While we were preaching the word, suddenly in rushed

A BLACK MOB

About fifteen or more of the baser sort, who were drunk and mad on the wine of Babylon, with their faces blackened, sprang into the room and seized upon us and started to take us out. Brethren quickly saw the situation and were not slow in our help. But the room being seated with backed seats, and the space between us and the door being all occupied by the sons of Belial, not many saints could get near us. The enemies of the Lord all having hold of each other and the front ones hold on us, we were pretty rapidly drawn to the door. But a few of the little ones were pulling back with all their might. Brother Barney and Sister Frankie Miller were in the hottest of the fight! Mother and Nan could not get to us.

Halleluiah! We praised God every step and felt the perfect peace of God in our souls. Bro. George Roush had hold on our left arm and was our principal stay. The black clan, knowing him as a very strong man, thought to beat him loose from his hold on us; but he received the blows on his face without slacking his hold. God bless that brother. The Lord did not suffer him to be hurt to amount to anything. One of the black clan brought with him a pretty wieldy little cudgel, which Bro. Jacob Roush grabbed and wrested out of his hands. And being an officer of the law, of whom the Word of the Lord says, "He beareth not the sword [or club] in vain," he began to apply it vigorously on the black heads. Up to this second the contest stood in breathless uncertainty. We were hauled to the very threshhold, and all the desperadoes were determined to have their victim. Once the threshold crossed, we were to be dragged out into the dark night to suffer all that Satan might dictate in the hearts of fiendish Catholic sect idolaters and wicked sinners. But all at once the Spirit said to our soul, "I will not leave thee in the hands of the wicked." Almost immediately every black hand let go and fled. Glory be to our God, he always causes us to triumph through Christ Jesus.

The little ones said it looked as though we should be pulled to pieces, but, praise God, not a hair of our head was harmed, not a muscle strained, and not a thread of our clothes torn. Glory to Jesus for his precious deliverance of us out of the jaws of the fierce beasts! It was reported that their intention was to strip us and give us a good lashing with whips and then serve us with a dessert of rotten eggs. We praised God for their defeat, but believe we should have praised him and leaped still more with the glory in our soul had he seen fit to let the wicked accomplish their end. After the struggle we sang a hymn of praise to God and resumed our discourse in the Spirit of the Lord.

Before we came to the place, our eyes rested on 1 Thess. 2:1, 2, and as we read, the Spirit gave us the words as descriptive of what we should meet. Praise God, we were willing to be shamefully entreated for Christ's sake and were none the less "bold in our God to speak unto you the gospel of God with much contention," "knowing that our entrance in unto you was not in vain."

The night before the black mob came we dreamed of fighting black dogs, which finally fled from before our face. Some were apprehensive they would repeat the attack, and there were all kinds of "rumors of wars." Had we not been saved above all fears we should have escaped out of that place as soon as possible, but we remained over the following Sabbath.

From Ohio the course of our little company of evangelists turned westward again. While they were holding meeting at Payne, Ohio, Brothers Williams and Yoder, from LaGrange County, Ind., arrived to convey them seventy-two miles back to Brushy Prairie, Ind. On their return they reached a point near Antwerp, Ohio, the first evening. As soon as they came into the neighborhood the news was sounded out, and the house where they were stopping was quickly filled with people who had come to hear the words of eternal life.

When we landed there, we began to think of our bodies, and felt sorry the word had gone out announcing a meeting. We had been up, some until twelve, and others until two o'clock, the night before, and wishing to start by daylight on a fifty-five mile drive the next day, it seemed that the rest was a matter of necessity. But as the people came together, our hearts, burdened for lost souls, soon forgot circumstances, and the meeting continued till eleven o'clock. All glory to our God, who is 'able to make all grace abound unto us, so that we always having all sufficiency in all things may abound unto every good work.'

Meetings were held in LaGrange County, Ind., after which the company were conveyed in a two-days journey by lumber-wagon, to Beaver Dam.[20] While engaged in meetings in this part of the State he was called home to the Office again, to assist with the third edition of the song-book. The Publishing Office by this time had been moved to Grand Junction, Van Buren County, Mich.

> Brother Fisher, having gone to the Office, wrote for us to come also, as we were needed. The interest of the meeting was such that we thought we should by no means leave. But as we fasted and prayed, the Spirit of God bade us go immediately, assuring us that he would put his Spirit on dear Bro. Barney Warren and cause him to preach the word to the people....

> Though the little ones were loath to have us leave so suddenly, the grace of God enabled all to say, "Amen," and in a few moments we were on our way to the station, and several hours ride on Father's swift chariots landed us at the Trumpet Office once more, after an absence of five months.

> Oh, praise God for his glorious blessings upon our soul and body! Having had no ministerial help, preaching nearly all the time twice a day, with much altar-work, singing, etc., besides doing one man's writing keeping the Trumpet filled and attending to a large correspondence, hymn-writing, etc., it is wonderful, a constant miracle, how God can do so much through a poor, naturally frail body. We scarcely get six hours sleep out of twenty-four.

[20] An interesting episode in connection with this trip is related by Bro. D. Leininger, of Beaver Dam, whose mother, known as Mother Krause, was at this time not expected to live. Mother Krause had for some cause held a slight grievance against Brother Warner. Early in December, on the night before she died, she declared she must see Brother Warner and begged to have him sent for. She was told that Brother Warner was over in LaGrange County, quite a distance away, and that if the Lord wanted her to see him he would spare her life until she should have that opportunity. Scarcely had this been said when Brother Warner arrived, to the surprize of all.

Two days before, where he had been holding meetings, he expressed the conviction that the Spirit bade him go to Beaver Dam. Accordingly it was decided to go, and he resumed his writing, at which he had been engaged, until the time to start. Perceiving that no preparations were being made he dropped his pen and asked the cause. He was told that the weather was inclement and that traveling would be disagreeable. He said, "Never mind the weather; the Lord can take care of that. The Lord says, 'Go to Beaver Dam'." Thus it was that he and his company were prompted to make the trip. Landing at Bro. William Ballenger's, they stayed over night. In the latter part of the night Brother Warner awoke Brother Ballenger and said he must go to see Mother Krause immediately.

Mother Krause died the following evening, but not before she was comforted by the presence of Brother Warner.

Glory to God, we do love this holy war for our God against the powers of hell and for the rescue of perishing souls. If the Lord saw fit to keep us working the whole time day and night, and sustained us, we should say, Amen.

Oh, how glad we were to see the beloved little ones at home once more! God bless their souls. How grateful we are to God for the faithful labors of these dear ones. Truly they endure all things for the elect's sake, that their fingers may send forth the bread of heaven to the hungry souls. Dear brethren, when you read the Trumpet so eagerly do not forget to pray for those blessed children who are so devoted to this great work. We were in hopes that God would give us the sweet luxury of some nights' rest with the little ones at home. But lo, here came the dear saints from every direction wishing Brother Joseph and us to come here and there to preach for them....

When we left our little company we expected to return soon again, but as the second edition of Songs of Victory is nearly exhausted we have to remain here to help print the third edition soon.

Praise God, nearly thirty-five hundred books have gone forth singing the praises of God. May God speed all his flying angels with the everlasting gospel to this dark and wretched world, so near its awful doom. Amen.

Brother Warner remained at the Office until early in March, when, by agreement, he met his little company again at Walkerton, Ind., where they had held meetings almost a year before. Frankie Miller refers in her diary to their meeting in Walkerton on the night of their arrival there.

That night we all met at Brother Barden's to worship God. After the meeting had nicely begun, in walked Brother Warner. Well, it is needless to say we were all very thankful to see his dear face again. He said that this was the second time he had been mobbed. The first time was by the black mob near Rising Sun. Ohio, and the second time was this time by the White Horse Cavalry.

Sister Miller also relates an instance of healing that occurred before they left Walkerton.

Wednesday morning, the 13th, Brother Wolfenberger came out to Brother Barden's, where we were, before breakfast. His little boy five years old was very sick with spinal disease and had high fever. The doctors held a council over him the day before. We all went over about nine o'clock. The doctor was there. The little fellow was crying, and burning up with fever. He had not eaten anything but a little scraped apple since Saturday. The doctor tried to open his eyes, and wanted to put a fly blister on his spine. Brother Warner told the parents that if they wanted to put the case in God's hands they must drop the doctor and his medicines and take Christ alone for their physician. They were both willing, and said they believed God would heal the child. After looking to God in prayer, Brother Warner anointed the child in the name of Jesus, and we laid on hands, and God healed the little sufferer. Oh, praise God for his goodness! The fever was broken, and he sweat freely and opened his eyes very bright and asked for a cookie. He ate two cookies and some bologna very greedily, and teased to be dressed and go to the depot with his papa after his sister's satchel.

The daughter had been attending school in Auburn, and they telegraphed for her, thinking the child could not live. Before we reached the place, the daughter had gone to God in prayer asking him to pardon her sins and to save her little brother. After the child was healed, a young woman working in the family, who had been bitter against the power of God and against us, fell on her knees and cried to God for mercy, and she received the spirit of adoption. She was a member of the United Brethren without a spark of salvation.

We present extracts from Brother Warner's report of this second meeting at Walkerton.

Here we set the battle in array last April in a two weeks siege. Hell was moved to the bottomless pit. Babylon foamed and howled, and, like the ancient Pharisees, stirred up the people to "shamefully entreat us," as they did Paul at Philippi. But, thank God, in the fires of persecution and storms of opposition God saved a few souls, and these we find standing fast; and a few others the Lord has added to his own church, who are praising God for the great salvation. We soon found that the gospel of Christ had grown much in the favor of the people. The Lord God of power had greatly turned the minds and hearts of the people to endorse and love the truth. Men of principle gave all to understand that if they attempted to disturb our meetings again as they had before they must suffer the application of the law. Praise God, the people heeded the warning, and God also inclined them to give good attention.

We occupied a very large hall for two weeks and had it well filled with hearers. Multitudes were under deep conviction, but were unwilling to pay the price of real salvation. Several, however, were saved by the power and grace of God, converted and sanctified, and a few made their escape fully out of Babylon and were wonderfully blessed of the Lord. Were it not for shoddy holiness and stagnant pools of sectish religion in the way of God's salvation, a great harvest of souls could be brought to Jesus. But the corrupt preachers in this place will have to answer for the awful influence that is damning multitudes of poor sinners, both in and out of their sect enclosures. On the last two nights of our meeting, there was also meeting in the Methodist house in the town. Some of that sect were greatly convicted to escape out of her; but we could feel the influence of those meetings as sensibly as if the Holy Spirit were incarnate and were being literally crucified in the town, as the Spirit and Word were killed "in the streets of the great city, which spiritually is called Sodom and Egypt" (Rev. 11:8). Oh, how sensibly we felt the "fellowship of the suffering" of Jesus Christ! While the sweet peace of God flows a deep, everlasting undercurrent in our souls, we often feel the slaughter of immortal spirits in the streets of Babylon until our heart sickens and we long to leave this world and be with Jesus. But like the apostle, we always conclude that "for us to live is Christ"; and the rescue of perishing souls from the brink of hell fires us with a willingness to expose our soul to the hatred and jeers, violence and murder in hearts that are drunk on the wine of beast religion. The United Brethren preacher at this place, whom Satan used with such diligence against the work when we were here last year, was much tormented by our return. "The wine of the wrath of her fornication" so foamed in his heart that, we were told by good authority, he said that he wished we were stripped, tarred and feathered, and then set on fire, and added that he would like to touch the match himself. And this wretched priest of Baal professes sanctification, and frequently leads the Babylon holiness band's meetings. Today we were told that he regretted much that his words came to our ears. That is like the thief that repented bitterly, not of his theft, but that he was caught in the deed.

A sister came in from the country and received full salvation. There being a union meeting-house in the community, she and others desired us to come there and preach the gospel. We agreed to do so on Sabbath evening if the house could be obtained. She thought there would be no difficulty. But as soon as the matter became known, a Methodist local preacher of the vicinity began to rage. He came to Walkerton on Saturday and, "foaming out his shame" before the people, declared that if we attempted to enter that pulpit he would "break our head," "break our neck," "kill us," etc.

Bishop Foster speaks of his M. E. sect as follows: "Oh, how changed! A hireling ministry will be a feeble, a timid, a truckling, a time-serving ministry, without faith, endurance, and holy power." Through this corrupt ministry "worldly socials, festivals, concerts, and such like, have taken the place of the religious gatherings, revival meetings, class- and prayer-meetings of the past. Oh, how changed!" Yes, saith the prophet, "How is the faithful city become an harlot! it was full of judgment; righteousness lodged in it; but now murderers. Thy silver is become dross, thy wine mixed with water: thy princes are rebellious, and companions of thieves: every one loveth gifts, and followeth after rewards" (Isa. 1:21-23).

Surely we have come to the last days. For, "this know also, that in the last days perilous times shall come. For men shall be lovers of their own selves, covetous, boasters, proud, blasphemers, disobedient to parents, unthankful, unholy, without natural affection, trucebreakers, false accusers, incontinent, fierce, despisers of those that are good, traitors, heady, highminded, lovers of pleasure more than lovers of God; having a form of godliness, but denying the power thereof: from such turn away" (2 Tim. 3:1-5).

Yea, "Babylon the great is fallen, is fallen, and is become the habitation of devils, and the hold of every foul spirit, and a cage of every unclean and hateful bird."

Oh, the rottenness, fierce hatred, and soul-murdering wickedness of sect Babylon! If there were only one hundred professors of Christ in the United States, and they all holy men and women of God, filled with faith and the Holy Spirit, walking unto all pleasing before God and exemplifying the pure life of Christ before men, and this generation had never known any other kind of professors of Christ, the masses of the people could be rapidly reached by the gospel of Jesus and saved from sin. But the devil has the world piled up with corrupt, proud, filthy, sectish religionists, 'professing that they know God; but in works they deny him, being abominable and disobedient, and unto every good work reprobate' (Tit. 1:16).

And because God has given us an honest heart to confess the sins of the professed Christendom and show the people that Christ is not the author of this mass of spiritual whoredom and abominable wickedness, which has filled hell with lost souls and covered the earth with blackness and infidelity, the devil howls and rages in his sectish priests, who are ready to murder us as the Jews did Christ, Stephen, and thousands of other martyrs who testified against them and their evil deeds.

As we shall have to meet the people of Walkerton and surroundings face to face in the day of judgment, God holds us responsible to tell them that the greatest obstruction to the salvation of souls is their shoddy, sectish holiness and their abominable, worldly religion.

Up to the summer of 1887 the evangelistic efforts of Brother Warner and his company were confined to the States of the Middle West. But now came a more extensive tour, that should take them as far West as Denver, Colo. On June 24 they left the Office and after a few meetings in LaGrange and Jay Counties, Ind., departed for the West. They stopped at Gilman and Onarga, Ill., and Hayesville, Iowa.

From Keokuk, Iowa, they traveled by steamboat to St. Louis, where the following report was written:

"Oh, praise the Lord with me, and let us exalt his name together!" We have just landed here from the steamboat Sidney, having had a very delightful trip down the Mississippi from Keokuk. We made the trip of two hundred miles in twenty hours. The river being very low at this time, much caution was necessary to avoid running aground. Doubtless one hundred miles were traveled in passing from one side of the river to the other to keep the deepest channel.

We were a day and a night at Keokuk, waiting the coming of the boat. The Gem City was to have reached Keokuk the first day and then return down the river; but being late she turned around at Quincy and started back, leaving us to wait until the next day. Praise God, we confessed his all-wise hand in the matter and thanked him for the prolonged wait, believing it was all ordered of him. This morning about daybreak we passed the Gem City, she having stuck fast in the sand. So the Lord was good to his little ones and gave us a safe and very joyful voyage. Oh, the goodness and wisdom of God our heavenly Father for placing the great rivers and lakes in the earth as a beautiful means of travel! It is so much more pleasant than by railroad. Though the speed is not more than half so great, we can very pleasantly improve the time reading and writing. However, this trip was so wonderfully enjoyed by us that we could do no more than feast upon the beauties of nature and praise the Lord. The river abounds in beautiful green islands, and all her verdant banks are delightful. Just below the mouth of the Illinois river, for a few miles, the hand of God has skilfully carved out of the high rocky shore very beautiful scallops and great piers and towers, and even some appearances of partly ruined mansions and rustic stone buildings.

*   *   *   *   *

No one else on board the vessel seemed to be delighted with these vast and beautiful works as were our company, because unacquainted with our dear Father, whose hand of love has formed them all. Oh, how blessed the pure in heart who see God all along the voyage of life! What a vastly different aspect everything wears when looked at in the light of God! Oh, how poor and meager the pleasures of the children of this world! How utterly tasteless and empty their thoughts and conversation! No place on earth serves better to call out the glories of a life hid with Christ in God in its striking contrast with the dark minds and almost senseless twaddle of the aliens than the deck of a steamboat. Even the more elevated seldom have a worthy thought on immortal mind; while every object our eyes lighted upon in the passing panorama of nature inspired our souls with joyful acknowledgments of God, and moved our hearts and lips to praise his name. Oh, what a rapturous and heavenly kingdom we live in, all flashing with glory and yet hidden from the blinded sinners! Having lost our lives for Christ's sake we are raised to the heavenly joys of the life of God in us, a life of bliss, that already transcends the sinner's loftiest ideal of heaven itself. Oh, the beauties of holiness! "Out of Zion the perfection of beauty, God hath shined." Never in all past experience has our heart flowed out more in gratitude to God for the inexpressible bliss of a pure conscience, a pure heart through the blood of Christ, an innocent life through grace divine, a conversation in heaven flowing from a good treasure in the heart, and, above all, a soul illuminated and inspired to see and enjoy God in every bright sunbeam that gleams on earth and sparkles in the silvery stream and every object upon the footstool of God.

> God is love; the angels know
> That Father dearly loves us so.
> But, oh, the ransomed feel within
> The burning love we try to sing!

This evening we start for St. James, Mo., the Lord willing, where we expect to meet once more our dear Bro. J. Cole, and many others dear to our hearts by the fellowship of the Spirit whose faces we have never seen. And best of all, we are expecting a glorious harvest of souls turned to righteousness by the mighty power and love of God.

The next report was written from St. James, Crawford County, one hundred miles west of St. Louis. Bro. B. E. Warren says that after buying their tickets for St. James they had but seven cents left, and that after arriving at the latter place Brother Warner went to the post-office and received a letter containing five dollars from S. L. Speck, who felt led of the Lord to send that amount. Brother Warner's account of their reception in St. James, as follows, is interesting:

The night following our last report, which was from St. Louis, Mo., we landed at St. James, at 12:30 A. M. The Lord directed us to a friendly inn, where we rested until the morning. As we sat at the breakfast-table our grateful hearts flowed out in our sweet little table thanksgiving song. The Lord wonderfully blessed that sweet offering of praise. It rang out and greeted the ears of all in hearing as the music of heaven. After meal, requests soon came in for songs. The Holy Spirit gloriously inspired our voices to sing his praises. Many people soon collected in front of the room and some came in. After a few hymns, we had family worship. We invited all that would come to come in and bow with us in prayer. Some did so. The Lord blessed our souls. Soon Bro. J. H. Morrison came into town, and seeing the throng in front of the hotel he asked the cause, and was told that "your people have come to town." He came into the waiting-room and introduced himself, and the Spirit of God gave us a joyful meeting. Sinners looked on with wonder and amazement, and were led to say, "These are truly the real children of God, and this is the right way," according to the words of our Savior, "By this shall all men know that ye are my disciples, if ye have love one for another." Many seemed quite serious. Had we tried to respond to the requests of the people we should have kept singing all day without cessation.

The people desired Brother Morrison to keep us right there and have a meeting that night in town, saying they would see that all our expenses there should be paid. The landlady and family were also very anxious we should stay, and treated us with much kindness. The Lord reward them. The Methodist preacher also came to see what this Pentecost fire was that had come to town. When asked if we could have their meeting-house that night he replied that he was going to "begin a protracted meeting tonight." Suddenly the preacher concluded a protracted meeting was needed in his charge. Whoever heard of a Methodist minister commencing a protracted meeting in the month of July in the latitude of central Missouri, especially since that sect has gone spiritually to the frigid zone where, as their oldest living bishop says, "spirituality is frozen to death"? Quite a capacious hall was procured and well filled, and we enjoyed preaching the precious gospel to the people. About all received the word. The M. E. meeting consisted of three or four women, and was not further protracted.

The day of our arrival here came also dear Bro. C. C. Knight, from Fulton, Ill., with tent and equipment to accompany us on our Western campaign. He is full of faith and the Holy Ghost and is a good help in the work.

The next day we moved out to the camp-ground, which is about ten miles from St. James and near the Merrimac River. Here we met our dearly beloved Brother Cole, who spent a year with us in Michigan a few years ago; also his sister Mary, a chosen and anointed instrument of God to preach and testify the gospel of the grace of God.

At this camp-meeting the little company were to encounter a new problem. As soon as they arrived at the place of meeting they were accorded a strange reception. Those who were supposed to be saints at that place came to meet them, some dancing on one leg, some rolling their eyes in their head, others gibbering in tongues, or jerking, or falling stiff, etc. At first they did not know what to make of the strange performance. At this place also was another attempt by a mob to capture Brother Warner. His report continues:

We met also a much larger host of saints than we had expected to find in this country. Praise God for this! But oh, how soon we saw and felt that Satan, the deceiver, had passed a dreadful network of deception over them, or nearly all of them! Unseemly and even hideous operations and contortions were carried on and called the manifestations of the Spirit and power of God. We began at once to rebuke it in the name of the Lord Jesus. God gloriously blessed our souls in preaching his word and assured us that he had much people there who were honest and sincere at heart and who would be delivered by the presentation of his word. The supposed gift of tongues was alarmingly increasing. Indian war-dances, etc., had turned the church of God into something quite different, a disgusting maze of confusion. We were helped of God in teaching them "how they ought to behave themselves in the house of God, which is the church of the living God."

A terrible nervous jerking had seized upon many in the meetings, which in some cases resembled much St. Vitus' dance. We speak of these things in order to give the saints of God everywhere the benefit of what these precious souls have learned in the dear school of experience. We had never seen such manifestation except in persons possessed with devils, and yet the Spirit of God showed us these were not so possessed, but were, for the most part, still owned of the Lord. We read 1 Cor. 12, 13, 14, and showed the beautiful harmony of the church under the control of the Spirit of God; that 'love does not behave itself unseemly'; that the gift of tongues was not of general usefulness, and was a sign to the Jews, not generally edifying to the church; that other gifts should be sought in preference, and unless he or some one else interpret, the person having the gift should keep silent or speak to himself; that 'five words with the understanding is better than ten thousand in an unknown tongue'; that spasmodic jerking is not mentioned in the Bible as a manifestation of God's Spirit, but is ascribed to a malignant spirit.

We renounced that working as of the devil. It seems that one brother who had been powerfully charged by the Holy Spirit had become puffed up, which gave place to this satanic working. Then Satan made it the standard of being filled with the Spirit and power of God; therefore many earnestly prayed for it. They forgot that the Holy Spirit makes intercession for us only according to the will of God, and whatsoever one prays for outside the will of God must be suggested by some other spirit. And as God has not promised to answer such a prayer, the devil steps in and answers it. And now, since delivered, the dear saints see and confess that the incoming of this power dimmed their faith, joy, and peace. It was nothing less than Satan touching and playing upon their nerves and upon their imaginations. Their motives having been good, namely, to seek the real power of God, their consciences were not defiled—at least, with most of them. But some were much blinded and puffed up of the devil. Satan had free access to their minds under the cloak of the Spirit of God. Those who were not affected by the foolish jerking of the devil were judged by the devil and made to believe they did not have the Spirit of God because they did not jerk. Thus all were under depression and more or less bewildered. Oh, how our souls were saddened at the sight! O dear saints of God everywhere, do not ascribe to the Spirit of God ludicrous and unbecoming conduct, such as chattering like a coon or barking like a dog, and all hideous looks!

Well, praise God, the word of God was received. Some at first resented, but God soon convicted them and they became teachable. Nearly all the foolish stuff was rid out of the camp after one discourse explaining and renouncing it. Intelligent sinners respected the truth of God that exposed the devil's counterfeit, and some who loved the true church wept for joy to see the abomination put away. From that time God led one after another to confess that spiritual joy and true faith began to depart out of their hearts from the time of receiving the jerks. Many came bowing at the altar, and the glorious work of cleansing went forward.

The truth of God was published against all the works of the devil by the power of the Holy Spirit. Some sect preachers, filled with the beast spirit and the very devil himself, were very much enraged against the word of the Lord, which had laid open the rottenness of their hearts. Hence they spewed out their shame and foamed exceedingly. On Tuesday night, after meeting, we all lay down to rest, being wearied with the arduous labors of the day. A masked mob aroused us from our much-needed sleep and ordered all to pack up and leave the grounds in half an hour. They were armed with staves and rocks. Well, the saints arose and packed up, praising God for peace and comfort in their souls, not fearing the poor set of sinners who knew not that they were persecuting the Savior. They made diligent inquiry for us all about the camp. We were doubtless the special victim marked by their rankling hatred; but the Lord delivered us out of their hands. Oh, praise the Lord with me and let us exalt his name together!

The next morning early some saints drove back to the ground to get some things that had been left, and there came the preachers who had been howling with torment and sorrow because of the sword of the Lord, and even gnawing their tongues for pain, and who were generally believed to have been in the clan the night before, and one of them even recognized. They asked with much affected surprize what had happened, and began to declare and even to swear in the presence of God that they knew nothing of the movement and were not in it, though one of them confessed he was glad of it. This they did without having been accused. One brother said, "A guilty conscience needs no accuser; you plead guilty before accused."...

Well, praise God, the next morning, after a few hours' sleep, we were called up to join some little ones in asking God to heal a child that was suffering with the croup. The good Lord instantly did the work. Others followed, some for healing, others for complete deliverance from every taint of the devil. God himself gathered the saints at that place, and the day was devoted to salvation work. Probably twenty-five or thirty souls were delivered from all the works of the devil and filled with the Spirit of God. Oh, what a mighty change has taken place here! Instead of gloomy and hideous looks, now shines the glory and beauties of holiness, upon the joyful faces of the redeemed, and clear, ringing shouts of praises are pleasing to God.

No meeting was announced for the next day, but the Lord gathered quite a number together again, and salvation work was resumed. On both days God so filled and possessed the meetings that there was not time for the slightest allusion to the mob workers of the devil. A stranger might have sat in the meeting the whole day and not received the faintest information of what had happened two nights ago. Praise God, these two days after driven out of camp were the most glorious and fruitful of all that we spent in these wild thickets. In spite of all that poor, pitiable ruffians could do, hissed on by wicked Babylonians, we are filled with joy unspeakable and full of glory.

We are now holding meetings a few days in the village of St. James. A large hall is crowded with attentive hearers, and the truth is mightily prevailing. Let all the saints of God pray for us. We will continue to preach the whole truth and rebuke the works of the devil, even if this tour should end in heaven. Halleluiah!

Of these strange manifestations Bro. T. E. Ellis, who was one of those living in the vicinity and affected by the peculiar power that possessed the saints there, says:

We were under an influence similar to what the modern tongues people are under. We had different manifestations. Some would jerk spasmodically, some would fall and become stiff, some would dance, some would seem to have a kind of trance and a vision. Healing was claimed and the work seemed to be done. We had what we called the "unknown tongue" and an interpreter. A few talked similarly to the way modern tongues people talk nowadays.

From St. James the company continued their tour to Carthage, in the southwestern part of the State. They also held meetings at a number of different points in southern Kansas and in southeastern Nebraska, The first paragraph of his report from Chanute, Kans., was written while he was sick. We quote the first two paragraphs:

It seems as distance stretches out between us and the dear loved ones with whom we have so often and joyfully worshiped God, that the love of God in our hearts is drawing us nearer together. I have never before felt the blessed, pure love of God burning so intensely in my heart for the dear household of God as lately. I can scarcely write to the beloved saints without tears dimming my eyes. O dearly beloved, we can feel your daily fervent prayers in our behalf, and all our company desire to thank you, for them.

We want to testify to the goodness of God. The foregoing lines were written by a very sick man, but now we continue writing, a well man. Oh, praise the Lord with me and let us exalt his name together! From early morn until 3 P. M. today we were very sick, unable to eat. Tried to write, but had to take the bed. Finally the Lord impressed us with earnest prayer. We called the little company and kneeled before God, and oh, our dear heavenly Father instantly healed our body, took away all bad feeling, raised our voice from the faint tones of a person just beginning to rise from a hard sick spell to clear loud shouts of praise! He also sent through our entire system the strength of high leaps, as well as the high praises of God.

In a later report he shows how his health was maintained by faith.

For some time we have felt called of God to devote ourself more especially to the great duty of writing some works of present truth, and we expect to do so after the present tour. With this fact coming oft before our mind, we began unconsciously to relax our faith by which in our natural frailty we kept up sufficient strength for field labor. The presence of the ministerial brethren with us for some time also helped ease up our mind and drop our shield of faith by our side. The result was the devil had afflicted our poor weak body for several weeks. But, praise God, the Lord having in answer to prayer shown us what the trouble was, last Sabbath we rebuked the devil in the name of the Lord Jesus with a holy vehemence, and our soul and body sprang forth with a shout of victory, and, glory to our God, we have been wonderfully well and spiritually glorious ever since.

From Waco, Nebr., the company traveled westward to Denver. The following are extracts from his report at that place:

We stopped over a few hours in Lincoln, the capital of the State. We viewed with surprize the young city. Fourteen years ago when we visited the place it was small—now it numbers over twenty thousand inhabitants, more than double the size of Lansing, Mich.

That night, for the first time in all our travels, an accident occurred to our train, a slight collision with a freight-train several miles out of Lincoln. The engine being injured, we had to wait some hours until another was brought from the city. During this time there was a very violent wind. The car rocked on its springs like a load of hay passing over a rough road. But we lay down and slept sweetly, committing ourselves unto the Lord. That evening dear Bro. E. E. Byrum, at the office, had a great burden for our safety, as he wrote us the next day. But he prayed for us until the Lord by the Spirit answered him that we should be delivered from all harm. Oh, praise the Lord for his goodness and mercy toward us! For our safety he placed a burden on one nearly a thousand miles away, but allowed not the slightest anxiety on our minds....

Tuesday evening, December 6, our little company took train for Denver, five hundred miles more toward the setting sun. That night we stopped over and had a good night's rest at McCook, Nebr. Took train again at 7 A. M. and went flying over the prairie at a swift rate. Oh, what vast expanse of the broad prairie! Some parts are rough and broken, but the larger portion is beautiful and even and wanting only showers or irrigation to make a beautiful farming-country....

When about fifty miles from Denver, we observed strange blue banks to the west, which we first took to be dark clouds, but which we soon perceived were distant foot-hills of the Rocky Mountains. Plainer and higher they loomed up before our eyes as our swift train kept darting like an arrow toward the base. How beautiful and sublime the sight! Here at Denver we are twelve miles from the foot-mountains. They seem but a very short distance, especially when the morning sun shines brightly against their eastern sides. It seems impossible that they can be more than a mile and one half away. A person would surely suppose that he could walk over and back before breakfast. The foot-hills, rather mountains, are of a dark color, being covered by timber, and to all appearance just beyond them rise up the beautiful snow-covered range. To our astonishment we are told that fifty miles stretch out between them and that there is a fertile valley there with towns, etc. The snowy range being so much farther off seems to be but a little higher than the foot-mountains, and both ranges seem to stand together. In the morning they all seem so close that one would surely suppose a man could be seen if standing there in the snow....

It was quite a novelty to the company to see the many sod-houses we passed and dugouts in the hillsides. Sometimes there was scarcely anything to attract attention but a window door in a steep little hill. Sometimes we saw upon the level ground a roof about eight by ten covering a little underground house. Most of such were but herdsmen's dens. We have not yet begun to work here. Let all the saints pray earnestly for the work of salvation.

The company remained in Denver ten weeks, holding meeting in various places. When they went to that city there were only four persons who were in the light of the truth, but they left a congregation of about forty who had taken their stand for the truth. Returning eastward they stopped in York County, Nebr., where Brother Warner had labored in his Nebraska mission in 1873–4. A portion of his report from Wayland reads as follows:

> We preached and lived in this community thirteen and fourteen years ago, then a member of the sect wearing the stolen name of Church of God. The Lord blessed our labors in the salvation of some souls from their sins, and we had good meetings. There were very dear brethren and sisters here. But since our departure the work has retrograded. Some of their preachers became horse jockeys, others jealous-hearted, dead formalists, too cold and dry to keep men awake, much less awaken and get any one converted. The one on the work up to the time of our coming here has preached here four years without the conversion of a single soul. During our meeting he resigned his charge, and we are told he has now hired himself to preach for the Christian sect at Wayland, some of the members of which were the most malignant enemies and opposers of the work of grace. An unsaved citizen declared the other evening that about all the bad behavior and interruption he had seen during our meetings was by the sinners of the sects.

From Wayland the company went by way of Meriden and Atchinson, Kans., to Whiteside County, Ill., where they held meetings near Albany and also near Fulton. The following is the report, in part, from Albany:

> We were happy to meet our dear beloved Brother Knight at his prairie home, four miles east of Fulton, and he leaped and skipped like a lamb to see us. The next day we all came eleven miles south to Bro. A. Byers', whose house is a happy home for the war-worn pilgrims. The people are receiving the word with much interest. After several days' work here and as long at Brother Knight's neighborhood we go on homeward, for there is a great deal to do at home, some small works to print and the new songbook, Anthems From the Throne. Praise God for the precious and glorious songs he is sending us! The music is nearly all written by Brother Barney, whose inspiration in this gift is a marvel....
>
> O beloved, will you help us? A great responsibility rests upon us. While we are praising God for the precious light of heaven let us not forget others in darkness and exposed to the numer-

ous pitfalls now threatening souls for whom Jesus died. Let no spirit of the devil nor any of his children tell you that we have any selfish motive in enlisting all willing and obedient hearts and hands in doing our duty in the rescuing of souls from Satan in every possible way. In the name of Jesus we spurn such meanness. God knows we do not draw a breath for self, but 'for us to live is Christ.' Are we seeking self-interests, as wicked men have belied us? Where can any facts be cited upon which to base such an unkind assertion? On the present tour of nearly a year we have used about every cent we have received from the sale of books to supply the needs of ourself and little company. So we go forth preaching night and day, exposing this poor frail body to the cruel, biting frosts and beating storms, and toiling about every moment with the pen except when in meetings or going to and from, and in about six hours sleep, asking nothing for our labors either from God or man but the salvation of souls and the glory of God....

Life will soon be over. You must leave your earthly treasures in the hands of others. Whether they will leave it to serve God or the devil is not yet known. Therefore, had you not better put a little of it at least into God's bank, laying it up in heaven, where thieves do not break through and steal and where moth and rust do not corrupt? As we return home from this long tour we feel impressed of the Lord to devote ourself more fully to the preparation of matter for the press; and we shall pray God with all our soul to move men and women to provide the means to purchase paper and other supplies to send it forth. There should be some works sent forth by the million, free of cost. We feel sure that God will find willing hearts to help in the work, and shall toil on in full assurance that when we breathe our last we shall have this consolation, that we have done what we could to enlighten and save souls, for whom Jesus died upon the cross.

The company arrived at Grand Junction, Mich., on April 25. Thus ended their Western tour, in which seed was sown in many hearts to spring up and bear fruit for God.

Sister Frankie Miller said of this tour that it was marked by wonderful answers to prayer for rain. It seemed that wherever the company stopped on their way West in Illinois, Iowa, and the other States the country was suffering on account of drought. At every place their visit was either attended or followed by copious showers. At one public service Mother Smith prayed earnestly for rain. There was not a single indication of rain, but before the service was over the heavens blackened and rain fell in abundance. Thus all along their course the drought was broken.

The summer of 1888 was spent in attending camp-meetings and visiting the churches in various places in Michigan, Indiana, Ohio, and Pennsylvania. Early in the winter a tour was made into Ontario. They found a good many souls in that country who had come out for the truth. Their labors there were blessed in the salvation of others and in the sowing of the good seed. Of the country and people Brother Warner had this to say:

> We can say that we find a moderately fair farming-country, and we can not observe the slightest difference between the people here and in the States. More than ever we have learned that so long as governments allow a free, conscientious worship of God, their form is quite immaterial. We do not see that people have any special advantages by living in the States over what are enjoyed here. If any difference, farmers do not pay as heavy taxes here as in the States. Local option temperance laws are given to the people, and some counties have no saloons. And one blessed thing Canada has reason to thank God for is the fact that all liquor-selling establishments are strictly compelled to close early Saturday evening and not open until Monday morning. This law enforced cuts off nearly one half the mischief of the nefarious business. Sabbath-observance is also far more complete here than in the States. We were blessed with good order and find the way open for the gospel freely.

In August of the year 1889, the company again made their way Westward, going as far as Nebraska and returning through Kansas and Missouri. They held meetings again at St. James, Mo., where a mob had given trouble two years before. Some of those who were guilty of that disturbance had become friends to the truth. One old preacher, however, continued to abuse the saints in his preaching until one Sunday evening, after expressing his usual opposition to the saints, he went home and dropped dead near his gate. Before this second visit of Brother Warner to this place one of the Baptist Church members made it known that he intended to break up this meeting also. It was reported that he actually began to work up a mob; but his child had a bean to lodge in its windpipe and died, and this put a stop to the carrying out of his evil design.

Brother Warner intended to spend the winter in Missouri, but he felt drawn back to Indiana. Having a great desire to settle down for a while, he wrote as follows, in December, 1889:

> For a long time we have felt the call of God to shut ourself away with him for a while and let him teach us the deep things of God, that we may be able more perfectly to follow out the glorious lines of present truth. We have a great desire to do so, and yet when hungry souls in every direction are calling for the saving truth of God it is hard for us to keep from running; but if the Lord will, we shall pass the calls around to the many able-bodied and warm-hearted soldiers of the "white horse" cavalry, who are ready to rush to the battle wherever he leads. We began preaching, a poor, frail invalid, over twenty-two years ago, and God has sustained us in a most remarkable manner during all these years of intense labor and great exposure. Oh how grateful we feel to

our heavenly Father that we are blessed with such good health! But nevertheless we feel that more regular diet, sleep, etc., for a season will prove a great blessing, and increase and prolong our usefulness on earth. We shall devote ourself principally to Bible-study and poetical labor.

By the close of the year 1889, it was seen that the work had been almost doubling itself annually. That year there had been held twenty-five grove-meetings, fourteen camp-meetings, besides several general assemblies. Quite a strong working force was by this time in the field, and evangelists were scattered out in the more distant parts of the country.

The next tour of any considerable extent was one that took them into the Southland. This trip was made in November, 1890. They intended to make the trip by boat down the Mississippi, but found the water at a low ebb and traveling very slow. They took a steamer at Cincinnati, but had to wait two days before it started; and then it took them four days to reach Cairo. After waiting three days for a boat overdue from St. Louis, they made the rest of the journey by rail, and landed at Meridian, Miss. In this part of the country Brothers Bradley and Bozeman and others had opened up the work. The people were very hungry for the preaching of the word. Brother Warner and the company spent several weeks in the eastern part of the State. His bold manner in uncovering sin and false religion occasioned considerable opposition from various sectarian sources. The country was cursed with a false holiness element called "Straight Holiness," representing the Good Way, a paper then published at Fort Scott, Kans. Its teachers failed in the South to be uncompromising against tobacco and other evils and they incited no little opposition and prejudice against the New Testament standard held by Brother Warner. At Beech Springs, Miss., the mob element was encountered, as is shown by the portion of Brother Warner's report here given:

At that place there are a few Babylon hearts of the most pernicious hue, men steeped and dyed in tobacco and drunk on Babylon's worst wine, the wrath of which they infuse into the baser sort. Brothers Bradley and Bozeman have both been threatened in that place with violence and, we believe, even with murder, and we could expect the same animus toward us. Hence, the second night several pieces of brick and clubs came crashing through the window, all doubtless hurled in wrath at us. Nearly half of the sash was broken in and the glass flew over the house. The unsaved were much frightened, and the whole house was thrown into confusion. The glory of God was greatly upon us through all the evening, and with the cowardly onslaught the heavenly tides so wondrously swelled in our soul that we had to leap for joy in the midst of the uproar. Oh, the mighty river of peace and joy! The excellent tide of glory only subsided into sleep at a late hour, and it arose again with our waking in the morning. We stood only about seven feet from the window and nearly opposite; but the hand of God protected us from serious harm. However, the Lord saw he could overrule a slight glancing wound on the side of our face and nose for his glory, and so permitted the same. It was very evident in the meeting the next day that either Satan had made a great mistake or else his children were more wicked than he wanted them to be, so that he could not restrain them from their wicked deed, which proved a great blessing to the cause of Christ. All the saints were able to see more clearly than ever before the track that Christ and his primitive saints had trod. And about all testified that they had reached a clearer experience, stronger faith, and more joy in the Lord through the last night's meeting than ever before. The meeting that day was indeed very glorious.

The spiritual condition of the people as countenanced by the "Straight Holiness" teachers in that part of the South is set forth in the report written from Spring Hill, near Meridian:

> Our last report was from Oak Grove neighborhood. When we entered there we found the powers of darkness and wickedness fierce and black. Threats were breathed about and written notices deposited in the dark. After one night's meeting in the old meeting-house, which is a neighborhood building, it was locked up. We went into the small schoolhouse near by and the Lord most wonderfully blessed our souls. Satan then had the schoolhouse locked, and though certain citizens had jerked the staples out of the old meeting-house and the doors stood wide open, and the Methodist class-leader, being in favor of the right and truth, invited us to enter, yet because others were raging we preferred to hold a little service in the public road, in the bright moonlight. God blessed the songs, prayer, and a few words of exhortation, and all the people seemed touched. Nearly every person present kneeled during prayer.
>
> All these circumstances God overruled to the good of the people and the cause of Christ. The schoolhouse was again opened, and we went on a few nights longer, with glorious victory. Only a few sought the Lord; but there was a general blessing effected on the community in the removal of prejudice and hatred out of many hearts that had been influenced through lies and slanders, such as of promiscuous kissing, free-love, etc., propagated chiefly by the little Fort Scott-creed sect.[21]
>
> It is a bad and fallacious cause that depends upon defamation of others. The course these schismatics resort to occasions some persecution and no little hatred, and even danger of violent treatment, which they will have to answer for in the day of judgment. But the cause thus bolstered up can not stand, and truth

---

[21] In addition to this a letter had been received in the community, from Carthage, Mo., written by an opposer who misrepresented the saints as believers in amalgamation with the colored people, the purpose of the letter being, of course, to stir up prejudice.

crushed down by foul means is sure to rise again; and just in proportion as there has been evil-speaking against the truth will it enlist the hearts of the honest, and at the same time forfeit all confidence in and elicit contempt for such as have defamed it and its lovers. In accordance with these principles truth rose triumphant at Oak Grove. The people saw we had been slandered, yea and Jesus Christ also.... The Lord has raised up many friends for the whole truth in that place, and could we have remained long enough to make a thorough effort, doubtless a number of souls would have been saved. But the way is opened for the true work of God to prosper there. Some who were much prejudiced when we went there, seeing that the truth of God is in us, had their minds changed, and their countenances were divested of the sour and took on the pleasant. God bless the people of that community.

From that place we came to Spring Hill, several miles east.... Here were a few pure children of God, whom we found yoked up with a majority who were professing salvation and yet "walking after the flesh in the lust of uncleanness." In our lifting the standard of God's Word against such inconsistencies, the wicked spirits were stirred in the baser sort, so that many threats of violence were blown about in the neighborhood. But the hand of God being over us, we suffered no harm....

Oh, how our soul longs to be excused of this most unpleasant task of lifting the gospel standard of holiness where profession has been countenanced in lives of filth and idolatry! The preacher that simply tells the people he could not use tobacco, and even earnestly admonishes men to quit, and yet receives the testimonies of men who use it, sets at naught the Word of God, pampers men in their sins, and prepares a storm of persecution to fall on the head of the man who comes after him showing the real Bible line between the works of God and the works of the devil, between real holiness of heart, soul, spirit, and body on the one side, and all filthiness of the flesh and spirit on the other. If holiness-teachers, on going into a new field where people know nothing about the doctrine and experience, would faithfully tell them at once that entire sanctification, the second work of grace, cleanses out of man all filthiness of the flesh and spirit, which includes all unholy tempers and appetites, that it can be obtained only by abandoning every sinful and unclean habit and giving the whole man—soul, body, and spirit—up to God for perfect purity of life and being, no person is prepared to contradict him, and such as conclude to seek that grace will expect to pay the full price....

But when men are allowed to profess holiness without contradiction and yet practise the sin of tobacco-using or anything else contrary to godliness, they, in imagining themselves holy while living in unholiness, as well as sinners in general, learn to associate holiness and filth, and the difficulties in rooting out the abomination, are many times increased. Men, by getting a degree of blessing of God upon their souls in consequence of abandoning some evils, or at least imagining themselves blessed, take the same as an endorsement from God upon the filth they yet continue in. The longer they continue in their delusion the more they are confirmed in it and the more they will fight for their idols. And their practise justifying the lusts of the wicked, these are ready to assault and abuse God's ministers, who must declare the whole counsel of God. And so a lax preacher gives place for the devil and wrath of men to assault the faithful herald of God that follows him. So by the fruits of the devotees of rehashed Methodism in the Fort Scott creed, which has cursed the South and filled hearts with bitter hatred toward all who follow Christ, and by their strife and contentions having brought a general contempt upon the name of holiness, and also by their lack of radicalness against sin in every form, our work here is beset with dark mountains, which God alone can remove, but which, thank his holy name, have been much obliterated in all places where we have labored.

Later, at Spring Hill, the mob element was further encountered. Here, as was always the case where a mob gathered to do violence to Brother Warner, the chief instigators were sectarian preachers and professors who were incensed by the preaching of the truth that condemned them.

From Spring Hill meeting-house, where we last wrote, we went about seven miles to the southeast through a wild and almost mountainous woods, to the house of Brother and Sister Irby, in whose dwelling we remained and held meeting about one week.... A goodly number of hearers came out through the wet weather, and the dear Lord was pleased to pour his Spirit upon us gloriously. It seemed that God had taken us up upon the Delectable Mountains. The leaps in our soul were too high for the height of the room, as the house had a ceiling, whereas, nearly all the country houses here have nothing overhead but the roof, and never has a whitewash brush touched the walls. Scarcely one out of ten of the houses in the country has a pane of glass in it. The sisters talked with some women who did not know what a carpet is. We have seen no such thing here. The people in the South seem contented with fewer domestic comforts than any people we ever before met. As one sister remarked the other day, "they take it out in tobacco." There is much truth in this statement. That weed deprives them of nearly all comforts and many actual necessities of life. Of course, there is not the same need of carpeted floors here as in the North; but how people can live for years in a house without a window is a mystery.

Well, our stay at Brother and Sister Irby's seemed to my soul like old Brother Elijah's hiding-place in the wilderness, where he dined on food brought by angels. We also feasted on heavenly manna, and shall never forget it. Some came to the altar, and a few cast away their filthy idol; but we hope the day of judgment will reveal much more good done than was manifest....

Some of God's little ones came over from Spring Hill, who informed us that some were anxious for our return to that place. Now, at that place is where Satan's seat is. Before we left there we were much impressed that the mob spirit was at work, and one night when the rain prevented our going to the place, a disguised crowd was seen going there. But now, hearing that some souls were hungry for salvation, we ventured back in the name of Jesus.

When reaching the neighborhood, we were joyfully surprized by the coming of our dear young brother Andrew L. Byers, from Illinois, who has come to join our little company. Having had a great deal of trouble and several days' ramble before he found us he was reminded of Stanley in search of Livingstone. Truly our hearts were mutually refreshed by his arrival.[22]

The first night of meeting three souls came to the altar, two consecrated for entire sanctification and one was gloriously pardoned. The next night the fierce powers of hell were fully awakened from their brief slumber occasioned by our absence. A couple of lead balls called buckshot were thrown through the open window by means of a rubber concern that we are told is even dangerous to life. These wicked wretches also threw stones with slings at some of God's saints on their way home that night, even regardless of women and children in the crowd. One woman was hit. That was a little the lowest and most cowardly work we have ever yet met with. The next day four of Satan's chief servants rode out in four directions five and seven miles to enlist by his lies and slanders such as were base enough in a great mob to assault us that night. During the day we learned all about the movement, and at a meeting at a brother's house we recalled the meeting for night, seeing no possible chance of doing good.

Hear O heavens, and be ashamed O Babylon, when we tell you that one of the four spirits that went forth to gather together Gog and Magog was of the Fort Scott creed, or the Good Way sect, and the father of the only family of that sect in the neighborhood. And at his cotton-gin was the appointed place for the mob to meet. Some five miles away he called on some young men

---

[22] These meetings in the vicinity of Spring Hill were almost the author's first experience in gospel work. I was asked to join the company to supply a missing part in song, Mother Smith having dropped out previously. After arriving at Meridian it was some time before I could locate Brother Warner.

who are reputed pretty wicked and invited them to join the mob, telling them base lies. But they, having more principle than he, said they would have nothing to do with it. They also came and informed some friends of the Lord all about the plot. These told the Fort Scott man to his face what he was guilty of, and he said he did not deny it.... We expected to meet that creed with the Word of God and had hopes of seeing some saved. But they shun Scripture investigation as a wolf shuns daylight. Brother Bradley invited the editor and two of the leading preachers to meet him in discussion, but they have failed to do so; and now we have discovered their tactics. They seem to regard slandering and mobbing as better calculated to subserve their cause than would honest discussion. While we are happy to think that most of them in person would not condescend to mobbing, it is only too true that many of them have given their tongues to slander whereby the other measures have been infused in the baser sort. May God forgive them for Christ's sake.

There being no meeting at which the mob could assault us, they beset the house where we stayed until about twelve o'clock at night. They reported their number between seventy-five and one hundred. They were armed with guns and revolvers. There were in the crowd a Methodist preacher, a class-leader with his axe, many old gray-haired sectarians, men recently out of jail; the basest men in the country mixed up with a majority of sectites—so we were informed by brethren that knew the majority that came up to the house, for a part kept in reserve with most of the guns. They stated that their object was only to give us orders to leave the country next day. A brave army, about a hundred strong, gathered from several miles around, just to tell a few little children of God to leave the next day, after we had announced in the meeting that we were going at that time! There were a few fearless souls present who told them to their face that they were actuated to their dark work by the lies of Satan and the wickedness of their hearts, and shamed the Babylon professors there mixed up in common cause with base outlaws.

The mob hung around until about midnight, clamoring for us to come out, stating they would not hurt us, etc. But when men are low down enough to fling buckshot into a congregation and rocks into a promiscuous crowd, you might as well tell us that wolves and hyenas do not care for meat as to say that such did not want to hurt us. Doubtless some in the crowd did not, and for what we know such as said so did not; but judging the mob by what we had seen in the past we had good sense enough to avoid such beasts....

After all left the house, not a great way off, they fired off their pieces, which, for a few seconds, mimicked the din of war.[23]

May God ever bless and keep the few pure children of God in that wicked region; and may he reward their kindness to us and also that of the few non-professors, whom we shall not soon forget and for whom we shall pray that God may bless and reward them with his great salvation.

Following the campaign in eastern Mississippi, meetings were held in northern Alabama, near Hartsells and near Athens, after which the company returned northward, Brother Warner into Indiana and the others into Ohio.

On the way north the author had the pleasure of making a trip through the Mammoth Cave, in Kentucky, in company with Brother Warner, whose description of this trip appears in the Trumpet of April 15, 1891, but for want of space is not reproduced here. He had great capacity for enjoying the wonderful in nature.

In a report written from Markleville, Ind., he tells of a visit to Indianapolis,

[23] To one unaccustomed it was hard to realize that opposition to the truth would take the form of a mob. We were quartered at the house of a Brother Smith. When the mob first came, Brother Warner asked if I wished to join him in his escape from the house. I then accompanied him to the pine woods some distance from the dwelling, and we remained there until we could hear that the mob had left. Bro. B. E. Warren had found a hiding-place under the house. The first company of men that came proved to be only a detachment, and the mob afterward came in greater force. This second time I remained in the house with the women folks, while Brothers Warner and Warren took the hiding under the building. The men wanted Brother Warner and lingered at the gate for some time talking with Brother Smith, who would not allow them within the gate except to see for themselves that Brother Warner was not in the house. Finally, after learning that I was present, they asked to see me, whereupon I went out and talked with them from the porch. They asked a number of questions and then left.

Trumpet Family, 1895, at Grand Junction, Michigan.

where the Trumpet passed through the first year and a half of its existence.

We came on to Indianapolis, where we began the blasts of the Gospel trumpet. We remained all night, and early in the morning walked out to the spot where we labored and prayed and trusted God nearly two years in great trials. Abandoned and hated of all the world, opposed by all of Babylon and rejected by the sectish associated holiness forces, we were forced out upon the promises of God and endured a great fight of faith. All the earth seemed dark as midnight, and growling letters came thick and fast and friendly ones few and far between. We were where, a stranger in a city, without money, friends, or credit, "give us this day our daily bread," was not a mere formal prayer. Oh, the riches of the goodness and the wonders of the mercy of God! Surely he hath never yet forsaken the righteous. Here we labored and prayed in intense poverty, while the word of the Lord tried us; but his strong arm hath gotten him the victory over all the powers of hell and earth. Here we had a temporary summer office on our lot and occupied a room of the house, about 10×14, in winter. Now a large two-story building is occupied with the business, and the circulation is rapidly enlarging.

We went back to the room we had occupied through the night and cast ourself down on the carpet in gratitude to God. Glory be to God for the triumph for his mighty present truth!

Lena Shoffner. Hattie Rupert. J. H. Rupert.
The Gospel Van, Birkenhead, England. — 1894.

Little did Brother Warner realize, when he was at Markleville describing the facilities of the publishing work in Indianapolis shortly after it started, that he was then within ten miles of where (at Anderson) the publishing office should be permanently located fifteen years hence. Since he is making comparisons of the beginning of the publishing work with its status at the time he wrote, it may be well to make some comparisons with the present.

At the time he wrote, the publishing force numbered twelve persons; now, thirty years later, there are about two hundred persons employed. Then the building located at Grand Junction, was a two-story frame structure, 40x70 in size, with a small lean-to; now the publishing machinery is housed in a building of concrete and steel containing more than an acre of floor space. The yearly expense for paper was then $500; now the cost of paper and printing-plates for the periodicals alone is $37,000, all materials together $ 1 34,000. Postage then $300, now more than $17,000. Fuel then $200, now $10,000. The printing-plant as well, it may be added, is one of the most up-to-date in the country. How greatly the work has grown! And yet the growth has been sufficiently slow to be substantial.[24]

The tour into the Southern States was the last tour Brother Warner made in company with his little band of singers and helpers. After holding a couple of grove-meetings in Ohio and attending the Beaver Dam meeting in Indiana, during the summer of 1891, the company did not travel together any longer. Brother Warner visited the churches in Pennsylvania and Ontario and then spent the following winter, or most of it, at the publishing office. In April, 1892, came a visit to the churches in the West, including the one at Denver. Before leaving home for this trip he suffered from a severe attack of rheumatism, and recovered only by a constant fight of faith. His report from Denver furnishes an example of how he frequently had to contend with afflictions and how he found his victory only in the Lord.

> Through exposure in a cold rain at Kenesaw, Nebr., I was taken with a bad lung-trouble; was quite poorly and had lost about all appetite. But, thank God, we held on by faith in him and he raised me up. I was rapidly regaining strength when we left there. But an apparently congested state of my lungs seemed still to oppress my being. As the onward-flying train carried us higher and the air consequently became more and more light, the difficulty of breathing increased. I also found myself under a fever and lay one day very weak.

---

[24] Besides the Gospel Trumpet, a young people's paper and a children's paper are published. Tons of literature in the form of books, tracts, and periodicals are sent out each year. A general ministerial assembly and camp-meeting, attended by thousands, is held annually at Anderson in an auditorium seating over five thousand. Missionary centers are established in many foreign countries. It is God's work and is destined to spread over the whole earth.

Present publishing office and plant of the Gospel Trumpet, Anderson, Ind.
50,000 feet of floor space. Built of concrete and steel.

Gospel Trumpet Home, Anderson, Ind. For employees and Bible students.

Oh, how my poor soul cried out all the day long for the blessing of health and strength once more to this frail temple that had been so long crushed down with one affliction after another! But there was searching of the heart and consecration as well as prayer. I realized a sweet willingness to suffer on more and more all the days of my life, and almost more than a willingness to quit the theater of this life and of this dark world, which had pressed so many bitter cups of tribulation to my lips. I did not know, indeed, but that I had come here to join the dark train that moves silently and almost constantly out of this city to the large city of the dead, where thousands who come here to regain health are furnished a grave instead of health. But these thoughts brought no gloom to my redeemed soul. Three glorious things lit all up brightly:

First, I knew my soul was all arrayed in the pure righteousness of God, without spot, and that by the grace of God I had kept the faith, obeyed God, and done what I could to glorify his holy name on earth.

Second, whether we wake—remain in the body—or sleep—leave the body—we shall live together with the Lord. I shall still have a conscious and joyful existence in a more near and blissful presence of the Lord after leaving this clay house.

Third, this mortal body also shall put on immortality and be fashioned like Christ's glorious body. Oh, bless God for the beautiful hope of a child of God!

Before sundown I awoke from a short sleep, and instantly felt heavenly sweetness in my soul and comfort in body. Behold, the Lord had taken away all the fever! That night some of the beloved came together and anointed me for complete healing. We believed the Lord granted the petition, and after much trial of my faith I am now feeling well in body once more and rapidly gaining strength.

His account of his visiting the natural wonders at Colorado Springs is interesting and shows his love for the handiwork of God.

Yesterday we all improved the time in visiting some of God's wonderful works about Manitou and what is called the Garden of the Gods. Here we praised and worshiped the true God and creator of all things in heaven and earth, when we beheld the wonderful works that his hands had wrought. Here rise from a level surface, or, rather, project out of the earth, yellow rocks to the height of over three hundred feet. Some of them look like a great castle, others are a few thin slabs standing side by side with very fine crevices, between which were doubtless at one time veins of rock more soft than the rest, and the stream of time has worn them out. Some of these majestic formations could be ascended to a considerable height from one side. On these elevations we shouted the praises of God, feeling his presence with us. Many smaller rocks of very peculiar shape are seen in this romantic region.

From here we proceeded to the town of Manitou, which is a small but very attractive town in a deep passage of the mountains. Here we found a family that was interested, in full salvation. We talked with them and prayed with them, and perhaps they will find a door open for Jesus in that place. We then drove about one mile beyond up the Ute Pass to Rainbow Falls, after which we visited the celebrated Iron Springs. The water is so highly charged with mineral substances that it is nearly as strong as hard cider; and yet it has what most pronounce no unpleasant flavor. It tastes like strong soda-water. It is very electrifying to the system, and the constant tide of visitors goes there to drink the healing waters. Near the upper springs is the beginning of the cog railroad that transports travelers up to the summit of Pike's Peak. The distance up the mountain is about nine miles.

Returning to Manitou we stopped and drank freely of the soda spring, of which soda-water is a good imitation. Visitors may freely drink of all these springs and each may carry away one quart of the precious water. We brought some home, and by adding sugar and lemon-juice the water foamed up and made a delicious drink.

Here we sit and write in Colorado Springs on a plain that rises nearly six thousand feet above the place of our home. How pure and light the atmosphere is! And Pike's Peak near by us lifts its snow-covered summit over eight thousand feet still higher in the skies.

His return to Michigan was in time to attend the general camp-meeting, which this year was held on the new ground at Grand Junction. Before the summer was over he received an urgent call to go to the Pacific Coast and to attend the tabernacle-meeting at Los Angeles, Cal., in October. Feeling it the will of the Lord that he go he started on this journey in August. After a few meetings in Missouri, Iowa, and Kansas, he proceeded to Los Angeles, which he reached in time to attend the meeting appointed there. His first report from the Coast, written at National City, is in part as follows:

We were three days and nights making the trip, with very little stopping. We came over the Santa Fe system. We passed over much wild and mountainous scenery, but the lofty peaks called The Needles we passed at night and failed to see. Our chariot brought us over one thousand miles of desert. The awful blank was broken only by an occasional Indian camp or village, or a mining-point. For perhaps a hundred miles or more the earth was as bare as the paved streets of a city, and for many hundred miles nothing but tumbleweed had ventured life upon the dry region. But it is believed that nearly all that lifeless desert would be productive if irrigated or blessed with summer showers. One thing that broke the awful monotony of the long, weary plains was the fact that we were seldom out of sight of mountain ranges. In Arizona we reached a very high altitude. The morning found the ground covered with snow and the temperature quite cold. In eastern California we traveled for hundreds of miles in the midst of a wild mountainous scenery, much of the time running on or near the summit, giving us a grand and awful view of the mountains for a vast distance around. Finally, fertile nooks, little houses, and orchards made their welcomed appearance, which began to relieve the mind wearied with the long scene of barren emptiness. At San Barnardino everything began to look as though we had returned to the land of the living.

A few hours more through almost perpetual vineyards, lemon, orange, and fig orchards, etc., brought us into Los Angeles, and seeing our dear Bro. J. W. Byers through the window, we felt like climbing over the slow-moving people to reach the door. Oh, praise God for the privilege of greeting our dear fellow laborer in the gospel of God! We found him and family well, and he and Sister Byers wonderfully devoted to their calling, laboring day and night with unwearied zeal for the salvation of lost men and women, who are on the brink of everlasting ruin. Praise God, we soon saw that their labors have been owned and blessed of God. We found a precious and very zealous church in Los Angeles....

Truly dear Brother and Sister Byers have been working the richest mine of gold ever opened in California. Their toils have known no moderation. They have indeed, according to apostolic example, "given themselves continually to prayer and to the ministry of the word." And, thank God, there are those in Los Angeles who labored with their hands for the direct object of saving lost men and women, using only enough to supply nature's wants. Oh, that everybody who professes consecration of self and all to God would show it forth by a life wholly devoted to the spread of the pure gospel of Christ and the deliverance of the lost!...

His stay in California was confined to the southern part of the State, where he spent two and one half months laboring in various places. On his return he wrote from Denver and described some of the sublime scenery he witnessed on the line of the Denver and Rio Grande Railroad.

Some of the most sublime scenery was passed in the night. At Glenwood Springs the train stopped an hour and a half, giving passengers a much-appreciated relief from long confinement and a very much enjoyed ramble amid the beautiful scenery of the little city, which lies in a small glen, surrounded by towering mountains on all sides. Here, for the first time in our life, we saw hot springs. The weather was cold and snow was on the ground, and the many stony springs and the great hot-water reservoir caused a steam to arise that made a person feel as if the infernal fires were not far off. A stone wall separates between two large pools, in one of which arise many cold springs, and just over the wall the hot water boils up. At this place is the junction of the Grand River and the Roaring Fork. Our line followed up the Grand River, the canyon of which was very delightful. The great red, stone mountains towered up on both sides in the form of large old castles, many of them nearly square and others oblong but with square corners like a building. Finally we left the Grand River and followed the winding course of a tributary. Now the scene became yet more wildly grand, which we greatly enjoyed.

At some time past eleven at night we reached the Royal Gorge. Having requested the porter to notify us, we lay down without undressing, and so, blessed with good starlight, we were enabled to behold one of the most sublime and awful scenes we ever witnessed in all our travels. Here the almighty hand of God had cleaved a narrow passage through the rocks, which tower up thousands of feet on either side. On our left we passed close to the base of the mighty wall; on our right only a small stream lay between our track and the awful elevation. This indescribably awful gorge extended perhaps for two or three miles. We stood upon the platform of the car, at first turning our eyes right and left, beholding with solemn wonder the vertical cliffs that seem almost to touch the stars. Finally we had but to direct our eyes straight up between the two cars and behold, by one straight upward gaze, the cliffs on both sides as their proud summits seemed to draw together. As we stood on the platform nearest the rocks we frequently saw the great peaks leaning directly over our heads. We could not refrain from crying out, Oh! oh! wonderful! wonderful! Never shall we forget that impressive sight! It seems to us that we would have but to make that trip by daylight to be satisfied that nothing more sublimely awful and inspiring need be looked for amid all the wonders of this creation of God. We would not have missed it for a great deal, and hope it may please God to let our eyes behold the same by daylight.

On the previous afternoon we passed a freight-train that had the day before been wrecked by running upon a heap of earth and rocks that had broken loose perhaps a thousand feet up the sloping mountains and, rushing down, covered the track. The engine and tender were pitched down the hill and lay upside down, under which, alas, the fireman had met his death, or rather he lay with his limbs crushed beneath the engine for over four hours and expired a short time after being taken out.

But as we went flying along under the lofty cliffs and around the short curving niches that were cut out of the solid rocks, sometimes at a height that made one feel giddy to look down, we thought how the strength of the everlasting hills is our Father's, and that his wings overshadowed us by the way. We felt no fear of harm.

His poem Good-by, Old Rockies, was written at this time. He arrived home February 16. With the portion of his report written after he had returned from his California tour we close this chapter.

Never in all our past journeyings did our soul seem so thankful and joyful before God for the privilege of greeting all the dearly beloved ones at home once more. Oh, bless the name of the Lord. We knew not how to thank God enough nor scarcely how to act for the great joy of our heart. Let all the dear saints help us bless the name of the Lord for his wonderful care over us during the travel of over ten thousand miles since our departure last July.

Our flying abroad has not been in vain. All along the line of our tour God has been with us and saved souls at every stopping-place, with perhaps two exceptions. Thank Heaven also for the blessing of good health! How wonderfully he strengthened us to preach his everlasting gospel, often twice a day and sometimes on Sabbath three times, putting in as much as eight hours swift talk in one day, added to which was the earnest altar service and the care for immortal souls! We feel especially thankful to God for the grace of our Lord and Savior that we find resting upon all the beloved family.

Sing It Again.

Sing It Again.

D. S. Warner.   B. E. Warren.

1. Let us sing the name of Jesus, oh, that name we love so dear! Sweetest anthem

2. Sing the love-ly name of Jesus, oh, the precious Lamb of God! Lo, he died our

3. Sing, oh, sing the name of Jesus, he is wor-thy, he a-lone, Glo-ry, hon-or,

4. We will sing the name of Jesus all a-long the path of life, We will sing it,

earth or heaven ever breathed on mortal ear; In that name we have salvation, oh, how

souls to ran-som, he redeemed us by his blood; Let the joy-ful o-ver-flow-ing of our

and salvation, chant with angels round the throne; Sing it soft-ly in the Spir-it, sing it

hal-le-lu-jah, 'mid the battle and the strife; We will sing it all to-geth-er when we

pre-cious is the flow! Sing, oh, sing the name of Jesus, for it makes us white as snow.

hearts so full of love, Sound aloud the name of Jesus with the might-y host a-bove.

loud as thunders roll, Sing with rapture, hallelujah, to the Lamb that saved my soul.

meet upon that shore, Oh, we'll sing the name of Jesus, blessed name forever-more.

Chorus.

Sing it a-gain,... sing it a-gain,... Sweetest of all the names that
The precious name, the precious name,

an-gels sing a-bove,... Jesus, thy name's a fountain of redeeming love....

CHAPTER XVII

THE MINISTRY OF SONG

Adaptation of existing hymns—Occasions that suggested various hymns—Instances of the effect of song.

Scarcely a spiritual movement in the history of Christianity has been without its service of song. The emotions, whether of victory or of devotion or of interest in the salvation of the lost, naturally flow out in singing. Far back in Biblical history we find songs of victory attending the triumphs of the people of God.

The Wesleyan reformation, through its gifted hymn-writer, Charles Wesley, furnished many of the standard spiritual hymns that are in use today. Witness also the immortal gospel hymns that originated with the Moody and Sankey revivals of the last century. Likewise the holiness movement of forty and fifty years ago was characterized by its holiness songs. And so in these last times, when we have come to the full standard of truth and the full development of the church independent of human creeds, when the "ransomed of the Lord" are returning over the "highway" prepared, what wonder is it that they should "come to Zion with songs and everlasting joy upon their heads" (Isa. 35:10)? In no respect was the inception of the present reformation more marked than in its ministry of holy song.

For the writing of spiritual hymns Brother Warner had a wonderful endowment. It seems that the development of this gift came, however, only with his entrance upon the special work of the reformation. In his earliest writings we find no examples of hymns or poems of any merit. A few verses in his diary betray a lack of familiarity with the principles of prosody, or hymn-writing. Considering the little time he had to devote to the study of those principles, it is marvelous that he produced so many useful, and we may say excellent, hymns during the few short years of his intensive ministerial labor.

His first effort appears to have been the adaptation of existing hymns either by rearrangement of the words or by composing new words to fit the tunes. Thus we have the Glory, Halleluiah song with new words appearing in an early copy of the Gospel Trumpet. The chorus is familiar to all and we omit it.

> On the mountain top of vision what a glory we behold!
> Eighteen hundred years of victory are tinging earth with gold;
> For the saints are overcoming with their testimony bold,
> The truth is marching on.
>
> For the glory of the Father Jesus taught in Galilee,

And preached the great salvation that delivers you and me;
And a million voices shout it, "Redemption's full and free,"
The truth is marching on.

From the cabin on the prairie, from the vaulted city dome,
From the dark and briny ocean where our sailor brothers roam,
We hear the glad rejoicing like a happy harvest-home,
Salvation's rolling on.

Eighteen hundred years of marching, eighteen hundred years of song,
The Conqueror advances, and the time will not be long,
When he shall come in glory and overthrow the wrong,
Our God is marching on.

Nahum's chariots are speeding as the lightning on their way,
And their flying torches tell us 'tis the preparation day;
For the bride is getting ready and the Lord will not delay.
The marriage feast is near.

Precious knowledge is increasing, evening light begins to glow,
With the trump of full salvation many running to and fro;
And the song of glory echoes, Christ has washed us white as snow,
All glory to his name!

The long dispersed remnant of Jehovah's chosen race
Are flying from all nations to their ancient dwelling-place;
And the sinful world is surely in its closing-day of grace,
The Lord is just at hand.

In the valley of decision there's a battle drawing near,
Sectish Gog and Magog powers round about the saints appear;
But our God is our munition and our hearts shall never fear,
The victory is sure.

On the blissful heights of glory we will shout the battle o'er,
And in the golden city we will join the Conqueror,
And when the war is over, with the saints forevermore
And crown him with all praise.

On the subject of the church—a prominent subject with him—we have Brother
Warner's arrangement of Frances Ridley Havergal's poem, Church of God. We
give but two stanzas.

Church of God, thou spotless virgin,
Church of Christ for whom he died,
Thou hast known no human founder,
Jesus bought thee for his bride.
Sanctified by God the Father,
Built by Jesus Christ the Son,
Tempered by the Holy Spirit,
Like the Holy Three in one.

God himself has set the members

In his body all complete,
Organized by Jesus only,
Oh, the union pure and sweet!
Church of God, the angels marvel,
At the music of thy song;
Earth and hell in terror tremble
As thy army moves along.

Another of the class of adapted hymns was one on the exercise of faith for sanctification, sung to the tune of Beulah Land.

Why should a doubt or fear arise,
As this poor little all of mine
I lay a living sacrifice,
All on the altar, Christ divine.

Chorus
I'm fully thine, yes, wholly thine,
All on the altar, Christ divine.
The word of Jesus I believe,
The Sanctifier I receive;
All on the altar I abide,
And Jesus says I'm sanctified.

Ah, not a moment more I'll doubt,
And not a moment longer wait;
He shed his blood to sanctify,
He suffered death without the gate.

By faith I venture on his Word,
My doubts are o'er, the vict'ry won;
He said the altar sanctifies,
I just believe him, and 'tis done.

Through all my soul I feel his power,
And in the precious cleansing wave
I wash my garments white this hour,
And prove his utmost power to save.

Still another was The Hand of God on the Wall, of which we quote but two verses.

See, the great king of Babel in these latter days of time
Makes a feast that's universal, all the nations drink her wine;
As they eat, drink, and revel in her lofty steepled hall,
God proclaims her desolation by his hand upon the wall.

How the nations are drunken and are sporting in their shame!
Even scoffing at our Savior and profane his holy name;
Far more blind than Belshazzar, who so trembled with appal,
They still riot on to judgment, with their doom upon the wall.

Brother Warner was not gifted in writing tunes. This necessary counterpart was supplied in J. C. Fisher and his wife, Allie R., also in H. R. Jeffrey, a brother who lived in northern Indiana. Fisher frequently wrote both words and music, as did also Jeffrey. One of the first hymns of which both words and music were original with this reformation was The All Cleansing Fountain, by J. C. Fisher. The first stanza and chorus are as follows:

> There's a fountain opened in the house of God,
> Where the vilest of sinners may go
> And all test the power of that crimson flood,
> Of the blood that makes whiter than snow.

Chorus

> Praise the Lord, I am washed
> In the all-cleansing blood of the Lamb,
> And my robes are whiter than the driven snow,
> I am washed in the blood of the Lamb.

Another early one was H. R. Jeffrey's Songs of Victory, of which the first stanza and chorus will also here suffice.

> Songs of victory bringing
> Unto the Lord most high,
> Victory, victory singing,
> Let all the saints draw nigh;
> For there can be no failure
> While Jesus leads the van,
> And victory, victory, victory,
> Is heard on every hand.

Chorus

> Vict'ry shall be the chorus,
> Vict'ry our watchword and song,
> Jesus is marching before us,
> Leading his army along.

A hymn that breathes a deep spirit of devotion was Brother Warner's I Ought to Love My Savior, music by Fisher. There were five stanzas in all. We give it with music at the beginning of Chapter IX of this book.

> I ought to love my Savior,
> He loved me long ago,
> Looked on my soul with favor,
> When deep in guilt and woe;
> And though my sin had grieved him,
> His father's law had crossed,
> Love drew him down from heaven
> To seek and save the lost.
>
> I ought to love my Savior,
> He bore my sin and shame;
> From glory to the manger,

> On wings of love he came.
> He trod this earth in sorrow,
> Endured the pains of hell,
> That I should not be banished,
> But in his glory dwell.

We shall refer, in what follows, only to Brother Warner's hymns. One that sung of the times as being prophetic was entitled Prophetic Truth, and is shown with music at the beginning of Chapter XIII.

> 'Twas sung by the poets, foreseen in the Spirit,
> A time of refreshing is near;
> When creeds and divisions would fall to demerit,
> And saints in sweet union appear.

Chorus
> Oh, glory to Jesus! we hail the bright day,
> And high on our banner salvation display,
> The mists of confusion are passing away.

> We stand in the glory that Jesus has given,
> The moon as the dayspring doth shine;
> The light of the sun is now equal to seven,
> So bright is the glory divine.

> Now filled with the Spirit, and clad in the armor
> Of light and omnipotent truth,
> We'll testify ever and Jesus we'll honor,
> And stand from sin Babel aloof.

> The prophet's keen vision, transpiercing the ages,
> Beheld us to Zion return;
> We'll sing of our freedom, though Babylon rages,
> We'll shout as her city doth burn.

> The fig-tree is budding, the "evening" is shining,
> We welcome the wonderful light!
> We look for the Savior, for time is declining,
> Eternity's looming in sight.

As he saw the church of God emerge out of confusion into the brightness which should characterize the evening of time, he wrote the following, which is given with music at the beginning of Chapter I.

> Brighter days are sweetly dawning,
> Oh the glory looms in sight!
> For the cloudy day is waning,
> And the evening shall be light.

> Misty fogs, so long concealing
> All the hills of mingled night,
> Vanish, all their sin revealing,
> For the evening shall be light.

> Lo, the ransomed are returning,
> Robed in shining crystal white,
> Leaping, shouting, home to Zion,
> Happy in the evening light.
>
> Free from Babel, in the Spirit,
> Free to worship God aright,
> Joy and gladness we're receiving,
> Oh, how sweet this evening light!
>
> Halleluiah! saints are singing,
> Vict'ry in Jehovah's might;
> Glory, glory, keep it ringing,
> We are saved in evening light.

Another hymn of the return, and also embodying Sister Fisher's vision of the stone tower, was the following:

> We are coming, halleluiah! we are coming home to God;
> Jesus only we're beholding, who has washed us in his blood:
> We are marching back to Salem at the trumpet's joyful sound,
> And we're building God's own temple on it's ancient holy ground.

Chorus

> We are coming, Oh, we're coming, with the glory in the soul!
> Grace we're shouting as we're bringing Christ, the headstone we extol;
> Though as captives long we've suffered, we do feel the royal blood,
> And we're rising to our freedom in the fulness of our God.

> While we're working, we are fighting all the mighty foes around;
> Tho' in wrath they do oppose us we will not desert the ground.
> O my God, do thou remember all those wicked plotting crews,
> Hear them saying in derision, "Now what do these feeble Jews?"

> Thou art coming, mighty Jesus, in the power of thy grace;
> Now our souls break forth in singing at the smiling of thy face:
> Fear of sect, a mount of terror, thou hast made an open plain,
> And the misty fogs of error all have vanished in thy name.

> Our foundation strong is Jesus, he the topmost, crowning stone;
> Halleluiah! we adore him, king upon his living throne:
> And his crimson glory streaming through each crystal stone below
> Tints the whole ecstatic temple with the beauty of its glow.

> Oh, the glory of this temple far exceeds the former one!
> All its stones are bound together in Love's dear eternal Son:
> In this building, what a wonder! there's a dwelling-place for me;
> Yes, thy beauty, O my Savior! I shall here forever see.

Many of his hymns, as is usually the case with hymn-writers, were prompted by some particular occasion or suggestion. Thus in connection with the terrific furnace trials at Bucyrus, Ohio, in 1883, he wrote:

Why should a mortal man complain
At his trials in this wicked world?
Nay, let us thank God's holy name
For all his love o'er us unfurled.

Chorus
   O Jesus, bear our souls above
   Each wave of trouble that we meet!
   Then in the furnace of thy love
   We'll sing thy praise with joy complete.

Oh, why should any one oppressed
Forget the promise of our God!
To thee each providence is blessed
If in love thou bear the chastening rod.

Oh, who would cast away the gold
We have gathered in the furnace flame!
And who would wish again the dross
Here purged in our Redeemer's name?

Once when a new printing-press was installed in the Office (he always rejoiced when there was an increase of printing equipment), he wrote the following in anticipation of the Trumpet's being raised to louder blasts. See the music at the beginning of Chapter XIV.

Onward moves the great eternal
In the order of his plan;
Louder, nearer rolls the thunder
Of his awful word to man.

Since by sin this earth was blighted
God has whispered of his love.
Dreams and visions by his prophets
Breathed of mercy from above.

Louder speaks his love in Jesus,
Heaven sweetly chants his fame;
Earth receives its glorious Savior,
Halleluiah to his name!

Yet the world is wrapped in slumber;
Louder raise the Trumpet's blast;
Oh, in mercy let it thunder,
Ere the day of mercy's past!

In the cages of deception
Souls are pining to be free;
Quickly sound the proclamation
Of the glorious jubilee.

The hymn, Perishing Souls at Stake, was one of the early productions. We quote this hymn and its history as it appeared in the Trumpet of Dec. 15, 1885. The music will be found at the head of Chapter XVI.

> Perishing souls at stake today!
> Says the banner of Christ unfurled;
> Pleading in love for help to save
> Blood-bought sinners o'er all the world.
>
> Perishing souls at stake we see,
> Yet the Savior has died for all;
> Go and invite them earnestly,
> Some will surely obey the call.
>
> Perishing souls at stake today,
> There's a famine in all the land;
> Many are dying for the bread
> Freely given by Jesus' hand.
>
> Perishing souls at stake, go tell
> What the Savior has done for you,
> How he redeemed your soul from hell,
> And is able to save them, too.
>
> Perishing souls at stake we know,
> Oh, do pity the sinner's fate!
> Brother and sister, will you go,
> Give them warning before too late.
>
> Perishing souls at stake today,
> Can you tarry for earthly dross?
> Fly to the rescue, don't delay,
> Bring the needy to Jesus' cross.

The foregoing song was suggested to our mind by a solemn vision given to Bro. C. Ogan, of Latty, Ohio, on the night previous to September 19. He saw Christ displaying a banner upon which was written these words: "Perishing Souls at Stake." That day we had a very solemn meeting at Jerry City, Ohio. The Spirit of God was present, making imperative calls for workers in the vineyard. Our soul was burdened with an awful sense of perishing souls at stake. All hearts were melted before the Lord. A number acknowledged the solemn commission. Dear Brother Ogan was one of them, relating this solemn and beautiful vision.

We pray that all who that day confessed the call of God may go forward, lest that "woe is me" be upon them, and perishing souls be lost for whom the blessed Savior died. In about all the meetings this fall the same great burden has come upon our soul for men and women of God to go forth and hold up the light of his saving truth. O ye that have the real fire of God in your souls, can you tarry at home to watch a few earthly effects, when there is such a sore famine in all the land! And you who have found the true salvation of Christ Jesus are the only ones that can bring the living bread to others. College bread will not do. 'Dumb dogs can not bark'; Babylon priests are full of darkness, and souls are dying all around. Oh! if you have any gratitude in your hearts for what Christ has done for you, go and tell others, and some will surely receive the joyful tidings. Oh, how sad this world with no gospel but the wretched stuff given by Babylon priests! And most everywhere there are at least one or two honest souls who long for the light. Can you stay at home for the sordid dust of earth and let them perish? Oh, fly to the rescue, don't delay; bring the needy to Jesus Christ!

After a few years both Fisher and Jeffrey dropped out of the ranks and ceased to contribute their melodies to Brother Warner's hymns. In their place God provided Brother B. E. Warren. No sooner did this young brother become a part of Brother Warner's company than he began to display a marvelous gift for writing melodies. In the years that followed he filled a large place as a writer of music, and he also learned to write the words as well.

When the company were on their Western trip in the autumn of 1887, Brother Warner wrote the hymn Sowing the Seed, in anticipation of their having to brave the chilling blasts of the winter which was before them.

> Unheeding winter's cruel blast,
> We venture heaven's seed to cast;
> Both late and early plant the truth
> In aged hearts and tender youth.
>
> Shall we be found with only leaves
> When Jesus comes to gather sheaves?
> Nay, sowing daily o'er the land,
> We'll come with joyful sheaves in hand.
>
> Nor is the precious labor hard,
> Its glory is its own reward;
> We plant in hearts of grim despair
> A life that blooms as Eden fair.
>
> Oh, were this life the utmost span,
> The closing destiny of man.
> No toil could half so blessed prove
> As sowing seeds of peace and love.
>
> But heaven's bright eternal years
> Have bottled up our sowing tears;
> There we shall greet in holy bliss
> The souls we turned to righteousness.
>
> Then sow the seed in every field,
> And grace will bring the golden yield;
> We soon shall sing the joyful song,

And shout the blessed harvest-home.

The song Who Will Suffer With Jesus? had its origin while the company were in the South in the winter of 1890–91. It was written at the time a mob assaulted the house in which Brother Warner was preaching and a sharp, flying missile struck him on the side of the face, causing it to bleed.

> Who will suffer with the Savior,
> Take the little that remains
> Of the cup of tribulation
> Jesus drank in dying pains?
>
> Who will offer soul and body
> On the altar of our God;
> Leaving self and worldly mammon,
> Take the path that Jesus trod?
>
> Who will suffer for the gospel,
> Follow Christ without the gate;
> Take the martyrs for example,
> With them glory at the stake?
>
> Oh, for consecrated service
> 'Mid the din of Babel strife!
> Who will dare the truth to herald
> At the peril of his life?
>
> Soon the conflict will be over,
> Crowns await the firm and pure;
> Forward, brethren, work and suffer,
> Faithful to the end endure.
>
> Lord, we fellowship thy passion,
> Gladly suffer shame and loss;
> With thy blessing pain is pleasure,
> We will glory in thy cross.

One of the prominent features of the reformation was the sweet, heavenly singing of the saints. Wherever Brother Warner's company went the people were attracted by the singing. They were not what the world would call "trained singers"; they were not even adept at reading music. But God blessed the singing, so that the songs, sung in the element of the Spirit, were simply heavenly. At the time the company held the first meeting at Walkerton, Ind. a theatrical troupe came to the town. So many people had flocked to Brother Warner's meetings that the house was packed and there were not many left to attend the theatrical concert. The troupe, not having a sufficient audience, came to the place of meeting and gave some instrumental music just outside in order to attract the people. Of course it interfered with the preaching. Brother Warner said, "Sing a song." Sister Nannie Kigar, who was the soprano of the company and always ready with a suitable selection, started a song. The people decided to remain. Many and powerful were the effects of these heaven-inspired songs.

Mention has been made already of the instance where the cattle listened and gazed with wonder when Brother Warner's company were singing at a place where they had stopped in the edge of the woods for dinner. Brother Warren says that once when they were traveling on the road and singing they were passing a field where there were cattle, horses, and other live stock, and that all of these followed along inside the fence until they reached the corner of the field, seeming to be attracted by the wonderful charm of the singing.

At the time the company visited St. James, Mo., on the second Western tour, Brother Warner wrote the hymn Sing it Again, at a place where they were stopping in the country. Brother Warren then composed the music, and they began singing it. When the time came for them to be taken to the train to leave that part of the country, it was decided that they should be conveyed to Jefferson City in order to afford a little country ride for a change. They camped out the first night, and reached Jefferson City the second day, early in the afternoon. They decided to visit the State prison, and as the weather was warm they left their wraps in the baggage-room of the railroad-station until they should return. When they came back the baggage-room was locked, and the temperature was falling and becoming just a little chilly. Everything was quiet around; not a sound could be heard except the clicking of the telegraph instrument in the office. The train they were to take would not be due until in the night, and as the waiting-room was open they gathered a little fuel and built a fire. When this was done Brother Warner gave a little jump (he always seemed happy enough to jump at any time) and said, "Let us have a song." Naturally enough they sang the new song, Sing it Again. Soon the door opened and in came the operator, and then shortly, almost before they were aware of it, a number of others had gathered and were listening intently. When the song was ended, the operator said, "This reminds me of my childhood days; won't you sing that song again?" They sang it again, and then Brother Warner, as his manner frequently was, took out his Bible and said, "Perhaps you would not object to a little of the Word of God." The operator had to attend to his office duties, but the others listened. Next testimonies were proposed. And so they had a precious little meeting in the waiting-room of the railroad-station, and the new song had already begun to be useful. We here reproduce the words. The music is given at the head of Chapter XVII.

> Let us sing the name of Jesus, oh, that name we love so dear!
> Sweetest anthem earth or heaven ever breathed on mortal ear;
> In that name we have salvation, oh, how precious is the flow!
> Sing, oh, sing the name of Jesus, for it makes us white as snow!
>
> Sing the lovely name of Jesus, oh, the precious Lamb of God!
> Lo, he died our souls to ransom, he redeemed us by his blood:
> Let the joyful overflowing of our hearts so full of love
> Sound aloud the name of Jesus with the mighty host above.
>
> Sing, oh, sing the name of Jesus, he is worthy, he alone,
> Glory, honor, and salvation chant with angels round the throne;
> Sing it softly in the Spirit, sing it loud as thunders roll,
> Sing with rapture, halleluiah, to the Lamb that saved my soul.

> Yes, we'll sing the name of Jesus, 'tis the only name that's giv'n
> That can save a guilty sinner, and no other under heav'n.
> Oh, we love the name of Jesus, his salvation we adore!
> Blessed be the name of Jesus, we will sing it more and more.
>
> We will sing the name of Jesus all along the path of life,
> We will sing it, halleluiah, mid the battle and the strife;
> We will sing it all together when we meet upon that shore,
> Oh, we'll sing the name of Jesus, blessed name forevermore!

I shall never forget the time when Brother Warner and his company first came to my father's home in northwestern Illinois. I have always considered it the brightest event in my life's career. Today, as memory carries me back to that time, and I imagine myself in that same situation, I have indescribable feelings. They arrived on a Saturday afternoon in the spring of 1888. My father and I had gone to engage a schoolhouse for the meetings when the company arrived. My sister had been converted the previous year; but during her attendance at school through the winter she had become somewhat cold spiritually and so had no particular pleasure in anticipating the coming of "Warner's band," as she had heard them called. When the company arrived in the house, wearied with much travel, they seemed particularly to enjoy the sense of home, and they sang the hymn,

> Home, home, brightest and fairest,
> Hope, hope, sweetest and best.

My sister simply melted. That song introduction was enough. Then they had prayer, and their hearts welled up in thankfulness to God for his blessings and care over them. If there ever were men who could pray, Brother Warner was one of them.

After my father and I returned home, my sister and mother wanted me to hear the company sing, and of course another song was requested. They sang this time, The All-cleansing Fountain, and it seemed to be the sweetest singing I had ever heard. During their stay in our home Brother Warren did some composing at the organ, and this seemed wonderful to me. I had never seen such people, whose countenances were aglow with the victory of salvation and who were so filled with praise and song.

While the company were at our home we decided to give them a little outing by taking them across the Mississippi to the city of Clinton, Iowa, then remarkable for its lumber trade, and for having eight large sawmills, one of them the largest sawmill in the world. As we were driving along the road and singing The All-cleansing Fountain, a neighbor who was working in a field near by but who on account of an intervening ridge could not see us, heard the song. Not knowing from whence the sound came he concluded it was angel music, and when he went to his house he declared to his wife that he had heard the angels sing.

A large class of songs that were used were such as expressed victory and worship. Another large class were those of invitation and warning to sinners. In the later books, about all topics that are useful in Christian work were represented.

Songs of Victory was the name of the first book published. It was issued in 1885. This was followed in 1888 by Anthems from the Throne. The third book was Echoes from Glory, published in 1893. Following these a new book of songs has been issued about every four to six years.

CHAPTER XVIII
POETIC INSPIRATIONS

Gifted as a poet — A book of poems — Various examples of poems.

To reflect on Brother Warner's career is to marvel at the accomplishment that was crowded into a few short years. He was active in several callings at one time. As a minister with the heavy burden of the gospel upon him he labored hard, preaching often and being everywhere in demand. On occasions he preached for three and even four hours in one discourse, the audience as well as the preacher forgetful of the passing time. Though in physical endurance he was weak, yet there were perhaps few speakers who could wear so well in the labor of the pulpit. His private work of instructing seekers, and his ministrations for the sick, requiring the exercise of prayer and faith, absorbed his strength and occupied much time. As editor of the paper, to which he contributed articles, many of them doctrinal and requiring study, and for which he had to edit articles written by others, it was necessary that he spend much time with the pen. His correspondence also was considerable, and as stenographers were not so available then as now he had to do his writing with his own hand. Where would he get time for study and prayer, and for writing hymns or poetry? And yet he accomplished all of these.

In the latter years of his life he apparently was declining to some extent in ministerial vigor; but as a writer his productions seemed only to grow richer with his years. Had his life been prolonged to the full period of what is commonly expected of man, he would have given to the world some of the finest poetical productions. His poems are not at all inferior, though written during a strenuous career.

In 1890, he collected and published his poems in a book entitled Poems of Grace and Truth. It contained 343 pages. With the exception of a small book entitled Bible Readings, and the limp-cover binding of a song-book, this book of poems was the first cloth-bound book ever made at the Gospel Trumpet publishing office. The press-work is imperfect owing to the poor stereotyped plates from which it was printed. A number of beautiful poems were written since the publication of this book and therefore were not included in it.

His longest poem was his Meditations on the Prairie. It occupies eighty-four pages of the book mentioned and is written in ten-syllable iambic verse. It touchingly describes with beautiful imagery the author's acquaintance with and his subsequent marriage to Sarah A. Keller, and the circumstances that led to her deception and separation from him. His own description of its origin, as given in the preface to the poem, is as follows:

In the summer of 1873, the author took a mission-field in Nebraska, much of which had just been settled the previous year. My companion had died one year previously. Just before going West a correspondence was arranged with Sister Sarah A. Keller, which soon kindled into a glowing flame of love. A year later I returned and we were happily joined in marriage. With her precious company I came again to this blooming plain, where one year was sweetened with the most transporting conjugal bliss. In 1875 we returned to Ohio, where life and labors flowed on in uninterrupted happiness, until in 1884 the dear object of our love was deceived by the wily foe and torn from our soul, a crisis that threatened our frail life, and which we survived only by the grace of God.

In the fall of 1887, while on an extensive Western tour, we came into a new part of the great prairie, which strikingly reminded us of our travels on the new plains twelve and thirteen years before. There the Spirit touched our mind with vivid recollections of that cherished one, who made for us this prairie a blissful Eden. An inspired imagination also portrayed what dire wreck of our own life might have ensued from the crisis of broken love had not the grace of God averted the sad issue. This cast us on the sod beneath a load of gratitude, where the poem was inspired as our heart's humble tribute for Heaven's pity and sustaining arm.

A quotation from this poem appears in Chapter XV of this book.

Brother Warner was a great admirer of nature as the handiwork of God, and several of his poems are on nature subjects. What we give here are in most cases but selections from the poems named, the omissions being indicated by stars.

AUTUMN

Gone is the spring with all its flowers,
And gone the summer's verdant show;
Now strewn beneath the autumn bowers,
The yellow leaves await the snow.

Behold, this earth so cold and gray
An emblem of our life appears;
Its blooming robes sink to decay,
To rise again in round of years.

Earth cheers its winter sleep with dreams
Of springtime's warmth and gentle rain,
When she shall wake to murmuring streams
And songs of merry birds again.

So we come forth like springtime flowers,
Soon into manhood's summer go,
Then, like the leaves of autumn bowers,
Lie down beneath the winter's snow.

And there our bodies slumb'ring wait
Till time's short winter day has fled,
And Christ, our Lord and Advocate,

Shall come again to wake the dead.

Then winter's storm and summer's heat
Shall end in everlasting spring,
And all immortal we shall meet,
And round the throne of glory sing.

NEW YEAR'S GREETING

January 1, 1890

Another year has come and gone
So swiftly flows unceasing time.
Forever on and on and on,
With sorrow's groan and merry chime.
Commingled in its surging tide,
Time bears along upon its flood
Poor human wrecks by sin destroyed;
Yet o'er its stream, the hand of God
Still bends his bow of hope divine;
Its hues of love in beauty shine.

Another year of hope and fear
Has swept around its dial-plate,
And with it thousands disappear
To higher bliss or awful fate.
God grant to us who yet survive
A heart of fervent gratitude,
And grace that we may wholly live
To glorify the Source of good;
Then, should this be our final year,
We'll sink to rest without a fear.

Another year hath brought its store
In rich profusion at our feet,
That we should, heart and soul, adore
Our Maker's love so broad and deep.
And have you cast your bread upon
The waters of the passing year,
In hope that what your hands have done
Will in much future good appear?
Then as thy faith so shall it be;
In coming days thine eyes shall see.

*　　*　　*　　*　　*

The poem To the Alien, is addressed to his wife, Sarah, who, early in the year 1884, through the influence of a spiritual deceiver, as already stated, left her husband.

TO THE ALIEN

Three years have fled since billows wild
Wrecked our domestic bark,
And chilled your love for husband, child,
Mid waters cold and dark.

"How wonderful the mystery,"
Astonished men exclaim,
"That hearts so knit in unity
Could ever part in twain!"

  *   *   *   *   *

We suffered some adversities,
A portion all must find,
When compassed round by devotees
Whose creeds we'd left behind.

When pressing to the harvest-field
Of everlasting truth,
And just before the golden yield,
Alas! you turned aloof.

Oh, how I wish that you could share
In these ecstatic days,
Enjoy the light of God so pure,
And help to sing his praise!

My soul had longed for more of God,
More glory in the cross;
But never dreamed that it must come
Through such a bitter loss.

I can not chide his providence,
But count it all the best;
For in each storm of violence
I sink to sweeter rest.

  *   *   *   *   *

'Twas not a rival filled thine eyes
With colored fancies rare;
But Satan came in deep disguise,
And wrought the dread affair.

  *   *   *   *   *

We still are joined in Eden's bond
Of matrimony true;
While life endures, yet undissolved
It binds my heart to you.

No court of man nor Satan's power

Can disannul the tie;
Though spirits rent, in evil hour,
"One flesh" are you and I.

No face so fair, no heart so warm,
Upon this verdant sod,
Shall alienate with rival charm
The wife received of God.

So I will walk with God alone,
And bless his holy name,
Till he shall bring the alien home
To dwell in love again.

In vision of the night I saw—
And woke to joyful praise—
True nature reimprint her law
That ruled thy former days.

From nature's pure affections then
Grace led to love divine;
Then heaven's bliss alone can bound
Our mutual joy sublime.

God grant that this may real prove
Through coming years of time,
And in his shining courts above,
An endless crown be thine.

The hand of God alone can take
The broken chords of love
And knit them in a union sweet
As love's pure reign above.

Here I will close my present rhyme;
But ever pray for you,
That God may give you back again
The heart of woman true.

Then touched by sweet seraphic strains,
With all the heavenly throng,
I'll shout aloud my Savior's praise,
And sing another song.

TO MY DEAR SIDNEY

The heart that feels a father's love
And swells with love's return,
Will kindly bear this overflow
Toward my only son.

Yes, Sidney's love so blent with mine,

A poem shall employ —
A token left to coming time
That father loved his boy.

One gentle vine — thy tendrils sweet
Around my soul entwine;
A comfort left in sorrows deep,
One heart to beat with mine.

Thy life has dawned in peril's day.
Mid wars that heaven shake;
Thy summers five, eventful, they
Like surges o'er thee break.

Thy little soul has felt the shock
Of burning Babel's fall,
When hell recoiled in fury black
And stood in dread appal.

But wreaking out his vengeance now,
Like ocean's terror dark,
Hell's monster came athwart the bow
Of our domestic bark.

Thy guardian angel wept to see
This brunt of fury sweep
The girdings of maternity
From underneath thy feet.

But pity still her garland weaves
Around thy gentle brow,
And angels on thee softly breathe
Their benedictions now.

They soothe and bless thy manly heart,
And wipe away thy tears;
So tempered to thy bitter lot,
The bitter sweet appears.

An exile now is each to each,
As banished far at sea;
A martyr on his island beach,
I daily think of thee.

And stronger love has seldom spanned
The mocking billows wild,
Than are the chords that ever bind
To my beloved child.

Though sundered not by angry main,
Compelled from thine embrace,
We flee abroad in Jesus' name
To publish Heaven's grace.

Thy little heart can not divine
Why Papa stays away,
But coming years will tell, if thine,
The great necessity.

When sickness crushed thy little form,
I knew my boy was ill;
I heard thee in my visions call,
But duty kept me still.

A trial deep, to feel thy pain,
And yet debarred from thee,
To show that sinners lost are in
A greater misery.

Oh, may this lesson speak to thee
When Father's work is done!
And highest may thy glory be,
A soul for God is won.

And now, my son, attentive hear
My benediction-prayer,
And ever tune thy heart and ear
To heaven's music rare;

For ere the light of day had shone
In thy unfolding eyes,
We gave thee up to God alone,
A living sacrifice;

And oft repeated when a babe,
To God our child was given;
And Jesus heard the vow we made,
And wrote it down in heaven.

So, like a little Samuel, you
Must answer, "Here am I";
Give all your heart to Jesus, too,
For him to live and die.

Like Samuel, serve the living God,
His temple be thy home;
In love obey his holy Word,
Thy gentle heart his throne.

The Lord is good, my darling boy;
He made thy body well,
And he will bless thee evermore,
If in his love you dwell.

A new edition may you be
Of Father's love and zeal,
But yet enlarged so wondrously

That earth thy tread may feel.

The poem Throwing Ink at the Devil, refers to the printing and publishing of the Gospel Trumpet. The place "where two lightning tracks lie crossing" is Grand Junction, Mich., where the publishing office was then located.

At Wartburg Castle sat a son of thunder
Dealing heaven's dynamite,
When, lo! before him 'peared an apparition,
Fury-threatening demon sight.

The piercing words of truth, so long besmothered
Flashed the burning wrath upon
The devil's patent monk and pope religion,
Which confronts the dread reform.

*   *   *   *   *

Before the dauntless, lion-hearted Luther
Forth the hellish monster stood,
Drawn from his prison by the scattering theses
'Gainst the Romish viper brood.

He lifted up his eyebrows knit with thunder,
To the hellish specter said,
With stern address, „Du bist der wahre Teufel!" —
Hurls an inkstand at his head.

The doctor's splattering missile, proving potent,
Drove old Satan from his door;
But ink he threw on paper at the devil
Battered down his kingdom more.

*   *   *   *   *

Not now, as did the sturdy Wittenberger
Fling an inkstand at the foe,
But by the mighty force of steam, much faster
We the battle-ink can throw.

Just at a point where lightning tracks lie crossing,
Northward, southward, east, and west,
The Lord has planted his revolving cannon,
Firing ink at Satan's crest.

*   *   *   *   *

Not only toward the main forewinds of heaven
Sin-consuming ink is shot,
But right and left in force, 'tis outward given,
Striking sin in every spot.

When round "Mansoul" Immanuel plants his army,
To retake the famous town,

On "eye-gate" hill he plants this mighty engine,
Till surrendered to his crown.

If chance a pilgrim's shield of faith is drooping,
And his heart with fear oppressed,
Then comes the ink-winged angel, trumpet sounding,
And his soul anew is blessed.

TRUTH

"And what is truth?" asked Pilate, sober.
Immersed in deep perplexity,
And trembled while in judgment over
The One his final judge must be.
He asked, but waited not the answer;
For in his majesty there stood
The Truth himself at his tribunal—
Yea, the incarnate Truth of God.

Shine on with all thy constellation,
The precious attributes of God,
Love, mercy, justice, and compassion;
For second in thy magnitude
Thou only art in love's effulgence.
"I am the truth." and "God is love";
From both in one omnific fulness
Proceed the streams of truth above.

High honored and from everlasting
Thou art, O Truth, a pillar strong,
Upholding justice, faith, and virtue.
Before the stars together sang
Our ill-doomed planet's new creation,
Thy hand didst hold, on heaven's throne,
The balance weighing every nation,
Upon the worlds that round thee shone.

Thou art the firm and deep foundation
Of hope and universal good,
And on thy broad eternal bosom
Is based the awful throne of God.
The myriad stars that gem the ocean
Of boundless space, at thy command
Pursue their even-tenored motion,
And are supported by thy hand.

*   *   *   *   *

AUTUMN LEAVES

A mournful sermon greets my ear!
The pensive season of the year
Now preaches in a muffled tone,
From nature's fast-decaying throne.
Come to the woodland's cold retreat;
The leaves that rustle at thy feet,
With all that linger o'er thy head—
Commingling, yellow, green, and red—
And all that, trembling, leave their place
And softly greet their mother's face,
As sailing from their lofty top
They in your presence mournful drop,
Remind the thoughtful passer-by,
Thy falling autumn, too, is nigh.

Life has its gay and happy spring,
When birds of every feather sing;
Its warm and verdant summer, brief,
Which hastens to the yellow leaf,
Soon winter's icy hand will lie
Upon our cold and lifeless clay.
But oh! our soul—where will it be
Throughout the long eternity?
How can this question pass your mind
As falling leaves drift in the wind?

     *   *   *   *   *

Ah! there's a sweet and sacred spell
That draws me to the shady dell;
Here could my soul with God remain
In meditation's holy frame.
Ho! all ye men that know not God,
Come seek him in the shady wood;
And, all ye saints of feeble love,
When will ye come and wisely prove
The blessedness that crowns the hour
That's spent with God in leafy bower?
If only heard your prayers ye say,
Then unto God ye never pray;
For did ye truly seek his face
And pray to win his saving grace
You'd pray when mortals are not near,
Right in your heavenly Father's ear.
In public, too; yea, everywhere,
But most of all with secret prayer;
Where only silent leaves applaud,

There would ye bow and worship God.

    *   *   *   *   *

Then in the hush of solitude
Come listen to the voice of God;
Come oft, and he shall teach thine ear
His gentle words of love to hear.

There is no place on earth so sweet
As forest shades, where streamlets meet
And sing aloud their rocky ways,
With birds, and universal praise.
Do not the lover and his maid,
Delighted, walk the balmy shade,
And there unlock, with words so blest,
The pent-up love within their breast?
The crazy-quilt spread on the ground,
Of beauty-tinted leaves around,
Each bright sunbeam and fragrant flower,
And nature's music in the bower—
But, most of all, the cooing dove—
Lend inspiration to their love.
And does not nature's solitude
Inspire a soul to worship God?
Behold, he framed her majesty,
Cast up her hills, and carved the way
For babbling brooks that flow between
And tread the winding valley's green.
The many lovely trees that spread
Their sheltering wings above our head,
Rose up by his supreme behest,
With all their nuts and fruitage blest,
He taught the vine their trunks to climb,
Like cords of love their boughs entwine.

    *   *   *   *   *

Hear thou, O man, our autumn chant
While sunbeams coldly o'er us slant,
And mournfully we fall so low·
To don our winding sheet of snow,
There doomed in silence to decay.
So, too, thou, man, must pass away;
Thy springs of love shall lower run
Until thy life's last setting sun;
Then in thy grave-suit, coldly wound,
Like us return to mother ground.

But we are not without a seed,

From which anew there may proceed
Our kind to grow and multiply,
As round and round the seasons fly.
So, man, within thy mortal breast
There is a soul, immortal quest,
That shall reanimate thy clay,
And both, immortal, live for aye.
Thou shalt from winter's sleep arise,
And meet thy Savior in the skies.
With this blest hope so sure and bright
All seasons beam with golden light,
In winter's storm and summer's heat
The pure in heart have joys complete;
And when the close of life appears,
Their pleasures ripen with his years—
Unlike the sinner, dark and cold
Who graceless, godless, hopeless, old,
Sits lowly down in autumn's vale,
His life all fruitless to bewail.
Each falling leaf his conscience stings
And thoughts of future judgment brings;
Yea, warns him that the time is nigh
When he in black despair must die.
Unlike the life in folly spent,
And now with sinful years is bent
Low at the grave with dismal moan;
Nay, "for the righteous light is sown,"
Yea, light that brightens in the vale
Of falling leaves, where he can hail
The glories of another world;
Where mortal shafts are never hurled,
Nor cruel frosts can ever sting.
There life begins another spring
To flourish in eternal green,
In heaven's high celestial scene.

BEAUTIFUL SPRING

Ah, gentle spring, thy balmy breeze,
New chanting 'mid the budding trees,
A glorious resurrection sings!
And on thy soft, ethereal wings
Sweet nectar from ten thousand flowers,
That bloom in nature's happy bowers
Thou dost as holy incense bring
To Him who sheds the beams of spring.

Far in the South thy bloom appeared,
And all our journey northward cheered;
A thousand miles in sweet embrace,
We northward held an even race;
Or if by starts we did outrun
Thy even tenor from the sun,
Ere long we blessed thy coming tread
And quaffed the oders thou didst spread.

O brightest, sweetest of the year!
When all is vocal with thy cheer,
Thy lily-cups and roses red
With us some tear-drops also shed.
The cherry-trees, in shrouds of white,
Bring back to mind a mournful sight—
A coffined brother 'neath the bloom,
Just ere they bore him to the tomb.

Ah, yes, thou sweet, beguiling spring,
Of thee, my inmost heart would sing.
"The time of love," all bards agree
To sing in merry notes to thee.
Yea, such thou art, and happy they
Who walk in love's delightful day
Along the path thy flakes hath strewn,
And know indeed her constant boon.

But what of him who walks alone,
With past love fled and turned to stone?
Shall not the springtide music's roll
Mock withered joys and sting the soul?
Not in the heart embalmed in love
Transported from the worlds above,
Nor seasons, no, nor else can bring
Heartaches where only God is king.

That soul an endless spring enjoys
Where life the will of God employs.
He 'mid the fields of bliss may tread,
And feast on joys that long have fled,
By sacred memories' glowing trace
More than the heart untouched by grace,
Can drink from full fruition's stream,
Or paint in fancy's wildest dream.

O God! thou art the life of spring,
The source of all the seasons bring,
The soul of all the joys we know,
The fountain whence our pleasures flow.

> While nature wakes from winter's sleep,
> And gentle clouds effusive weep,
> We join creation's grateful lays,
> And celebrate our Maker's praise.

The deaths of individuals furnished inspiration for many a verse from Brother Warner's pen. Celia Kilpatrick Byrum was one of the early workers in the Gospel Trumpet Office, when the paper was published at Grand Junction, Mich. Her death occurred on the 11th of December, 1888.

> And is she gone—dear Celia gone?
> Such news would tax credulity
> Did not the Spirit's previous tone
> Toll in our bosom mournfully
> The thought, "She's left this mortal clime,
> And we shall see her face no more
> Until we pass the bounds of time
> And meet upon celestial shore."
>
> 'Twas in our heart to tune our lyre
> To sing thy cheerful wedding-day;
> But debts are made by fond desire,
> More than our fleeting time can pay.
> So now we sing our mournful lay—
> Another epoch followed soon
> To thy poor soul, a brighter day
> Than that when blessed beside thy groom.
>
> The Author of these feeling hearts
> Chides not affection's flowing tears;
> But with them soothing balm imparts,
> And in his arms of love he bears
> Poor nature's heavy burden up:
> So when bereavements press our mind,
> Grace drops such sweetness in the cup
> That even then we comfort find.
>
> But is she gone whose heart e'er burned
> With such devoted, fervent zeal?
> To bless mankind her spirit yearned,
> Wished every heart God's love might seal.
> She thought no sacrifice too dear,
> No painful toil and care too great,
> That all this world the truth might hear
> And gain redemption's blissful state.
>
> O sister, while thy eyes beheld
> Whate'er thy willing hands could do,
> No needed rest thy footsteps held,
> No moderation couldst thou know;

Regarding not thy slender frame—
To pious toil so passionate—
Till thy enfeebled limbs refrained
To execute thy heart's mandate.

       *   *   *   *   *

When sickness had already cast
Its waning paleness on thy cheek,
God folded thee within the breast
Of love, connubial, warm and deep.
Thank heav'n for this provision kind,
To bless, support, and comfort thee;
On those strong arms thy life declined
Till from thy suffering body free.

       *   *   *   *   *

Dear Celia's gone! How sad the news,
Dear saints, this mourning Trumpet brings!
The hands that dropped refreshing dews
Upon its flying-angel wings
And toiled so hard to set the lines
That burned upon your hearts with love,
Inspired your souls a thousand times,
Has gone to blissful toils above.

       *   *   *   *   *

Ah! now invert the column rules,
And dress the Trumpet sad with crape,
That all who read may know it feels
And weeps the loss of friend so great.
Her artful fingers shall no more
Set up its many vocal peers,
Nor shall her anxious heart yet pour
Upon its sheets her moist'ning tears.

Her gentle voice, so fine and sweet
The Trumpet organ's highest key
Is singing now, at Jesus' feet,
With heaven's joyful minstrelsy.
Oh! could we near the pearly gate
And listen to her ransomed song,
Our souls would more felicitate
The bliss of that immortal one.

The poem The Marriage of a Mr. Hope, is a play on the word "hope" and has a slight touch of the humorous.

It appeared that Mr. Hope,
Entertained the pleasing hope

That some hopeless one among the fair
Was seeking hope from life's despair,
And was pleased with Hope to share,
The cheerful name of Hope to wear.
And so good Hope went smiling 'round
Till the object of his hope was found;
Then sitting by the fair one's side,
Hope beamed with prospects of a bride.
The question asked, the prompt decision
Turned hopeful's hope to full fruition,
And so it happened very soon,
The beau of hope became a groom.
Then hopeless changed to Hope by name,
And two hopes but one Hope became.
Their bark now launched on the stream of hope,
May all the blessings hope bespoke
Their voyage crown along the way
Of hope's uncrowded blissful day,
And may their happy little bark afford
A lively crew of sunny Hopes aboard;
And when to anchor in the harbor driven
May all their hopes be realized in heaven.

An interesting imaginative story of some length is his poem Soul Cripple City, in which he represents sectarian religion as a city wherein the inhabitants walk on crutches. The following is the first stanza.

Not a mere imaginary
Object, borne on fancy's wing,
Is the city of this story,
But a real historic thing.
Though by troupes and proper figures
We delineate her fame,
Though she has some mystic features,
She's an entity the same.

He takes up the different denominations as particular brands of crutches on which people hobble.

But whereunto shall we liken,
Or with what similitude,
Paint this foolish generation?
Ah! behold the sinful brood!
All within that mystic city
Walk not upright on their feet,
But on crutches play the cripple—
'Tis a custom they must keep.

Not a man in all Soul Cripple,

Not a woman, girl, or boy,
But must go it on quadruple,
Must the wooden legs employ.
Not one ever tried it walking
On created feet alone;
Not on crutches to be stalking
Were a scandal to the town.

       *   *   *   *   *

Next appeared the English crutches,
And the High Episcopal.
Thence the mania fast increases,
Every style conceivable.
Wycliffe crutches, Calvin crutches,
Quaker, Shaker, Mennonite,
Wesley crutches, twenty branches,
M. E. crutches, black and white.

       *   *   *   *   *

Then there are the Baptist crutches,
Hard-shelled and inflexible,
Free-will Baptist, bond-will Baptist,
And the creed Six Principle.
There are Baptists called Ephrata,
Saturnarian Baptists, too,
Anabaptist, Calvinistic
Baptist crutches we'll undo.

       *   *   *   *   *

In this mart of vain religions
You will find on Water Street,
And at all her river stations,
Crutches vaunted as complete.
But the clubs that they are vending,
Are as hollow as a horn;
They that buy need no repenting,
In cold water they are born.

       *   *   *   *   *

All these bapto 'sociations
Have a god of water made,
Leaving fire and salvation
And the blood without the trade,
More than all the sects who clamor,
Just to make the sinner wet,
Who have swallowed down a Campbell,
And are straining at a gnat.

He allots special "Additions" to the city for Adventism, the Salvation Army, Russellism, and Lyman Johnson of the Stumbling stone. The last of the poem is devoted to God's call to his people to come out of Babylon. We give but three stanzas.

> But adieu, for we must travel
> With the remnant who return,
> Fleeing from the fall of Babel,
> To the new Jerusalem.
> Hark! a noise like many waters!
> 'Tis the captive's jubilee,
> Like the voice of mighty thunders,
> Halleluiah! we are free!

*   *   *   *   *

> Jesus is our head and ruler,
> And his Word our only guide,
> And his gentle Spirit leader,
> He our peace, a constant tide
> Flowing in our tranquil bosom,
> Where is reared the mystic throne
> Of the King of peace eternal,
> Where he dwells and reigns alone.

> Oh, the glorious hope of Zion!
> Oh, the riches of her grace!
> Ever happy are the people
> Who abide in such a place.
> God is over all in glory,
> And is through them great and small,
> And he's in them by his Spirit,
> Jesus, Jesus, all in all.

The Crusades of Hell is the title of a serial poem describing the fall of man, the plan of salvation, and the different epochs of Christian history. It shows how Satan attempted to destroy the church by martyrdom and, failing in that, next attempted counterfeiting the church by making false churches.

His poems To the Ocean and Good-By Old Rockies were written on his Pacific Coast trip in the autumn of 1892.

TO THE OCEAN

> Help me, O sweet voice of inspiration,
> Help me sing one gentle lay
> To the ocean's wide and deep creation,
> Singing for us night and day.
> And thou restless sea, with all thy wonders,
> Touch my heart with melody;
> For no bard can sing thy awful numbers

Uninspired indeed by thee.

'Twas a balmy evening in October,
As our train sped on its time,
That we came in sight of God's great ocean,
To the old Pacific brine.
Swiftly gliding down its ancient orbit,
The great monarch of the light
Dropped his golden smiles upon the water
Ere he bid us all goodnight.

     *   *   *   *   *

Thou a preacher art to all the ages,
And thy audience all the world;
Lo! we read thy sermon on the pages
Of the book that God unfurled.
And to all that tread thy sand evirons
Thou dost thunder, yea, and show
How the human heart in sin's dominion
Never, never peace can know.

As thy waves in ceaseless turmoil labor,
And in fury beat the shore,
As they writhe and moan and dash asunder,
Rise and fall for evermore,
So the blasting hopes and guilty terrors
Of the sinner's wretched heart,
Restless, fearful, and despairing ever,
From his bosom never part.

Only One has sailed upon the bosom
Of the tempest-troubled sea,
Who could hush the winds and calm the billows—
He who spoke to Galilee.
Only he can break the storms of passion,
And rebuke the fears of hell;
Only he can calm the struggling spirit,
Speak the word, Be still, be still.

     *   *   *   *   *

Oh, I bless thy kindness, friend Pacific,
For thy temporizing breath;
For the climate wafted from thee truly
Is an enemy to death.
Sweet and soft and balmy are thy breathings,
Keeping winter blasts away;
And I thank thee, Providence, that brought me
Here to San Diego Bay.

* * * * *

On this seacoast I would fondly linger,
Where the zephyrs gently breathe
O'er the vineyards vast, and lemon orchards,
Where the bright pomegranates wave;
And the golden orange, figs, and guavas,
Apples, pears, and prunes abound;
With delicious nectarines and peaches,
Blessing all the season round.

Where the ocean moans its solemn numbers,
And the sun outpours its gold
On the clouds which hang, while twilight lingers,
O'er the sea-waves rising bold.
And the glorious king of day, descending,
Bids the vintage toilers rest,
While he cools his fevered brow each evening
On the great Pacific breast.

GOOD-BYE, OLD ROCKIES

I love your wild, romantic beauties,
Ye forms that seem to vie
Each with the summit of his neighbor,
And pierce the giddy sky.
Old Rockies, now to you
I bid adieu, adieu,
But hope we part not here forever.

I leave you as I found you, covered
With winter's chilly shroud,
Reaching toward the starry heavens,
And manteled in the cloud.
While I God's mercy preach,
And you his greatness teach,
We jointly glorify our Maker.

I read upon your lofty bulwarks
The might of nature's God,
What fortresses thy hands have builded
Where human feet ne'er have trod!
The strength of these are thine,
And round their apex shine
Jehovah's bright creative glory.

* * * * *

Divine Guidance was a poem of his later years in which he reflects on the kind hand of God upon his whole life.

> I own a providence supreme, divine,
> Has ruled and overruled this life of mine,
> Yes, ruled in all that heaven's love bestows,
> O'erruled in that from ill-intending foes.
> But oh, what mystery
> Veiled all his policy,
> And made this life a solemn wonder!
>
> To trace the mystic path my feet have trod,
> And note how every step is marked of God,
> How mercy hovered o'er my single blank
> Till at Love's throne my haughty spirit sank,
> And saw my pardon free
> Flow down from Calvary,
> Unlocks my bosom's grateful fountain.
>
> But greater, wider, higher, O my Lord,
> My humble walk with thee unfolds thy Word,
> Unfolds thy plenitude of love and grace,
> And helps thy hand in providence to trace.
> And yet high o'er my soul,
> Like ocean billows roll,
> Unsolved, ten thousand sacred wonders.
>
> I bless thee, O thou wise and loving Guide,
> That thou didst lead to full salvation's tide,
> And there my heart didst wash in crimson blood,
> Restore into the image of my God.
> Thenceforth my soul hath been
> The palace of a King;
> The joyful place of royal banquet.
>
> And I, who kingly honors never dreamed,
> Am raised with him who hath my soul redeemed,
> To jointly reign On Love's eternal throne,
> His peace and joy and glory all my own.
> O mystery Providence!
> Why lavishly dispense
> Thy gifts on one so meanly suited!
>
> Lord Jesus, when I retrospect my life
> Down through the varied scenes of mortal strife,
> At every change I stand in wonder wrapt,
> How thou hast saved and used and blessed and kept,
> And by thy blood hast bought
> A thing of utter naught;
> And well may all the angels marvel.

Besides the foregoing were a number of short poems, also a lengthy poem on Faith, which covers over sixty pages in his book. His poem on Innocence is referred to in our first chapter.

CHAPTER XIX

LAST YEARS

Hoped for long life—Difficulty in combining writing with evangelical work—Could not remain long out of the field—Begins to write a book on prophecy—Third marriage—Ohio River campaign—Last New Year's greeting—A school on the camp-ground—Last sermon—End of the journey.

During the last years of his life Brother Warner's time was devoted in greater proportion to writing than during the preceding years of more active ministerial work in the field. Possessing a weak physical constitution he aged rapidly and seemed elderly at fifty. Due to an earnest desire to accomplish much for the cause of God he had, however, a hope that the Lord would 'satisfy him with long life,' as the Psalmist expresses it. Whether he had any idea that his life might soon draw to a close, it is not known, but at any rate he felt prompted, after the few years he spent in evangelistic tours, to devote more of his time to writing on specific lines of truth. He wished in particular to write a book on prophetic subjects.

He spent the winter of 1891–92 mostly at home writing, but he was not altogether satisfied to be out of the field entirely. He desired in some manner to combine writing with field work.

> We have been very desirous that God should manage this poor frail temple so as to get the most effectual service and highest degree of glory. That he has enabled us to preach the gospel for twenty-six years through constant weakness and many infirmities has been a marvel of divine grace and a miracle of divine power. Should any one ask why he did not heal us up soundly, we answer. Many years ago as we cried to God to remove this thorn from our flesh, he taught us that he had weighty responsibilities to lay upon us, and that our afflictions would contribute to that humility and utter dependence upon God that were necessary to fill our calling; that in our weakness he would manifest his own power. So the Lord chose to display his power in upholding us in our afflictions rather than in utterly removing them. So we with the apostle 'glory in afflictions, that the power of Christ may rest upon us.'

> Of late years our experience has been something like this:

When out in the gospel field and spending our time between meetings chiefly in conversation with the dear brethren, who are always eager to talk about the good Lord and his dealings, an uneasiness would arise in our heart, a conviction that could we be away quietly with the Lord writing the precious things he has given us to set forth, time would be better used and God more glorified. These feelings created a longing to retire to our editorial sanctuary.

But remaining at home this winter, our mind has not yet been exactly satisfied, owing to the many earnest calls to the field. Last fall in Wooster, Ohio, we were kindly provided with a room to ourself. It being only a few moments walk from the hall, we could retire in good time, arise about three in the morning, have a good long time to wait before God, and yet get an early start to work. During that time the Lord blessed us in preaching daily, and we got more writing done, it seems to us, than if at home. Ever since, that arrangement has appeared to my mind as the best possible plan for effectual service to God. Since the Spirit seems to stir our heart to go forth and preach the word and at the same time requires our time uninterrupted by surrounding company and conversation, except when we can be a special help to some soul, we can see no way but to labor chiefly in towns and cities and have a retired place to spend the intervals between meetings before the Lord. This will enable us to make the best use of our time and also avoid the exposure and fatigue of going about from place to place. God knows it is not because we are not willing to endure hardness as a good soldier of Jesus Christ, but only for the glory of God, that we may do more good in this short life.

He never could remain long out of the gospel field. It was not his privilege, however, to carry out the plan of working in cities while engaging in writing. He rather had to be subject to calls as they came. To remain in one place very long and engage in writing he found to be weakening, due to the fact that he was likely not to take sufficient exercise. We have already noted his illness with rheumatism just before making the trip to Denver in the spring of 1892, and his sickness he had during that trip. He was not at home long after this trip until he was called to the Pacific Coast. While on the latter tour he spent two weeks, during the holiday season, at Farmersville, Cal., writing on his book on prophecy, The Cleansing of the Sanctuary. He returned in February and attended some of the camp- and grove-meetings during the summer. In the latter part of the following winter he spent some time in the home of Bro. B. E. Warren, in Springfield, Ohio, writing hymns for a new song-book he was helping to edit. This book, Echoes from Glory, was ready by the time of the June camp-meeting at Grand Junction.

On Aug. 12, 1893, he was married to Frances Miller. This was his third marriage, his second wife having died in Cincinnati some time previously. During the summer Brother and Sister Warner made a tour to Illinois and Missouri, and later to Pennsylvania.

Facsimile of D. S. Warner's handwriting.

The Family of D. S. Warner, as it last Appeared.

In the New Year's Greeting, in the Trumpet, for 1894 he expressed a desire to make a world tour. He thought seriously of doing so, but concluded later that his health would not permit. His years were drawing to a close. At the end of the Greeting he wrote the following verses:

> My years of time all flee away,
> And, swifter than an arrow,
> I glide along my pilgrim way,

And hasten to the morrow.
Away, away, see the moments fly,
We can not hold them waiting;
Then on their pinions let us try
To drop a future blessing.

My years of time, how fast they flee!
And yet the scribe of heaven
Records whate'er my actions be,
The thoughts my life has given.
Thanks be to God for his boundless grace
That keeps the record holy;
Just ready, Lord, to see my face,
And enter into glory.

My years of time are meted out,
A moment of probation,
Upon which hangs the awful weight
Of endless destination.
Press on, press on, O my soul, and seek
Eternal life's fruition,
Since everlasting ages reap
The fruits of short duration.

My years of time run on in peace,
All seem a golden summer;
And each one, blessed with heaven's grace,
Shines brighter than the former.
O God, thou crownest the happy years
With thy unbounded goodness,
Thy wondrous love has changed my tears
To songs of joy and gladness.

My years of time will close ere long
Where blooms an endless spring,
Where all the ransomed swell the song
The angels can not sing.
Roll on, sweet years, for I know my last
Will end high up in glory,
The toil I love will sweeten rest
And gem my crown of duty.

In the meantime there had opened up a rather unique method of evangelistic work. Bro. G. T. Clayton, who had been engaged in the Eastern field, had planned an Ohio River campaign. He had purchased a boat 26 × 80 and fitted it up for a dwelling and a meeting-hall. The plan was to float down the Ohio and tie up at every town on each side of the river and hold meetings for a season. January and February of 1894 were spent on this Floating Bethel, as it was called, with Brother and Sister Clayton. By this means he could do writing and at the same time hold meetings.

Late in May, 1894, he held a discussion with an Adventist leader. He attended during this summer, as usual, the general camp-meetings and grove-meetings. He began the erection of a house on the camp-ground near Grand Junction and by the following winter it was sufficiently completed that it could be occupied.

We are making some quotations from his New Year's Greeting for 1895. Little did he know that this would be his last message of this kind. He died in December of that year.

> To all our dear friends and readers we devoutly wish a happy New Year. May each of you enter the year with a holy zeal to glorify God in your soul and body, which are the Lord's. Nothing better can we wish you than the meekness of Christ in your heart and life and the omnipotence of faith in your work for him.
>
> How solemn and awful the place where we stand today! We have been carried down the stream of time until we approach its very outlet into the boundless expanse of eternity. Upon us have fallen the ends of the world. We are called in the providence of God to take a part in the last great struggle against the principalities and wicked powers of this sin-stricken earth. Oh, how significant to us are the words of John, "Beloved, it is the last time"! The harmonious testimony of all truth and of current facts on earth show us that we are rapidly approaching the last day of the last days.... But we know nothing with any degree of certainty. God alone knows the awful day and hour, and we may err even in naming the approximate time. Yea, before another New Year's bells ring on earth the trump of God may proclaim the death of time. One thing is sure, the Lord's coming is not very far off, and men of all creeds and faiths seem to agree in this....
>
> ... In great weakness of body we began the erection of a house last September. Bless God, he has in every way wonderfully blessed us in this work; and now we expect in a couple of weeks to move into our house on the camp and take up the writing of prophetic truth with a physical and consequent mental energy we never before possessed.
>
> We were consecrated to go to the foreign lands, and indeed thought the Lord would soon send us forth. But he showed us we were physically unfit. However, we may yet go. Our only wish is that God may get the greatest possible glory out of all our remnant of time and feeble abilities, coupled on to his omnipotent power and infinite wisdom.

At the close of the Grand Junction camp-meeting of that year, the last year of his life, he wrote the poem After the Battle.

Lo, they are gone; that armored host
Whose feet have daily pressed
These grounds have fled their several ways,
And all is hushed to rest.
But hark! the leaves upon the trees
In echoes lisp their song,
And on the wings of every breeze
Salvation floats along.

Oh, sacred ground! oh, honored site!
Behold, Jehovah's feet
Have stood among us here, and light
Eternal, pure, and sweet
Has glittered from his sword of truth,
And from his awful eyes
Two fiery streams have issued forth,
Revealing sin's disguise.

No battle-field where armies stood
In rank, with musketry,
And garments dyed in human blood,
Achieved such victory,
Or turned a scale of destiny
Of such momentous weight,
Or ever reared a monument
Of liberty so great.

Not with the cannon's roar of death,
Nor din of battle wild,
But by the burning fuel of fire
Salvation won the field.
'Twas not a crown of earthly state,
Nor freedom's empty boast,
But souls upon an awful brink
Called forth this mighty host.

The thrones of earth must crumble down,
All nations fade away;
Dominions of antiquity
Can not abide for aye:
But spirits captured here from sin,
And marshalled with the free,
Shall live and reign and sing and shine
Through all eternity.

But they are gone, those heralds strong,
Who stand within the sun,
And all that army dressed in white
To other fields have run:

And from this holy battle-field
New waves of glory roll,
And these, in turn, will others wake,
To spread from pole to pole.

Amen! amen! let heaven shout,
And earth break forth in song!
A thousand camps, ten thousand groves,
In every city throng.
Along the rivers, o'er the sea,
In Jesus' mighty name,
The present truth that set us free,
To all aloud proclaim.

This was his last poem, so far as is known, excepting a few verses he wrote in connection with obituaries. He assisted in meetings in the northern part of the State during the summer. In this series of meetings he obtained very little rest or time for writing, which emphasized the desire to devote more time to pen preaching at home. It was always hard for him to deny himself the glory of the field work, for he enjoyed it; but he felt he *must* settle down to write.

Besides some other small works, he prepared a new tract showing the fallacy of the millennium tradition, revised the tract on Marriage and Divorce, and wrote a book entitled, Salvation, Present, Perfect; Now or Never. His major work, however, to which he had for some time given attention, was his book on prophecy, The Cleansing of the Sanctuary. Of this he had written nearly four hundred pages.

By this time a children's school was started on the camp-ground, near Grand Junction. He took quite an interest in the school. Among the last things that engaged his mind was the arranging of a system of Bible-study. It is evident that he had in mind some sort of training-school, for he had planned courses in history, music, penmanship, etc., in addition to Bible-study.

And now we come to the end of the journey of life for Brother Warner. That frail body which had often been so wondrously touched and sustained by divine power was to be left in the grip of an affliction that should end his earthly career. His work was done. The purpose to which God had called him had been accomplished. He was to give place to others. This wonderful man of God, whose physical temple had so often by the Holy Spirit been quickened to new life when about to fall, and through whose touch the same divine power had many times brought help to the afflicted bodies of others, must himself now succumb to the hand of Death, for in this world all must die. His vitality, always weak, and now declining, had but slight resisting power against the forces of disease and decay that humanity is subject to in this life. An undermining affliction seemed to be at work in his body. On Sunday, Dec. 1, 1895, he preached a sermon on Christian Growth in the schoolhouse (also used for a chapel) on the camp-ground. That he should preach while physically weak was no uncommon thing and no one realized that he was so near the end. That discourse was his last.

Library and Home of D. S. Warner, Grand Junction, Mich.

Camp-ground and Lake, Near Grand Junction, Mich.

The following Sunday he suffered very much from an attack of lung trouble and was unable to speak above a whisper. But after prayer was offered he arose, walked across the room, and praised God aloud, also joining in singing. Thus he fought the fight of faith till the very last. His illness soon developed into pneumonia, and he went down rapidly. About midnight on the night of December 11 his watcher, noticing that he seemed to be resting easy, left the room to have his midnight lunch; but ere he returned the spirit of Brother Warner silently took its flight to the glory world above. Thus he died in solitude, at about 12:30 A. M. Thursday, December 12.

> "Our friend and brother dear, whose life
> Made bright this world of ours,
> Has passed away mid early snow,
> Soon after Autumn's flowers.
>
> No days of lingering sickness came
> To warn us of his death;
> No vision from the silent land
> To tell of parting breath."

A post-mortem examination revealed an enlarged heart but no trace of tuberculosis, which he had in his younger days and from which he was miraculously healed and preserved.

His spirit was very tenacious of life. As ill as he was, he arose every morning at his regular early hour, and through the day engaged to a slight extent in writing. Even the day before he died he was on his feet a part of the time.

The funeral was held on the camp-ground on Sunday, the 15th. A brief notice of his death was inserted in the Gospel Trumpet of December 12. In the succeeding issue the obituary appeared in full between draped column rules.

Of the last hymn he attempted he completed only the first stanza, one half of the chorus, and the first line of the second stanza, the hymn as he left it appearing thus:

> Shall my soul ascend with rapture
> When the day of life is past?
> While my house of clay shall slumber,
> Shall I then with Jesus rest?

Chorus.

> O my soul, press on to glory,
> Worlds of bliss invite thee on.
>
> Oh, shall my immortal spirit

This hymn was afterward completed by Sister Georgia Elliot. Music was composed for it, and it appears as Number 365 in Select Hymns.

CHAPTER XX

AS OTHERS KNEW HIM

Statements of various individuals—Author's statement—Reflections
at his grave.

The following statements by individuals who knew Brother Warner personally are of interest.

Our home was at Lindsey, Ohio, when we first met Brother Warner. We were then members of the Evangelical Association. We were both sanctified, but were dissatisfied with the formality of sectism. We attended the regular appointments faithfully; but we craved for deeper spiritual devotion and felt the need of special services where we could talk freely of the glorious doctrine of sanctification. When the people throughout the country heard what we taught, many doors opened among the denominations and many were converted. This stirred the ministers with envy, and they tried to stop the work, but failed, because it was God's work.

This continued for five years. We felt we should be better out of the Church than in it, and often wished to withdraw, but did not know where to go. We made this a subject of special prayer and meditation. We were assured God would bring us and lead us in a way we did not understand.

We had not known Brother Warner, but had heard that he was a deceiver and that everywhere he went he caused the most spiritual to believe his doctrine. We received a card from him stating that he had just closed a meeting and that the Lord was directing him north for the next meeting. He said if we could furnish a place for meeting, either public or private, he with his company should be glad to visit our place.

I asked husband what to do. He said, "Mother, do you know this is the man that we were warned against?" I said, "Yes, I know, but we are praying for God to send us a man who will preach and practise the whole truth. Now, if this man is of God we must receive him." I went to the Lord with the matter and said, "Lord, if thou dost want these people to come and hold a meeting and can use them here, send them right on, without my answering this card." This was on Monday morning. At one o'clock a load of six drove up to the gate. Brother Warner came to the door and knocked. When I opened he said, "Peace be unto this house." I can not tell my feelings, but after I gave them a hearty welcome I was conscious they were of God and decided they should stay as long as God could use them.

While I was preparing the noon meal for my new guests and my family, they sang numbers 43 and 72 out of Songs of Victory. [These songs were, 'Twas Love that Found Out Me, and, The Hand of God on the Wall, respectively.] We never before heard such heavenly music. The tears streamed down husband's cheeks. My daughter was so affected she left the house; it made such an impression on her she afterward gave her heart to God.

God used Brother Warner to help us discern the one body of Christ and the evils of sects. We rented a hall. Sometimes it was crowded with earnest listeners, and I am sure much good would have been done had it not been for the five ministers who lived in our town. One night Brother Warner preached with such power one of the preachers said, "This is too strong for me," and went out. The hall was closed against us and we held our meetings in private homes. On occasions rotten eggs, gravel-stones, and mud balls were thrown at us, and through it all Brother Warner praised God and manifested such a calm and gentle spirit one could not help but feel he was a man of God. During these meetings some walked thirty miles to hear the truth.

Brother Warner had been undergoing the great trial of his wife's separation from him, and many earnest prayers went up for her. He gave us some of his letters to read, which he wrote to her, and oh! the gentle spirit, and the kind pleadings which he wrote, were enough to break any heart of stone.

Later we moved to St. Louis, Mich., and it was our privilege to have him in our home often. He always preached with power. I can say his life and conduct were worthy of imitation.

Mrs. Elizabeth Walter,
St. Louis, Mich.

The first time I met Brother Warner was in February, 1883. He came to our home and assisted in cottage-meetings. He was a very humble man of faith and one I dearly loved. At the first camp-meeting at Bangor, Mich., in 1883, he was called away, and I took him to the train. As he stepped from the vehicle I handed him eleven dollars. He raised both hands and praised God, as he had had no money for car-fare.

I was with him one time in Chicago in search of a printing-press. At the breakfast-table in a restaurant he poured out his heart to God in deep, earnest prayer and thanked God for the food, which drew the attention of many listeners. At noon we bought a lunch, so as to save the Lord's money. In an alley just off a busy street we found a dry-goods box, which served as a place for our meal. Here he again lifted up his hands and in a deep sense of gratitude gave thanks to God.

S. Michels,
South Haven, Mich.

In October, 1881, I was visiting in North Eagle, Michigan, at my father's, Daniel B. Howe. A brother sent us a Trumpet, the first we had seen. In a few days J. C. Fisher and wife came there. Father asked him to come and hold a meeting, which he did in December, and was there all winter. Many received the light. In October, 1882, Brother Warner came and some others, and held a meeting lasting several days. That was a wonderful meeting to us. When Brother Warner came he seemed to be under a heavy trial on account of some difficulty that had come into his life, and was very sad, apparently unreconciled.

He stayed at our house, and while there God wonderfully blessed him and the clouds began to lift. When he was preaching on Sunday morning, the power of God came down on him and on the people. All wept and shouted. He leaped up a foot or more, turned completely around, and came down facing the audience. From that time the sorrow and sadness were gone.

I did not see him again until in 1894 at the June camp-meeting at Grand Junction. I went to where he was staying at the Trumpet Family residence and met him at the breakfast table. He asked me how the people were at North Eagle. I told him all were well. He put his elbow on the table, his face in his hand, and wept like a child for a few moments. Then he said, "Pardon me, I have to think of how the Lord blessed me there. I never knew that the Lord could bless a mortal man as he blessed me at that meeting."

In 1895, in March, he came to preach my father's funeral. While he was waiting for the train at Grand Ledge he wrote a poem and read it at the funeral. I next saw him at a grove-meeting south of Eagle. He preached a great sermon on the Church. He said nothing of other ministers or denominations, but his discourse when finished left no place for any other church, no possibility of there being another. I never saw him again, as he died the following December.

In my estimation, there never lived a more holy or godly man than he. I doubt whether any other reformer was any more devoted to the cause of Christ than he, or ever preached sermons that were more deep or soul-stirring than his. He lives in the hearts of the people today, and in his writings will be heard until the end of time.

Julia M. Cheeseman,
Liberty Center, Ohio.

Brother Warner was one of the most godly men I ever met; he was so consecrated and devotional. He had great power with God and men; was very humble, and all persons, regardless of rank or position, could approach him for help.

I was at a meeting at Carthage, Mo., where he was preaching. An awful storm came up, and we were in its path with a cloth tabernacle. At the roar of the wind people became alarmed and began to run. Brother Warner cried out, "Stay in the tent; not one shall be hurt." Lifting his eyes and raising his hand heavenward, he said, "Father, calm this storm so thy word can be preached." The storm ceased within a short distance, not more than a block, away. Much damage was done to buildings. The top was blown off the large woolen-mill and box-cars were thrown from the track. I was amazed and said, "What manner of man is this that even the winds obey?"

At another time some boys whose people opposed the truth gathered in a body and began to drink, and finally came to disturb the meeting. They did this on two nights. On the third night, when Brother Warner was preaching he heard them coming. He said, "Father, rebuke the devil in these carousing boys." That was the last of their disturbance. He was a man of faith and was always praising God, even in the deepest trials. He was a reformer indeed.

Lena L. Matthesen,
Moore, Okla.

My memory is poor and I now recall but a few instances. At one time while Brother Warner was preaching a terrible storm came up. The heavens were black. The congregation was becoming uneasy and fearful. He told them to remain seated; that God had given him a message and would not let it rain. He asked God to hold the rain till he had delivered the message. I do not know how long he was preaching, but it was unusually long. God surely held the rain, for when he had finished and the people reached their homes the rain poured down tremendously.

Once when sectarians were framing all manner of falsehoods

and sending them broadcast over the country, some of his friends came to him saying, "How can you stand all this?" He paused a moment and then said, "This all came about since I died."

William N. Smith,
North Star, Mich.

Once when he was away from home holding meeting, Brother Warner felt a strong impression that he should return home. Some one offered to take him to the train, though the time was short till the train was due. Brother Warner was praying the Lord to hold the train. When they came in sight of the station, the train was there and soon began to move off. He cried aloud, "My God, stop that train for me." The train slowed down. The conductor signaled to back-up and stop, and took him on. He expressed his gratefulness to God and to the railroad men and confessed God in it.

He told me that at one time he received a telegram from the West requesting him to come in haste. He went to his room and placed the matter before the Lord. He had no means; but the Lord told him to go, doubting nothing, that all things were possible with Him. He then packed his grip and hastened to the depot. When he arrived there he continued in supplication to God. People began to gather to take the train. All at once his eye caught sight of a man hurrying toward the station. The man came in, and when he saw Brother Warner, rejoiced, and said, "Well, I see you are packed to go." "Yes, I received my orders from God to go on a Western trip." "Well, a man needs money to travel on," the man replied, and then handed him a bunch of money. After he had purchased his ticket he noticed he had plenty of change left to defray all necessary expenses, and he went on his way rejoicing. He arrived at his destination and had success. When he was ready to return and was in a conveyance to go to the depot, an old sister called to him to stop and said, "Here is a little budget; take this." As he was in a hurry he just put it in his pocket. Later, when he opened it, he found one hundred dollars in gold. He came home rejoicing, like the disciples when they were sent out without purse or scrip.

A. J. Shelly,
Alma, Mich.

I was much impressed with Brother Warner's remarkable patience under trying circumstances, and when his frail body was racked with pain. On one occasion he and I were on our way to a tent-meeting on the north side of Denver. Being quite late on account of having gone to pray for the sick, we were waiting for a car at a transfer-point, and it seemed to me the car never would arrive. I became anxious and paced up and down the sidewalk (as though in so doing I could hurry up the car), because it was then time for meeting to begin. But to my astonishment, Brother Warner was humming a song and 'making merry in his heart to the Lord.' I said, "Brother Warner, do you ever become impatient?" "Impatient!" he replied, "I have not felt impatient for fifteen years." I believed it then and I believe it now and have ever since that evening. I was striving to overcome anxiety and restlessness because of pain, delay, or opposition, and have succeeded to a great extent in submitting all to the One who is able to cause all things to work together for our good.

John E. Roberts,
3830 Stuart St.,
Denver, Colo.

A TRUE EXAMPLE OF HUMILITY

One of the most striking examples of true humility that I ever saw was on the day I first met and became acquainted with Brother Warner. With his company of workers, he came to the place where I was expected to preach that day. I was just beginning in the ministry, and had a very high ideal of a minister, to which I was trying hard to attain. When I arrived at this place, the company had already come, and we simply met and were introduced before the Sunday-school began. After the exercises were over, and before time to begin preaching, Brother Warner came to me and said he understood that I was expected to preach that day. I answered yes, but not when a man of such reputation and ability as he was present. He insisted that I go ahead, as he was very tired from the labors he had been in and from the trip which they had just made from the West. I answered that I could not preach much yet, and if he would speak only a little while, it would be a treat to the congregation and me. He still insisted that I should preach, and did not seem to care to take the pulpit. I plead with him to do so, and said, "Brother Warner, I simply could not preach in the presence of such a great man as you are." He came up to me and placed his arm around my neck and his head on my shoulder, and said, "God bless you, my brother, I am only one of God's little ones."

This action seemed very strange to me, as I was not acquainted with such a spirit in a man of such reputation; but I kept insisting that he take the pulpit, if not for more than but a few minutes. He then said, "Well, then, if you feel that way, I will; but I need your prayers." He really did look weary, and seemed so frail in body that for a moment I feared I did wrong in urging him so hard.

Well, he began, and I felt that I should be prepared to follow him in case he should stop suddenly, and I would finish the sermon. He preached on the subject of sanctification, and I was so desirous that he might be able to give us a full sermon on this precious subject. Well, he had hardly begun when he seemed to change into another man, and my fears were soon gone that he might have a physical breakdown before the close. That weary look and the appearance of frailty soon disappeared, and the wonderful words that he spoke were full of power and authority. I was soon lost in the glorious truths of the sermon and was unconscious of my surroundings. When he sat down, we were surprized to find that he had preached just three hours, which seemed such a short time to all of us.

The deep impression of the humility of this man of God and the divine power with which he preached had this effect upon my heart: If this is "but one of God's little ones," where will there ever be a place for such an ignorant beginner as I? My ideal of a minister was wholly changed, and it was for some time that I had great difficulty to believe there was a place for me. But having the privilege of sitting at Brother Warner's feet in a series of meetings following that day, I was greatly helped to try to sink into deeper humility, and through the grace of God find my place in the body, the church. This impression of humility has remained with me these years, and has often been a protection when at times there would be presented temptations to self-exaltation.

A WISE ANSWER

In one of the meetings that Brother Warner and his company held in our home neighborhood my older brother had become very much interested in the good singing of this company. He was passionately fond of good singing, and though working hard all day, could not stay away from the evening meetings. But he had become backward in his spiritual life, and knew he was living far below the standard that Brother Warner was holding up. At the close of one of the evening services Brother Warner met my brother and asked him how it was with his soul. The answer was this: "I simply confess to you that I don't have enough brains to understand sanctification." These words were spoken in a spirit of resistance and self-justification. Brother Warner looked into his face with a kindly and humble smile and said: "God bless you, Brother John, it doesn't take brains."[25]

[25] It was characteristic of Brother Warner to give ready and wise response and oftentimes to answer an objector on his own ground or in his own terms. It is related that in a certain meeting after he had preached on holiness an opposer arose and vociferously de-

HOW A VICTORY WAS WON BY PRAYER

While Brother Warner was with us in San Diego, Cal., he gave a series of lessons on the Revelation, and preached hard against the errors of Millennialism. A man who had come amongst us, who was a preacher, and seemed to be accepting the truth very well, but had not received the light on this line, became very much offended at the sermon Brother Warner preached that evening. He seemed to lose his patience altogether, and manifested anger. He came forward to Brother Warner before the congregation had left the hall and in a loud voice and with a face expressing real bitterness said, "The Lord shows me that you are of the devil." He had hardly finished his words when Brother Warner fell on his knees and began to pray, right at the feet of his accuser.

I never before heard such a pitiful prayer, as he poured out his heart to God for this dear man who had brought such a charge against the servant of the Lord. He prayed that the man might be able to see his wrong, that God would reveal the truth to his understanding, and also bless the people who were standing and looking on at this scene of Christian discourtesy, etc. We were all so shocked at the unusual act that it was hard to know just what to do but stand there, which we did, until the prayer was over. After finishing the outpouring of his soul in prayer, he quietly rose from his knees, and went away. The accuser was one of the most surprized people I ever saw. During the prayer he stood as though riveted to the floor, his deathly pale face turned down toward Brother Warner. His hands hung by his side, and he had the appearance of one paralyzed. For a while after Brother Warner had risen from his knees, the man remained fastened to the spot. The congregation began going out, and finally the man also took his hat and left, without one word.

The next night, in the presence of a large audience, this man arose and came forward to Brother Warner, weeping and humbly asking that he might be forgiven for the great offence toward him and the people. He said the Lord had shown him that Brother Warner was right, and he did all that could be expected to right himself with God. From that time he was a strong advocate of the truths of the reformation.

The wisdom of God that was manifested in this moment of sudden surprize, in this critical condition, had a wonderful effect upon the people.

J. W. Byers,
618 Palm Ave., Fresno, Cal.

nounced the doctrine, saying in his closing remarks, "I pray God to scatter this old holiness doctrine to the four winds of the earth." Immediately Brother Warner responded with a shout of "AMEN"! The effect was terrific, and the opposition was confounded.

Very early in my experience in the reformation I was staying at the home of Brother and Sister Fry, in Michigan. I had been under accusation for some time. Brother Warner was coming to hold a tabernacle-meeting right near their home. I determined that when he came I would go to him and tell him I was backslidden and ask him to pray with me. I did not go to see him until just before he arose to preach, hence said nothing to him regarding my condition; but I shall never forget that sermon. He arose, and with his eyes filled with tears he broke the bread of life, and my accusations were swept into oblivion, and my soul received a glorious refreshing. It made one think of the saying of Jesus, "Feed my sheep."

At another time, on the old Deerfield (Ind.) camp-ground, I fallowed him to the meeting one morning, and though he was always frail it seemed he was worse that day, so that he almost reeled as he walked. After singing, we all knelt in prayer, and Brother Warner prayed, "Now, Lord, thou hast laid this message upon me; give me strength." He sprang to his feet and leaped all over the floor. He preached for a long time. That made a lasting impression upon me, for I knew he received help directly from heaven.

J. W. Daugherty,
Glenville, Nebr.

It would require much more space than is at my disposal to narrate even half of the things that stand out prominently in my memory concerning the life of D. S. Warner and its influence upon me. As his last years were spent in my home community, and he was often in the home of my parents, I was intimately acquainted with him from my childhood's earliest recollection until I was past fifteen years of age, when he died. This association being at the impressionable period of my life, multitudes of events were stamped indelibly upon my memory.

I shall mention but three of these incidents. The first occurred in the autumn of 1890. An assembly was being held at Geneva Center, a short distance southwest of Lacota, Mich. One day while a special service for children was being held I sat upon the front seat, listening to the kind, persuasive words of instruction and admonition being given by Brother Warner. At the close of a short talk he asked, "How many of you children want to give your hearts to the Lord?" and then without waiting for a reply he turned to me, and with love and tenderness beaming from his kindly eyes, asked, "Do you not want to get saved now?" Instantly my heart was stirred. I knelt at the altar and Brother Warner came and prayed for me. Laying his hands upon my head, he said, "Lord, give this boy a new heart; take away from him the stony heart and give him a heart of flesh." I felt immediately the touch of God. I was born of the Spirit. My young heart was filled with holy joy. Can I ever forget that glad moment? Not so long as I have a being. When time, as we know it, has ended, when old earth itself has grown weary and ceased to go round, and when all the stars of the heavens have forgotten to shine, I shall still praise God for the revelation of divine life that thrilled my soul on that glorious morning. And when I wander over the green fields of the heavenly paradise, or sit down with my Lord in the city of God, I want to renew that association with Brother Warner and thank him for what he did for me.

Brother Warner's preaching always possessed for me an irresistible charm. His doctrinal sermons took hold upon me, especially those devoted to prophetic subjects. I remember distinctly one sermon on prophecy, delivered at the camp-ground, near Grand Junction, Mich. It created a lasting impression upon my mind. Although he preached for four hours and ten minutes, the time did not seem long. I have no doubt that my later interest in doctrinal themes is due, in a great measure at least, to those early impressions, when the Spirit of God stamped the truths of his Word upon my soul.

The third incident that I shall mention was a sermon preached by Brother Warner, just a short time before his death. It was delivered at the camp-ground. The subject was Heaven. So inspiring was this message that it created in me an intense longing to go to that place of light and life—a longing that abides with me still.

F. G. Smith,
Anderson, Ind.

I can not find words to express the help and comfort Brother Warner was to me. I well remember the bitter persecutions he and his company met while here in the South. His pure, holy life and the radical preaching are still living in the South. I remember hearing him preach one night, in a private house, on the oneness of God's people. He was so filled with the Holy Spirit he would leap and praise God. The ceiling overhead was very low. He said the leaps in his soul were higher than the ceiling of that house. I thought every time he left the floor he would hit the ceiling. He and his company were in our house at Spring Hill when the angry mob came after him; but the Lord took care of him.

Mrs. Demaris (Smith) Vance,
Meridian, Miss.

Brother Warner was the man under whose preaching I was

convicted for salvation. I had gone fifteen miles to hear him, and when I arrived on the ground I was met by an old friend of mine who had been one of the worst men I have ever known. He said to me, "Praise God, I am glad you are here." This made me feel that after all there might be a chance for me to obtain freedom, from the sins that held me. When I went to meeting that night and Brother Warner was pointed out to me, I thought to myself, "I fear there is not much to him." But they sang and Brother Warner began preaching. I never had heard a man preach as he did. After the meeting, several were prayed for and healed. Something came over me as I stood and seemed to go off the ends of my fingers, and I said to myself that this was the first camp-meeting I ever attended that was not ruled by Satan, and that if I could get this religion I could keep out of hell.

One day some one arose and testified that he was still "chawing" tobacco and asked all to pray that he might hold out. Brother Warner remarked that all the saints were testifying for Jesus but this man got up and testified for his tobacco. This was a new kind of talk to many of us. Brother Warner was one of the greatest preachers I ever heard. God was with him in such power as no one else seemed to have in those days.

R. H. Owens,
Mt. Pleasant, La.

At a grove-meeting near Antwerp, Ohio, some roughs came to break up the meeting. They divided into two squads, one to pass to the one side of the congregation and the other to the other side. They were prepared to throw eggs, but the leaders of the two squads said, "Don't throw until something is said to justify." They marched to their places and waited. Brother Warner was preaching with wonderful anointing, and shouting. Finally the leader on one side said, "There shall be nothing thrown at that man by my consent. He is preaching the truth; he is a man of God." So they started back. Strange to say, those on the other side did the same, and the two parties met. One said, "Why didn't you throw?" The other said, "Why didn't you?" The leader repeated as before remarked. Finally one big fellow said, "Well, I am going to take one shot, anyway," and he threw an egg right into the congregation. There was a man sitting near the front who was a sectarian; the egg struck him directly in the face and broke over him. He made quite a splutter.

At a meeting at Rising Sun, Ohio, Brother Warner was praying in an opening service when some one threw a pack of cards over their heads. After the preaching the people were gathering up the cards. He said, "Amen, gather them up; the devil has surrendered; he has given up his testament."

J. N. Howard,
Nappanee, Ind.

It was in the spring of 1891, in southern Indiana, that I first met Brother Warner. I shall never forget the impression he made on me as he stepped into our home. I felt so sensibly the presence of God with the man. He held a two weeks' meeting at our place at that time. A number of souls were saved. Opposition ran high. The meeting was held in the schoolhouse near to a sectarian meeting-house. The preacher who preached at this place tried to get a revival started, but failed. One minister rode all day on a Sunday trying to gather up a mob to drive the brother out of the country; but the people so much enjoyed his preaching and were so won to the man by his gentleness and the clearness of his teaching that they would not rally to the opposers' standard.

I had the pleasure of having him in our home at a later time for about three months. It was at this time that we learned more about his prayer-life. My father-in-law once drove him out of the woods where he had gone for prayer. Those prayers, however, and his patience and calmness while being driven out of the woods resulted in my mother-in-law's salvation.

He had a great, sympathetic heart and consequently could comfort the sorrowing as few men could. He preached the funeral of my little boy, and his words of comfort were as a healing balm. He and I roomed together at one time, when he held a ten nights' debate with a Seventh-day Adventist preacher. Here he again impressed me with his mighty prayers. After going to our room he would wrestle long and earnestly with God in prayer before retiring. I have always felt much indebted to him for his example in prayer and holy living.

C. E. Orr.
Everett, Wash.

For about seven years we traveled with Brother Warner in the ministry. Our work was incessant, winter and summer. My intimate association with him impressed me with his deep devotion and sterling Christian character. He was a student of rare ability and an efficient New Testament minister and writer. He was not given to lightness, sentimentality, or idle words. He was sober, serious, and impressive in both words and actions. No one could enjoy his presence and association unless he, like him, would live spiritual and close to God. His whole life and ambition were the spread of the pure gospel and the well-being of souls. He used no empty words in his manner of preaching. His messages were weighty and impressive.

I remember one time in Canada where God's presence was so manifest in one of his sermons that when he was through preaching the entire congregation to an individual knelt in prayer and sought the Lord for pardon and peace. He was a very busy man. He was up early in the morning and late at night studying, writing, preaching, or helping some needy soul. He was charitable, sympathetic, hospitable, and self-denying. His life was full of constant peace and victory. I can not estimate the value and worth to me of my intimate association with him through those years.

He was evidently chosen of God as a great reformer. While he was meek, mild, and gentle, he was heroic and fearless as a Martin Luther. We shall do well to preserve his words of writing and to remember his example, for we shall thereby be worth more to God and souls.

B. E. Warren,
Springfield, Ohio.

It is indeed a pleasure to me to contribute a few lines of kindly remembrance of our departed brother D. S. Warner. It was the good pleasure of our heavenly Father that my dear wife and I live with Brother and Sister Warner as members of their household for some fifteen months before he died. I can say with all truth that the gospel he preached he lived. He was always cheerful, kindly, and affectionate in brotherly love to all about him, ready to give wise and fatherly advice and counsel. He was very devoted and much given to prayer in his home. He spent much time in his library with his books and translations of the Scriptures, and did much writing and correspondence, his wife assisting him much. The book Salvation; Present, Perfect; Now or Never, he wrote at this time and he read the manuscript to us before it was printed.

He loved to talk of God's dealings with him; how God led him step by step out of error and confusion and many deep difficulties, how he was violently persecuted by false brethren, how his wife became deceived and separated from him, etc. He would tell of how God revealed to him the sect Babylon of the Revelation and gave him to understand that he must cry out against her and expose her sins; how Babylon loomed up before him as a great black mountain, and that God was taking him as a worm to thresh it, and how he shrunk back at the thought of being thrown against such a seemingly impregnable wall, "God made me see," he said, "that I was nothing but a little mouse, but that he had his hand over me," then he would feel encouraged.

What God accomplished through him some of us know something about, and the results are glorious. Verily he being dead yet speaketh!

Curtis W. Montgomery,
27 Chestnut St.,
Marcus Hook, Pa.

In the winter of 1888–89 Bros. Geo. T. Clayton and Charles Koonce came to our community, near Cochran's Mills, Armstrong Co., Pa., preaching what was generally termed "a new doctrine," a "turning the world upside down." I was a boy sixteen years old, and the first night of the service walked four miles to the meeting. The first sermon made a deep impression on my mind. During that meeting quite a congregation was raised up for the truth.

A few weeks after the close of this meeting, Brother Warner and company came. They arrived in spring wagons from Blanco, Pa., a distance of about thirty miles. I was working with my father in the field when they passed down the road, singing The River of Peace, and shouting, "Halleluiah!" We never witnessed such a scene. Singing and shouting along the public road was character-istic of Brother Warner's company in those days. At night people would rush to their windows to hear the singing, and remark, "The angels are coming."

In this meeting Brother Warner's preaching was all doctrinal. It was all new to us; but I never was able to shake off the convic-tions that fastened on my heart that these people had the truth. I said I wanted their kind of religion.

In August of 1892 we attended the Perryville (Pa.) camp-meet-ing. I well remember going to the depot from the camp-ground for some baggage, and of meeting on the way Brother Warner and company, who had just arrived. At first they did not recognize me; but when I said, "Praise the Lord," Brother Warner arose in the spring wagon and lifting his hand to heaven shouted at the top of his voice, "Halleluiah! praise our God for eternal salvation!" and all the company joined with loud amens and, "Glory to God!"

At this meeting also Brother Warner's preaching was about all doctrinal. The great fundamental truths of full salvation, holiness, the church, unity, the downfall of sect Babylon, and the command to come out of her, the great apostasy, the last reformation, divine healing, etc., were preached uncompromisingly. I will say, breth-ren, this kind of preaching confirmed the saints and brought out clearly the holy remnant from the folds of confusion and drew the line in the manner that people knew the way to Zion and re-joiced in their freedom. Sinners were soundly converted under this preaching. They were not born dead. People usually came through at the altar shouting. It was not unusual during a sermon to see one hundred saints on their feet shouting and Brother Warner leaping and crying, "Fire! fire!" We all got this inspiration, and leaping and shouting were characteristic of most of the early preachers in the pulpit.

In the summer of 1893, wife and I attended the Grand Junction, (Mich.), camp-meeting. When the train from South Haven stopped at the station I heard a great shout, and looking over near the Trumpet Office saw Brother Warner leaping and shouting, crying at the top of his voice as the saints were getting off the train, "The holy remnant is pouring in." That was a great meeting, the most powerful I ever attended. Miracles were wrought and devils "crying with a loud voice, came out of many that were possessed with them."

Brother Warner impressed me as a man of deep piety and spirituality. He was very humble and tender-hearted. Many were the warm-hearted counsels and admonitions he gave to the younger ministers, and these were delivered in tears, with a, "God bless you, my dear brother." He was a very able man in the Scriptures, and one of the deepest in prophecies I have ever heard. He was slow to see the faults of others; but able to expose wrong-doing when he clearly discerned it in any one. He was very definite and radical in his preaching, and eternity alone will reveal what he suffered because of his bold defense of what he believed to be the truth. We who knew him best would never question his sincerity. He was a reformer in every sense of the term. The influences of his life and ministry will sweep onward till time shall end. The principles he advocated are more and more being recognized by spiritual people everywhere, and the fires of reformation are destined to sweep the earth until

> "We girdle the globe with salvation,
> And holiness unto the Lord;
> Till light shall illumine each nation,
> The light from the lamp of his word."

H. M. Riggle,
Akron, Ind.

As a young worker in Brother Warner's company for a few months I was deeply impressed with his kindness, courtesy, and humility. He often exhorted the young ministers and workers to seek humility of heart, and often related an incident of his personal experience in talking with the Lord, when the Lord said to him, "Be humble, my child, be humble."

He had a great burden for the gathering of God's people, the prosperity of Zion, and the salvation of the lost. To this end he dedicated his time, talents, and means, and was so self-denying that he would share his last penny with those in need. He said, when he finished a Bible subject or outline for a sermon, "There's the skeleton, I'll trust the Lord to put the meat on it." I heard him say, "Satan puts us in his sieve that he may sift all the good out of us; God puts us in his sieve that he may sift all the bad out of us."

Brother Warner was a son of thunder in delivering truth against false religions, but as wise as a serpent and as harmless as a dove in dealing with the erring ones.

Nora Hunter,
San Diego, Cal,

I also wish to bear personal testimony of Brother Warner. The first time I met him was on Apr. 7, 1888, at our family home, near Albany, Ill. He with his company were on their return from their Western tour. I had been teaching school in Iowa during the previous winter and had also engaged myself for the spring term, but had a two weeks' intermission for vacation, which I decided to spend at my home. How wonderful that the course of life may turn on a mere decision, which at the time may seem to involve no particular consequence. It was during that two weeks' interval that I met Brother Warner and came in contact with the reformation movement.

On the date mentioned, the little company of evangelists arrived at our house. They were brought thither by Brothers Knight and Daniels from the former's home, near Fulton, where they had arrived the day before. My father and I had gone to engage a schoolhouse for meeting. When we returned two men were standing at our front gate conversing, one of whom was Brother Warner. My father made himself acquainted and then introduced me, informing Brother Warner that I had been converted only a short time before. As he reached to shake my hand he said, so appreciatingly, "Well, that's good news," and there beamed out of those soft blue eyes a Christian love and tenderness that made a lasting impression on me. That he should so rejoice in spirit at the knowledge of my conversion seemed to give me a spiritual uplift and to place my appreciation of things spiritual on a higher level. It seemed that during that week when Brother Warner and company were with us our home was a heavenly paradise. I regard that week as the brightest and most full of destiny to me in all my life's history. There was something about the happy, victorious spirit of those dear saints that exalted Christianity in my conception and made it a thing very much to be desired. The impression made upon my young heart at that time can never be erased.

My mother had been reading the Trumpet and had formed the opinion of Brother Warner that he was a great and wonderful man. So when she met him she exclaimed, "And is this Brother Warner!" His reply was, "Yes, and he is the *least* man you ever saw."

In the meeting that followed he instructed me in my consecration for sanctification. As I arose, ready to venture on God's promise, he discerned my faith and broke the way before me by claiming the promise with me.

When my mother died, in July, 1894, I was engaged in the publishing work at Grand Junction. The telegram notifying me of her death said also, "Bring Brother Warner." This message was received late in the evening, and Brother Warner had retired. I went to his room and informed him of the request. He was feeling bad physically and wondered if Brother — — could not go instead. I knew that no other person available could give the satisfaction Brother Warner could, and so expressed myself to him. Finally he consented. Although he was weak and tired he arose from his bed and prepared to go. It was never in him to shirk what might be interpreted as duty. He believed in taking the Lord for his sufficiency, and the Lord did not disappoint him. We had to take a night train for Chicago, and before we reached the city he said he felt stronger than when he started, and this in spite of his having been deprived of rest. He preached the funeral discourse, wrote quite a lengthy obituary and poem, and even responded to a request to preach in an evening service. It was wonderful how he could take God for his strength and his every need. His life seemed to be a constant miracle.

I have traveled with him, slept with him, taken part in his meetings, and have been associated with him in editorial work, and thus have known him at close range and he was always God-fearing, humble, loving, devoted, full of faith, and possessed of singleness of heart, to a degree rarely known among men. His life, so exemplary, was an object lesson of Christian attainment and of what God can do for and through weak humanity. It was an inspiration to feel the touch of his Christian spirit. And thus we exalt, not the man—for apart from the divine influence that ruled his life he would have been very commonplace—but we exalt the God who can take such humble instrumentality and by a transformation of being use it to accomplish his work in the earth. It is the Christ in man that we are to exalt and to follow.

*   *   *   *   *

The body of D. S. Warner lies, near where it fell, in a rather lonely spot some distance off the thoroughfare, in the sparsely-wooded edge of the camp-ground near Grand Junction, Mich. This place, where are situated a few other graves and where the proximity to the empty cottages on the camp-ground gives an aspect of desertion, is a place for reflection. Here nature undisturbed, through the succession of bursting buds of spring, refreshing dews of summer, sighing breezes and gently falling leaves of autumn, and rigorous storms of winter covering all with a shroud of snow, is heard to speak silently but eloquently of the brief cycle of life on this earth, of the grave as our last resting-place, and of the fact that "here we have no continuing city, but we seek one to come." One thinks, when standing beside this grave, of the wonderful accomplishment crowded into that short career, and of the reward of a life of faithful service. And one feels springing from the depths of the heart this choice, that come what may of toil and self-sacrifice in the Christian service, come what may of reproach and persecution for Christ's sake, "let me die the death of the righteous, and let my last end be like his."

Grave of D. S. Warner, Near Grand Junction, Mich.

The New Monument.

END OF ORIGINAL BOOK

SUPPLEMENT FOR
THIS REPRINT EDITION

On the following pages are added pictures of ministers for this reprint edition, most of whom were co-workers with Bro. Warner in the Reformation.

E. E. Byrum.

Editor of Trumpet after Warner's death.

Mary Cole. Geo. L. Cole.

Superintendents Faith Missionary Home, Chicago, Ill.

F. G. Smith, Lacota, Mich.

J. W. Byers, Lodi, Cal., and Jennie Byers, Wife of J. W. Byers.

S. M. Helm, Stafford, Kans.

Ella and Drusilla Trent.
C. A. and S. S. Sunderland, Granby, Mo.

Wm. G. Schell, Moundsville, W. Va.

Geo. E. Bolds, Brice, Mo.

R. H. Owens, Sherwood, La.

Julia Myers, St. James, Mo.

Lena L. (Shoffner) Matthesen.

Ostis B. And Mattie (Bolds) Wilson.

F. M. Williamson, Hammond, La.

Elder H. M. Riggle.

Ministers at Church of God Camp-meeting, Carthage, Missouri in 1905.

Names of Known Ministers appearing in the Picture on the opposite page

W. J. and Luella Henry	Fred Rapp
Drusilla and Ellen (Trent) Porter	S. M. Rich
Cornelia A. Sunderland	James Trask
George W. Johnson	Charles Mansfield
E. M. Zinn	Charles Williams
Sam McAlister and wife	W. H. Smith
J. W. Youngblood	Grant Teter
George E. Harmon	W. T. Seaton
Henry W. White	A. D. Seaton
Clara (McAlister) Brooks	C. W. Seaton
Mabel Hale	A. C. Bennett
W. H. Shoot	R. B. Stafford
L. L. Porter and wife	Frank Porter
Willis M. Brown	A. L. Hutton
S. G. Bryant	M. L. Hutton
J. B. Peterman and wife	Annie Shipley
Samuel M. Helm	Claudine Heald
George E. Bolds	Sister Pearce
J. D. Ferrill	Bro. Keeran
Hugh Caudell	The other ministers
George Cole	have not been identified.

Cornelia Bateman, Wichita, Kans.

Willis M. Brown, Hickman, Ky.

Chas. E. Orr, Federalsburg, Md.

Charles E. and Sadie Orr in 1928 at Guthrie, Okla.

Bro. Charles E. Orr, co-worker with Bro. D. S. Warner, began about 1910 the publication of the paper, **Herald of Truth**, contending for the reformation truths and against the worldly innovations that had been accepted in the movement by the majority. Also, many other ministers and saints would not bow to the goddess of this world, so the "holy remnant" continued in "the old paths" and "the good way." Jer. 6:16,19. However, this paper was suspended in the early 1920's. Then in 1928 Bro. Orr began editing **The Path of Life**, a paper especially for children and young people. He continued this publication until 1932, when he merged it with the **Faith and Victory** (begun in 1923), and assumed the editing of six pages of this monthly paper until his death in Sept., 1933. Now in its 44th year of publication, the **Faith and Victory** stands for the teachings of the Reformation prior to 1910 and open for more light on God's Word, but not the "new light" which hides or eclipses the precious truth which brought forth this "evening light" Reformation in fulfillment of Bible prophecy.

We quote and emphasize the exhortation by Bro. Orr in 1932: "Let us unite our efforts in upholding those glorious truths and keep this reformation moving on in purity and power." —Lawrence D. Pruitt, Editor

Lector House believes that a society develops through a two-fold approach of continuous learning and adaptation, which is derived from the study of classic literary works spread across the historic timeline of literature records. Therefore, we aim at reviving, repairing and redeveloping all those inaccessible or damaged but historically as well as culturally important literature across subjects so that the future generations may have an opportunity to study and learn from past works to embark upon a journey of creating a better future.

This book is a result of an effort made by Lector House towards making a contribution to the preservation and repair of original ancient works which might hold historical significance to the approach of continuous learning across subjects.

HAPPY READING & LEARNING!

LECTOR HOUSE LLP
E-MAIL: lectorpublishing@gmail.com